Saga of

AMERICAN SPORT

Saga of
AMERICAN SPORT

JOHN A. LUCAS, D.Ed.
Professor of Physical Education
Penn State University
University Park, Pennsylvania

RONALD A. SMITH, Ph.D.
Associate Professor of Physical Education
Penn State University
University Park, Pennsylvania

Lea & Febiger • *1978* • *Philadelphia*

Library of Congress Cataloging in Publication Data

Lucas, John Apostal, 1927-
  Saga of American sport.

  Includes index.
  1. Sports—Social aspects—United States.
2. Sports—United States—History. I. Smith, Ronald
Austin, 1936-   joint author. II. Title
GV706.5.L82   301.5′7   78-1889
ISBN 0-8121-0485-4

Published in Great Britain by Henry Kimpton Publishers, London

PRINTED IN THE UNITED STATES OF AMERICA

Preface

A close look at the history of American sport indicates to us that sport has reflected the dominant social themes in American society. Increasingly, to know the sporting and leisure habits of Americans is to know something significant about this modern society. To concede that sport generally has not been an important cause of change or condition in no way rules out the contention that its study will reveal important information about the American experience. Long ago, the English historian of sport, Joseph Strutt, explained his book on sports and pastimes as a viable attempt "to form a just estimation of the character of any particular people. . . ." Sport does mirror society. It is a felt need of many Americans, filling a void of a restless citizenry. This search for self and collective fulfillment provides an excellent focus for the great changes that took place in sport as America passed first from a self-sustaining agricultural economy to the productive and interdependent economy of the industrial age, and then finally entered a consumer period within the present post-industrial age. This socio-economic transformation is of incalculable importance and, according to futurist, Herman Kahn, capable of providing "a basis for a relatively peaceful and smooth evolution to all kinds of 'futures'—many of them, by current standards, almost utopian in their possibilities." Recreational pastimes, both passive and participatory, will probably play a large role in such a twenty-first century ideology.

In a search for the prevailing ethos of the American people, J. Franklin Jameson, in a presidential address to fellow historians, concluded that "of all means of estimating American character from American history, the pursuit of religious history is the most complete." And he was probably right in 1908. There seems no need today to identify a dominant theme, a single trait that most closely approaches a central and continuous record of American history. It is enough to say, for example, that sport, games, and recreational habits are a perpetually important American preoccupation. Sport in America has reflected the nation's dominant social themes. The social milieu of any era has to a great extent dictated the sporting activities in which Americans have participated, passively or actively. Thus, in the colonial Puritan theocracy and the old aristocratic-like society of the South, sport took on vastly differing hues. The continuing English influence plus a host of other immigrant people have stamped American sport. The inexorable change from an agricultural to an industrial society changes everything in America, including sporting habits. Civil rights, women's rights, minorities, and the so-called mass of middle America all have had something to tell us about the direction of sport in this country. Lastly, the pioneering spirit, both brilliant and brutal, had much to say about being "number one" in all facets of American life—not the least of which is competitive athletics. It appears that all truly important manifestations of our culture filter into the deepest membranes of our sporting habits, rules, strategy, organization, ethics, and make it all a heady area of inquiry.

Finding a single central theme in the history of America sport is a task of extreme difficulty. Possibly it is enough to identify a continuing stream of ideas—ideas contiguous to the nation's European-North American sporting heritage. America's extraordinary proliferation of ideologies, theologies, social and cultural mores has created a unique society, and in the process gained a certain "unity through diversity." For well over a hundred years this country has moved from rural individualism to urban collectivism—a phenomenon explaining, in part, the changing character of sport in the United States. No less important are the spirit of adventure and the competitive rise of the common man. National literature from the time of Fenimore Cooper to the astronauts joins with sporting heroes and heroines to portray a theme of speed, power, daring, and the pursuit of excellence.

Other themes appear to exist. American institutions, especially sport, have flourished on the belief that most citizens have the opportunity for success and mobility. America's traditional sense of optimism continues despite attacks from late twentieth century events. As if to balance things a bit, two powerful forces have emerged in the modern age and have, in their own way, touched sport. The ascendance of anti-intellectualism, embodied in some art, music, literature, innocuous radio, frivolous and frenetic television and films, are joined by an ever increasing display of gladiatorial sport. The spectre of "vulgarity and pragmatic materialism" seems stronger than ever. In some ways the American free enterprise system has bred "the parallel threads of violence and humanitarianism." Inevitably, this two-edged sword of cruelty and chivalry, so marked in our society, is present in sport of Americans. Sport, it appears, has not been primarily demonic; neither has it been all good. It has become pervasive. In the last analysis, a central theme of fulfillment seems an all-encompassing American dream. The need for sport, vicarious and participatory, seems a felt need for millions; it fills a void; it will likely not go away and may even increase significantly in these last decades of the twentieth century and into the next.

University Park, Pennsylvania   JOHN A. LUCAS
                                    RONALD A. SMITH

Contents

x

Part I.

Colonial and
Early American Sport

CHAPTER 1

The Colonial Puritan— Moral Athlete of Yesteryear

THE PURITAN MIND

The puritan mind was one of the toughest with which the world ever had to deal. Life was hard for the early colonists. But there existed among the founders of the Virginia and Massachusetts colonies a kind of mental and moral strength that has come to represent a significant facet of America's greatness. During the first half-century of the nation's existence, life was an endless struggle, pleasurable diversions nearly nonexistent, organized and commercial amusements out of the question. The earliest settlers found sport enough in taming the land, establishing a cluster of families, and singing praises to and trembling before an omnipotent God. They made a virtue of qualities which eventuated in political stability and economic success—self-reliance, frugality, industry, and energy. Play and the levity of leisure time was an adult luxury; the children managed with quiet pastimes and games. These early men and women saw rest as something for the next world; here on earth man must "do the works of him who sent him, as long as it is yet day." Activity rather than enjoyment seemed to serve to increase the glory of God. Wasting time was conceived of as the deadliest of sins and jollification deserved absolute moral condemnation. Yet strangely and wonderfully, the tenuous beginnings of the Virginia and Massachusetts colonies planted deep roots that would grow and flower into societies of orderliness and, for most people, ones filled with purpose and deep satisfaction.

THE FOUNDING OF THE VIRGINIA COLONY

Toward the close of the sixteenth century, England's efforts to establish an empire in the New World began to assume great

3

importance. On the eve of English colonization in America, Queen Elizabeth's subjects, people of all classes, were characterized by a supreme sense of patriotism and filled with a restless energy. Catholic missionaries and explorers had beaten the English to the New World and there was strong feeling among the latter that permanent settlements must be established. On April 10, 1606, King James I of England established the Virginia Company; the following spring an expedition of three ships arrived in the lower Chesapeake Bay and settled some thirty miles upland on the north bank of the James River at Jamestown, both named in honor of their king. The remarkable Captain John Smith stepped ashore, and the first permanent English settlement was founded.

RELIGION AND ECONOMICS IN THE NEW COLONY

Economics brought people to the new land; it was economics buttressed by religion which founded the Virginia Colony. The patriotic and persevering men of the Virginia Company hoped to (1) increase British trade, (2) enlarge the English nation, and (3) perpetuate the Church of England. Religion was a powerful if not singular reason for establishment of the colony. English customs, ideals, and the Anglican Church were quickly planted in Jamestown. Commerce, a more convenient route to the South Sea, possible discovery of gold, and revenge against the Spanish monarch, were all valid reasons explaining the presence of colonists at Jamestown. Finally there was a religious consciousness that fused in the minds of the settlers a view of the new land as both a source of riches and redemption. Religion and economics merged into one conception, with a strong missionary fervor a compelling force. The ascetic puritanism of the Virginia Anglican Church in its early history was a reflection of its membership—pious, hard-working, mostly middle class, many of whom accepted literally and solemnly the tenets of Puritanism, original sin, predestination, and election.

GERMINAL SPORT IN EARLY VIRGINIA

Sir Thomas Dale, the new governor, arrived in Virginia on May 10, 1611, with a new code of laws to bring order to a colony on the brink of extinction. Many were Puritans—men and women of an English dissenting mind, imbued with a deep and serious Calvinistic metaphysics. Martial law was declared in Jamestown and on June 22, 1611, Sir Thomas issued his code of laws, "The First Criminal Code in Virginia." It was reported that the previous month, as Sir Thomas came ashore, he witnessed a game of bowls in the streets of Jamestown and was not at all pleased. Dale's sixth order to his colonists was a puritan warning that:

No man or woman shall dare to violate or breake the Sabbath by any gaming, publique or private . . . upon paine of the first fault to lose their provision, and allowance for the whole weeke following, for the second to lose the said allowance, and also to be whipt, and for the third to suffer death.[1]

Little is known of the meager recreational activities of the earliest Virginia settlers; however, amusements of any kind were anathema on the Sabbath. This day was to be kept duly sanctified. All were instructed to worship God publicly—with dice, card playing, gambling, swearing, and all forms of loud noises absolutely forbidden.

Almost from the beginning, Virginia colonists learned to fear the Indian. Yet, a certain Henry Spelman, companion to the remarkable adventurer, Captain John Smith, observed Indian dances in 1613. Women and young boys played a form of soccer, while the warriors "play with a little balle lettinge it fall out of ther hand and striketh it with the tope of his foot, and he that can strike the ball furthest winns what they play for."[2] The first picture of the sports of the American colonists is an idealized engraving by Theodore DeBry, published in 1619, illustrating the "Recreations of Gentlemen in Virginia." The highly improbable picture shows one planter on a horse and accompanied by a dog chasing a stag, another fishing, and still another with a gun on his shoulder. The image of the English leisured class is represented, astonishingly, by several planters engaged in falconry, two men carrying hawks on their wrists while another is reaching for the quarry.

The Virginia Company, an English and Church of England enterprise, was strongly Puritan during the first tenuous generation. Religion was looked upon by most as the strongest energizing and propulsive force in the new colony. The Company received self-government on November 28, 1618—a Virginia legislature that was

The English leisure class participated in falconry.

designed to repeat in America the political philosophy and moral as well as civil code of England. A governor sailed for Virginia and on July 30, 1619, a company of twenty-two men, the first representative assembly in America, passed laws for the punishment of idleness, gambling, drunkenness, all ungodly disorders, and excess in dressing apparel. Early Virginia law makers and clergymen, thoroughly loyal to the Church of England but Puritan in social and moral habit, found no inconsistency in the 1619 Proceedings of the Virginia Assembly which outlawed drunkenness, excess in apparel, gaming, and stood firmly "against Idlenes."

> First, in detestation of Idlenes be it enacted, that if anyman be founde to live as an Idler or renagate, though a freedman, it shalbe lawful for that Incorporation or Plantation to which he belongeth to appoint him a Mr. [Master] to serve for wages, till he shewe apparant signes of amendment.[3]

The early Virginia General Assembly strictly conformed with the canons of the Church of England. Instructions from London to Governor Wyatt, dated July 24, 1621, reminded him "to be industrious and suppress drunkenness, gaming and excess in cloathes, not to permit any but the council and heads of hundreds to wear gold in their cloathes or to wear silk till they make it themselves." Of the thirty-five laws passed in 1623-1624, seven dealt with churchly matters. Hard times and admonitions against frivolity kept sporting activities to a minimum. Laws of 1624, 1632, 1643, and 1644, warned against swearing, drunkenness, riotous living, idleness, dice, cards, unlawful games, and excessive travel on the Sabbath. Yet some amusements existed; early Virginians played ninepins, either in alleys specially built for the purpose, or in large rooms of private residences. The arm of the Church apparently failed to reach the Eastern shore where ninepins was already a popular sport in the 1630s.[4] A certain William Ward, of Accomac County, found ninepins so absorbing a diversion that he is reported to have spent the whole day engaged in it.[5] Jane Carson, in her book *Colonial Virginians at Play*, indicates that even in the early history of the colony horse racing was a popular sport. Repressive legislation against idleness and diversions was already losing effectiveness in the face of an ideal outdoor climate, a new, rapidly growing plantation community, and mankind's inexorable play instinct.

THE MORAL ATHLETE OF THE MASSACHUSETTS COLONY

Among Massachusetts colonists in the early seventeenth century, religion served as a powerful instrument of social discipline—even greater than in the South. The settlers of Virginia and Massachusetts came from the same English middle class, with an intermingling of a few persons of gentle birth and breeding. Massachusetts settlers were resolved to build in America a purified counterpart of the society they had left at home. In a life devoted to hard work, an unqualified faith in an all-powerful God, and a proscription against any form of idleness or unproductive diversion, Puritan leaders attempted to set a standard for the colonists. Calvinists to the core, these men saw themselves as special or "elect" members of a spiritual hierarchy and envisioned God as "transcendent, terrible, incomprehensible, even while good and merciful."[6] The bulk of colonists or "non-elect" had less hope of salvation than the better educated and stronger leaders of the community who deliberately sought to perfect and prove their spiritual strength through unswerving faith in God, as manifested in a life of good works. "In order to perfect and prove his spiritual strength the puritan engaged in exercises and went into training, much as a youth now sets out to excell in sport," concludes Ralph Barton Perry in his examination of the early American moral athlete.[7] Through the exercise of his will rather than his body the earliest Puritan divine played his altogether serious game of morality and salvation. Self-righteousness and hypocrisy were more than balanced by qualities of manly courage, self-reliance, and sobriety. This unique American moral core was to make a deep imprint on the country's institutions and established a lasting American consciousness.

IN DETESTATION OF IDLENESS—A COLONIAL EDICT

Possibly too much has been made of the severity of the Puritan code of behavior in the virgin Massachusetts colony. Human nature demands recreation and even the Puritans had their diversions— although muted and inconstant. Yet it is a fact that an unfriendly New England environment conspired with a spiritual asceticism among the people—resulting in few recorded sporting pastimes. Spontaneous expressions of undisciplined impulses were under suspicion among first generation colonists. For example, on the hated Roman holiday, Christmas Day, 1621, Governor Bradford found recent arrivals on the ship *Fortune* "pitching ye barr" and playing "at stoole-ball." He ordered them to stop gambling and revelling in the streets, declaring that it "was against his conscience that they should play and others worke."[8] Several years later, in 1627, the pleasure-loving Thomas Morton was summarily censured for dancing and drinking around a May-pole with friends and Indian women—"frisking togeather like so many fairies or furies rather."

The founders of the Massachusetts Bay and Plymouth colonies were reformers, who sought to establish, in their eyes, a pure church and a sacred Sunday. The Sabbath was a special day for self-examination, self-discipline—a time one dare not spend except in deepest but restrained praise of the absolute sovereignty of God. All gambling and games of chance prostituted divine providence to unworthy ends. "God determines the cast of the dice or the shuffle of the cards, and we are not to implicate His providence in frivolity."[9] That everyone should have a calling and work hard at it was a first premise of Puritanism. With unremitting hard work, sermons, prayers, and school, there seemed little time for recreation and games. The latter were not looked upon as evil. Time spent on them was looked upon as sinful. In the Puritan concept everlasting rest is in the next world; on earth man must, to be certain of his state of grace, "do the works of him who sent him, as long as it is yet day." Not leisure and enjoyment but activity only served to increase the glory of God. The 1648 *Laws and Liberties of Massachusetts* ordered that no person "shall spend his time idly or unprofitably" under pain of punishment. Similarly, the General Court of Massachusetts set forth on August 30, 1653, a new law which made play, sport, and aimless sauntering on Sunday a positive misdemeanor. Small amusements and sporting diversions on week days—provided they were restrained and pretended practicality—were not disallowed. Abuse or excess was frowned upon. For the average colonist there was a "joi de vivre" all through his life, the perfect satisfaction of serving God to the utmost of his ability. For most Puritans of the period, life was hard but joyous to the degree that each felt certain of his obedience to God's demand for rational labor; each man must manifest evidence of redemption through unalterable faith, good and holy conduct. Time was the gift of God and should be used for His service.

ENGLAND'S SPORTING HERITAGE 1509-1660

The verdant British Isles, washed by the warm Gulf Stream, lay claim to the genesis of more sports than any other area of the western world. This is especially true of England. Sport and recreational pastimes have always been an essential and pervasive form of social action among these English peoples. English literature from the fourteenth century contains significant indications of the temper of the people and their leaders as gleaned by their leisure pursuits. The greatest English sport historian, Joseph Strutt, observed that "in order to form a just estimation of the character of any particular people, it is absolutely necessary to investigate the sports and pastimes most generally prevalent among them."[10]

Henry VIII, King of England (1509-1547), was a fine athlete, a skilled hammer-thrower, and "exceedingly fond of hunting, hawking, and other sports of the field." The reign of his second eldest daughter, Elizabeth (1558-1603), contained divergent elements of traditional mirth and gaiety and was opposed by the new cult—

The Puritans punished those who could not meet their standards of piety—and possibly enjoyed observing the punishment.

somber Puritanism. As a people, the Elizabethans set a supreme value on the active life. Elizabeth's brilliant, coarse and pleasure-seeking temperament was reflected in much of English society. "Merrie England" was more than a cliche. Opposing these excesses in amusement was Puritanism, the radical wing of the Church of England. It was fast becoming an ideal and a way of life—an excessive reaction to the lewdness and vulgarity of the Elizabethan age and the aggressive Roman Catholic Church. Puritanism represented an attitude of indignation regarding certain traditional forms of Catholic revelry, especially violations of the sacred Sabbath. The Puritan damned as sinful certain church festivals; he resented the amusements of the more wealthy, leisured class, making a moral issue of this discontent. These two forces, spiritual reform and economic envy, could never be disentangled among the new English rebels—many of whom would soon emigrate to the American colonies.

Confusion over Sunday amusements ushered in seventeenth century England. The Puritans were incensed at King James I and the publication of his 1603 *Basilikon Doron*, a directive to his son, a castigation to both Puritans and Jesuits, and a pronouncement for all to enjoy lawful amusements after observing Sunday worship. As if to still the querulous Puritans, as well as advise the natural successor to the throne, King James admonished his son, Prince Henry, to banish idleness, "the mother of all vice," with running, leaping, wrestling, fencing, dancing, tennis, archery, horseback riding, and all field sports. He reminded him "to exercise his engine, which surely with idlenesse will ruste and become blunt."[11] The Puritans were not amused at this champion of sport; they were further enraged at his next folly, the famous 1618 *Book of Sports*.

The Puritan addiction for continuous and organized activity—to banish idleness through work rather than play—was both Calvinist in origin and a primary form of the new disciplined middle-class English social reformers. The Puritans passionately desired a better life on earth as well as salvation. Frivolous sport seemed an unacceptable vehicle to attain either. Thus, they attacked with special vigor "The King's Majesties Declaration To His Subjects Concerning Lawful Sports To Be Used." King James repeated his desire for the "good people" of the land to engage in lawful recreation and honest exercises on Sunday and holidays—the logical days for sport— "seeing they must apply their labour, and winne their living in all working dayes."[12] James I lost no time in declaring his uncompromising hostility to Puritanism. "I will make them conform themselves," he cried, "or else I will harry them out of the land." His *Book of Sports* was a direct counterblast to Puritan teaching regarding the Sabbath. Mixed dancing, May-Day Games, Morris-dances, May-pole festivities "or any other such harmlesse Recreation," were allowed after Sunday service. Bear and bull-baiting plus bowling were still prohibited on the Lord's Day. The strong, vocal Puritan minority, fast gaining political power in these early decades of the seventeenth century, was horrified at King James' attack on their concept of Sunday worship. Puritans in Parliament as well as the pulpit had little to say in opposition to sporting amusements among the people on week days; the English sporting tradition continued as it had done for centuries. Sunday restrictions were the special target of the new political-social protesters. These Puritans, obsessed by the Old Testament interpretation of the Sabbath Day, totally rejected the relatively carefree ancient Catholic or Continental Sunday. A new kind of Sunday emerged—a Sabbatarian concept encompassing worship, rest, contemplation, and absolutely no forms of physical recreation.

King James I—"a scholar miscast as a ruler" received the sacraments of the Church of England and died (March 27, 1625) leaving a myriad of unsolved tasks for his successor and son, the tragic King Charles I. The new king continued to support the Anglican hierarchy which sought to enforce religious conformity. The *Book of Sports* was

Sport was sanctioned on Sunday in the "Book of Sports," but bull-baiting was not.

reissued in 1633, by Charles I, instigated by the fanatical Catholic-Anglican, Archbishop William Laud, and ordered read from all the pulpits. The chief enemies, politically and theologically, were Puritans—opponents of the King's ordinance permitting most popular sports on Sunday outside of church hours. Puritan clergy who refused to read the fourteen hundred word "Declaration" were ejected from their posts and punished. One preacher allowed his clerk to read the book from the pulpit, but covered his ears. Another read the book, then the Ten Commandments; the congregation was bidden to choose between the two. The target was the anti-authoritarian ascetic tendency of Puritanism, which seemed so dangerous to the State. Yet the seat of power gradually moved into the Puritan camp. "Merrie England" yielded to a Calvinist sense of sin, an awareness of God's awful power. The Puritan Parliamentary forces, called Roundheads, gradually defeated the Royalists; the Revolution was over, the whole British Isles were declared a republic with Oliver Cromwell at its head. On September 1, 1641, in the House of Commons, a resolution was passed reminding all that the Lord's Day shall once again be duly observed and sanctified; "all dancing or other sports, either before or after divine service, be forborne and restrained."[13] Politics and religion became more and more blurred; sporting edicts for some, both Parliamentary Puritan and Stuart King, became a devious means for party gain. The latter sought survival; national instability acted as a Puritan catalyst for unrelenting work, the banishment of idleness—the foundation of all their morality. Accordingly, in 1644, 25 December was ordered to be kept as a fast day, "in order that all might call to remembrance their own sins and those of their forefathers in transforming a day sacred to the memory of Christ into an occasion of revelry."[14] During the Great Migration 1629-1642, over 60,000 English Catholics, Anglicans, and Puritans emigrated to the West Indies, Maryland, Virginia, and the Massachusetts Bay community. The end of English Civil War and the restoration of the monarchy in 1660 saw the new colonies profoundly changed.

PURITAN AUSTERITY IN PERSPECTIVE

The Puritan preacher, Richard Baxter, once advised his company to be cheerful, godly, and to "converse with men of strongest faith who have this heavenly mirth." These men, only a small percentage of the English and colonial population of the seventeenth century, so dedicated themselves to religious and moral principles that to their practice they would subordinate everything else. An obvious manifestation of this dedication was their revolt against the acknowledged sensualism of the period. The Puritans did not fully turn their backs on the strong English heritage of sport and recreational pastimes. Only by contrast with the uninhibited revelry of previous Englishmen did the controlled mirth and pleasurable domestic life of these people seem the epitome of total gloom. Historians search in vain among Puritan legislation for restrictive measures against acceptable sport on weekdays. Puritans usually objected to the abuse and not the use of sport and mild amusements. The relatively manly games of the countryside were frequently advocated as substitutes for the effete entertainments of the town. Training days and election days in early New England assumed a holiday atmosphere; singing, feasting, and simple competitive games offered opportunities to break the harshness of colonial life. Sometimes the very laws against dice, card-playing, quoits, ninepins, bowling, and shuffle board—"whereby much precious time is spent unprofitably" were the best evidences of their existence among the unregenerate settlers. Clerical complaints alone would suggest the presence of "seasonable merriment," joyous Thanksgiving Days, simple soccer games, and target contests. By 1651, Boston and Salem shops supplied toys and dolls for children.

The leaders of the Massachusetts settlers were small in number, influential, usually well-educated, and convinced that they were the chosen elect of God. These self-elected "saints" rarely broke the law—moral or civil; yet they lived with deep anxiety. Their righteous, productive, no-nonsense lives were, hopefully, ample proof of eventual salvation. The remaining sinners or "strangers" lived with the small but perpetual hope that covenant theology might reveal God's mercy to man and assure them of everlasting life. Their resolve to lead a model Puritan existence broke all too frequently; it was the non-elect "stranger" that fills the statute books with acts of fornication, drinking, gross and illegal games, and idle play.

The God-fearing Puritan, the one we remember today, believed that "man's chief end is to glorify God and enjoy him forever." Amazingly, he held that God is more important than business, art, poetry, pleasurable and sporting activities. The New England Puritan loved life and was happy in his task of founding many of America's enduring institutions. He was, in the last analysis, a rebel who fought the established order. Puritanism was an ideology in which the idea of personal religious salvation was transformed into a model for the regeneration of society.[15] It succeeded to a remarkable degree, for the early colonial Puritan—the moral athlete of yesteryear—helped lay the foundation for a new and remarkable nation.

REFERENCES

1. George Maclaren Brydon, *Virginia's Mother Church* (Richmond, Virginia: Virginia Historical Society, 1947), p. 412.

2. Edward Arber (ed.), *Travels and Works of Captain John Smith*, Part I. (New York: Burt Franklin, 1910), p. CXIV.

3. Lyon Gardiner Tyler (ed.), *Narratives of Early Virginia 1606-1625* (New York: Charles Scribner's Sons, 1907), p. 263.

4. Jane Carson, *Colonial Virginians at Play* (Charlottesville, Virginia: The University of Virginia Press, 1965), p. 171.

5. *Accomac County Records*, Vol. 1632-1640, p. 59, Virginia State Library; cited by Philip A. Bruce, *Social Life of Virginia in the Seventeenth Century* (Lynchburg, Virginia: J. P. Bell Co., Inc., 1927), p. 193.

6. Perry Miller, *Errand into the Wilderness* (Cambridge, Massachusetts: Harvard University Press, 1964), p. 112.

7. Ralph Barton Perry, The Moral Athlete, Chapter X in his *Puritanism and Democracy* (New York: The Vanguard Press, 1944), pp. 245-268.

8. William Bradford, *Of Plymouth Plantation*, Samuel Eliot Morison, ed. (New York: Alfred A. Knopf, 1952), p. 97.

9. Perry Miller, *The New England Mind: The Seventeenth Century* (Cambridge, Massachusetts: Harvard University Press, 1963), pp. 15-16.

10. Joseph Strutt, *The Sports and Pastimes of the People of England* (London: Printed for Thomas Tegg, 1838), p. xvii.

11. James I, Basilikon Doron in *The Political Works of James I* (Cambridge: Harvard University Press, 1918), p. 48.

12. James I, The King's Majesties Declaration. To His Subjects Concerning Lawful Sports To Be Used, in *Smeeton's Historical and Bibliographical Tracts*, Vol. I, No. 4 (Westminster, 1820), p. 7.

13. Samuel Rawson Gardiner, ed. *The Constitutional Documents of the Puritan Revolution 1628-1660* (Oxford: at the Clarendon Press, 1889), p. 123.

14. Godfrey Davies, *The Early Stuarts 1603-1660* (Oxford: at the Clarendon Press, 1937), p. 304.

15. Michael Walzer, Puritanism As a Revolutionary Ideology, in *New Perspectives on the American Past 1607-1877*, Vol. I, ed. Stanley N. Katz and Stanley I. Kutler (Boston: Little, Brown & Co., 1969), p. 3.

CHAPTER 2

Sport and the Protestant Ethic

SPORT AND SOCIETY IN RESTORATION ENGLAND

The recalling of Charles II to the throne in 1660 marked the end of Puritan domination; it witnessed the restoration of the Church of England and Parliamentary power. A natural reaction against twenty years of Puritan control was inevitable. Enforced sobriety turned to merry-making; popular festivals boomed and rural sports, never effectively repressed, burst forth with new vigor. Once again Puritans and other minorities became the targets of oppression. But these Puritan Englishmen fought back; their faith was a fiery combination of religious and social dynamism—little resembling modern Fundamentalism. Unswerving faith in God and the Holy Bible would, they prayed, guide the believing pilgrim "onward through dangerous country to the Celestial City." John Bunyan's 1678 classic, *The Pilgrim's Progress*, arrived just in time to sustain the harassed rebels. Life, Bunyan said, was a confrontation between the powers of light and the powers of darkness. This new kind of Englishman, the militant Puritan, could endure any earthly hardship in his inexorable search for "the everlasting prize." Bunyan, the uncompromising evangelical preacher, possessed a vivid imagination; he knew his subject and he knew the audience for which he was writing. Picturing the dangerous journey from the City of Destruction to the Celestial City, Bunyan cried:

> I seek an inheritance, incorruptible, undefiled, and that fadeth not away; and it is laid up in Heaven, and fast there, to be bestowed at the time appointed, on them that diligently seek it.[1]

It was the perfect book for pilgrims and pioneers—one of the most influential religious books written in the English language. There was, of course, little room in such a philosophy for games and idle recreations. Such actions were considered wasteful and even dangerous for "one leak will sink a ship, and one sin will destroy a sinner."

Throughout history, waves of asceticism are followed by periods of moral relaxation. Such was the case in Restoration England. Sports were restored to the people. Traditional sporting textbooks, like Markham's *The Art of Archerie*, Roger Ascham's *Toxophilus*, Henry Peachman's *The Compleat Gentleman*, were dusted and re-read. Charles Cotton's *The Compleat Gamester* appeared in 1674 and remained for decades a standard text on billiards, bowling, chess, and other sporting activities. Yet the nation's new boom in trade and economics plus a sticky Puritanism helped to prevent a complete restoration to the old ways. "The old Catholic pattern of the Church's calender with its frequent seasonal feasts had received a sufficient battering from Puritan attacks to make sure that it could never be restored to its full significance."[2] A more balanced attitude towards sport and exercise was one permanent effect of the social, political, and religious upheaval in seventeenth century England. Another important change impinging on sports and games was in the recreational use of Sunday. It became a quieter and holier day in England. And so it was in the colonies. The ties between England and her American tendrils were

The art of archery had been taught in England from medieval times.

still very close. Every profound action and change in English society was recognized, mirrored or rejected by the colonists. Their reaction to sport, recreational pastimes, the use of leisure times was, for a long time, the manifestation of an ancient English heritage and a new Puritan sobriety.

SPORT AMONG VIRGINIA'S LANDED GENTRY

The Anglican Church had always been officially recognized in Virginia. The blue laws of very early Virginia were fully as puritanic as those of Massachusetts itself, revealing the extent to which Calvinistic ethics had penetrated the Anglican body. Nevertheless, the Virginia Church had developed distinctly differently from that of the Massachusetts Bay Colony or the English Church. In England the church was struggling for its very life; colonial cries for assistance and requests for bishops and episcopal supervision had necessarily gone unheeded. Thus, the Virginia Church never did become one with the Church of England. No bishop ever visited America. The colonists molded the church to their local needs and interests.

During the 1650s, several thousand English loyalists or Cavaliers escaped Cromwell's Commonwealth and emigrated to Virginia. Many returned to England a decade or so later but enough stayed to increase the ever-growing number of Virginia plantation aristocrats. The word "cavalier" was not a social class but a political party fleeing the homeland and the violence of civil strife. The arrival of these reluctant colonists coincided with an embryonic and affluent tobacco plantation aristocracy. A quasi-feudal society emerged, one that aped the landed nobility of England—even though they themselves were not of that class. Though this Virginian was no aristocrat by birth, he longed to be one. The brief history of Virginia asceticism, at least among the ruling class, rapidly merged into a longer period of moral liberation. For many generations these plantation gentry remained a working aristocracy. But a concomitant love of pleasure characterized prosperous Virginia landowners. What these middle-class Englishmen wanted above all else was land—the life of the country gentlemen— the English gentleman. "Virginia was not looked upon as a new country; it was simply an outlying possession."[3] The powerful English impulse, temporarily frustrated in Virginia's first half century, emerged inevitably, first among the affluent planters and later with the middle classes. A rich sporting heritage, a part of this impulse, began in earnest during the last decades of the seventeenth century.

By mid-century the publicly supported Anglican Church began to fall under the secular influence of its wealthier members. Virginia congregations became notoriously independent and self-sufficient—a certain bending of the outward form without breaking the inner spirit. The Puritan emphasis weakened. Perhaps it had never been a pervasive element in the colony. Perhaps the general tone of the social life in which the average Virginia landowner moved prompted him to make the most of the few pleasures offered, whether they be a glass of wine, a dance, a game of cards or, especially, a good horse race. The disposition to entertain and to be entertained grew rapidly. This proliferation of amusements and leisure pastimes was ineffectively countered by an ever-weakening Puritan ethic. The legendary Robert Beverly (1673-1722), planter, minor statesman, and author, speaking of the days of his youth, discussed Indian games, fishing, fowling, turkey shoots, and "the hunting of wild horses." From the beginning, riding, horsemanship and racing were the most popular sports in colonial Virginia. Skill in horsemanship was expected of every gentleman; in fact, even the poorest planters took pride in their horses and as riders. John Clayton, English rector and visitor to the colony in 1688, observed that the Virginia gentlemen "ride pretty sharply, a Planter's Pace is a Proverb, which is a good sharp hand-Gallop."[4]

Horse racing dominated Virginia amusements. Betting on horses was pervasive; county courts recognized them as contracts and often settled disputes growing out of irregularities in performance or in payment. For this reason the early history of the sport is recorded in the county records. Saturday afternoon and holiday tests of speed were common in late seventeenth century Virginia.

> The seventeenth-century track was a straight path about a quarter of a mile in length, laid out in an abandoned field near a convenient gathering place—a church, a court house, or an ordinary [eating-house] located at a cross-road. The narrow path, ten or twelve feet wide, had an open space at each end large enough for the horses to maneuver into position and pull up to a quick stop. The finish end of the track was customarily marked by upright stakes or poles, where the judges stood.[5]

These races attracted large crowds but only gentlemen could compete. The well-known case of a common tailor named James Bullocke, who entered a horse against a gentleman in a race for two thousand pounds of tobacco, is carefully recorded in the court records. Bullocke won the race but "it being contrary to Law for a Labourer to make a race, being a sport only for Gentlemen," was fined one hundred pounds of tobacco, while Mr. Mathew Slader, the gentleman, was ordered to be put in the stocks for one hour for allowing Bullocke's horse to win, "which is an apparent cheate."[6]

Cockfighting, hunting, and shooting matches were popular among most elements of Virginia society. The rougher English pastimes of bear and bull baiting failed to gain universal sanction. Wealthy Virginians continued their mimicry of English aristocracy. The favorite vice of the colonial gentry (if we exclude a tendency for heavy drinking) was gambling on games, sports, and cards. The secularized Anglican Church, dominated by this same social class, may not have condoned gambling but few if any restrictive measures are found in the law or literature after 1680. These Virginians had strayed somewhat from an earlier Puritan tendency that looked upon all games of chance as a prostitution of the divine order. By the end of the century, interest in athletics prompted the governor, Sir Francis Nicholson, to proclaim in 1691 an annual field day. Nicholson, a bachelor, directed the sheriff of Surry County to give public notice that:

> I will give first and second prizes to be shott for, wrastled, played at backswords, and run for by Horse and foott, to begin on the 22nd Day of Aprill next St. George's Day, being Saturday, all which prizes are to be shott for by the better sort of Virginians only, who are Bachelors.[7]

As the century came to a close, the sessions of the General Assembly brought people together in "Publick Times." Foot racing, chasing the greased pig, lotteries, raffles, primitive prize fighting (cudgeling), gouging or no-rules-wrestling, the theatre, puppet shows, beauty contests, lawn fetes, and fireworks, were all new forms of public entertainment. Virginia had come a long way from the harsh days of Sir Thomas Dale. Even James Blair, appointed American Commissary in 1689 by the Episcopal Bishop of London, was not immune from a newer sense of freedom to use leisure time in frivolous or rather, non-productive pursuits. The distinguished clergyman (and founder of William and Mary College in 1691) served as endman [finish judge] in a horse race that took place in Henrico County.

Amusements in late seventeenth century Virginia were varied and numerous but by no means consistent throughout all social classes. Colonials of the upper class had some leisure to indulge in English-like sporting pastimes. The rest participated in physical activities that satisfied an urgent utilitarianism with an equally strong desire for recreation. The pristine Virginia Church rapidly evolved into one emphasizing ritual rather than theology. This tendency toward secularism, combined with a growing affluence, created fertile ground for the spread of sporting amusements. In less than a century, the Virginia colony had prospered and matured to a point where it selected as it saw fit many of those temporal and spiritual manifestations of the mother country and nurtured its own unique characteristics. The country house was the rising Englishman's way-station to heaven. The Virginia landowner found his "heaven" in quiet devotion to the Anglican Church, in gracious living, in deep devotion to the rich Virginia soil with its abundant opportunities for sporting pastimes, and in a new and precious passion for independence.

Upper class colonials indulged in the English pastime of cock fighting as noted in *The Compleat Gamster* (1674).

DUTCH COLONIALS AT PLAY

The coming of the White Man as a permanent settler precipitated the transfer of a European culture to America. The small and tenuous Dutch community in seventeenth-century New York is a perfect example of a new people in a strange land making every effort to live as they had at home. The colony barely survived its first forty years (1624-1664) and quietly conceded control to the English Duke of York and his representative, Governor Richard Nicolls. Little changed in the daily life of the robust Dutch after the English conquest of 1664. Only in the richness and durability of their social customs had the Dutch made a profound impression. The official Dutch Reformed Church, far less rigid than the one in Massachusetts, took on a cosmopolitan air, and New Netherlands soon harbored Presbyterians, Congregationalists, a few Roman Catholics, numerous

Quakers, members of the English Church, and some Jews. Sport and the maypole came with the baggage of European civilization.

The Dutch were a most tolerant people, possessing a sense of world-mindedness that looked upon sport, revelry, and certain intemperance as a natural carry-over from their lives in the old country. Of course, the Protestant Sunday was sufficiently ingrained to disallow "illegal exercises" of any kind and that included both work and sporting activities. But how they did enjoy themselves after trade, agriculture, and household chores were completed!

The Dutch loved snow sports and winter recreational activities. New York's weather was ideal for sledding, skating, coasting, and hockey—reminders of merry times in Holland. State Street in Albany was long a famous resort of young people with sleds. The maze of ponds, marshes, and watered meadows on Manhattan—very much like the fatherland—made grand skating rinks. Children learned to skate very early and kept it up all their lives. Marketmen brought back loads of provisions into New York City on skates. Rapid transit on steel was common whether for business or fun—either singly, or with a dozen people grasping a pole while keeping a rhythmic motion over the ice surface. "Every habit and each trick known on Holland canals or ponds was reproduced on the Mohawk and Hudson."[8] Ice-boating, distance skating, and carnivals on ice enriched the traditional winter Christmas and New Year's holidays.

As early as 1665, Governor Nicholls announced that a horse-race would take place on the Long Island barrens at Hempstead, not so much for amusement we are told, "as for encouraging the bettering of the breed of horses which through great neglect has been impaired." Daniel Denton, one of the early settlers of Jamaica, Long Island, wrote in 1670, of a vast and level plain ideal for racing horses. "Once a year," he tells us, "the best horses in the island are brought hither to try their swiftness and the swiftest rewarded with a silver Cup."[9] Other popular sports were contests in marksmanship, golf, bowling, and truck, a game played at a table or on a lawn in which an ivory ball is driven under a wicket with a cue. Throughout the English occupation, certain "blood" sports satisfied some; cockfighting, fox hunting, and "riding the goose" found adherents. The later was an attempt to pull down, while riding on horseback or moving through swift water, a greased live goose suspended on a wire stretched between two poles. The fun-loving Dutch had discovered the pleasures of cricket, tennis, fishing and hunting, skittles or pin bowling, ninepins, archery, shooting with the crossbow, and a variety of ball games using stakes, gloved or ungloved hand, a racket, stick club or mallet. The "Klos" or "Klootbaan," was an ancient game of royalty—a farmer's game in late seventeenth century New York.

The blood sport of gander-pulling had its following.

At the end of a long alley two iron staves or pieces of wood were fastened in the ground and made to join at the top so as to form a sort of gate, and through this gate, from the end of the alley and at a set distance, the player had to throw a round disc. If he missed, he had to take up the disc where it landed and throw until he hit one of the posts, which counted one. Throwing through the gate counted two; and this continued until one of the players had reached the number of twelve, or any other number agreed upon.[10]

In an age when the bigotry of Old World religiosity was still the binding tie in most New World transplantations, the tolerant, industrious, and fun-loving Dutch must be said to have made a great contribution to American society.

SPORTING PASTIMES IN EARLY PENNSYLVANIA

The remarkable William Penn, nonconformist and zealous Quaker, had conferred upon him, in 1681, the proprietorship of Pennsylvania. Penn's *First Frame of Government* was adopted in England on April 25, 1682, while the *Great Laws* were passed by the first Pennsylvania Assembly at Chester on December 4, 1682. In the best Puritan and Quaker traditions, Sabbath regulations were included in these laws, and all "rude and riotous sports" plus organized Sunday entertainment of any sort were disallowed on pain of fine and/or imprisonment. More than a decade earlier William Penn had agonized through his passionate *No Cross, No Crown* and implored his fellow man not to "eat, drink, play, game, and sport away their irrevocable precious time, which should be dedicated to the Lord, as a necessary introduction to a blessed eternity."[11]

The Friends were Puritan in the matter of popular amusements, not so rigid as the New Englanders, but still finding it necessary to maintain a moral and godly Commonwealth. A certain Inner Light, called by Penn, "the most eminent article of our faith, is the spirit of God within man; it is his hope of glory and is not dependent upon dogma or even deep Bible study—not that which he professes, but that which he lives." Such an attitude discouraged plays, cards, may-games, bull and bear-baiting, cock-fighting, and the like, "which incite the people to rudeness, cruelty, looseness, and irreligion." Yet, ironically, in these very early years of the Commonwealth, Governor Penn was a man of great charm and persuasiveness, "tall and athletic, able to impress Indians with his prowess at running and leaping. He entertained lavishly and well; he appreciated a fine horse, a well-built ship, and a handsome woman."[12] Little is known about sporting activities in seventeenth-century Pennsylvania. Men and women did amuse themselves with light-hearted activities. Some were punished for excesses of these sporting moments. The pattern was the same nearly everywhere; conviviality was a precious commodity—natural and acceptable—except on Sunday. Still, the Sabbatarianism of William Penn's colony, the result of a deep belief in the mystical and altruistic Quaker faith, was milder than the searing New England Blue Laws.

PLAY AND THE NEW ENGLAND WORK ETHIC

The seventeenth-century New England Puritan was an unusual Christian. In most cases, his was a dynamic sense of life—a moral process originating in sin and proceeding first through faith in God and then quite naturally by practical Christian endeavor to ultimate hope for salvation. Despite terrifying predestination, most Puritan preachers tended to emphasize the assurance that if man vigorously sought the grace of God, he might—just might—receive the most precious gift of immortality. Such a heavy atmosphere made "seasonable merriment," music, play, and sporting interludes—all part of New England life—unadorned pastimes. Moderation in all these was allowed (except on the First Day of the Week); immoderation was sinful. For example, dancing "where it may be done without offence, in due season, and with moderation . . . is a natural expression of joy." But, warned Increase Mather in his 1684 "Arrow Against Profane and Promiscuous Dancing," all intimate "Gynecandrical Dancing" is utterly unlawful and "cannot be tollerated in such a place as New England, without a great Sin."[13]

Too much of what we know about these New Englanders comes to us from the religious elite—who also tended to be the social elite. Most settlers were not a dour sort only interested in religious affairs. Often they were joyous, loving, playful, and slightly wicked at times. A 1648 law called for a five shilling fine for those "who expend time in unlawful games. . . ." But the prohibition was so lightly regarded that by 1671, the penalty was increased twenty-fold. Selected recreational activities, song, instrumental music, and dancing enriched the spartan lives of early New Englanders. Of course anyone joining Indians in their dancing, games, gambling, "fooleries and Divill worship" were subject to a heavy fine of ten pounds. Thus, despite "a lurking inherited distrust for enjoyment," the young people cultivated a certain dry humor and enjoyed simple amusements such as house-raisings, dancing parties, husking, spinning, quilting, apple-paring bees, and a whole host of nearly-forgotten children's games. Puritan laws, especially blue laws, were not always the expression of the people but frequently the mandates of a ministerial oligarchy. For example, at a hierarchical council held in Boston on April 9, 1677, it was announced that "that vanity of Horseracing for money" was forbidden within 4 miles of the city.

We hear of a kind of foot-ball being played by boys in Boston's streets and lanes. By the end of the century, the once-serious Training Day had become irksome; playful sham-fights became common and many Boston gentlemen and gentlewomen dined in the tents set up on drill fields for much more serious, military purposes. A kind of amusement hunger turned many to any kind of exhibition. There were signs that the heroic age of Puritanism was passing, some of the old zeal lost. In the Massachusetts of 1684, Puritan theocracy was legally and theoretically brought to an end by royal edict. Many were losing confidence in the power of the saintly aristocracy. A new community conscience was emerging in these very early days of New England mercantilism. The golden age was slipping away; by 1685, the Puritans had become involved in "a great and visible decay of godliness." A turning point in the amusement field was reached. An ancient English sporting heritage was slowly and imperfectly winning out over the religion of Puritanism.

PIONEERS AT PLAY—THE COLONIES IN TRANSITION

By 1680, the native-born were the dominant element in colonial society. They were not carbon copies of their European born and bred parents. In the South, newly affluent families had learned to work hard and enjoy leisure hours in horse racing, dancing, cockfighting, hunting and fishing. The Dutch, never seriously burdened by anti-amusement sentiments, slowly emerged from a primitive society into a richer setting where sport played an ever-growing role. William Penn's colony, still tiny amidst the vast Pennsylvania forests, waited longer before indulging in any significant recreational activities. Three fun days in New England were the Harvard Commencement, Training or Muster Day, and Election. After that, God-fearing folks found enjoyment in community work projects and in elemental games during the few precious free moments. There were visible signs of change in the Puritan community. The Puritan's unique achievement of giving an intellectual structure to their religion without depleting it of emotion resulted in distaste for excess and an abhorance of conspicuous mirth. For them, it helped greatly if any form of merry-making had even a partly utilitarian function. "Sport grew up through Puritan life like flowers in a macadam prison yard."[14] Yet, despite magistral and theological denunciation that most sport was a great "mispense of time," proper sporting amusements were always a part of seventeenth-century New England life.

In New England, the golden age of Puritanism was beginning to slip away. Many of the second generation failed to "feel the spirit that was being poured upon them." The Holy Commonwealth was invaded by secular ideas, a less austere Anglicanism made a strong thrust in the last years of the century; the Massachusetts Charter was revoked, thus eliminating the right to vote only to church members. Still Puritanism continued to be a vital and dynamic faith for a very long time. Throughout the colonies new families of wealth emerged; in the South large landed estates and new fortunes ushered in a luxury class; white servants and African Negroes increased leisure for the few. New England's Puritan oligarchy, if not in retreat, was weakened and the eighteenth century arrived heavy with anticipation of increased opportunities for leisure time sporting pastimes.

REFERENCES

1. John Bunyan, *The Pilgrim's Progress* (Baltimore: Penguin Books, 1965), p. 42.
2. Dennis Brailsford, *Sport and Society. Elizabeth to Anne* (London: Routeledge and Kegan Paul, 1969), p. 206.
3. Philip Alexander Bruce, *Social Life of Virginia in the Seventeenth Century* (Lynchburg, Virginia: J. P. Bell Co., Inc. 1927), pp. 109-110.
4. Peter Force (Ed.) *Tracts and Other Papers*, Vol. III, No. 12 (Washington: Wm. Q. Force, 1844), p. 35.
5. Jane Carson, *Colonial Virginians at Play* (Charlottesville, Virginia: The University of Virginia Press, 1965), pp. 108-109.
6. *York County Records*, Vol. 1671-94, p. 34, as cited in William G. Stanard, Racing in Colonial Virginia, *Virginia Magazine of History and Biography*, II (January, 1895), p. 294.
7. Nicholson's Proclamation . . . , *William and Mary Quarterly*, XI (October, 1902), p. 87.
8. William Elliot Griffis, *The Story of New Netherland* (Boston: Houghton Mifflin Co., 1909), p. 152.
9. Alice Morse Earle, *Colonial Days in Old New York* (New York: Empire State Book Co., 1926), p. 219.
10. Esther Singleton, *Dutch New York* (New York: Dodd, Mead and Co., 1909), p. 291.
11. William Penn, *No Cross, No Crown* (New York: Collins, Brothers and Co., 1845), p. 69.
12. Samuel Eliot Morison, *The Oxford History of the American People* (New York: Oxford University Press, 1965), p. 129.
13. Increase Mather in Perry Miller, *The Puritans* (New York: American Book Co., 1938), p. 412.
14. Robert H. Boyle, The Bizarre History of American Sport, *Sports Illustrated*, XVII (January 8, 1962), p. 56.

CHAPTER 3

Colonial Diversions in Conflict With the Gospel of Work

THE AGE OF ENLIGHTENMENT BEGINS IN ENGLAND

John Locke, whose philosophy may have exercised undisputed sway over the ideas of the entire eighteenth century, began his *Thoughts Concerning Education* with the famous first words—"A sound mind in a sound body is a short but full description of a happy state in this world." His pronouncement was educationally and philosophically reminiscent of an ancient Greek concept and a newer intellectual view of the inseparability of man's mind and body. Yet Locke's voice was no clarion call for universal sport and physical education—certainly not license for the masses to engage in disoriented play devoid of obvious health and moral benefits. The Puritan influence was strong in the Englishman Locke and persisted—without dominating the eighteenth century. For many Englishmen, idleness was suspect unless it was looked upon as respite from work—a refreshing interlude insuring a greater measure of work to follow. Rural Britain, at least, continued as it had for a thousand years—a green and flourishing, opulent land. Here, beyond the teeming cities filled with vital political, social, and economic changes—all heralding the industrial revolution—oarsmen, anglers, hunters, and archers practiced their hoary, sometimes aristocratic sports. "Less moneyed Britons amused themselves with cricket, tennis, fives ('handball'), bowling, horse racing, cockfighting, bearbaiting, and boxing matches—between women as well as between men."[1] Beyond her shores, England had turned back the power of Louis XIV and became mistress of the seas. Affluence, science, sophistication, literary brilliance, the transcendence of Parliament over the Crown, a wider degree of religious toleration, and freedom of the press, were countered by materialism, moral laxity, political corruption, internal strife, and a persistent negative attitude among many toward religion—especially the Established Anglican Church. Thus England was locked in an era of profound change that would, inexorably, spill over to her most precious colony.

Colonial history of the eighteenth century lacked a unifying theme as each colony worked out its own pattern of life—its political practices, its economic system, its cultural advancement. Each persisted in acting as a miniature England—a mutation governed by a North American environment. Sporting amusements received a boost in the colonies during the years 1690-1740. Lurking persistently in the New England territory, especially, was a Protestant gospel of work that continued to see merit in the relaxed moment only in the form of blameless and spiritually revivifying recreation. There were significant exceptions to this measured rationale for sport and amusement, particularly in the Dutch settlement and among many southern aristocrats. Here, the new merchant and plantation elite thrust themselves forward. New families on large landed estates, both in the North and South, emerged seeking diversions in their successful quest for a place in the sun. A carefully stratified society along the eastern seaboard welcomed a period of expansion, prosperity, population influx, and after the 1713 Treaty of Utrecht, an era of peace. Many of the ingredients for a more active sporting colonial involvement were present. In predictable fashion, many seized the opportunity.

SPORT AMONG THE FIRST GENTLEMEN OF VIRGINIA

As usual, historical records reveal more of the wealthy man's pastimes than of poor whites and slaves. This is regrettable yet understandable; the rich had far more time and energy to indulge in a melange of sporting activities. Nowhere in the colonies was this truer than with the Virginia affluent of the eighteenth century. They enjoyed horse races, gambling and cards, formal dinners, dances, music, and the most universal sport, hunting. So much of colonial work was a kind of play that the line of demarcation is difficult to distinguish. Plantation owners worked hard and played hard. Despite the fact that Virginians and New Englanders were both recruited from the same type of Englishman—pious, hard-working, middle-class Puritans—geographic, cultural, and economic factors in the main, transformed an early aversion to sport into a sybaritic Southern ethic. By and large, the Southern aristocrat "shamelessly and notoriously stole time for sociability." The elite escaped the direct thrust of the Puritan Ethic. "It is extremely unlikely that a sports event—horse race, fox hunt, cock fight, or gander pulling anywhere from the Tidewater to the Delta—was typically preceded by a prayerful debate over whether it 'served a rational purpose' or was 'necessary for physical efficiency.' "[2]

Hunting, horse racing, and cockfighting were the three most popular sports in eighteenth century Virginia, and developed in that order. Fishing, hunting small game, shooting wild turkey and deer in the virgin woods was great sport. Robert Beverly, writing in 1705, tells of nocturnal as well as daylight diversions called "Vermine Hunting" (minks, polecats, wolves, and foxes). Hounds were not used in this exercise as they often broke their necks running into trees. Virginians in this early period hunted bears, panthers, amused themselves with rabbits, beaver, otter; organized hunting parties with horses and dogs and sought out large numbers of wolves. Beverly, the Virginia historian, states that he had often, while going at full speed, run down wolves in the untamed forests. Again, writing in 1705, he tells of young people hunting wild horses. He found the ponies so swift and wild "that tis difficult to catch them; and when they are taken, tis odds but their Grease is melted, or else being old, they are so sullen, that they can't be tam'd."[3] The genesis of formal, English-style fox-hunting was delayed till the fourth decade of the century after the wolf population had been reduced and the harried fox chased into the open areas of the Virginia uplands.

Virginians made every effort to preserve the traits of English country life. Among the gentry of both England and her colony, horses were a delightful passion. Virginia alone had more than a dozen race courses before 1700, although there is no evidence that horses were kept especially for racing before 1730. Horses were introduced early and increased rapidly; the planters, especially,

Cock fighting was one of the most popular sports in Virginia. (Courtesy of Library of Congress.)

became unsurpassed riders. William Randolph was typical of early Virginia supporters of the turf; his own Henrico County boasted five racecourses (Bermuda Hundred, Conecock, Varina, Ware, and Malvern Hill). This cradle of American horse racing was witness to excess as early as 1696 when citizens of Northumberland County complained to the House of Burgesses that Saturday races led to Sunday re-matches after all-night parties. "Climate, geography, occupation, and English tradition all helped foster the cult of the horse in Virginia."[4] The records are replete with picturesque names, places, and famous races of the period. Young Fire, Smoker, Folley, Edgecomb, the famous imports, Monkey, Traveller, Jolly Roger, Fearnought, and Janus, "the most perfect horse in colonial America," were central figures on the sporting stage of early Virginia history. William Randolph, William Byrd, Thomas Chamberlaine, Stephen Cocke, and others are representative of the Virginia upper class that the Reverend Hugh Jones, professor of mathematics at William and Mary, described in 1724, as "leading easy lives [and] don't much admire Labour or many Exercises except horse racing." Frequently, they spent the morning in search of their mounts "only to ride two or three miles to church, to the court-house, or to a horse-race."[5]

The aristocratic outlook on life was already firmly entrenched among the landed gentry in the Virginia colony. Their social ideology aped the nobility of England. Virginia society was becoming stabilized, and unlike most Puritans and Quakers who frequently felt uneasy at the prospect of leisure, "your genuine Southerner did not even bother to *appear* industrious."[6] Card playing, gambling, constant visitations between plantations with rounds of dances, fox hunting, horse racing, bowls, quoits, skittles, and endless "Diversions for the Entertainment of the Gentlemen and Ladies" were genteel preoccupations before mid-century. Vivid pictures of Virginia society at play are contained in the *Virginia Gazette* of the period. For example, on November 30, 1736—St. Andrew's Day—"a generous bachelor" of Scotch birth, Mr. Augustus Graham, provided handsome entertainment for his guests: a three mile race between twenty horses and mules, several novelty wrestling matches, a boy's sprint race, music, dancing, singing, lots to eat and drink—provided all such mirth be innocent and free from immorality. Thus, leisureliness was an essential mark of the Southerners' identity; they seemed never to pretend to love their amusements less than they loved work.

RECREATIONAL PRACTICES OF THE KNICKERBOCKER SOCIETY

Only the aristocrat of this period indulged in any significant and recorded forms of amusement. The poorer New Yorker or

Skittles play was popular in the south and in Dutch New York. (*Skittle Players*, by Jan Steen. London, National Gallery of Art.)

Philadelphian found his time mainly occupied with work, church, and family matters, with deliciously small pleasures and games at the local tavern. Many of the well-to-do New York Dutch followed a tradition of early rising, their major meal at noon, and evening recreation. Sleighing parties in winter and fishing picnics in summer were common and very popular; private theatre, balls, concerts, and an astonishing number of joy-filled secular and religious holidays marked Knickerbocker society of the early 1700s. Madame Sarah Knight, visiting Manhattan in the winter of 1704, was met by "50 or 60 sleys." This penchant for cheerfulness was the result of an even earlier inclination among significant New York populations. Hunting, cockfighting, race meetings twice a year at Hempstead, raucous court trial attendance by all classes, "mirth, jolity, and frolicks," animated these spirited people. Among many colonists, including the Dutch, a noticeable decline of interest in religious faith and practice up to about 1734 was a factor in awakening latent recreational tendencies. "Life in the colonial towns from 1690 to 1720 was far more pleasant than it had been in former years. Wealth and leisure commanded new forms of entertainment."[7] The gap between the social classes continued to widen perceptibly. The absence of anything approaching asceticism, especially among the gentry, created serious social and legislative problems. Drinking and gambling increased alarmingly with "pernicious consequences to the public." Innkeepers were reprimanded for not showing restraint with their billiard tables, truck or shuffleboard tables, lotteries, dice, and cards.

Outdoor games and sports were pervasive indulgences in the New York settlement. Good marksmanship was valued as much in the city as it was on the frontier. Shooting matches were held in the form of a sweepstakes—the prize being some object of value instead of money. Besides, games of fives, tennis, cricket, bowling on the green, and golf were no strangers. In 1729, Governor Burnet's inventory mentions "nine gouff clubs, one iron ditto and seven dozen balls." This enthusiastic sportsman-governor also owned five cases of foils, three fowling-pieces and a cane fishing-rod. Dutch tapsters or innkeepers kept truck tables—much like a pool table, on which an ivory ball was struck under a wire wicket by a cue. The same game was also played on grass—a modification of croquet. "Of bowling we hear plenty of talk; it was universally played, from clergy down to Negro slaves, and a famous street in New York, the Bowling Green, perpetuates its popularity."[8] As always, horse racing was strong at fair grounds and on special Manhattan and Long Island courses. Whichever way one turns in reviewing the contemporary literature, there remains the view of a fun-loving Dutch society that managed to make significant contributions to colonial culture in spite of (or maybe because of) its spontaneous play instinct.

PHILADELPHIA SPORTS IN THE OLDEN TIMES

William Penn's "Holy Experiment" was forced very early to assume a defensive posture against certain worldly contaminations. It was of their own doing. "The quiet, simple Quakers, most of them from the humbler walks of life, suddenly found wealth dumped in their laps."[9] Contemporary defenders of the faith found a "barrenness overspread the Society"—a weakness caused by a relative luxurious style of living and an imagined unwholesome passion for games and frivolity. It was inevitable that a Philadelphia court ordered a warrant issued to "Negroes and loose people" for playing about the streets on Sunday. In the same year, 1695, the city council demanded a check be put on horse racing which "begets swearing and blaspheming God's holy name." The passage of restrictive legislation in 1700, by Quaker leaders who made up less than half of Philadelphia population, was evidence enough of the growing pervasiveness of "rude or riotous" sports. This law prohibiting plays, games, bullbaiting, cockfighting, cards, dice, lotteries, "vain and evil sports" so enraged the populace that it was repealed by the Queen's Privy Council in 1705. Alarmed Quaker leaders quickly countered with punitive laws (mild in comparison with the Massachusetts Bay Colony); all Sunday diversions were outlawed along with outright disapproval of nineholes, ninepins, quoits, bowles, bearbaiting, dog-matches, cudgels, backsword, throwing at cocks, rowley-powley, loggats, shovegroat, shovel-board "or any other kind of game whatsoever, now invented or hereafter to be invented."[10] The Quaker oligarchy, perhaps the most logical of all the Puritan groups, continued to inflict on the larger population "a well-formulated conviction regarding the deletereous effects of worldly pursuits."[11] Nonetheless, significant portions of these colonists, clustered in Philadelphia, along the Schuylkill River and in Southeastern Pennsylvania, continued to indulge in these sporting "worldly pursuits." Gaming, sports and pastimes, races on horseback or on foot gained greater appeal among many in spite of the ancient adage that "our time swiftly passeth away, and our pleasure and delight ought to be in the law of the Lord."

The Society of Friends did not approve of horse races, but others did, and races were held early in the century. Race Street in Philadelphia got its name because it led directly to the race ground—a circular course through forest trees. As early as 1726, the city's rapid growth made horse racing at the Sassafras Street fair "very dangerous to life." Almost as popular as racing was fishing on the

The Schuylkill Fishing Company was a sporting club founded by Philadelphians in 1732.

Schuylkill River; America's oldest sporting club, the Colony, was founded in 1732. Only a few years later the unnatural marriage of sport and politics manifested itself in the celebrated "Walking Purchase" swindle. It seems that in 1686, the peace-loving and skilled Indian peace maker, William Penn, had arranged for the purchase of Indian lands along a boundary parallel to the Delaware River and running inland as far as a normal man could walk in a day and a half. It was left to Penn's son, Thomas, to carefully lay out the route, clear the trail, and hire the three fastest pedestrians in the Province to consummate the task. Edward Marshall, James Yates, and Solomon Jennings, set a blistering pace on the morning of September 19, 1737, and were accompanied by pacers on horseback and several astonished Indians. The Indians protested that the trio were "lifting" or running rather than walking; they gave up at noon gasping, "No sit down to smoke, no shoot squirrel, just lun, lun, lun all day long." One runner quit, the second fell into a creek and was drowned; but the third pumped through till noon of the next day, grasped a sapling ending the "race," and gasped that the eighty miles covered and the half million acres of Indian cornfields and hunting grounds now belonged to the Penn family.[12] Generations of Indian troubles followed on the heels of this historic cross-country performance.

The pure Quakerism of George Fox and William Penn was rapidly diluted as second and third generation colonists were joined by a new stream of German and Scotch-Irish immigrants. Astonishing numbers poured into Philadelphia beginning about 1717; the promise of cheap lands and religious freedom offered strong inducements to poor Europeans. Most worked very hard in the new land. Most would learn to rise above total austerity and enjoy the fruits of their labor— including a relatively free conscience regarding worthy use of leisure time. Indigenous Quaker families were beginning to lose full political power in Philadelphia, "yet retained the serenity, the high ideals, and the sturdy pacifism that are the finast flowers of their sect."[13]

NEW ENGLAND'S STOLEN TIME FOR SPORT

The period 1690-1740 in England was one of brutal amusements and much gambling, and colonial life reflected these tendencies in milder form. The period was also one in which orderly colonial policy and administration reached a peak—a state of affairs conducive to the growth of nonproductive and relaxing sport. Yet the spectre of Indian wars was always present, adding to a low point in New England intellectual achievement and spiritual commitment. The rapidly growing revolt against the dogmas of Calvinism created a theological vacuum that had to be filled; a growing humanism soon manifested itself in a metaphysical and intellectual new view of God as a "merciful and compassionate Parent." Along with a swelling mercantile success, many New Englanders advanced steadily toward greater earthly comfort—and often with little accompanying feelings of guilt. The rigidly introspective, class-conscious, and ascetic New England leaders had great difficulty adjusting to the changing intellectual climate of England and to the rich material growth of America. Some of the laws designed to regulate personal habits and customs broke down. "The builders of the Bible state had focused so narrowly on their own sainthood that they failed to see the growing discontent and power of the large unsanctified majority."[14] This same larger group had long since decided to enjoy a Christian life punctuated with bouts of recreational sporting pastimes.

The lack of organized recreation and the ever-present statutory restrictions guaranteeing a quiet Sabbath, did no more than blunt the presence of a variety of sports, games, indoor and outdoor amusements. The absence of the theatre plus a muted music and dancing expressiveness narrowed the New Englander's cultural horizons. Community leaders like Cotton Mather and Judge Samuel Sewall had little sympathy for untrammelled mirth. The Reverend Mather was shocked in 1711 when the youngsters of his congregation held "a Frolick, a revelling Feast, and Ball" on Christmas night. We have no record of his main objection—the activity or the unfortunate time chosen for play. Possibly the former, for the New Englander of the period had little to do with Catholic holidays. "How displeasing must it be to God," observed sober Judge Sewall, "the giver of our Time, to Keep anniversary days to play the fool with ourselves and others."[15] However, times were changing albeit slowly. Less objection was encountered to pleasant, healthful divertissement. Benjamin Coleman's conception of humor combined traditional Puritanism with the new eighteenth-century English non-conformism:

> A great deal of Pleasantry there is in the Town, and very graceful and charming it is so far as it is Innocent and Wise . . . We daily need some respite and diversion, without which we dull our Powers; a little intermission sharpens 'em again. It spoils the Bow to Keep it always bent, and the Viol if always strain'd up. Mirth is some loose or relaxation to the labouring Mind or Body. . . .[16]

The key words of the time were restraint and utilitarianism. Satisfying merrymaking could be found at baptisms, weddings, barn-raisings, cornhuskings, quilting-parties, church and house-raisings, ship-launchings, and even ministers' ordinations. A public bowling green was advertised in Boston in 1700—as was a public billiard room. Dice, cards, backgammon, tally bowling, and nine pins were reluctantly permitted. Cotton Mather inveighed against cock-fighting in 1705. A growing foreign trade in toys reflected an easing Puritanism and a changing view of children. Youngsters played stone tag, wood tag, squat tag, marbles, leapfrog, and singing games. In "Deer and Hounds," one boy took the place of a deer and a number of others pursued him through the woods. Singing schools, spelling bees, and sleigh ride parties offered young people opportunities to approach uninhibited joy. Boston Common was the scene of a general town revel on annual training days. Running, leaping, wrestling, cudgel, stool-ball, quoits and back-sword or single-stick were practiced. But the favorite competition on these days was shooting at a mark for a handkerchief, a prize, or a wager. Over at Harvard, Commencement Day always brought the gentry together for good times. At Charles Town the common people indulged in crude English sports and games—so much so that in 1712, the Assembly declared them illegal near taverns on Sunday. Throughout, of course, hunting and fishing remained among the most satisfying of the approved sport in early eighteenth-century New England. Social histories throw a penetrating light on how a very considerable number of people were spending such free time as they had. Always there was the central problem of the Puritan Elect—the problem of doing right in a world that does wrong. No Puritan objected to recreation as such; indeed only if he saw in such activity the smallest deviation from the glorification of God and his prescribed pathway to moral perfection would sport be condemned. The puritan work ethic in its purest form must have allowed that "it was necessary for a man to indulge in frivolous pleasures from time to time, in order that he might return to his work refreshed."[17]

New England Puritanism—the traditional inhibitor of sport—was in truth one of the powerful American influences that led eventually to the introduction of voluntary school competitive athletics and compulsory physical education. National stability, rising expectations among middle and merchant classes, the beginnings of colonial university education, and an atmosphere of intellectualism received its most significant thrust in New England. This Puritanism was not, as we have seen, an immediate catalytic agent for the rise of sport in the American colonies. Rather, it was a substantial portion of the bedrock upon which certain moral traditions, intellectual origins, and capitalistic institutions rested. Only out of these beginnings of the new nation was a pervasive system of sport and physical education to slowly emerge. As long as a society struggles for preservation, it cannot endure sport. Civilization is born the moment that life satisfies its primary needs and begins to enjoy a little leisure. The New England work ethic of the seventeenth and eighteenth century took firm root in a primitive country, helped it grow, and made an immense contribution to an atmosphere where most people might eventually find time for conspicuous play.

Because the Puritan found contentment in his daily work, he contributed to a later age's increased leisure through the building of a responsible society by individual passion for God and a cheerful diligence. These Puritans were not ignorant, fanatic, nor prudish. They were moral athletes dedicated to a "gospel of work," trained to sedulously observe a Protestant ethic emphasizing sobriety, thrift, and earthly comforts without forgetting the highest joy—devotion to a sovereign God. They were not opposed to diversion and recreation, provided it was truly refreshing, not excessively time-consuming, and not immoral or sensual by their definition. Seasonal merriment must somehow contribute to their brand of Christian living; it must be a beautiful and harmonious experience. In their profound respect for beauty, the Puritan rejected all forms of barren estheticism. "In fact, no people ever hated lower and frivolous forms of beauty more than the Puritans."[18] These people had high expectations. Their life style made material success for the majority an inevitability. For those who think the Puritan had no time to enjoy his success, one has only to investigate the colonial New Englander's extraordinary talent for combining work and play in his daily life—six days a week.

REFERENCES

1. Will and Ariel Durant, *The Age of Voltaire* (New York: Simon and Schuster, 1965), p. 78.

2. C. Vann Woodward, The Southern Ethic in a Puritan World, *The William and Mary Quarterly*, Third Series, XXV (July, 1968), p. 357.

3. Robert Beverly, *The History and Present State of Virginia*. Louis B. Wright, ed. (Chapel Hill: University of North Carolina Press, 1947), p. 312.

4. Dixon Wecter, *The Saga of American Society. A Record of Social Aspirations 1607-1937* (New York: Charles Scribner's Sons, 1937), p. 430.

5. Hugh Jones, *The Present State of Virginia*. Ed. by Richard L. Morton (Chapel Hill: University of North Carolina, 1956), p. 84.

6. C. Van Woodward, The Southern Ethic in a Puritan World, *The William and Mary Quarterly*, Third Series, XXV (July, 1968), p. 347.

7. Carl Bridenbaugh, *Cities in the Wilderness* (New York: Ronald Press, 1938), p. 280.

8. Alice Morse Earle, *Colonial Days in Old New York* (New York: Empire State Book Co., 1926, original in 1896), p. 209.

9. Thomas Jefferson Wertenbaker, *The Founding of American Civilization. The Middle Colonies* (New York: Cooper Square Publishing, Inc., 1963), p. 200.

10. *The Statutes at Large of Pennsylvania 1705-6*, p. 187.

11. William S. Dye, Pennsylvania versus the theatre, *The Pennsylvania Magazine of History and Biography*, LV (1931), p. 340.

12. William J. Buck, *History of the Indian Walk Performed for the Proprietaries of Pennsylvania in 1737* (Printed by the author, 1886).

13. Samuel Eliot Morison, *The Oxford History of the American People* (New York: Oxford University Press, 1965), p. 130.

14. Roger Burlingame, *The American Conscience* (New York: Alfred A. Knopf, 1960), p. 73.

15. Samuel Sewall, *Samuel Sewall's Diary*. Edited by Mark van Doren (New York: Macy-Masius Publishing Co., 1927), p. 245.

16. Benjamin Coleman, *The Government and Improvement of Mirth* (Boston, 1707), as cited in Perry Miller and T. H. Johnson. *The Puritans*, Vol. II (New York: Harper & Row, 1963), p. 392.

17. Edmund S. Morgan, *The Puritan Dilemma, The Story of John Winthrop* (Boston: Little, Brown & Co., 1958), pp. 9-10.

18. Paul K. Conkin, *Puritans and Pragmatists* (New York: Dodd, Mead and Co., 1968), p. 31.

CHAPTER 4

Sport During and After the Great Awakening

RELIGIOUS REVIVAL AND THE GREAT AWAKENING

The quiet and pervasive liberal view of Christianity, characteristic of the early decades of the colonial eighteenth century, was fractured by the Great Awakening—an emotional revival of orthodox Calvinism. Attitudes toward sport and frivolous use of leisure time were caught in a squeeze play between a century-old condemnatory outlook and a newer and softer Arminianism.* Uncompromising in his orthodoxy, Jonathan Edwards (1703-1758) represented a New Divinity, a restatement of Calvinism. Preaching at Enfield, Connecticut, on July 8, 1741, Edwards terrified the weeping and groaning congregation with the pronouncement that sin is the ruin and misery of the soul—that Christ was their only refuge and salvation. "Therefore, let everyone that is out of Christ, now awake and fly from the wrath to come," cried Edwards to all backsliders. He looked upon youthful amusements and frolicking as a dreadful manifestation; that "the corruption of the heart of man is immoderate and boundless in its fury."[1] Religious toleration, however, had gained a foothold even in Puritan Massachusetts, and the pleasant village citizenry of Northampton dismissed him in 1750. "He had offended influential citizens by denouncing the 'frolics' of their young people—which amounted to nothing worse than sleigh rides to a neighboring town to indulge in country square dances and rum and water."[2] The genius of Jonathan Edwards was that of an earlier Puritanism combined with an extraordinary eighteenth century intellectualism. Edwards' chiliastic predic-

---

* Arminianism opposed absolute predestination and preached universal redemption through Christ who died for all men and not only for the elect. It saw salvation as the direct result of a free spirit and good works.

40

Youthful amusements, possibly even fishing, were among the list of Jonathan Edwards' corruptions of man's heart.

tions in the midst of the Great Awakening were incompatible with a growing colonial religious liberalism.

Possibly a manifestation of this liberalism as it relates to sport and recreation might be the thoughts of the Reverend Joseph Seccomb. Writing at the height of the sweeping evangelical fervor of the 1740s, Seccomb found that "Diversion in Proper Portions of Time, and other suitable Circumstances, are not hurtful, but very friendly to Religion." A colonial Izaak Walton, the Reverend Mr. Seccomb's "Discourse . . . in the Fishing-Season" is the earliest American book on the sports of field and stream. It is, more largely, a rationale for man's proper balance of work and play. For him, God is an active Being to be emulated.

> When the Body has been long wearied with Labour, or the Mind weakened with Devotion, it's requisite to give them Ease; then the use of innocent and moderate Pleasures and Recreations is both useful and necessary, to Soul and Body; it enlivenes Nature, recruits our Spirits, and renders us more able to set about serious Business and Employment. . . . For to intermix no Gratifications, nor Diversions with our more serious Affairs, makes the Mind inactive, dull and useless. . . . Our Diversion, if rightly used, not only fits us for, but leads us to Devotion.[3]

The Great Awakening was an intercolonial evangelical movement which attempted to stem the tide of irreligion, moral laxity, and alleged over-intellectualism that swept Europe. The colonies, as always, felt these continental tremors. A freer, more daring and democratic atmosphere, unexpectedly, resulted from the Great Awakening. It was, after all, a parallel thrust of the western world's Age of Reason—a further effort at responsible freedom of man's spirit as well as his body.

SPORT AND THE COLONIAL ENLIGHTENMENT

The Colonial Enlightenment, an adaptation of a brilliant eighteenth century European intellectualism, was a positive factor in the growing acceptance of sport and recreational diversions as a natural part of individual and family life activities. Relative affluence, a certain national optimism, and individual buoyancy of spirit appear as prerequisites to any sport pervasiveness. These ingredients were conspicuous in colonial America during the century's middle decades. In 1743, Benjamin Franklin, the leading citizen in the colonies and already well known in Europe for his scientific discoveries, wrote: "The first drudgery of settling new colonies is pretty well over, and there are many in every colony in circumstances which set them at ease to cultivate the finer arts and improve the common stock of knowledge." As often was the case, Franklin was both correct and

prophetic; the European intellectual impetus was immediately reflected in the American colonists' more widely accepted role of sport
and leisured activities. American contributions to this Age of Progress
were still slight but there was a mood of optimism in the land. "The
World is now daily increasing in experimental knowledge, and let no
Man flatter the Age, with pretending we are arrived to a Perfection of
Discoveries," stated the *American Magazine* in a balanced but optimistic
editorial.[4] A growing secularism, especially in the cities, combined
with new wealth and an inquiring, relatively sophisticated intellectualism to bring about a desire in all classes to spend money on
something more than mere existence. The tavern and the horse
racing track were the two most conspicuous areas of sporting indulgences during the colonial period 1740-1781.

HORSE RACING AMONG THE ELITE

The rebellion against Calvinism took place in earnest during the
1740s. "Liberal seams were clearly visible in the Puritan granite," is
one modern historian's assessment of the time. Churchmen conceded
the decline of religiosity, of morals, and standards of conduct after
1740. Yet, it is easy to exaggerate these individual and collective
human desires. From the very earliest Puritan beginnings, the people
in the American colonies had always laughed and enjoyed
themselves—difficult as it was at times. The aura of the Enlightenment blended with the earlier ecclesiastical culture and helped
produce an urbane gentleman—in many cases a most notable elitist
who looked upon horses and horseracing as one of the several
passions of his ample leisure time.

Excepting the founding decades and the Revolutionary War
period, there was no time in Maryland and Virginia colonial history
that a rich tradition of horse racing did not exist. The middle of the
eighteenth century was especially important in the history of the
sport. After 1740, the systematic breeding of horses from imported
English thoroughbreds resulted in formal course or circular track
racing replacing the primitive matched affairs of quarter-racing.
Almost simultaneously, jockey clubs emerged in South Carolina,
Virginia, Maryland, and New York. The distinction between spirited
or blooded horses and those of the common sort took on new
meaning as horsemen learned fundamental principles of breeding,
and jockeys, trainers, and stablemen emerged as part of a systematic
and organized sport—possibly the most romantic and pervasive one
in American history.

Surprisingly, horse racing on the circular-mile track as well as
organized racing originated in the North.[5] Early in the eighteenth
century the New York Subscription Plate was being run and by 1750,

Circular tracks began to replace quarter horse straight racing in the 1700s. (Courtesy of Harvard University Theatre Collection.)

things were booming; a spectator charge of six pence was levied as early as 1736. The Maryland Jockey Club was founded around 1745—the predominantly Catholic colony not strongly against racing—only gambling. Races usually consisted of three heats of 2 miles although the 4 mile heat winners were considered the truest champions and received prizes accordingly. Governor Samuel Ogle returned from England in 1747 with a blooded stallion and mare. The superiority of the English thoroughbred was evident from the start. "Ogle's importations started the trend toward thoroughbred domination of the Maryland turf. Some races were closed to the thoroughbred and eventually weight was added to horses with as little as one-eighth English blood in them."[6] Most Maryland fairs featured horse racing. A typical affair is described in the *Maryland Gazette* of September 20, 1745. In addition to handsome cash prizes to the winning horses, contests included cudgelling bouts, wrestling, and foot races for Negro girls.[7] The Jockey Club Plate, the Town Purse, and the Free Mason's Plate were all handsome prizes, and to heighten gala Maryland occasions, ladies' galleries or grandstands were provided.

Between 1730 and 1770, some 176 stallions and mares had crossed the Atlantic—mostly to the Tidewater area of the Virginia colony. "A new and perfect type of race horse" had been bred in England—the stimulus of three legendary Oriental stallions, the Godolphin Barb, the Darley Arabian, and the Byerly Turk. The size and endurance of the Virginia horse increased rapidly as a result of thoroughbred importation; by mid-century foreign visitors were commenting on the high quality of Virginia-bred horses. Both the improved stock and the increasing formality of the sport were part of the economic prosperity of the Old Dominion. The taste for luxury was already ingrained in upper-class Virginians; "the Race Horse Region" was replete with stud farms. Fairfax Harrison identified and listed twenty-seven such farms in pre-Revolutionary Virginia.[8]

The handsome animals from these farms were built for endurance as well as speed. In the subscription races so popular in the era, each horse ran three heats—the winner of two heats gaining the purse. In each heat the slower horses were eliminated if they were "distanced" or trailed the winner by a furlong. Each heat might be four times around the mile course; a horse that ran all three heats covered twelve miles—a test requiring "bottom" as well as speed. One of the greatest subscription racers was Selima, daughter of the Godolphin and the best horse in Colonel Benjamin Tasker's Maryland Belair stable. Selima's crowning achievement as a racer came when she entered the Inter-Colonial Sweepstakes in December of 1752, defeating William Byrd's Virginia chestnut horse, Tyral. A fortune was bet on the race and the winner, Selima, the first great matriarch in American breeding history, was acclaimed in her life-time as "the best of the best." The indissoluble connection between a growing wealthy Virginia class and horse racing history is typified by the exploits of Selima and her progeny.

SURCEASE FROM THE CULT OF WORK

For ages the chief creative force in western civilization was Christianity. Then, rather suddenly, in the eighteenth century, it declined amidst a new kind of spiritual reform. With the notable exception of the Great Awakening, "colonial Americans continued to drift either into spiritual indifference or into the rationalistic religion fashionable in contemporary Europe."[9] In either case, for a large number of people, it resulted in an unsatisfactory state, an uneasy partial vacuum that demanded a belief in something outside themselves. This partial collapse of the Christian faith first occurred in England. The French philosopher Montesquieu noted that "there is no religion in England. If anyone mentions religion people begin to laugh." Such attitudes, more noticeable among intellectuals and the wealthy, resulted in a surge of interest for art, music, literature, splendid homes and furniture, theatre, fashionable sport and ostentatious amusements. Some of this, in modified form, percolated down to the masses and significant numbers sought escape from vespers and relief from work.

An activity perfectly suited to accomplish both these ends was fox hunting with a pack of hounds. Surprisingly, the sport began awakening in America at about the same time it did in England. For many colonial aristocrats, it became a passion, and a long, unbroken history began in the fifth decade of the eighteenth century. Dr. Thomas Walker, scholar, sportsman, and explorer, of Castle Hill, Albemarle County, Virginia, imported hounds from England in 1742—the only pre-revolutionary pack to pass into the twentieth century without losing its specific identification. Earlier, in 1730, the English red fox had been imported to Maryland's Eastern Shore. Still earlier, in mid-seventeenth century, the cavalier, Robert Brooke, the first known master of foxhounds in America, sailed for Calvert County, Maryland, in his own ship, taking with him his family, a large retinue of servants, and his pack of hounds. The sport grew slowly in these early days. Before leaving England in 1747, Lord Fairfax shipped two dogs and a bitch to William Fairfax, his cousin at Belvoir, Virginia, dispatching him a note to take good care of them as they were well-bred, and that a cross should improve the native breed. In 1751, George Washington entered in his diary, "Although a heavy man, he [Lord Fairfax] was a fine horseman; and, as I was never tired of the saddle, we were much engaged in the hunting of wild foxes." The

George Washington and Lord Fairfax went fox hunting in Virginia around 1750.

sport grew rapidly after the Revolutionary War and before the Civil War, particularly with the landed gentry of Virginia, Maryland, and Pennsylvania. A woman-satirist, with a spirited pen, had her fling in rhyme at fox hunting:

> "A fox is killed by twenty men,
> That fox perhaps had killed a hen.
> A gallant art no doubt is here,
> All wicked foxes ought to fear,
> When twenty dogs and twenty men
> Can kill a fox that killed a hen."

An item in the *Virginia Gazette* of 1751, said that taverns had been "perverted" from their original purpose and the least desirable townspeople indulged in "prohibitive and unlawful Games, Sports, and Pastimes." There is considerable proof that in England as well as the American colonies, the poor squandered their wages in taverns while the rich gambled their fortunes in clubs or private homes. During the period, taverns were the most flourishing of all urban institutions; men gambled on backgammon, shuffleboard, cards and games of chance. Billiards became the rage everywhere.[10] Recreational opportunities became more pronounced for many, but were a special accompaniment of gentility. Dancing, horse racing, the theatre, cockfighting, games of fives, tennis, and cricket all had their following among an ever-growing strata of the population. Cricket had become the national sport of England and spread to Georgia, Maryland and New York. In 1751, an international cricket match between eleven colonists and an equal number of Londoners resulted in a surprising victory for the Americans.[11] It was undoubtedly the first American international sporting event.

America was coming of age and several of her leading citizens felt the need to discuss the deleterious effects of physical inactivity. As a youth, John Adams spent much of his time making and sailing boats, in making and flying kites, driving hoops, playing marbles, quoits, wrestling, swimming, skating, "and, above all in shooting, to which Diversion I was addicted to a degree of Ardor which I knew not that I ever felt for any other Business, Study or Amusement."[12] A short time later, in 1750, Adams' biographer noted that the future president's freshmen duties at Harvard included furnishing upper classmen with bats, balls, and foot-balls.[13] Benjamin Franklin, America's Renaissance man, was fully aware of the writings of Milton and Locke—in particular with those dealing with exercises. In his *Proposals Relating to the Education of Youth in Pennsylvania*, Franklin urged that all expected college students "be frequently exercised in running, leaping, wrestling, and swimming."[14] The remarkable Mr. Franklin, himself, was a skilled and pioneer swimmer and repeated more than once the need for a sound mind and a sound body. The list of leading colonial Americans that urged a fuller interpretation of worthy use of leisure time includes William Byrd, II, George Washington, Thomas Jefferson, and others.[15]

Most colonists of the mid-eighteenth century, even New Englanders, were less handicapped by religious restraints. As soon as most could find relief from the daily struggle against elemental nature, they began to enjoy certain sports and pastimes. Winter and water sports abounded. Boating, hunting, and fishing were everywhere present. In New York City, out-of-door games were extensively played on the Common, while bowls and golf were no strangers to the gentry. The uninhibited Dutch enjoyed cockfighting, horse racing, and bull-baiting.[16] Similarly, the dilettantish set of Annapolis and Williamsburg enjoyed equally its literary clubs, dances, dinners, its jockey club, the theatre, gambling, cockfighting, and the like. Low and high brow amusements were seized upon by some indiscriminately. Billiard tables were part of the standard furniture in taverns and planters' homes throughout the Virginia colony. The game was an adaptation of an ancient outdoor form of bowls, brought indoors and raised from the ground to an oblong table, surrounded by a low railing and covered with green cloth. At one end stood a sort of wicket made of ivory, called the port, and at the other end a pointed

An international cricket match was played as early as 1751.

Billiards, brought to America from England, graced many homes of well-to-do southerners.

ivory peg called the king. There were six pockets or "hazards"—one at each corner, and one in the middle of each of the long sides. Two small ivory balls, and wooden sticks shaped like miniature hockey sticks completed the equipment. The player held the stick between his forefingers and thumb and struck his ball smartly with the flat side of the curved end. He scored in several ways: (1) sending his ball first through the port (2) touching the king without knocking it over or (3) sending opponent's ball against the king or into a hazard.[17] In predictable fashion, the sport became a positive obsession with many.

The pioneering families forging westward, the rough and peripatetic woodsmen all had an ever-present fabulous kind of sporting amusement. During this period, 1740-1781, the richness of children's games seems particularly noticeable. Stool-ball, cricket, fives, tip-cat, baseball, oystering, street games, marbles, hop-scotch, leap-frog, blind man's bluff, hide and seek, prisoner's base, hoop rolling, kite flying, and many others were easily identified as period activities. Yet the truest picture of the changing tapestry of sporting interests was found in the five major colonial cities of Boston, New York, Philadelphia, Annapolis, and Williamsburg. Basking in the broadening influence of overseas commerce, stimulated by the quickening effects of a decade or more of war between France and England, affluent colonists made an extraordinary effort to emulate the sophistication of Old World cities.

SPORT DURING THE PERIOD OF COLONIAL RESISTANCE 1758-1781

John Adams saw the American Revolution as a "radical change in the principles, opinions, sentiments and affections of the people," and thought it was, above all, "in the minds and hearts of the people." The new nation, conceived in liberty, was, from the beginning, dedicated to the proposition of free enterprise. In the years before the war, great economic growth combined with social and military tension. The middle-class, self-made man had already made his mark while the elitist, landholding class gained even firmer control of the social and political life of the Atlantic seaboard. A pervasive materialism and confusion regarding the role of Christianity began to whittle away at the foundations of the family, community, church, and other institutions of the social order. One common interest, even passion, was the growing desire to utilize leisure time in recreational activities and sporting pastimes. It was a sentiment that cut across social lines and persisted through the next two centuries.

Throughout colonial history, social stratification was very discernible in the amusements of gentlemen and the ruder diversions of the common people, particularly those in the backwoods. While seventy-one "Gentlemen of the Turf" in Philadelphia were donning pink coats and riding to hounds at the new Jockey Club of 1766, the lower classes on the frontier found rougher amusements in shooting and no rules boxing and wrestling. In 1769, rude North Carolina farmers entertained themselves by fighting, bruising, gouging out the eye of an opponent, biting, "balloching" or "Abelarding" (emasculation). The ever-fitful diarist and school teacher, Philip Fithian, described a form of crude boxing popular late in the eighteenth century:

> Every diabolical strategem for Mastery is allowed and practised,
> of bruising, kicking, scratching, pinching, biting, butting, trip-
> ping, throtling, gouging, cursing, dismembring, howling, etc.
> This spectacle (so loathsome and horrible!) generally is attended
> with a crowd of people![18]

The Reverend Doctor Joseph Doddridge, in his travels through
western Virginia and Pennsylvania from 1763 to 1783, explained such
barbarous frontier sport as natural for survival among a people who
"set a higher value on physical than mental endowments." Running,
jumping, wrestling, shooting, dramatic narrations, singing, and especially dancing, were all western settlement games and diversions.

As the revolution approached, radical colonists, striking back at the
crown and the conservatives, attempted to pass legislation against
certain extravagances and dissipations—especially horse racing,
gambling, shows, plays, cockfighting, "and other expensive diversions
and entertainments." The American Revolution showed a Puritan
streak common to most revolutions; in March of 1779, the Pennsylvania Assembly enacted "An Act for the Suppression of Vice and
Immorality." Sunday work and play were strictly forbidden; cockfighting, horse racing, shooting matches, and any form of gambling were
punishable by heavy fines. "Idle sport" of any kind was not permitted
in local taverns and inns. During these critical years, middle class
virtues and a natural resentment towards aristocratic pleasures combined with war-time austerity to temporarily dull the edge of a people
rapidly learning the delights of leisure time sporting activities.

All along the seacoast the life of the people was very much altered
by the war. Intemperance, changes in morality, a new social order and
a new outlook upon life and leisure were coming into being. The
Reverend Joseph Strong, who preached in New London just after the
war, was alarmed at the vulgar conduct among the boys. Boys and
girls called to each other across the church and before he had reached
his lodging the boys were already playing ball and pitching quoits.
Quaker morality stiffened in the face of the growing threat and the
Philadelphia society lobbied directly against the theater, dram shops,
and idle and vulgar sport. Alarmed by the participation of common
people in "deceitful" games of chance, the South Carolina Assembly
voided all gambling debts, made provision for the recovery of money
or goods lost by playing cards, dice, bowls, tennis, betting,
shuffleboard, billiards, skittles and ninepins. And in 1773, Josiah
Quincy, Jr., a dyed-in-the wool Yankee, spread his Puritan prejudices
over the pages of his journal during a Virginia visit.

> I spent yesterday chiefly with young men of fortune; they were
> gamblers and cock-fighters, hound breeders, and horse-jockies.

To hear them converse, you would think that the grand point of all science was probably to fix a gaff and touch with dexterity the tail of a cock while in combat.[19]

Another small manifestation of the American Revolutionary conflict between traditional Puritan conservatism and a newer liberalism occurred in 1779, between Henry Laurens, South Carolina millionaire president of the Continental Congress and liberal Carolina lawyer, William Henry Drayton. The advocate had urged Congress to authorize the celebration of Independence Day by an elaborate display of fireworks. In what Laurens called "a funny declamation," Drayton praised the Olympic games and other festivities by which nations celebrated their nativity. Laurens, outraged by the extravagance of celebrations in general answered that "the Olympic games of Greece and other fooleries brought on the desolation of Greece." When Drayton won approval for his motion and pointed out that the Olympic games "were calculated for improving bodily strength, to make men athletic and robust," Laurens was left to reflect in his diary, "Is drinking Medeira Wine from 5 to 9 o'clock, then sallying out to gaze at fireworks, and afterwards returning to wine again, calculated to make men athletic and robust?"[20] This emergence of sport and recreational pastimes as a regular and frequent American experience—approaching in importance the work ethic, was an ideological struggle that persists to the present day.

REFERENCES

1. Jonathan Edwards, Sinners in the Hands of an Angry God, in Vergilius Ferm, ed. *Puritan Sage. Collected Writings of Jonathan Edwards* (New York: Library Publishers, 1953), p. 368.

2. Samuel Eliot Morison, *The Oxford History of the American People* (New York: Oxford University Press, 1965), pp. 152-153.

3. Joseph Seccomb, *Business and diversion inoffensive to God, and necessary for the comfort and support of human society* (Boston: S. Kneeland and T. Green, 1743), pp. 17-18.

4. *American Magazine*, October, 1743, as cited in James Truslow Adams, *Provincial Society 1690-1763*, Vol. III of *A History of American Life*, Arthur M. Schlesinger and Dixon Ryan Fox, ed. (New York: The Macmillan Co., 1927), p. 273.

5. John Hervey, *Racing in America 1665-1865*, Vol. I (New York: The Jockey Club, 1944), p. 33.

6. Alexander J. Young, Pre-Civil War Horse Racing in Maryland (unpublished M.A. thesis, University of Maryland, 1963), p. 68.

7. *Ibid.*, p. 48.

8. Jane Carson, *Colonial Virginians at Play* (Charlottesville: University of Virginia Press, 1965), pp. 114-115.

9. Rowland Berthoff, *An Unsettled People. Social Order and Disorder in American History* (New York: Harper & Row, 1971), p. 110.

10. Carl Bridenbaugh, *Cities in Revolt. Urban Life 1746-1776* (New York: Alfred A. Knopf, 1965), p. 157.

11. Charles Blancke, Cricket in America, *Harper's Weekly*, XXXV (September 26, 1891), p. 725.

12. John Adams, *Diary and Autobiography of John Adams*, L. H. Butterfield, ed., Vol. I (Cambridge: Harvard University Press, 1961), p. 100.

13. Page Smith, *John Adams*, Vol. I (1735-1784) (Garden City, New York: Doubleday and Co., Inc., 1962), p. 20.

14. Benjamin Franklin in Carl Van Doren, *Benjamin Franklin* (New York: Viking Press, 1938), p. 190.

15. Thomas R. Davis, Sport and Exercise in the Lives of Selected Colonial Americans: Massachusetts and Virginia, 1700-1775 (unpublished Ph.D. dissertation, University of Maryland, 1970).

16. Part VI titled, Amusements, in Esther Singleton, *Social New York Under the Georges 1714 to 1776*, Vol. II (Port Washington, New York: Ira J. Friedman, Inc., 1969).

17. Jane Carson, *Colonial Virginians at Play* (Charlottesville; University of Virginia Press, 1965), pp. 82-84.

18. Philip Vickers Fithian, *Journal and Letters of Philip Vickers Fithian, 1773-1774*, Hunter Dickinson Farish, ed. (Williamsburg, Virginia, 1943), pp. 240-241.

19. Josiah Quincy, Jr., Journal, Massachusetts Historical Society *Proceedings*, XLIX, p. 467.

20. Edmund S. Morgan, The Puritan Ethic and the American Revolution, *The William and Mary Quarterly*, Third Series, XXIV (January, 1967), pp. 31-32.

CHAPTER 5

The National Period and America's Efforts at Leisure

CULTURAL INDEPENDENCE AND NATIONAL OPTIMISM

New England's scholar-patriot, Noah Webster, was one of the many Americans at the close of the eighteenth century who reflected a European enlightened thought welded to a peculiar national spirit of independence and optimism. Writing in *The American Magazine* for December, 1787, Webster entreated all Americans to unshackle their minds, to establish a national character, and, above all, to create a system of broad and liberal education. "Before this system can be formed and embraced," he said, "the Americans must believe and act from the belief that it is dishonorable to waste life in mimicking the follies of other nations and basking in the sunshine of foreign glory."[1] The new nation of optimists—many in a frenzy of movement—very early began the shaping of a national character. Samuel Harrison Smith, Jefferson's party journalist and editor of the *National Intelligencer*, remarked in 1796 that the American man "would feel himself in possession of two extensive sources of enjoyment, the exercise of the body, and the reflection of the mind."[2] The new American would need both of these faculties, for he faced the dichotomy of continuing to borrow the essence of European liberal thought while at the same time creating a brand new and stubbornly independent American. It never wholly came about, yet the nineteenth century effort was a magnificent chapter in American history. The American's euphoric state at the turn of the century, the nation's economic revolution, the rise of American nationalism, religious liberalism, and an extraordinary individual creativeness, vigor or self-reliance encouraged most men to play hard when they could, as well as work hard.

FRONTIER SPORT

The American historian, Frederick Jackson Turner, looked upon the frontier as the line of most rapid and effective Americanization. Pioneer work and play was crude, contentious, individualistic, and supremely pragmatic. Their recreations reflected their environment—hard and lonely. Frequently, the colonial pioneer associated pleasurable recreation with necessary industry. But, as Foster Rhea Dulles points out, "when the craving for comradeship could no longer be ignored, when the need for amusement had to be satisfied, there were no artificial constraints or polite conventions about the pioneer celebrations."[3] An Anglo-Saxon heritage and a newer New England Puritan conservative background had less influence on the early frontiersmen than environmental forces which sharpened already inherent personal qualities of self-determination, aggressiveness, and rugged individualism. One writer exaggerates only slightly when she says that "our cultural institutions stopped being English as the first settlers crossed the Appalachians."[4] The tendency of this peculiar American was to evaluate a man on his physical performance rather than on title or financial status. Most pioneers were restless, optimistic, boastful, ardently nationalistic, firm believers in the "manifest destiny" of their country. When he could find time, he danced, attended weddings, enjoyed barn-raisings and cornhuskings, and threw himself into individual participatory activities such as wrestling, shooting, running, jumping, horsemanship, and a host of bizarre feats stressing bravery, stamina, and skill.

Every man on the frontier felt as worthy as every other. These frontiersmen were optimistic; the spirit of conquest and competitiveness ran strong in the veins of these vanguards of major settlements. Their sports were the same way, and even after strenuous physical labors in harvest field or timber clearing, there always seemed a surplus of energy for feats of strength and skill or competitive cornhusking, logrolling or house-raising. These men glorified in the exercise of their muscles. Spectator sports had little importance in the rural communities; these pioneer extroverts preferred "athletic and healthy diversions." Track and field events, baseball, boxing, lacrosse, and weight lifting—all modified to meet wilderness exigencies—caught the fancy of the frontiersman. Survival and momentary levity were far more important to him than any kind of physical exercise directed to purely educational ends. The strong code of sportsmanship so characteristic of upper-class Englishmen found little philosophical acceptance among American frontiersmen. Traditional religions also found difficulty in penetrating the inhospitable back woods. Besides, the frontier people had little taste for doctrinal

Frontier sport was unrestrained as in this, *The Jolly Flatboatmen*, by George Caleb Bingham. (Courtesy of National Gallery of Art, Washington, D.C., Collection of the Honorable Clairborne Pell.)

dialectics. Theirs was a world of immediacy and unbridled physicality. Their lives and recreational pleasures reflected these characteristics. Mike Fink, notorious king of Mississippi keelboatmen, was always "chock full o'fight" and bragged:

> I can hit like fourth-proof lightnin'; an' every lick I make in the woods lets in an acre o' sunshine. I can out-run, out-jump, out-shoot, out-brag, out-drink, an' out-fight, rough-and-tumble no holts barred, any man on both sides of the river from Pittsburgh to New Orleans, an' back again to St. Louis. Come on, you flatters, you bargers, you milk-white mechanics, an' see how tough I am to chaw! I ain't had a fight for two days, an' I'm spilein' for exercise. Cock-a-doodle-doo![5]

Foreign travelers to the new America left us precious, although sometimes jaundiced, accounts of pioneer sports in the early decades of the westward migration. One of the most vivid accounts of gross lower class sport entrusted us was by the Englishman, Thomas Ashe, during his *Travels in America* in the year 1806. While passing through Wheeling, West Virginia, he encountered a "rough and tumble" fight between a Virginian and Kentuckyman. Nearly the entire community was on hand to see this cruelest of sports—an English import. Launching themselves at one another with complete abandonment, the two fought like wild animals. The crowd roared its approval as the Virginian "expressed as much beauty and skill in his retraction and bound, as if he had been bred in a menagerie." Never losing his hold, the Virginian fixed "his claws in his hair, and his thumbs on his eyes, gave them an instantaneous start from their sockets." The sightless warrior roared with pain but continued fighting until forced to quit, his nose and lips now also totally mutilated. The gouging contest over:

> the poor wretch, whose eyes were started from their spheres, and whose lips refused its office, returned to the town, to hide his impotence, and get his countenance repaired. . . . I had had sufficient sports of the day, and returned to my quaker friend . . . [who] informed me further, that such doings were common, frequently two or three times a week;[6]

Other uncommon sports, the result of frontier mutations, were throwing the maul (caber or hammer), pitching quoits (twenty to sixty pound stones), running, jumping—high, broad, half-hammon (hop, step, and jump)—pole jumping for distance, tug-of-war, crack the whip, horseshoe pitching, leap frog, town ball, "stink base," "chicken," "slap jack," and "I spy." "Even grown men played industriously at marbles, to the neglect of more serious labors."[7] In throwing the tomahawk, youngsters mastered the difficult skill of burying the weapon in nearby trees. These same boys learn to "bark" a squirrel— to stun the animal with wood chips by firing a bullet just above or below the animal. Apocryphal stories notwithstanding, the early American frontier produced an extraordinary breed of men and some magnificent athletes. Robert McClellan, from Cumberland County, Pennsylvania, was a man of average height and slight physique, but the pioneer biographer John McDonald called him "one of the most athletic and active men that has ever appeared on this globe." McClellan could leap over a standing horse or a yoke of oxen. On the parade ground, with a slight downgrade to help him, he cleared a canvas-arched wagon. The Indians could not catch him in a footrace or match him in a broad jump.[8] These rough, crude men pushed the frontier west, helped form a "composite nationality," and exerted a strong influence on American thought. The half-century after American independence was dominated by the influence of the frontier. A certain important and primeval youthfulness existed among these early settlers of the frontier. When the frontier closed in the 1880s, the habit of a physically vigorous alfresco life was too strong to be discarded as millions streamed into the city. It may be that Frederick L. Paxson was right when he said that "the search for sport revealed a partial substitute for pioneer life."[9]

SPORT IN AN ERA OF RELIGIOUS DIVERSIFICATION

The new nation in 1800 was bursting with energy, optimism, and a proliferation of ideologies. Perhaps the strongest single element in young America's march toward the millennium was religion and, except in the South, the period was marked by a renewed theological conservatism regarding sport. The Calvinistic austerity that had steadily lost touch with the secular spirit of the late eighteenth century attempted a comeback in the decades following the American Revolution. Some later historians called it a Second Great Awakening. This transitory religious revivalism only lasted a generation and bridged the period from the 1790s to the second decade of the new century. The denigrating social effects of the war, increasing urbanization, new wealth and leisure, plus the influx of immigrants belonging to religious sects which did not so strictly adhere to traditional Sabbath laws brought about an increasing number of violations of these laws. An alarmed Pennsylvania legislature, for example, passed a 1794 statute restraining "disorderly sports and dissipations"; furthermore, cockfighting, cards, dice, billiards, bowls, shuffleboards, bullet-playing, and even horseracing were deemed illegal pastimes on the Sabbath-day. The fraudulent "Peter's Blue Laws" of Connecticut were bizarre exaggerations in many instances but they did not seriously misrepresent the spirit of an early nineteenth century New England legislation.[10] Sport existed and persisted through the period but most official and ecclesiastical comments on fun and games were adverse unless there was an obvious gain therefrom in virtue or usefulness. "Usefulness and innocent" were the outstanding characteristics of any approved recreation. Virtue must be inherent in the leisure activity; utility was essential. Excess in sport was anathema as it was believed to lead to excess in other things. The *Massachusetts Missionary Magazine* for 1803 warned parents that intemperate recreational habits waste "the golden days of youth." Except in the South, the preachers' role in sport was that of offering criticism, even admonishing the people to refrain from participating in such vice as amusements if they expected to be ushered in at the throne of God.

Yet the voice of liberal theology was also in the land and its message of hope for man in his worship of a Perfect Creator must have been a factor in reducing the stigma attached to uninhibited play. American Deism or free thought rejected the Calvinistic concept of man's depravity and concentrated on man's inherent ability to perfect his own institutions. In New England, such radical ideas hastened the intellectual emancipation of many who had managed to amass a goodly share of the world's profit. The theocentric piety of an older Calvinism seemed to have little relevance to an expanding mercantile society which believed in natural rights, social contracts, and foreign trade. The Puritan preoccupation with other worldliness did not fit with the upper class Bostonian or Philadelphian's interest in the state of his pocketbook and the amusements of this world. The revolt against Calvinism reached its apogee as Unitarianism and Universalism preached a loving God, the nobility of man, and the salvation of all people. Thus, the deeply ethical core of Puritanism—its greatest strength—emerged perfectly into alien currents of thought, first Deism, then Unitarianism and Universalism, and soon into the philosophy of Transcendentalism. New models of man were being created in an America where the proliferation of churches and faiths were unprecedented in world civilizations. Bit by bit, thinking Americans "learned that they were vindicating a radical thesis unprecedented in the history of Christendom: they were proving that a wide diversity of churches within a single society could survive and prosper."[11] The rise of sport in America, beginning just before the Civil War and emerging full-blown in the 1870s and 1880s, could never have occurred without the revolution of religious and intellectual diversification so prominent at the beginning of the century.

PARTICIPANTS' SPORT IN THE NEW NATION

Most sports during this period of high American individualism were participatory—some because of their intrinsic nature, others due to immature organizational development necessary for attracting spectators. Prominent and happy events for the farmer and frontiersmen continued to be (whenever they could afford the time) recreational hunting and fishing, shooting matches, athletic contests, house-raisings, corn huskings, and a host of fun activities indigenous to what was still the major population segment of the nation. In the cities and on certain campuses the germ of an idea began to circulate. A few intellectuals and some students saw in exercise and games a temporary but totally satisfying release from new and disconcerting pressures. Yale president Thomas Dwight, puritanical disciplinarian, disapproved of the crude campus football games but allowed them to continue. At Harvard and Yale, a yearly game took place between the sophomores and freshmen. The honor of the class was at stake and the rudimentary battle-game lasted for weeks, the ball being put in play at the noon hour, and kept very much in play until the commons bell tolled at twelve-thirty. At Princeton the faculty forbade students from playing field hockey, on the grounds that it was ungentlemanly and unhealthy. Still the idea persisted, especially among the young, that there was something to be gained from such ostensibly unprofitable pastimes.

The idea that artificially induced exercises might be manifoldly

Corn husking festivals were popular in rural areas in early American history. (Courtesy of Library of Congress.)

beneficial received further credence from several prominent literary, educational, and political figures of the time. Thomas Jefferson had read John Locke's advice of a sound mind in a sound body. This American renaissance man saw moderate exercise as "the sovereign invigorator" of the body as well as the mind and recommended two hours each day be devoted to it. Franklin was especially convincing in his arguments that learning to swim might save one's life but was also a genuinely satisfying experience. Philadelphia's eclectic physician, Benjamin Rush, advocated a variety of exercises—"even carrying stones from one stop to another and carrying them back again"—in order to harden the body. In a remarkable article titled, "The benefits of exercise, in preference to medicine," Dr. Rush indulged in a symbolic narrative in which the spirit Hygeia, omnipotent guardian of mankind's health, descends upon the islanders of Ceylon, prescribing the formula for life-long health and happiness. Hygeia, this "Venus of Medicis," held high a bough of evergreen and addressed the unhappy audience:

> My name is Hygeia. I preside over the health of mankind. Descard all your medicines, and seek relief from Temperance and Exercise alone. . . . Shun sloth. This unhinges all the springs of life—fly from your diseases—they will not—they cannot pursue you.[12]

Here she ended, dropping a parchment of instructions for each; a cloud received her and the natives began their appointed tasks of hiking, gardening, riding, and bowling. Within months, physical and psychological maladies disappeared; the natives returned to the assembly place singing praises. "Temples were erected to her memory; and she continues, to this day, to be worshipped by all the inhabitants of that island." Far less eloquent was Shadrach Ricketson, New York City physician, who proposed that "a certain proportion of exercise is not much less essential to a healthy and vigorous constitution than drink, food and sleep." The Reverend John Bennet's "Letters to a young lady" pointed out that continual religious worship is exhausting, and frequent intervals of innocent amusement are "as much a part of true wisdom as employment itself." Again, Samuel Knox, minister and president of Frederick Academy in Bladensburg, Maryland, found moderate exercise "salutary to youth." Noah Webster, addressing young Hartford gentlemen in 1790, urged regular exercise in order to develop the whole man.

The North American Review of December, 1818, wrote "On the health of Literary men," pointing out that Europeans tend to eat more intelligently, worry less, and exercise more than urban American intellectuals. "Here, certainly, is a combination of circumstances admirably adapted to preserve the sound mind in the sound body."

The trickle of advice was just that, but it persisted through the first decades of the century—a necessary precursor to the profound discontent regarding personal and community health voiced by many during the years immediately prior to the Civil War. Sports and games had never really been out of favor with Americans at any point in history. Daniel Webster's years at Dartmouth College (1797-1800) were dotted with ball games and athletic exercises. Presbyterian preacher, Lyman Beecher (1775-1863), recalling the days of his youth in Connecticut, found the smell of spring inexorably drawing him to his fishing tackle. He often drove to Three-mile Harbor, got some clams "and rowed out to the Chicquot ground—easy exercise—opening the chest, and breathing the fresh air; how good it was!"[13]

SPECTATORS' SPORTS IN THE NEW NATION

Regrettably, one of this period's popular pastimes was watching and wagering on the blood sport of cockfighting. The age-old European and American diversion appealed to men in most sections of the country, and to all social classes, with the so-called "lower element" finding it particularly zestful. The Marquis de Chastellux was amazed to find in his 1782 travels through northern Virginia, flocks of rural folks asleep on the floor next to the arena awaiting the following day's cockfight. The birds were armed with long steel spurs. The wagering and the blood were equally profuse. A child of fifteen, said the disapproving Frenchman, kept leaping for joy, crying, "Oh!, it is a charming diversion." The Marquis was unable to determine "which is the most astonishing, the insipidity of such diversion, or the stupid interest with which it animates the parties."[14] In Tidewater Virginia, teams of two dozen gamecocks were sometimes matched in a two-day series of battles to the death. Cockfighting in Hampton County, Virginia, in 1787, attracted hundreds of blacks and whites to spacious mains or cockpits. Beautiful cocks, armed with long steel-pointed gaffles were dropped.

> The little heroes appeared trained to the business—advancing nearer and nearer, they flew upon each other at the same instant with a rude shock, the cruel gaffles being driven into their bodies, and at times directly through their heads. Frequently one, or both, would be struck dead at the first blow.[15]

In the South, from Maryland to New Orleans, cockfighting was a popular sport and pits were visited by all classes of people. Great attention was paid to the breeding and training of the prospective fighters. According to English experts, the desired cock was one whose head was small, with a quick, large eye, and strong back. The beam of his leg ought to be very strong; his spurs rough, long and sharp. The courage of the animal was known by his proud upright posture and stately tread.[16] Universal acceptance of the sport was accompanied by uncompromising condemnation by many clergy. It was contended that cockfighting was unfriendly to morals, encouraged idleness, fraud, gambling, and vulgarity of all sorts. Yet, as late as 1821, cockfighting was carried on in Philadelphia; but the pit was shunned by all who laid a claim to social standing. In that city, the blood sport continued into the fourth decade of the century, but only "under the superintendence of men who have nothing further to dread from the opinion of the world." Many Southerners, conservative and well ordered, thought Providence had designed cocks for man's amusement; the sport lingered there for many more generations.

By the 1820s, Eastern cities in such far apart ports as New York and Savannah reported a quickening of interest among spectators for foot racing, walking contests, wrestling bouts, water sports and boat races. Spectators were numerous at most of these contests. In November, 1820, at the close of a matched boat race, the Whitehallers of New York defeated a company of men from Brooklyn; the friends of the victorious crew took the boat from the water with the steersman in it, and bore it on their shoulders from Whitehall through Broadway to the Fulton Hotel.[17] Strangely, despite such burgeoning spectator sports, boxing received little encouragement in the states. Tom Molyneux, the powerful freed slave, who claimed the heavyweight championship of the country at the opening of the century, was more profitable to his promoters in his English fights than in his brief American tour. English pugilists, after encountering the vigorous hostility of the press from Boston to Savannah, frequently abandoned the prize ring to establish schools for teaching the "manly science of self-defense." Molyneux ran up a string of victories along New York's waterfront and went to England to have a go at Tom Cribb. They met on December 10, 1810, for 200 guineas and the championship belt. Molyneux was the better man that day. He had Cribb licked but was possibly cheated out of victory by the trickery of the Englishman's seconds. The black man was in front all the way, and, at the end of the twenty-third round, Cribb was so far gone that he couldn't answer the bell. The referee should have given the fight to Molyneux right then but instead he listened to Cribb's handlers, who claimed that the American fighter had leaden weights hidden in his fists. In the wrangling which lasted several minutes, Cribb recovered, and Molyneux, unused to the raw British climate, suffered a chill. The tide turned after that, and Cribb won in the fortieth round. They fought again the next year, and this time Cribb won against a badly conditioned Molyneux, who had taken to rum.[18]

English boxing and the "Fancy" as seen in the early 1800s. (*Boxing Match in London*, 1822. Schweizerisches Turn-und Sports Museum, Bôle.)

THE GREAT HORSE RACE—ECLIPSE AGAINST SIR HENRY

The growing American appetite for spectacles and spectator sport reached surprising and premature heights on Tuesday, May 27, 1823, at the recently constructed Union Race Course in Jamaica, Long Island. A horse race between Eclipse, the Northern champion, and Sir Henry, the fastest thoroughbred in the South, was responsible for one of the largest crowds ever to witness a nineteenth century sporting event in America. In addition to a competition of the highest order, the event was one of the first manifestations of intense and even bitter sectional rivalry between the South and the North. New York City was jammed far beyond capacity with 20,000 visitors, "chiefly Virginians and Southerners." An estimated 75,000 people overwhelmed the race course; the newspaper ballyhoo had been more than effective. An eyewitness, coolly detached from the madness of the day, found:

> It was really amusing to see the interest this race excited; indeed an election for a President would not have excited greater. In all the papers, and in every man's mouth, were the questions, "are you for the North or the South?" "The Free or the Slave States?" "The Whites or the Blacks?"[19]

It was the year before the presidential election and, in a desultory way, the campaign had already begun. It was to be the North vs. the South, do or die, and no quarter. The conditions of the race were to be the best two out of three victories at the heroic 4-mile distance; a thirty-minute rest period seemed sufficient (to the trainers) before returning to the mile-long track with its quarter-mile straightaways and quarter-mile turns. Each side put up $20,000, and the great dual began.

In the first heat Eclipse drew the inside position next to the pole. The starting signal was the single tap of a drum, the horses getting off evenly with Sir Henry gaining a three lengths advantage in the first quarter mile turn; "he then settled down to ride a rated heat at a blazing pace."[20] Positions remained unchanged until they reached the far turn of the fourth lap when Eclipse, the nine-year-old veteran, made his stretch run and closed Henry's lead to a length and a half. It was no use and the brilliant southern four-year-old won in 7:37—a world record. The northern backers were stunned, "the mercury fell instantly below the freezing point" and betting odds changed to three to one in favor of Sir Henry. The veteran thirty-eight-year-old jockey, Samuel Purdy, replaced the distraught Yankee rider and the second heat began. This time, with John Walden again on Sir Henry, the results were reversed and Eclipse ran a brilliant 7:49—the first authentic instance in which a second heat had been run in 7:50 or better. The situation was now completely reversed. Eclipse was made the favorite. The North was jubilant, the South in panic, and the immense throng in a lather pressing against the rail. A new jockey for the defeated horse was demanded and obtained. Arthur Taylor, who had not ridden for years, was drafted to ride Sir Henry in the final heat. But the day was lost for the South.

> The moment they got off, Purdy went at Eclipse with whip and spur and Henry's attempt to take the lead was thwarted. Taylor then took a pull on him and started in to ride a waiting race. For three miles and three-quarters he laid within striking distance until they were straight in the stretch the last time around. He then made a supreme effort, Henry tried to nail the old horse but was unable to do more than to get his nose up to his haunches, then fell back and was defeated by three lengths, finishing dead beat. The time, 8:24, told the tale of his exhaustion.

The ovation accorded Eclipse was one of ecstasy; the Southerners bore their loss like gentlemen. Later, as mail carriers passed through western New York, a red flag (Eclipse's color) was flown. On it was inscribed, "Eclipse forever—Old Virginia a little tired." At least a quarter million dollars had been wagered on the race. Many northerners took their horse's victory as an omen of political superiority. Even Josiah Quincy, later president of Harvard, and witness to Eclipse's victory, wrote in his *Figures of the Past* that the sporting madness foreshadowed the Civil War. "The victory," he said, "resulted in both cases from the same cause,—the power of endurance. It was, in the language of the turf, bottom against speed."

THE NEW NATION'S RECURRING INVOLVEMENT IN SPORT

The first American theatre production ever performed in public by a company of professional actors was Royall Tyler's "The Contrast," first delivered on April 16, 1787, in New York City. The contrast between the plain and simple honesty of purpose and breeding of American home life and the tinseled hypocrisy and knavery of foreign societies is finely delineated and suggests the name of the play. It also indicated the temper of the American public. The nation had emerged as an independent political unit although its social pattern was still equivocal. The prologue of "The Contrast" sounded the national note—a lusty embodiment of American ideals insisting that they could go it alone.

> Why should our thoughts to distant countries roam
> When each refinement may be found at home?

Nevertheless, American social patterns in 1800 were often indistinguishable fusions of European habits and peculiarly local customs. The unquenchable play instinct in man, so universal and timeless, manifested itself in unique ways on southern plantations, in Boston's Beacon Street homes, and in rough settlements at the confluence of the Ohio and Allegheny Rivers. Thus, American sporting practices of the period were an amalgam of (1) ancient British pastimes (2) European leisure time experiences, both intact and modified, plus (3) indigenous frontier games. Competition in the various participants' sports was generally on an individual basis; the cooperative efforts of team play still did not come naturally to most Americans. As Krout says, "In a generation which had not yet given substance to the concept of sportsmanship, the spectators' interest in sporting events was apt to center in the wagering of money on the outcome."[22]

Except in conspicuous areas of the country, the American concept of leisure was desultory and, despite powerful and permanent new ideas, heavy with evangelical and pietistic Protestantism. Most had but one day a week free from work, yet it was generally frowned on that any profanation of the Sabbath take place. There still existed during these early decades of the nineteenth century an excessive fear that games might be carried to excess and that the participants, weary from strenuous exercise, might temporarily drop their guard in the endless battle against temptation. Yet, the secularized work ethic that evolved from Puritan roots was more liberal than that of an earlier colonial period. It was no longer sinful, in most instances, to enjoy leisure time, if that time was earned by hard work. The modern view of leisure as an end in itself, popular among some today, was unacceptable one hundred and fifty years ago. Many at that time were just beginning to see leisure as a means of relaxation and revitalization—innocent moments preparatory to the consuming task of a seventy-five hour work week. Most were caught between the concept of nonwork as an opportunity for personal betterment in the service of God, and leisure time as a by-product of and respite from hard work. From then till now, the American tendency has been to accept more readily the latter.

REFERENCES

1. Noah Webster, Americans, Unshackle Your Minds, in Homer D. Babbidge, ed., *Noah Webster—On Being American. Selected Writings, 1783-1828* (New York: Frederick A. Praeger, Pub., 1967), p. 92.

2. Samuel Harrison Smith, Remarks on Education, in Frederick Rudolph, ed., *Essays on Education in the Early Republic* (Cambridge: Harvard University Press, 1965),p. 222.

3. Foster Rhea Dulles, *A History of Recreation. America Learns to Play* (New York: Appleton-Century-Crofts, 1965), pp. 69-70.

4. Phyllis J. Hill, A Cultural History of Frontier Sports in Illinois 1673-1820 (unpublished Ph.D. dissertation, University of Illinois, 1967), p. 124.

5. Walter Blair and Franklin Meine, *Mike Fink—King of Mississippi Keelboatmen* (New York: Henry Holt and Co., 1933), pp. 105-106.

6. Thomas Ashe, *Travels in America* (London: R. Phillips, 1808), Vol. I, p. 229.

7. R. Carlyle Buley, *The Old Northwest Pioneer Period 1815-1840* (Bloomington: University of Indiana Press, 1962), Vol. I, p. 316.

8. Walter Havighurst, *Wilderness for Sale* (New York: Hastings House, Pub., 1956), p. 8.

9. Frederick L. Paxson, The Rise of Sport, *The Mississippi Valley Historical Review*, IV (September, 1917), p. 167.

10. Samuel Peters, *A General History of Connecticut* (New Haven: Republished by D. Clark and Co., 1829). Royal Ralph Hinman in his *The Blue Laws of New Haven Colony . . .* (Hartford: Case, Tiffany and Co., 1838) exclaimed on page v that "no man can peruse these laws without a chill in every vein, and be ready to disbelieve that so uncharitable a spirit could ever have existed and been exercised in America."

11. Perry Miller, *The Life of the Mind in America* (New York: Harcourt, Brace and World, Inc., 1965), p. 40.

12. Benjamin Rush, The benefits of exercise, in preference to medicine, *The American Museum*, VI (July, 1789), pp. 45-46.

13. Lyman Beecher, *Autobiography and Correspondence*, Charles Beecher, ed., Vol. I (New York: Harper and Bros., Pub., 1865), p. 128.

14. Marquis de Chastellux, *Travels in North America* (London: G.F.J. and J. Robinson, 1787), Vol. II, pp. 31-32.

15. Elkanah Watson, *Men and Times of the Revolution*, ed. Winslow C. Watson (New York: Dana and Co., 1856), p. 300, as found in Robert Weaver, *Amusements and Sports in American Life* (Chicago: University of Chicago Press, 1939), p. 9.

16. Jennie Holliman, *American Sports 1785-1835* (Durham, North Carolina: Seeman Press, 1931), pp. 125-126.

17. New York *Evening Post*, November 13, 1820, as cited in Holliman, *Ibid.*, p. 157.

18. John Durant and Otto Bettmann, *Pictorial History of American Sports* (New York: A. S. Barnes and Co., 1952), p. 19.

19. William N. Blane, *An Excursion through the United States and Canada During the Years 1822-1823* (New York: Negro Universities Press, 1969), pp. 316-317.

20. John Hervey, *Racing in America 1665-1865*, Vol. I (New York; The Jockey Club, 1944), pp. 265-266. Hervey's unrivaled description of the famous race is an acknowledged reproduction taken from the July, 1830, *American Turf Register*, written by an eye-witness, Cadwallader R. Colden—"An Old Turfman."

21. John Hervey, *Ibid.*, p. 268; see also Max Farrand, The Great Race—Eclipse against the World!, *Scribner's Magazine*, LXX (October, 1921), 457-464.

22. John Allen Krout and Dixon Ryan Fox, *The Completion of Independence 1790-1830*. Vol. V of *A History of American Life*, Arthur M. Schlesinger and D. R. Fox, ed. (New York: The Macmillan Co., 1944), pp. 389-390.

CHAPTER 6

Health and Exercise During the Era of Reform

VESTIGIAL PURITANISM AND PHYSICAL CULTURE

On the wall of the old Amherst University gymnasium, there is an admonition to "Keep thyself pure: the body is the temple of the Holy Ghost." Old-fashioned Puritanism had lost most of its punch by the 1820s, but it persisted in peculiarly modified forms. Ministerial leaders, especially Unitarian intellectuals, enjoyed an unusual leadership and respectability. In New England history, the minister had enjoyed two periods of intellectual ascendency: "the first during the early days of the theocracy, when the commonwealth was ruled by the laws of God and John Calvin; and the second, between the years 1830 and 1850."[1] Despite a new and glittering optimism about man's heritage of perfection—the gift of a totally benevolent God—the thinly veiled Puritan remnant could not give full endorsement to undirected amusement, sports and games. Most influential religious leaders felt that recreational activities, like all human endeavors, must be sustained upon a personal and community conviction of their rectitude or rightness of principle. The pulpit and press persistently reminded dutiful Christians that amusements pursued as an end in themselves are among the most enfeebling and demoralizing of all influences. The softer and broader concept of Calvinism known as Unitarianism defended physical vigor as a deterrent to moral and spiritual intemperance. William Ellery Channing's magnificent effort to humanize society and awaken it to a nobler faith in its own destiny, observed that God has implanted in each of us a strong tendency for recreation after labor. The perfection of man seemed not only possible but relatively near at hand; a judicious use of recreational amusements seemed only logical in this early nineteenth century context.

70

The sporting practices of a nation must reflect the values of that culture or the subculture fostering it. The dominant ministerial idealism of the period was liberal in theological matters but conservative in well-nigh everything else. In an age when leisure-time recreations were growing in acceptability, "mere amusement" was still anathema. Conservative, sectarian, evangelical Protestantism was a dominant force on the American scene and made an uneasy bedfellow with the recently imported intellectual renaissance. For example, the Boston physician, John Jeffries, apparently saw no dichotomy in an 1833 paper titled, "Physical Culture, The Result of Moral Obligation." He presented an Athenian concept in which "the powers of the body should be cultivated because it is the workmanship of God."[2] Another medical doctor, Edward Reynolds, addressed himself to literary men and "especially to clergymen," reminding this traditional group of Americans that "the body, as well as the mind, was given to be cultivated for the glory of the Creator. 'Know ye not, brethren, that your bodies are the temples of the living God?' "[3] No less fervent in his desire to combine spiritual as well as temporal admonitions was Dr. William Alcott's resolution to The American Physiological Society "that we view with gratitude to Almighty God, the formation of Physiological and Health Societies in this country."[4] Alcott's religious disposition, medical training, forty years of teaching and writing, all in an era of reform, forged a view that looked upon the redemption of man's intellectual, moral, and physical capacities as essential and integrated—the only road to human improvement and eventual perfectibility.

The new optimistic faith demanded action. It had discovered the apotheosis of religion in "the adoration of goodness" and the active amelioration of the ills of mankind. Progress and perfectibility seemed possible through a deeply moral commitment and a life-time dedication to hard work. Most Americans had come a long way from the time when they had conceived themselves helpless sinners in the hands of an angry God. For example, the Reverend Dr. Philip Lindsley, graduate of Princeton University and president of Cumberland College, Tennessee, told the graduating class of 1826 that in addition to moral and mental education, their futures should include vigorous, graceful, healthy, active bodies—for themselves and the children they would teach. "Attach to each school house," he said, "a lot of ten acres of land, for the purpose of healthful exercise, gardening, farming, and the mechanical arts. For the body requires training as well as the mind."[5] The seering reexamination of old Calvinist dogmas in the light of a new liberalism brought with it, in part, a concern for man's health and fruitful use of leisure time. During these critical years the upholders of the traditional orthodoxy were most actively concerned to provide a defense for the sacred dogmas of their grandfathers. "The liberal advance produced a conservative reaction, and the lines of battle were sharply drawn."[6]

TRANSITORY SCHOOL PHYSICAL EDUCATION

The first volume of the *American Journal of Education* in November, 1826, beamed the good news that qualified instructors of physical education—"men of eminence in science, literature, as well as in the gymnastic art," were available for hire. Only the year before, Dr. Charles Beck of Germany, had met these qualifications and was hired to teach physical education at the Round Hill School in North-hampton, Massachusetts—the first instructor of gymnastics in this country. Another of his countrymen, and pupil of Germany's gymnastic patriarch, Friederick Ludwig Jahn, was the brilliant scholar-athlete, Dr. Francis Lieber. Father Jahn's letter to a patron of the new American physical education called Lieber an outstanding gymnast, pedestrian, and teacher, a man of high morals, "ingenious and clever," a zealous advocate of those "eternal maxims of truth, duty, and liberty, which form the only basis of the progress of human kind."[7] Leiber arrived in America on June 20, 1827, and joined the other member of the German gymnastic triumvirate, Charles Follen. For a brief period the three men, Beck, Leiber, and Follen, made every effort to introduce their kind of physical training from one end of Massachusetts to the other. German calisthenics put out no deep roots in the city of Boston nor at the grand experimental Round Hill School which closed its doors in 1834. American sport historian, Bruce Bennett, considered it a failure only in a crass, material sense. "Round Hill convincingly demonstrated that a high-quality education was not incompatible with extensive sports participation."[8] Joseph G. Cogswell and George Bancroft founded the school on the platform that a liberal education for boys must combine rugged academics with a unified physical and moral education. The concept was not without strong proponents in future American school philosophy.

The editors of the *American Journal of Education* anticipated a brighter day for gymnastics—the fledgling that must be recognized "by all who have acquired correct views of education" as of inestimable value. The new Boston Gymnasium was under the supervision of Dr. Charles Follen, former lieutenant of Frederick Jahn, and professor of Civil Law at the University of Basil in Switzerland, now new instructor at Harvard College. The gymnasium, it was said, could raise "the human system to any degree of vigor and health"; daily increase in physical strength would be realized, readers were told, along with an inexorable rise in intellectual perspicacity. Follen set up bars, trapezes, and flying rings for his Harvard students; he led them on cross country runs through Cambridge streets, frequently surprising and occasionally outraging property owners. Small overtures were made in the establishment of gymnasiums at Brown University, Yale, Amherst, Williams, Dartmouth, Virginia, and the College of Charleston, in South Carolina. All failed to survive the initial ardor or novelty for the activity, and the "precipitous decline in gymnastics" seemed yet another manifestation of the many ephemeral fads of the era.

Organized physical training and sports in the colleges seemed premature, although young men of special dispositions had always been aware of their muscles. Richard Henry Dana, Jr., reported to his parents in 1831, that Harvard students played cricket, had informal football games, and boxed, fenced, and swam for exercise. That same year saw unsuccessful efforts to erect a gymnasium at the University of Georgia, yet in front of several college buildings students jumped rope, swung on rings, and played town ball. As always, theory precedes practice; some educationists observed that so long as the body housed the mind and spirit "so long should we make the most assiduous and untiring exertion to give it the utmost degree of vigor and healthful activity." No one believed this more strongly than Charles Caldwell, M.D. In a speech delivered to a convention of teachers in Lexington, Kentucky, on November 6 and 7, 1833, he reminded them of the interdependence of moral, intellectual, and physical education. "What is man without a vigorous and well-trained system of muscles?"; harmful predispositions, he said, may be eradicated through a life-time of physical education.[9] In a near juxtaposition of Puritanism and the new education for women, Mary Lyon, founder of Mount Holyoke College, noted in 1832 that "those who enjoy bodily idleness enjoy sin. Exercise is part of the very constitution of man."[10] Several other women's schools, in part inspired by Catharine Beecher's 1832 *Course of Calisthenics for Young Ladies*, included opportunities for graceful carriage, walking, riding, dancing, gardening, and "hygienic exercises." Apparently for many men and women the whole new thrust for exercise appeared contrived and unreal. The movement failed to generate sufficient interest in eastern schools and soon lost ground with the students who seemed to await something more to their liking. It came, of course, but not without passing through the limbo of the next two decades.

A PASSION FOR HEALTH OF MIND AND BODY

Nowhere in American history, unless it be the contemporary scene, was there such total concern for personal and community health as the period 1824-1837. Combined with a powerful national spirit of social reform, many Americans embroiled themselves in a passion for health of mind and body. After all, the average life expectancy was

Catharine Beecher's "double stretching" movement was part of her attempt to get women to exercise.

still below thirty-five years and there were those who thought the American people were headed straight for physical degeneration. Yet faith in the inevitable perfectness of man was a current thought—the blending of new science and philosophical idealism. Improving the health of the masses became a powerful and realizable goal—a complex outgrowth of American idealism, moralism, growing commercialism and nationalism. "Thought on exercise and health trickled down slowly to the public";[11] few could deny the medical and educational credentials of those who passionately laid down the "general rules for the restoration and preservation of health." *The American Farmer* of May 28, 1824, strained even the language of the period by first advocating vigorous exercise for all, because "the delicate springs of our frail machines lose their activity and become enervated, and the vessels chocked with obstructions, when we totally desist from exercise." Influential educational magazines such as the *American Journal of Education*, the *Annals of Education and Instruction*, and *Godey's Lady's Book*, directed a rapidly growing reading public to the need for greater physical health through proper dress, diet, healthful exercise and innocent recreation. A rush of medical textbooks like Andrew Combe's *Principles of Physiology*, Dr. John Collins Warren's 1831 essay on the *Importance of Physical Education*, and the Philadelphia phrenologist, Charles Caldwell's *Thoughts on Physical Education*, all championed moderate and regular exercise. A review of Dr. Charles Londe's *Medical Gymnastics* concluded enthusiastically that "the importance of exercise and diet was perhaps never more fully acknowledged than by the physicians of the present day." British texts were having their effect. James Kennedy's *Instructions to Mothers and Nurses* and W. Newnham's *Principles of Physical, Intellectual, Moral, and Religions* both vividly pictured health and longevity as partly dependent on wholesome games and vigorous exercise.

Already, the eastern city dweller was apparently no paragon of physical fitness. Acid-tongued Frances Trollope "never saw an American man walk or stand well; . . . they are nearly all hollow chested and round shouldered." In an age of fits and fads, the new campaign for mankind's corporeal salvation had begun. Possibly the most influential physician of his time, Dr. John C. Warren, delivered a lecture "On Physical Education" to the American Institute of Instruction in Boston during August of 1830. His message was eloquent but already repetitious. Modern civilizations had freely supplied the means for intellectual improvement but "nearly in the same ratio, raised obstacles to the development of the physical powers." In a speech delivered at the Andover Theological Seminary on September 27, 1831, Dr. Edward Reynolds addressed himself to literary men and theologians. Hard physical work and vigorous exercise are good for the soul as well as the body, he said. These two, he went on, will "expel that cruel enemy of literature and religion—physical inaction." He reminded the audience that physical education is a subject of vital importance, capable of eliminating dyspepsia, and able to release each one from "the prison-house of his own digestive organs." Dr. Reynolds saved his most telling blow till last when he asked rhetorically, "How much sin does he accumulate, who, having enlisted as a soldier or leader in the cause of Christ, renders himself, by neglect, wholly or in part unfit for duty!"[12] Like so many reformers of the period, Dr. Reynolds saw the way to a man's salvation was, in part, through his body; the catechism of health comprised concepts of exercise in the open air, temperance, physical and mental cleanliness, and spiritual devotion. For many, this new preoccupation with physical health through exercise was a new kind of Christianity, honoring the body, and in the old vernacular, the proud temple of the mind and soul.

GAMES AND BALL GAMES AMONG THE INDIANS

The origins of sport among ancient and primitive peoples are shrouded in the desire for survival in this world, contained in man's realizable hope for immortality, and in his strong play and competitive instinct. Sports and games among the American Indians fulfilled primary wants; fertility rites, natural child birth, rituals of childhood and manhood plus proper preparations to meet one's ancestors help explain his play patterns. Seasonal changes, magical aspects, a universal love of play, and a compelling urge to excel were characteristic of Indians throughout the North American continent. The Indian's particular forms of divine worship were frequently manifested in a

Indians, such as Tullock-Chish-Ko of the Choctaw nation of the 1830s, excelled in lacrosse.

variety of ritualistic and often vigorous games. The study of Indian games has given scholars not only an understanding of Indian technology, but has contributed to an appreciation of Indian psychology and the impulses that underlie the conduct of primitive peoples in general.

During the period 1832-1839, George Catlin studied and painted the North American Indian. Once in a Mandan village on the Upper Missouri he spent the day watching Indians play, as well as throwing himself into the competitions "but with little success." Horse racing was described as one of their most exciting amusements, and one of the most extravagent modes of gambling. Catlin was amazed at the accuracy of the young men shooting arrows from atop a full galloping horse. In their "game of arrows," the one shooting the greatest number of shafts high into the air before any one of them landed succeeded in walking away with the shields, robes and pipes—all entrance fees for the competition. Catlin lingered long enough to note that:

> the people have many days which . . . are devoted to festivities and amusements. Their lives . . . are lives of idleness and ease, and almost all their days and hours are spent in innocent amusements. Amongst a people who have no office hours to attend to—no professions to study, and of whom but very little time is required in the chase, to supply their families with food, it would be strange if they did not practice many games and amusements, and also become exceedingly expert in them.[13]

Stewart Culin's massive study of American Indian leisure revealed two types—games of chance and games of dexterity. A rich tapestry of gambling games are complemented by skill activities such as shooting arrows at a moving target, sliding javelins over hard ground, snow or ice, scores of low order and highly organized games. Back of many games are found ceremonies of a magico-religious nature; frequently the ceremony had disappeared and the game survived as an amusement. Culin was puzzled by the frequency of the ball in play, its symbolism and possible reference to the earth, the moon, or the sun. The game of shinny or field hockey was practically universal among the tribes throughout the United States. The curved racket, analogous to the club of the war gods, was usually expanded at the striking end and was painted or carved. The ball was either a wooden knot or made of buckskin; the distance of the goals varied between 200 and 700 yards. The Indian game of lacrosse was even more universal and common to all the tribes from Maine to California, from the Gulf of Mexico to Hudson Bay. In 1834, a great game was played near Jasper, Georgia. Months of heavy training preceded the contest in which eighteen played on a side, the chiefs of the rival settlements wagered $1,000. Guns, blankets, horses—everything the Indians had

or valued—were staked upon the result. Secret ceremonies, incanta-
tions, fasting, bathing, sexual abstinence, and mystic rites attended
every step of the game. The rugged, skull-cracking ball game was
usually played on a quarter-mile field with two teams, often of
unequal numbers and from rival villages, fighting it out all day.
Courage, leadership training, preparation for war, winning prizes,
were realizable goals of a game that never lost its divine or religious
function as well—until the effects of white man's acculturation
strongly changed the concept of lacrosse.

Many North American tribes had legendary reputations for long
distance running. A Professor F. V. Hayden once described the
Manden foot race as Olympic in character. The 3-mile race course was
laid out on the level prairie in the form of an arc, describing
two-thirds of a circle with the starting and finishing posts only several
hundred yards apart. The athlete-warriors were matched in ability,
with blankets, guns, and other wagered properties piled high. The
runners were naked, except for moccasins, their bodies painted from

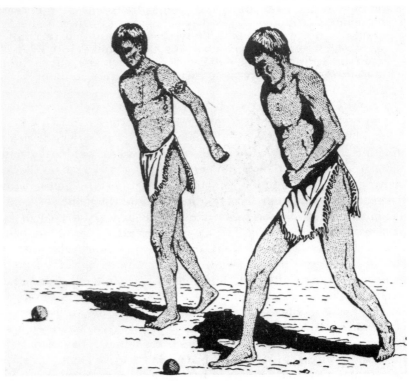

Southwest Indian kicking races used wooden sticks or balls to hurl
ahead in keen competition.

head to foot. Judges and hundreds of spectators lined the course which was run three times or nine miles. Special prizes were awarded to those winners displaying special speed, endurance, and courage. Professor Hayden called it "a fine national amusement" contributing to their magnificent physical condition. Immediately on finishing the race, "in a profuse state of perspiration, [they] throw themselves into the Missouri, and no instance is known where this apparent rashness resulted in any illness."[14] Legendary marathon feats of Southwest American Indians may be epitomized by the Zuni kicking-stick races. When the sun priest announced that the planting had been done, the usual deeply religious rituals and heavy betting preceded the 25 mile flight over the arid plain. Squads of runners stood poised at the starting mark—each leader with a little stick about the size of a man's middle finger balanced across his bare right foot just behind the toes. As the race begins, the stick goes hurtling through the air, thirty feet high and a hundred feet away in the sand. Immediately as it falls, a member of the team is ready to work his toes under it and relay it ahead to another team member. Guided by yelling horsemen, the group of runners sometimes clashing in a fierce melee as the sticks fall close to one another, turn at the half-way stone pile. The dust-blinded athletes increase the tempo as the flat roofs of the Zuni village and the finish line approach. The exhausted winners, finishing in under three hours, are closely followed by remaining teams. All is concluded by prayers, bathing, feasting, celebrations, and rest. The Zuni gods are pleased with the day's athletic worship.

EARLY NINETEENTH CENTURY SPORTING PERIODICALS

As early as 1824, some saw the restless flow of peoples into the urban areas as fraught with danger. That year, James Stuart Skinner was editor of the *American Farmer* and expressed pleasure at the thought that gentlemanly rural sports might soon influence the indolent city dweller. In typical hyperbolic language of the times, Skinner felt sure that hunting, fishing, and riding could "lead our young men . . . away from the vicious haunts of a populous city, into open fields, where no man ever contracted dyspepsia, or imbibed an ignoble passion."[15] Presidents Jefferson and Jackson took much interest in Skinner's *American Farmer*—its practical comments on efficient farming and frequent excursions into health practices and the re-creative powers of outdoor sports. Constantly opposing a lingering facet of Calvinism, Skinner argued that hunting, fishing, and outdoor sports were beneficial to both health and morals, even if they did afford pleasure in addition. He pioneered sporting editorials on horse racing and edited the *American Turf Register and Sporting Magazine* from 1829 to 1839. Skinner's persistence was rewarded by the introduction of agricultural fairs featuring trotting races, and initiating the first cricket matches in the United States. James Stuart Skinner very early joined the educational revisionists of the period and advanced a view of sport and recreation as both highly utilitarian and yet very British in its concept of sport for sport's sake.

One of the most important vehicles of the age for collecting and disseminating the subliterature of sporting amusements and recreational pastimes was *The Spirit of the Times*. Founded in 1831 by William Trotter Porter, a Vermont-born son of a horse fancier, the periodical called itself a "Chronicle of the Turf, Agriculture, Field Sports, Literature, and the Stage." Modern historian David Grimsted ventured that no magazine of the period "touches so evocatively on the ways in which Americans amused themselves" better than did the *Spirit of the Times*. For a quarter of a century it was the receptacle for literary and sporting news, for masculine anecdotes and humerous sketches sent from every part of the country. This first all-round sporting journal in the United States was closely modeled after the popular "Bell's Life in London." The average American four-page paper of 1830 was a dingy, ill-printed sheet; Porter had to do better to survive. He did, and undoubtedly helped give American sports a respectable standing. Still, a good yarn which stretched and tested the truth was most acceptable. Hunting and fishing stories took up much space. One of them, based on the 1823 *Travels of Baron Munchausen*, appeared in the 1837 *Spirit of the Times* and was called "Shooting Extraordinary":

> My grandfather, who was considered a man of truth and integrity, went hunting one day. He fired at a deer and found that the ball had killed it, passed through the head of a sturgeon in a nearby stream, and ricocheted through the body of a fox. In addition it had split the limb of a tree. The limb had sprung shut again, catching by the legs two pigeons, and came to rest in a bee-tree, from which a yellow juice was running down from a small hole——a ball hole—he put his finger to it, then to his tongue, and found that it was honey.[16]

Porter's essentially masculine publication reached 40,000 subscribers and many more readers. In 1839, he purchased the *American Turf Register and Sporting Magazine*. For the greater part of his life, he took a personal interest in many sports; he founded the New York Cricket Club and fought hard the deep-seated prejudice against activities on the turf in certain parts of the country. Porter's compendium of native tales, lively allusions to current attitudes, including the healthful and joyous benefits of participatory sport, must be considered a contributing factor in popular attitude changes in the pre-Civil War period.

AMERICAN SPORTS 1823-1837

The earliest history of American sporting habits—Horatio Smith's 1831 *Festivals, Games, and Amusements*—covered Indian games, and sport in every section of the country, including the Western States. Writing in the book's appendix. Samuel Woodworth, author and editor of the *New York Mirror*, observed that inventive Americans generally occupied themselves with practical and profitable subjects "and seldom, if ever, in multiplying the sources of amusement." It is true that the recent resurgence of religious fundamentalism along with the rise of the common man tended, for the moment, to mute much conspicuous sports display among the wealthy and leisured class. Augustus B. Longstreet, famous Georgia governor, author and sportsman, was a member of this upper class but his *Georgia Scenes* (1831) reflected a cross section view of all classes. His sports anecdotes are classics; "The Fight" describes a brutal back alley boxing match, "The Gander Pulling," "The Fox-Hunt," and "The Shooting Match" are unrivaled portraits of Georgia citizens in the early decades of the nineteenth century. In "The Turf," Longstreet and a friend arrived at the track early to study carefully human nature. Negro jockeys rode in the races. In the third mile of one race, the horse fell, killing the rider. " 'I declare,' said Mrs. Blue, as her carriage wheeled off, 'had it not been for that little accident, the sport would have been delightful.' "[17]

Significant leisure time was still a dream for the common man. But at least it was discussed. James Stuart Skinner's July 22, 1825 issue of *The American Farmer* urged the city dweller to take advantage of a Saturday afternoon hunting and fishing experience. After dinner, he suggested quoits, cricket, or bowl at nine-pins. "There is a time for all things," he said,—"for play as well as for work." Still, in most Northern sectors, sport for its own sake remained under suspicion; the moral earnestness of many Americans showed in the continual insistence that recreation have moral and educational values. Life on a southern plantation, on the other hand, was significantly different regarding amusements and attitudes toward sport and games. A white youngster often enjoyed idyllic hunting, fishing, riding, and shooting experiences. So did his parents, whom Thomas Nelson Page called "a careless and pleasure-loving people." The most important of pre-Civil War resort centers for Southern people of affluence were located at various sulphur springs in Virginia and the plush vacation spot at Saratoga, New York. Drama and music, reading and an appreciation of romantic literature vied for his time. The affluent southerner had golf clubs in Savannah and Augusta with a Quoit Club in the former city. Fishing, hunting, dueling, cockfighting, golf, boat

A turkey shooting match was a popular nineteenth century pastime.

and balloon races, medieval tournaments all took a back seat to riding and horseracing. Negro amusements during the 1820s and 1830s are little understood and, of course, infrequent. During his interminably hard work, the black man found time to make a jubilee of frolics, singing, dancing, music, Christmas festivals, and social barbecues.

America was coming of age in the 1830s and yachting had caught the fancy of southern and yankee aristocrats. Commodore John C. Stevens perfected the pleasure craft and in 1835 sailed his schooner, "Wave," to Boston where he defeated John P. Cushing's "Sylph." Sophisticated yachting competition had begun in America that year although on November 3, 1831, in Savannah, Georgia, the schooner "Jessy" was beaten by a sloop boat over a 36-mile course. "Considerable skill was manifested by the respective helmsmen" noted the contemporary account. In January of 1837, the Aquatic Club of Georgia met at Frederica, St. Simon's Island, for a series of four- and six-oared boat races. Colonel Dubignon's "Goddess of Liberty," Mr. Demere's "Columbia," and Captain Floyd's "Devil's Darning Needle" won all the honors. Several years earlier on Philadelphia's Schuylkill River, competitions between the "Imp" and "Sylph" attracted thousands. The seven oarsmen from the "Sylph," dressed in handsome Neapolitan caps, red striped shirts, black belts and white pantaloons, won the 3½ mile race. Later, in November of 1835, the first annual fete of the New York Amateur Club took place; thousands witnessed the "Wave" defeat six other crafts over a 5½ miles distance in 34 minutes. Judge John Lang awarded four silver pitchers and added that this historic first would promote health, strength, and longevity. If these races imitate the English Regattas, so be it, concluded the Judge, for "the most fastidious moralist cannot complain, while you devote no hours for rational exercise but those on which your various occupations have no claim."[18]

At the turn of the century the legendary Englishman, Captain Barclay walked a thousand miles in a thousand hours. So overpowering was the drowsiness which affected him during the last days of his walk, that he could be kept awake only by sticking himself with needles and by firing pistols close to his ears. Another Englishman, Joshua Newsam, walking in the private Labyrinth Garden, in Arch Street, west of Broad Street, Philadelphia, completed a thousand miles in eighteen consecutive days—easily surpassing Barclay's record. The date was November, 1830, and America's version of the peculiar sport of pedestrianism was born. One can discount as apocryphal the story of the Osage Indian who, starting from his post at day-break in April of 1835, with a bar of lead weighing 60 pounds, was ordered to reach his brother's post before midnight, a distance of nearly 120 miles. The Indian performed the distance without difficulty. Far more accurate and significant was the first time a man ran 10 miles in less than an hour. Thousands pushed their way into the Union Race Course, Long Island, on Friday, April 24, 1835. Nine men started but only one, a Henry Stannard of Stonnington, Connecticut, was able to run under an hour. The 35,000 spectators roared their approval as the winner pocketed his $1,300, mounted a horse and rode among the people, receiving their congratulations. "Looking like one of the victors of old, flushed from the triumphs of the tournament . . . he had exhibited genuine Yankee agility and bottom."[19]

AMERICA IN A FEVER OF ENERGY

Andrew Jackson, president from 1829 to 1837, was the embodiment of the common man—long remembered in his youth as a "most roaring, rollicking, game-cocking, horse racing, card playing, mischievous fellow." His personality helped in the emergence of the mass man. "Through his violent and impulsive person he projected the age's leading idea: that the unchecked development of the individual was paramount; . . . that thought should be subordinate to action"[20] This was the age of reform, religion, utility, and popular education, observed the *Knickerbocker* magazine in January of 1836. The new sense of political democracy created a new mass attitude towards politics; it became a main source of interest and entertainment, a national sport. Events of the previous half-century had convinced Americans that they could contribute to humanity the finest system of government ever devised by man. Social disorders and changes in home life were dominated by profound religious and philanthropic experiences. Sport and physical education enterprises were not exactly dormant during this era. Still the heat and degree of energy expended in other directions gave historians the distinct and correct impression that Americans were preoccupied elsewhere. A frequent blending of humanitarian and religious concerns with sport and physical culture began to develop. Dr. John Jeffries reminded Christians seeking the divine life to take greater care of their "mortal frame" through exercise and wholesome games. The inconsistency of expecting a vigorous mind in a sickly body was pointed out by the medical doctor turned theologian and physical educator. For him, exercise seemed to be interwoven with the very nature of man. "There must be peace and calmness in the soul, for the Spirit of God to dwell in the affections of the heart; and will more perfectly exist, with clearness of intellect and corporal strength."[21] The fever of reform and the romantic evangelical spirit of American religious life during the 1830s acted as an incubator for personal and community health concerns and for the expansion of spectator and participatory sporting amusements. The North felt this more than in the South where the ruling class derived their ideal from an image of the English landed gentry, who in the spirit of "noblesse oblige" assumed the gentlemen's responsibility for the maintenance of high culture, economic well-being of the community, political stability, and the perpetuation of ancient sports, games, and pastimes. The western frontier moved rapidly during these decades of the 1820s and 1830s. Unhampered by past institutions and conservative prejudices, western pioneer sports emerged as a vigorous meld of European games, Indian amusements, and unique American pastimes. In the North, especially New England, complex social and cultural changes were preparing the next generation and the one after that for greater opportunities to engage in frivolous and satisfying sporting experiences during their leisure time. John R. Betts attempted to outline some of the prevailing thought regarding mind and body when he said that:

> National pride was wounded when foreign critics referred to the underdeveloped physiques, wan complexions, and premature aging of Americans. Classicists and romanticists alike were inspired by the Greek Revolution; and ancient history was featured in the curriculum, which reminded the young of the gymnasiums of Athens and the vigor of Sparta.[22]

REFERENCES

1. Vernon L. Parrington, *Main Currents in American Thought*, Vol. II: *The Romantic Revolution in America* (New York: Harcourt, Brace and Co., 1930), p. 272.

2. John Jeffries, Physical Culture, the Result of Moral Obligation, *The American Quarterly Observer*, I (October, 1833), p. 252.

3. Edward Reynolds, On the Necessity of Physical Culture to Literary Men, and Especially to Clergymen, *The Biblical Repository*, II (January, 1832), p. 200.

4. William A. Alcott, as quoted in Paul R. Mills, William A. Alcott, M.D. 1798-1859—Pioneer Reformer in Physical Education (unpublished Ph.D. dissertation, University of Maryland, 1971), p. 69.

5. Philip Lindsley, The Cause of Education in Tennessee, *North American Review*, XXIV (January, 1827), p. 221.

6. Vernon L. Parrington, *op. cit.*, pp. 322-323.

7. Frederick L. Jahn in Teachers of Gymnastics, *American Journal of Education*, I (November, 1826), p. 700.

8. Bruce L. Bennett, The Making of Round Hill School, *Quest*, IV (April, 1965), p. 62.

9. The full context of Dr. Caldwell's speech may be found in his 133 page *Thoughts on Physical Education* (Boston: Marsh, Capen and Lyon, 1834).

10. Mary Lyon (1797-1849), as quoted in Margaret Duncan Green, "The Growth of Physical Education for Women in the United States in the Early Nineteenth Century" (unpublished Ed.D. dissertation, University of California, Los Angeles, 1950), p. 85.

11. John R. Betts, American Medical Thought on Exercise as the Road to Health, 1820-1860, *Bulletin of the History of Medicine*, XLV (March-April, 1971), p. 138.

12. Edward Reynolds, Physical Culture, *Annals of Education and Instruction*, II (September 15, 1832), p. 458.

13. George Catlin, *North American Indians*, Vol. I (Philadelphia: Leary, Stuart and Co., 1913), p. 159.

14. F. V. Hayden as quoted in Stewart Culin, Games of the North American Indians, *Twenty-Fourth Annual Report of the Bureau of American Ethnology 1902-1903* (Washington: Government Printing Office, 1907), p. 808.

15. James Stuart Skinner, Partridge Shooting, *American Farmer*, VI (November 12, 1824), p. 271.

16. Norris W. Yates, *William T. Porter and the Spirit of the Times* (Baton Rouge: Louisiana State University Press, 1957), pp. 173-174.

17. Augustus B. Longstreet, *Georgia Scenes* (New York: Sagamore Press, 1957), p. 146.

18. See The Regatta in *American Turf Register*, VII (November, 1835), pp. 121-122.

19. *New York Times*, Saturday, April 25, 1835, p. 2.

20. Francis Russell, The People's President, in *Age of Optimism*. Vol. V of *Milestones of History*, ed. by Alan Palmer (6 vols.: New York: Newsweek, 1970), p. 51.

21. John Jeffries, *op. cit.*, p. 256.

22. John R. Betts, Mind and Body in Early American Thought, *Journal of American History*, LIV (March, 1968), pp. 790-791.

CHAPTER 7

Sport and Recreational Practices of the Transcendental Man

AMERICA'S AWKWARD AGE

The fourth and fifth decades of the nineteenth century witnessed an unrivaled period of reform, some of it pervasive and lasting, some of it bizarre and transitory. "New winds" blowing over America introduced, among many things, powerful social changes resulting from the Industrial Revolution, a period of assertive patriotism among the common people, and an especially rich tapestry of religious-philosophical positions. An increase in spectator and participatory sport involvement was tempered by many Americans who still took their amusements somewhat surreptitiously. The centrality of the Protestant Ethic was strong in New England; earthly and, hopefully, heavenly fortunes awaited those who worked very hard and played with restraint. New freedoms and new ideas could not yet free New Englanders from those ingrained characteristics of the previous two centuries. Among the small Southern plantation aristocracy, an imported European romanticism further heightened their tenuous and unreal world. Sport and leisure activities reached a new summit with the political and social leaders of the South during this period. Ancient sports, fox hunting, and jousting tournaments were featured in every Southern state, and appeared as durable as their European origins. No sooner had Martin Van Buren been seated in the White House than the Panic of 1837 created disquietude everywhere. There were riots in New York over the high cost of flour. The financial crisis of 1841 was disastrous and the nation suffered lean years between these two dates. Sporting experiences for the masses were low priority during the difficult period. Americans were busy people, anyway, and had not yet learned how to employ leisure. As Samuel Morison says about the common man, "His pleasure came from doing; and as almost everyone worked for long hours six days a week, and (except in New Orleans) the Puritan sabbath prevailed, there was not much time for recreation." Yet, characteristically, the moment the exigencies of earning a living became even minutely easier, these same Americans, as they had always done, turned to sport, amusement, and recreation. On the far western frontier during the 1830s and 1840s, the era of the mountain men preceded the enormous rush of land hungry pioneers. "If anything in history approached an irresistible force, it was the pioneer who had learned that fertile fields to the west awaited his plow."[1] Survival was sport enough; the occasional foot and horse races, the vicious wrestling matches, and colorful Indian games were roaring overflows of animal energies. The existence of this vast area of free land drew men westward and the "Turner thesis" was born. Man in America was as much a product of the continent's unique environment as he was of his European heritage. Engrafted continental sport found a worthy soil in North America and a distinctly American sport variety took firm root during the two decades before the Civil War.

EMERSON'S TRANSCENDENTAL PHYSICAL CULTURE

Ralph Waldo Emerson (1803-1882) was unquestionably the most influential American philosopher during the first half of the nineteenth century. His concept of transcendentalism, touched with romantic idealism, taught self-reliance and a soaring spiritual greatness inherent in every man. He probably had a greater effect on the minds of generations of Americans than any other thinker. Emerson's transcending faith in the possibility of total human perfection gave to his time an almost ideal presentation—the freedom of the New World. His teachings appealed especially to the self-educated generation of that era—the philosophy of the reformers. Interestingly, the new morality of Emerson, despite its essentially metaphysical basis, also addressed itself to the physical health of Americans. The generously conceived transcendental man could not very well be consumptive; robust health seemed at least the outward manifestation of an inner divinity and spirituality.

Emerson reckoned that moral and physical courage were partly dependent on body fitness. "For performance of great mark," he said, "it [the body] needs extraordinary health." In his *The Conduct of Life*, Emerson noted that "the first wealth is health." He admired the great men of the past and urged young people to read their exploits. Yet sometimes youth does not take readily to books, he noted. "Well, the boy is right; and you are not fit to direct his bringing up, if your theory leaves out his gymnastic training. Archery, cricket, gun and fishing rod, horse and boat, are all educators, liberalizers."[2] With rare

"The first wealth," said Emerson, "is health"—a product of exercise.

Rousseauistic logic, Emerson saw youthful games as self-revealing and dramatically educative; riding, football, swimming, skating, climbing, fencing, and the like are "lessons in the art of power" and the main business of children. Undoubtedly a romantic longing for vibrant health (something he never attained), Emerson's view can be seen in a letter he wrote to Miss Elizabeth Hoar from Manchester, England: "When I see my muscular neighbors day by day I say, Had I been born in England, with but one chip of English oak in my willowy constitution!" Emerson visited England in 1833 and 1847, and observed that the English are far better athletes than Americans and have more constitutional energy than any other people. The English, he said:

> think, with Henri Quatre, that many exercises are the foundation of that elevation of mind which gives one nature ascendant over another; or with the Arabs, that the days spent in the chase are not counted in the length of life. They box, run, shoot, ride, row, and sail from pole to pole.[3]

Emerson saw greatness in every man. In his essay, "Success," men were portrayed as each having some triumphant superiority, which, through some "pugilistic or musical or literary craft, enriches the community with a new art." Emerson made people feel good, and fired the ordinary man with enthusiasm to discover his own unbounded greatness and worth. His faith in humanity was unclouded to the end. To the American of his own day, observed Alice Felt Tyler, "Emerson was the realization of his own highest ideal—the completely free and untrammeled individual, serene, civilized, and benevolent." American sport and physical education could only have been helped by so remarkable a man.

NEW ENGLAND EXPERIMENTS WITH LEISURE AND SPORT

New England, especially Massachusetts, during the period 1837-1844, was a center of social and moral reform. Public and private school education in the Bay State led the nation. It was a golden age of American literature and a period of frenetic business energy on the part of most Americans. James Silk Buckingham, British traveler, arrived in Boston during the fall of 1838; he noted the unresting hurry of the city dweller (New Yorkers were even worse, he said). Women, especially, appeared in poor health, ate hasty meals of cake and ice cream, and almost never exercised. Buckingham noted that physical training was not part of the curriculum of any school he visited and unlike the English "the vigorous exercise required for the young, in cricket, hoops, foot-ball, running, leaping, wrestling, etc., is almost unknown." Sir Charles Lyell, the English geologist who lectured throughout America in the 1840s, said the United States seemed to be a "country where all, whether rich or poor, were laboring from morning till night, without ever indulging in a holiday." The unkindest cut of all came from Thomas C. Grattan, British Consul from 1839 to 1846. Americans are born middle-aged he said; a "Boston boy" is a melancholy picture of prematurity. The speed with which eastern Americans live robs them of recreation, and prevents "gracefulness or strength to body or mind." Mr. Grattan saw little organized athletic games as was common back home. With olympian disdain, Grattan suggested that the physical powers of

Americans were retarded; "I doubt if there exists an American gentleman who could take a horse over a three foot rail in England, or an Irish potato trench."[4]

The ephemeral interest in gymnastics shown by Harvard and Yale Universities was already a thing of the past. A peevish Yale student in 1841 wrote that the English college students exercise two hours a day at hiking, riding, rowing, fencing, and gymnastics. No such thing existed at Yale. "The gymnasium has vanished," he pointed out, "wicket has been voted ungenteel, scarce even a freshman dares put on a pair of skates." Harvard students, no better off, sometimes resorted to time-honored informal rough play to discharge physical energies. Edward Everett Hale, Unitarian clergyman, author of *Franklin in France* and *The Man Without a Country*, was a Harvard youngster in the late 1830s. "Tumultuous throngs" of students pushed each other about in crude freshmen-sophomore battles; young Everett once had his fine coat and trousers badly torn and "ran against someone so forcibly as to give me a pain in my chest all the evening." Hale was a fitness enthusiast all his life and wrote that as a student he also played cricket and wildly irregular baseball.

The westward movement gained momentum after 1840. New Englanders, who a generation before had settled New York and Ohio, were pressing forward to the midwest. Most of those choosing to stay at home could not have failed to read the admonitions of two remarkable people, Lydia Huntley Sigourney and Horace Mann. Mrs. Sigourney directed most of her 2,000 periodical articles and 60 volumes toward the emancipation of women. A great deal of her work dealt with their physical and mental health. Her whole life was one of active philanthropy. She published in some 300 magazines, and during the 1830s and 1840s she must have been read by millions. She wrote frequently on diet, women's restrictive clothing, the wholesomeness and moral as well as physical necessity of family recreation and exercise. She directed much of her beneficent advice on the need for exercise to mothers. With unerring logic she reminded them that "if to a father the influence of continual ill-health in the partner of his joys is so dispiriting, how much more oppressive is it to those little ones. . . ." Women are obliged to care for their bodies, she said, for if they have received from their Creator "a sound mind in a sound body, teach them that they are accountable to Him for both."[5] Writing from a different platform but with a similar message, Horace Mann reminded all that "soundness of health is preliminary to the highest success in any pursuit." America's greatest antebellum educator pioneered the need for physical education in the schools. How bizarre, he pointed out, that physical vitality is not sought by clergymen, lawyers, writers, mothers "but by the wrestler, the buffoon, the

The gymnasium was uncommon prior to the Civil War. (Courtesy of Library of Congress.)

runner, the opera-dancer. There are ten professors of pugilism in our community to one of physical education in our seminaries of learning."[6] Mann recommended every day's school curriculum contain time for exercise, in order that city youngsters "with pale faces, narrow chests, and feeble frames . . . engage in some genial sport." Horace Mann served as secretary of the Massachusetts Board of Education from 1837 to 1848, and in the *Common School Journal* of January 1, 1842, pronounced that "the present generation is suffering incalculably under an ignorance of physical education." The next generation was to take this and other warnings as directives to modifying American life styles.

THE PAGEANT OF TROTTING AND THOROUGHBRED RACING

Americans who loved the sport of racing horses found in the 1830s and 1840s a period of singular interest. A genuine and universal interest in the sport, with several exceptions, had not taken place earlier. Horse racing was strong in the 1850s but baseball, rowing, foot racing, yachting, gymnastics, and prize fighting shared some of the growing national sport interest. The spectre of civil war made intersectional horse racing less viable as the conflict grew closer. Trotting and Thoroughbred racing survived the economic crises of the 1830s, marking the next decade as one of the most interesting in American turf history. The fresh, new sporting periodicals and eastern newspaper sports pages of the 1840s carried racing results everywhere.

Oliver Wendell Holmes, Sr. once wrote that the running horse was a gambling toy, but the trotting horse was useful and, furthermore, "horse racing is not a republican institution; horse-trotting is." There is some truth to this; horse racing's origins were aristocratic while harness racing popularity grew out of early New England agricultural fairs—the bailiwick of farmers and working people. The sport had its earliest formal introduction at Hunting Park, Philadelphia, the Centreville course on Long Island, and at the Cambridge, Massachusetts Trotting Park. Informal match races took place along newly constructed turnpikes in the New York, Philadelphia, and Boston areas. The first great American trotter was Lady Suffolk; she was foaled in 1833, first raced in 1838, won most of her 162 races in the next sixteen years, and earned a fortune before her retirement. Her campaigns carried her from Boston to St. Louis, from Baltimore to New Orleans.[7] On October 18, 1845, at Hoboken, she raced a mile in 2:29½ and set a standard for future pacers and trotters. Lady Suffolk's very first rider during the spring of 1838 in a race at Babylon, Long Island, was a young twenty-one-year-old named

Hiram Woodruff. The history of the American trotter in the years before the war centers about this remarkable reinsman and trainer. For thirty-six years he trained and rode trotters; he saw the sport grow tremendously and contributed much to the science of breeding good horses. John Krout said of him, "Though he loved the pageantry of the turf and the performance of the champion, he never forgot that the great objective was to bring the stock of the country up to the highest standard."

The period of the early 1830s was one of unprecedented expansion of thoroughbred horse racing. The twin economic depressions of 1837 and 1839 had a shattering effect upon racing, still a sport uncommercialized and relying for its main support upon men of wealth and property. At the same time the premier turf event of the era, and one of the most celebrated in American history, occurred at Union Course, New York on May 10, 1842, and did much to keep alive the sporting interest. This was another great North versus the South match race between Fashion and Boston for $20,000 a side. The preeminence of the Southern horse, Boston, as the best in America was well established. Foaled in Virginia in 1833, Boston won 40 of 45 races and took home $51,700 between 1836 and 1843. Fashion, greatest of American racing mares was born in 1837 on a farm near Madison, New Jersey. The chestnut filly was 15½ hands, rising high on the withers, with a light head and neck, faultless legs, an oblique, well-shaped shoulder running far back, and a roomy, deep, and capacious chest.[8] A brilliant racing season in 1841 led to the great match race of 1842. The aristocratic New York diarist, George Templeton Strong, noted the crush of people that witnessed the race between Boston and Fashion. "People came on from the East and the West and from all quarters to see the fun—some came from New Orleans."[9] The "outpouring of masses" was estimated at between 50,000 and 70,000. Forty United States Senators and an array of dignitaries occupied the ten-dollar seats in the new grandstand. Thousands were unable to see the race, train service broke down and the enraged mob smashed the ticket office. Unruly toughs demolished fences around the grandstand enclosure, repelling the security forces headed by prize fighters, Yankee Sullivan, Isaiah Rynders, and Jeroloman. Carrier pigeons were released carrying word of the race while the authoritative *Spirit of the Times* got out an extra edition.

Boston became the 5-3 favorite as race time approached. The first 4 mile heat saw Boston draw the pole and get away fast, leading the first 3 miles in 1:53, 1:50½, and 1:54, with Fashion hanging close. Boston brushed the rail, cutting a long, jagged tear on his flank, slowing him and enabling Fashion to win in 7:32½, a fraction away from the

The 1845 Fashion-Peytonia $20,000 race highlighted the 1800s. (Courtesy of Library of Congress.)

world's record. The second and last heat saw Fashion thunder through miles of 1:59 and 1:57. The magnificent 26 foot striding Boston blew past the Yankee horse, covering the third mile in 1:51½. But the old warrior tired badly and had nothing left, allowing Fashion to win by 60 yards in 7:45. Once again the North had triumphed. Both horses were covered with glory. Racing historian Trevathan called the contest beautiful and exciting. "There was no clambering, no faltering, no dwelling on the past of either; each ran with a long, rating stroke, and at a pace that kills." During the two succeeding seasons of 1843 and 1844, Fashion went on from conquest to conquest and in 1845, the great Peytona versus Fashion match drew even greater publicity and spectators. These two races and several others helped shore the faltering sport during the turbulent pre-war era, giving substance and fond memories to the horse racing game during its resurgence a generation later.

EARLY STIRRINGS IN BASEBALL AND PEDESTRIANISM

Baseball is an ancient and popular English children's game brought to America early in the history of the Republic. Historically, the games of "one-old-cat," "bat and ball," "feeder," "poison ball," "rounders," and others were legitimate precursors to the famous post Civil War version. The game in crude form was probably well known early in the nineteenth century when the journalist-politician Thurlow Weed (1797-1882), writing in his *Autobiography* about his youth, observed that young and old people of Rochester, New York, enjoyed the traditional game. He noted that "a base-ball club, numbering fifty members, met every afternoon during the ball-playing season." *The Boy's Own Book* (1829) by William Clarke, Robin Carver's 1834 *The Book of Sports*, and *The Boy's Book of Sports* (1839) all trace the fascinating evolution of baseball. Credit for bringing the game into maturity belongs to the Knickerbocker Base Ball Club of New York City. The Knickerbockers enjoyed their informal social baseball playing beginning in 1842, but in the spring of 1845, Alexander J. Cartwright enjoined a number of physicians, brokers, and merchants to form an organized baseball team. The Knickerbockers accepted the rules written by Cartwright later that year, and on June 19, 1846, at the Elysian Fields, Hoboken, the Knickerbockers were beaten 23 to 1 in an abbreviated game with the New York Club. Robert W. Henderson's authoritative baseball analysis points out that "there need be no mystery about the genesis of the Knickerbocker rules. They came directly or indirectly from those popular books of boy's games."[10] The popularity of baseball was more widespread and lasted for a longer time than any other American sport.

Pedestrianism, that persistent and peculiar professional distance running sport, had a banner year in 1844. On October 16, a crowd of nearly 35,000 assembled at the Beacon Course near New York to witness the "Footrace between England and America." *The Spirit of the Times* stated that the purse of a thousand dollars would be divided four ways with six hundred to the winner, "provided 10 miles is performed in an hour by the first, and 9½ miles by the 2nd, 3rd and 4th." The race was advertised in England, Canada and throughout the United States. Betting was unusually heavy on three Englishmen—John Barlow, John Greenhalgh and Ambrose Jackson against the field. The race was delayed an hour as nearly 10,000 "Oliver Twists—specimens of the tag-rag and bob-tail denizens of New York gained admission by breaking through the fences." Seventeen men started, including the American Henry Stannard, winner of the famous 1835 ten miler, the Indian John Steeprock (alias John Ross) and little regarded John Gildersleeve of New York.

Several days hard rain had left the half-mile horse track in poor condition. Just before the start, the strong wind subsided and the air was cool and bracing. At the conclusion of each three-minute period a bell was rung so that each athlete who wished might go a mile every six minutes. As the race began, the wildly enthusiastic crowd spilled out onto the track, a dozen horsemen just managing to keep open a narrow passage. Steeprock bolted into the lead and was ahead in 5:16 for the mile. His trainer then ordered him to "fall back and give up the track to Barlow," which he did. Barlow continued to lead the race through the ninth mile; Greenhalgh followed closely, took the lead and passed 10 miles in 57 minutes. Barlow was close, with Gildersleeve some 40 yards back and "running like a scared dog." With but three minutes remaining of the hour run, Gildersleeve continued "to go it like bricks" in pursuit of the Englishman, overtaking him just as the sixty minutes ended. A thunderous audience "shouting like devils" had witnessed Gildersleeve run over 10½ miles, the next three easily fulfilling their end of the bargain.

A return match came off on November 19th. The ballyhoo drew thousands. A single steamboat from Albany brought down four hundred; New Jersey, Long Island, and the river towns on the Hudson furnished more, while New York City sent over numbers "for an army three times larger than that with which Napoleon made his Italian campaign . . . ; thousands filled the stands, but it would have required the Amphitheatre of Titus to have accommodated all."[12] Essentially the same field lined up for this 10 mile race. After a few bizarre false starts, Mr. Barker gave the word "go" and the Lancashire professionals, Barlow and Greenhalgh, jumped into the lead. It was a determined John Barlow alias "Tallick" who passed through cracking

The 1830s pedestrians preceded America's greatest pedestrian, Edward Payson Weston, by a generation.

consecutive miles of 5:10, 5:15, 5:22, 5:25, 5:28, 5:31, 5:34, 5:36, 5:35, and 5:25. Barlow's time of 54:21 was the fastest ever run in the world. "They won't believe this in England," exclaimed the winner after the race. He had beaten the brilliant Indian, Steeprock (54:53), Greenhalgh (55:10), Gildersleeve (55:51), and McCabe of Ireland in 56:52. Barlow won the major share of the $1200 purse. All the contestants were in town "knocking about" during the evening, and the following morning most called at *The Spirit of the Times* office "looking as fine as bug-dust and feeling like perfect catbirds."

JOUSTING TOURNAMENTS IN THE OLD SOUTH

Three-fourths of the white population in the antebellum South were middle class, non slaveholding yeoman farmers. These plain people worked hard, hunted, fished, danced, attended camp meetings, sang spirituals, drank a lot, wrestled, indulged in practical jokes, shooting contests, barbecues, corn shucking, enjoyed ballads and folk songs. An 1860 census showed that of Dixie's eight million people, only 46,274 were classified as aristocratic planters—men who considered themselves the embodiment of the South. Only a few of them saw the necessity of improving conditions beyond their own plantation. Most continued to work hard at managing their own property and then indulge liberally in jockey club pursuits, card playing, formal balls, some organized golf, hunting, fishing, riding, boating, reading, and, frequently, simply doing nothing. Another social and sporting activity, one that has escaped the notice of sport historians, is tournament jousting.

In the dreamy South of the 1820s and 1830s, the plantation became, in the words of Oscar Handlin, "a manor, the slaves humble serfs, and the planter a mounted knight." Chivalric notions, strongly influenced by the *Waverly Novels* of Sir Walter Scott, dominated the thinking of many wealthy planters and helped to differentiate the Southern states from the rest of the Union. Scott's books graced every fine Southern library; his brand of romanticism made many planters feel like the chivalrous and athletic lord of the manor so vividly described in contemporary novels. Clement Eaton, historian of the South, pointed out that a passionate fondness for Scott's romantic stories by the Southern aristocrat tended to idealize their anachronistic society in terms of medieval chivalry. Significant leisure time and the influence of romantic literature resulted in the little southern vignette known as ring tournaments—inoffensive flummeries of a bygone era. In some long ago time and place, possibly Fauquier County, Virginia, in the 1840s, on an idyllic spring weekend, and in a broad, flat arena of several acres surrounded by high banks and shaded by embowering trees, a genteel ring tournament unfolded. The cult of chivalry, nourished by the myth that Southerners were descended from noble Cavaliers, led young gentlemen, clad as knights, to tilt with lances at suspended rings, while Southern belles waved their handkerchiefs. The first ring tournament in America was held on the estate of William Gilmore in 1840—a replica of the famous 1839 festival at Eglinton Castle, England. On August 28, 1841, the Virginia tournament was held at Warrenton Springs, Fauquier County. On the program local knights vied with contestants from Maryland, Texas, Mississippi, West Point, and the United States Navy. Tournaments also were held in the Southwest, the District of Columbia, Ohio, Pennsylvania, Delaware, New Jersey, and New York. Dewy-eyed knights took off on horseback with eleven foot lances, attempting to spear suspended rings varying in diameter from 2 inches down to half an inch. The rings were placed in a straight or curved line and about

25 or 30 yards apart. The entire course of 125 yards had to be covered in ten seconds. Considerable skill was required in threading the half-inch ring. In addition, life-size wooden Indians were used as targets; riding at full-tilt, the knights dispatched the enemy with pistol and saber.[13]

The *Waverly Novels* were America's first "best-sellers." The South assimilated Sir Walter Scott's romantic works into its very being. Virginia was the fountainhead of the chivalric stream in the antebellum South—a dislike for much of the present, a longing for the past. Professor Rollin G. Osterweis of Yale University noted that "of all the trappings of the Southern chivalric cult, the tournament most clearly exemplified the romantic mood."[14] One long-ago Maryland tournament featured beautiful maidens hoping to be crowned Queen, festive atmosphere, fervid oratory, and delicious flights of romantic fancy directed at the assemblage of youth calling themselves "Knight of Rose Lawn," or "Knight of the Lost Cause." Three rings, an inch and a quarter in diameter, were suspended 6½ feet above the ground; the lances were light, straight, wooden poles, 8 feet in length, sharpened to a fine point at one end. The knights were required to ride down the course at a great speed, on pain of being ruled out of the lists, the time allowed in making the distance being eight seconds. The task was difficult, for the rider must make the stab at the downward motion of the horse. The winner then placed the championship wreath "at the feet of his blushing and happy mistress, who is conducted to the stand and crowned by the victor, fair Queen of Love and Beauty."[15] Remarkably, these ring tournaments have not only survived to the present day but continue to be popular outdoor festivals in Virginia's Shenandoah Valley. General George S. Patton rode in the 1933 jousting "tunament" at Hume. The cult of chivalry remains alive; the dual, the hunt, the race and ring contest, emphasis on heraldry, ancestry, romance, hospitality, marvelous barbecued beef, and bingo playing far into the night continue to intrigue Warrenton County residents.[16] The 1972 Leeds Ruritan Jousting Tournament was won by the Knight of the Humites, T. Roy Wright, Jr. who lanced three rings in three and two-tenths seconds. Among the ancient locust trees a crowd of more than a thousand enjoyed the modified medieval ceremony and hearty good food. "All in all, for everyone, an exciting, relaxing fulfilling day at Hume" was the conclusion of the reporter assigned to cover the story.[17] Not far away, the century and a quarter old jousting tournament at Natural Chimneys Regional Park near Mount Solon reminds Virginians of an old nineteenth century sporting custom. The seven natural stone chimneys towering in the background resemble turrets of a medieval French castle. Contestants from several states hold their steel-tipped poles lightly in one hand as

George S. Patton rode in 1930s jousting tournaments such as this one in Acokeek, Maryland. (Courtesy of Library of Congress.)

they send their charges galloping down a 75-yard course to spear the tiny steel rings. "If a rider is good, he runs the course in not more than eight seconds, spearing all the rings." As the field of contestants dwindles, smaller rings are hung. The tournament begins in the afternoon and lasts late into the night. In addition to the jousting, there are exhibits of handicrafts, games of chance, and everything from country ham to fried chicken to ice cream.[18] Four thousand spectators braved damp weather and mud at the 1972 annual jousting tournament and saw thirty-one riders, including two women, participate in an effort to spear the three-quarter inch rings and witness the crowning of the lovliest "Queen of Love and Beauty."[19]

AMERICA TURNS THE CORNER IN SPORT

"There is a fine and beautiful alliance between all pastimes." Christopher North's observation in the October, 1842 *American Turf Register and Sporting Magazine* was another manifestation of the slow attitudinal change in the land—a public inversion that began to perceive national wealth as not all material but personal as well. Horace Bushnell's memorable Phi Beta Kappa oration on August 15, 1837, "The True Wealth or Weal of Nations," recognized the essential integration of man's mind and spirit with his body. He reminded the Yale student body that "the wealth of a nation is in the breast of its sons." By the fifth decade of the century the American character had definitely assumed a unique stamp. There was no idle aristocracy excepting those few Southern planters who took on this mantle; business enterprise was intense and common. Foreigners took back with them a strong impression of the aggressive egalitarianism of the American people. From the religious view and possibly in the psychological sense, most Americans were ready for leisure amusements, competitive and participatory. However, pervasive involvement in sporting activities came slowly, the result of American's passion for work and significant commitment to massive reform. Ray Allen Billington called the year 1844 America's year of decision. "Overnight," he said, "the American people awakened to their role in the Divine Plan." Few could clearly define this grand order but most agreed that "God is benevolent, Nature beneficent, and man divine."[20] If man was divine, therefore, and mankind perfectable, then it made uncommon good sense to many men that everything possible should be done to care for and strengthen the outer shell of man in order that his mind and spirit remain unclouded. The possibilities of sport or re-creative physical activities in the fulfillment of this glorious task was yet understood by only a few. The rest grasped precious leisure moments away from work and enjoyed them without the encumbrance of any such heady ideas. Beginning with Doctors Rusk, Warren, and Alcott, the medical profession urged their own more utilitarian suggestions for change. John R. Betts' perceptive comment stated that:

> A scientific and medical rationale for the movement toward health reform, physical education, field sports, athletics, and exercise for the masses had nonetheless been laid by scores of conscientious, observant, and informed physicians in the decades prior to the Civil War.[21]

The Industrial Revolution, the rise of large cities, a generation of social reform and ferment had begun to change ways of living and thinking. Physical education in the schools, recreational sport, and spectator athletics were beginning to receive a measure of attention. Outdoor activities for the new city dweller reminded him of his youth and his rural and frontier forebearers. Under suspicion for generations, sport for its own sake was emerging from a Puritan encasement. The full flowering of this concept would not take place for another hundred years. Despite some profound modifications, the majority of adult Americans in the 1840s regarded play and games as a waste of time. Fundamentalist churches frowned on many amusements; secular laws as well as ecclesiastical tenets threatened immoderate revellers. However, the imperative of crowded cities continued the rapid erosion of the Protestant Ethic with its "notion that earthly, and, hopefully, heavenly, fortune awaited those who toiled hard and continuously, and who avoided the temptations of luxury and idleness."[22] It was during this period that the idea of recreation and leisure merged with the work-status ethic and softened the sting of the latter. Indeed, during this pre-war period emerged the hybrid concept of recreation as individual re-creation of one's energies for more efficient work—a neat juxtaposition of the old and new.

REFERENCES

1. Ray Allen Billington, *The Far Western Frontier 1830-1860* (New York: Harper & Row, 1956), p. 91.

2. Ralph Waldo Emerson, *The Conduct of Life* (New York: A. L. Burt Co., n.d.), p. 125.

3. Emerson, *The Complete Writings of Ralph Waldo Emerson*, I (New York: Wm. H. Wise and Co., Pub., 1929), p. 439.

4. Thomas C. Grattan, *Observations of a British Consul, 1839-46* (London, 1859), as reprinted in Allan Nevins (ed.), *American Social History as Recorded by British Travelers* (New York: Henry Holt and Co., 1923), p. 251.

5. Lydia Huntley Sigourney, On Health to Mothers, *Southern Literary Messenger*, IV (1838), p. 477.

6. Horace Mann, On the Crisis in Education. Sixth Annual Report (1842) located in *Life and Works of Horace Mann*, Mary Mann/ed. (Boston: Walter, Fuller, 1865-1868), Vol. III, p. 5.

7. See Chapter 15, Some Super-Horses, in John Hervey, *The American Trotter* (New York: Coward-McCann, Inc., 1947), pp. 453-502. See also John R. Betts, Sporting Journalism in Nineteenth-Century America, *American Quarterly*, V (Spring, 1953), pp. 39-55; and John R. Betts, Agricultural Fairs and the Rise of Harness Racing, *Agricultural History*, XXVII (April, 1953), pp. 71-75.

8. Charles E. Trevathan, *The American Thoroughbred* (New York: The Macmillan Company, 1905), p. 249.

9. George Templeton Strong in Allan Nevins and M. H. Thomas (editors), *The Diary of George Templeton Strong—Young Man in New York 1835-1849*, Vol. II (New York: The Macmillan Co., 1952), p. 181.

10. Robert W. Henderson, *Ball, Bat and Bishop. The Origin of Ball Games* (New York: Rockport Press, Inc., 1947), p. 163.

11. *The Spirit of the Times*, October 19, 1844, p. 402.

12. *Ibid.*, November 23, 1844, p. 462.

13. Esther J. Crooks and Ruth W. Crooks, *The Ring Tournament in the United States* (Richmond: Garrett and Massie, 1936), pp. 2-3.

14. Rollin G. Osterweis, *Romanticism and Nationalism in the Old South* (New Haven: Yale University Press, 1949), p. 99.

15. Hanson Hiss, The Knights of the Lance in the South, *Outing*, XXXI (January, 1898), p. 341.

16. Blake Green, Jousting Tournaments in Virginia: The Age of Chivalry Lives On, *The New York Times*, August 22, 1971, p. 58.

17. Don Rypka, Knight of the Humites Leeds Ruritan Tourney's Champion, *The Fauquier Democrat*, August 17, 1972, pp. 1, 13.

18. Three Rings in the Chimneys, *Southern Living* (August, 1972), p. 10.

19. Annual jousting tourney winners announced, *The Staunton Leader*, August 21, 1972, p. 7.

20. Ray Allen Billington, The Far Western Frontier 1830-1860 (New York, Harper & Row, 1956), p. 143.

21. John R. Betts, American Medical Thought on Exercise as the Road to Health, 1820-1860, *Bulletin of the History of Medicine*, XLV (March-April, 1972), p. 152.

22. David Q Voigt, *America's Leisure Revolution* (Reading, Pennsylvania: Albright College Book Store, 1971), p. 29.

CHAPTER 8

Portents of Conflict and the Rise of Sport Before the Civil War

EMERGENCE OF A SPORT AND RECREATION PHILOSOPHY

Large scale recreational sporting activities continued to be a little understood and little practiced phenomenon till long after the Civil War. Yet the vision of a society caught up in sport and organized amusement amidst six days of hard work was understood by a few men and women of the period 1844-1858. Charles Francis Adams, Jr. (1835-1915), long after the fact, deeply regretted a boyhood without sport and blamed his father who "held in horror" such activities. The younger Adams, a noted economist, historian and the grandson of John Quincy Adams, lamented the loss of a carefree youth. "How irreparable," he said, "has been my loss in not acquiring . . . muscular aptitudes."[1] Yet, out of New England, home of such Puritan families as the Adams', emerged a new gospel proclaiming some doubt as to the virtues of total self-restraint. Historian Arthur C. Cole saw the antebellum period as one in which "Puritanical self-denial was at last forced to yield to the unimpeachable evidence that the American people were undergoing a serious physical decline."[2] The editor of *Harper's New Monthly Magazine*, in the January, 1857 publication, answered "nay" to his own question, "Are We Really Happy?" Americans are all-absorbed in a chaotic business struggle, he said; "the music of our social spheres is always out of tune." Relaxation and quiet enjoyment must become more widespread was his final charge. In a similar vein, Frederick Law Olmstead, architect of New York's Central Park in the 1850s, saw in this most significant recreational development a national mandate—the result of a "conscious effort of a democratic body to meet a proven need." American life in the first half of the nineteenth century was cast in the mold of individualism and democracy. The conflict between puritanism and the indigenous

Charles Francis Adams, Jr., lamented his loss of a carefree youth, here depicted by Winslow Homer's *Snap the Whip*. (The Metropolitan Museum of Art—Gift of Christian A. Zabriskie, 1950.)

pioneer concept of freedom, both of them having made profound contributions, continued to be resolved in favor of the latter. Urban dwellers, in many cases only recently arrived from the country, longed for exercise, for sport, and spectator athletics.

New knowledge of natural sciences, rising equalitarianism, and vocationalism or specialization was shaking the American universities to their foundations. The prestigious eastern schools gave their allegiance to German-inspired impersonalistic intellectualism. Students were to be considered adult men who needed no personal interest from their instructors. The boys, in some nearly automatic and counterbalancing fashion, reacted with a variety of debating societies, clubs, fraternal orders, and crude athletic adventures. It was to be a long time before faculties were to recognize the educational and therapeutic values of such activities. One pioneer who saw the need for faculty encouragement and involvement in student affairs, especially student health, was President W. A. Stearns of Amherst College. In his inaugural address of 1854, he said that "no course of education is complete without devoting special attention to secure a good development and health of the physical system." The Bostonian, Dr. John C. Warren, a few years earlier in his *Physical Education and the Preservation of Health*, had called for regular gymnastic training in all of the nation's colleges and seminaries of learning. The embryo of an idea was just beginning to catch hold. It took the remainder of the century for the concept of restorative exercise and enjoyable sport to become a major part of the American character.

REMINISCENCES OF ANTEBELLUM SPORT

The years before the Civil War saw a revival of ice skating, especially among city dwellers. Ocean bathing received notice, baseball grew steadily, while boxing and pedestrianism continued popular. Cricket was the rage in the Philadelphia area; its Newark Club was organized by men of English birth in 1849. So successful were the foreign born Americans in playing the game that the sport became surprisingly popular during the period.[3] A second wave of German immigrants brought the gymnasium movement to the United States in 1848. The Cincinnati and New York *Turngemeinde* were founded that year with three Philadelphia societies organized in 1849. The first national Turnfest was held in 1851. The nation's native-born began to take notice of the German-Americans and their strange gymnastic antics—especially after the American *Turnerbund* convention of 1855 took a decided political stand against slavery. When the Civil War began, the Turners comprised about 150 societies and 10,000 members. Unlike gymnastics which appealed to a smaller foreign element, field and stream sports, ever popular, reached new heights in the era 1844-1858. Directly responsible for this resurgence was Henry William Herbert, better known to his endearing American public as Frank Forester. His 1839 series of hunting and fishing articles in *The American Turf Register* got him off to a meteoric start. Born in England and trained at Eton and Cambridge, Forester had few equals in America as a classical scholar. His prodigious literary output, always engaging and authoritative, made him a legend in his own time. A contemporary writer saw in him the lover of Nature, the Shakespeare of sporting literature. "Herbert's name and fame have now become a species of American public property, as it were, in which every person using the English language takes a hearty interest."

College boat racing began at Yale University very early in the century. Shortly after mid-century, in a lovely bit of commercialism, the superintendent of the Boston, Concord, and Montreal railroad, propositioned a Yale undergraduate crew member, "If you will get up a regatta on the Lake [Winnipesaukee] between Yale and Harvard, I will pay all the bills." This first Harvard-Yale Regatta in 1852 marked the oldest of America's intercollegiate sports.[4] About this same time the fame of American pilot boats, both for seaworthiness and speed, had spread to English shipbuilders and yachtsmen. The opening of the 1851 World's Exhibition and the Crystal Palace in London created a business and sporting challenge intriguing to parties on both sides of the Atlantic. An American syndicate headed by Commodore John C. Stevens, ship designer George Steers, and a "smart crew" sailed for Havre on the schooner "America." She was 101 feet overall; a contemporary account described her bow "as sharp as a knife-blade, scooped away as it were outwards till it swells towards the stern, the sides gradually springing outwards as round as an apple. . . ." The surprisingly easy victory over fifteen British yachts around the Isle of Wight on August 22, 1851, brought world-wide fame to the clipper "America." The American ship won so handily that Queen Victoria, who was watching aboard the Royal Yacht "Victoria and Albert" is said to have asked a signalman standing nearby: "Who is first?" He replied, " 'America,' Your Majesty. There is no second." The classic competition continues to be a tradition well into the eighth decade of the twentieth century.

Another social and sporting activity with strong ethnic origins was the Scottish Caledonian Games. Heavy concentrations of Scots in the Boston and New York areas led these traditionally sports-loving people to organize the first American Highland or Caledonian Games in Boston during the summer of 1853. Philadelphia held its first Scottish Games in 1858. Conventional track and field events were spiced with music and dancing and good food, so like the old country.

Such fabulous events as tossing the caber, throwing the sledge, the heavy stone throw, the hitch and kick, the hop, skip and jump, hurdles and steeplechase were precursors to a more recognizable American track and field program. The author of *The Caledonian Games in Nineteenth-Century America*, correctly claims that "American track and field emerged from the influence of the early pedestrians, the rise of athletics in England, the appendages at the intercollegiate regattas, and the Caledonian Games."

AMERICAN MUSCULAR CHRISTIANITY

Charles Francis Adams deeply regretted not having had an education similar to the one offered at the English Public Schools in the second half of the nineteenth century. For him, inspirational daily chapel service, a challenging new academic curriculum, and being "rubbed into shape" during compulsory and highly competitive sports periods was the ideal education. The idea was new in England and newer in America, yet "Muscular Christianity," as it was called, rapidly became an acceptable philosophy in certain Anglo-American educational circles. Charles Kingsley, clergyman and influential author, always vehemently denied authorship of the phrase "Muscular Christianity." Yet, most of his writings glorify the Church's new social mission through the medium of the perfectly heroic man—the noble embodiment of moral, intellectual, and physical attributes. Kingsley envied English lads at Cambridge during their cricket, football, riding, hiking and cross country running. Spiritual consecration, hard mental work, and robust exercise forge an unbeatable Englishman, he said. It's all there in Kingsley's 1850 *Alton Locke*—an insufferable and

The Scottish Caledonian games combined sports, music, and dancing. (Courtesy of Library of Congress.)

quite heady self-concept that found immediate acceptance among many Americans.

I felt that in spite of all my prejudices—the stuff which has held Gibralter and conquered at Waterloo—which has created a Birmingham and a Manchester, and colonized every quarter of the globe—that grim, earnest, stubborn energy, which, since the days of the old Romans, the English possess alone of all the nations of the earth.[5]

"Muscular Christianity" was most dramatically introduced to American readers of the 1850s in *Tom Brown's Schooldays*, a huge best-seller by Thomas Hughes. It pictured life, especially the athletic atmosphere, at the Rugby School, during the years of the great headmaster, Thomas Arnold. The book's undeniable overemphasis on the role of athletics strongly influenced Americans of the period—not educators and intellectuals only but large numbers of so-called average people. Very quickly there arose a kind of mysticism about robust competitive athletics—a peculiar proneness to emotionalism and a fondness for romantic hero figures. The concept was to become one of the most significant in the English and American traditions. Leslie Stephen, Victorian writer and father of authoress Virginia Woolf, once defined "Muscular Christianity" as the duty of each to "fear God and walk a thousand miles in a thousand hours." The influence of Tom Brown on American sports, said William Blaikie, "has been greater, perhaps, than that of any other Englishman."[6] The movement launched the massive pursuit by thousands of young men for physical strength, beauty, courage, intellect, and virtue.

A PLEA FOR AMUSEMENT AND HEALTH PRESERVATION

Historian Arthur C. Cole saw the poor health of the American urban dweller in the middle of the nineteenth century as a reflection of lingering pioneer optimism and neglect. Serious signs of physical decline were noted by thoughtful critics. Personal habits of city folks "failed to reflect an adequate readjustment to the somewhat leisurely life that appeared with the recession of the frontier and of frontier conditions."[7] Poor eating habits, lack of recreational areas, and still fewer opportunities for regular participatory sport, made for unhappy conditions among the masses. Frederick W. Sawyer, in his 1847 *Plea for Amusements* repeated again and again the absolute need to balance hard work with recreational activities. Moderation and the Greek Golden Mean were urged as saviors of a sorely tested American civilization. "Temperance," cried the editor of *Littell's Living Age* in 1852, "is the very angel of health." Frank Queen, in an 1857 issue of the New York Clipper, urged that unless gymnasiums were considered as important as blackboards, the health of youngsters would be in jeopardy. These same children looked "pale and careworn" to Englishwoman, Isabella Lucy Bird, during her American visit in 1854. Another woman, the prominent physician, Elizabeth Blackwell, felt compelled to write in 1852, a lecture titled, "The Laws of Life in reference to the physical education of Girls." These were in the same years that Catharine Beecher's literary output chastised city parents for systematically educating the rising generation "to be feeble, deformed, homely, sickly and miserable." The reform spirit, so thick everywhere, was incapable of seeing that opportunities for sport and amusements were better than they had been, and the future of recreation bright with hope.

Healthful gymnastic exercises for girls were shown in the first volume of *Harper's Weekly*. "The physical deterioration of the Americans," stated the accompanying article, "is remarked upon by almost every traveler who comes among us." The pioneering *Godey's Lady's Book* gave constant attention to health and beauty hints. Good posture, fewer confining stays, and regular, moderate exercise were constantly presented to its readers. An advertisement in the January 14, 1854 edition of the *New York Tribune* called for all the family to attend gymnastic classes lest "in the absence of this health action, the system soon becomes deranged and disorganized." Education which fails to deal with physical health is no education, concluded an article, "Health and Disease," in the May, 1851 *The New Englander*. The parade of similar admonitions mounted through the 1850s. Too few city children exercised vigorously and regularly. "Young America is a man before he is fairly in his teens," pointed out *Harper's Monthly Magazine* for December, 1856. *The American Agriculturalist* reminded its rural constituents that the ancient Greeks had their gymnasiums for physical exercise. "Were not the Greeks wiser, after all, than we are, at least in this particular?"[8] A series of *Harper's* articles in 1857 and 1858 were titled "Our Daughters," "Our Sons," and "Our Husbands"; neglect of physical culture must be anathema reminded the writer. By 1850, cities were growing three times as quickly as rural places were expanding. This urban growth was recruited from a country exodus. Many educators, writers, and medical practitioners offered advice to a generally dispirited city dweller. Books like Dr. R. T. Trall's *The Illustrated Family Gymnasium*, his New York Hydropathic Establishment and flourishing Hygeiotherapeutic Medical School offered an incredible variety of posture training, medico-gymnastics, running, leaping, swimming, and "promiscuous exercises." Pure air, cleanliness, and universal exercise seemed an imperative need. Bigger guns from the intellectual and literary community leveled their attack on the problem.

AMERICAN INTELLECTUALS CRY FOR HEALTH AND SPORT

The decade of the 1850s saw a ground swell among certain American intellectuals regarding what seemed to be the wretched physical state of many city residents. *Harper's Monthly Magazine* reminded its readers that overindulgence combined with physical lethargy could only result in "enfeebling their strength, shattering their nerves, and fevering their blood." Too many Americans seemed irritable and plagued with a sallow complexion, the by-products, perhaps, of what foreign visitors and domestic critics invariably commented upon as the nation's barbaric eating habits, "the seed-time of dyspepsia." George W. Curtis (1824-1892), throughout his long career as editor of *Harper's*, waged a quiet war on "the impetuous haste with which we live," and urged daily vigorous outdoor exercise, as was his own life long habit. His own periodical's widely read columns, "Editor's Table" and "Editor's Easy Chair," made frequent mention of this concern. His October, 1853 column noted wryly that "in the proportion that the physique of young America diminishes, its clothes enlarge." The influential poet-novelist, Bayard Taylor (1825-1878), delivered a lecture on February 4, 1855, entitled "The Animal Man." There has been too much emphasis on spirit, he boldly asserted, and not enough on body. "In the name of physiology—what sort of a race shall spring from the loins of those tallow-faced, narrow-chested, knock-kneed, spindle-shanked simpering sons of rich fathers whom we see every day."[9] Our sorest need, as a people, he declared after a world tour, is recreation—relaxation from everlasting tension.

Many of those who should have known better, the upper classes, business men, and educated professional persons, were "continually bilious, dyspeptic, and altogether seedy."[10] The author of this statement, Charles Astor Bristed, in another book called *Five Years in an English University*, compared the spiritless academic life of American students with English school lads. "Constitutionals of eight miles in less than two hours" were everyday events. Rowing, cricket, foot-ball, riding, and all-day Sunday hikes marked young Englishmen.[11] The American *Country Gentleman*, in typical exaggeration found the English the most physically attractive people on earth. A June 8, 1854 column called American males "demi-dwarfs, and our females little more than house plants." Equally discouraging appraisals came from Edward Everett (1794-1865) who despaired of the American's habit of overwork. Sport and exercise, dual strengtheners of the mind and the body—that which brings "man into a generous and exhilerating communion with nature, are too little cultivated in town or country," he said.[12] In a similar vein, his nephew, Edward Everett Hale, delivered a public lecture on December 16, 1855, entitled, "Public Amusement for Poor and Rich." The errors of the Puritan theory must at last be laid to rest. In God's eye, the hours of rest are worth as much as the hours of labor. The education of the whole man—a kind of categorical imperative—was the message of the Boston Unitarian clergyman-author.

> We act . . . with a stupid inconsistency. I may dig in my garden, because there is a pretence of usefulness; . . . But if I spend a tenth part of the same time in playing ball, or in skating, or in rowing, my reputation, as a man of industry, and even of sense, under our artificial canons, would be gone.[13]

Almost with a sense of glee, foreign visitors Harriet Martineau, Charles Dickens, Fredrika Bremer, Sir Charles Lyell, and others commented on the poor health of Americans. Emerson and Thackeray, along with other well-informed Americans, mentioned the excess of physical fragility in too many countrymen. Discontent about poor health among city dwellers reached crusade proportions on the eve of the war. The two most prominent writers that served as a catalyst for such vexation were Dr. Oliver Wendell Holmes and Thomas Wentworth Higginson.

HOLMES AND HIGGINSON, EARLY APOSTLES OF PHYSICAL FITNESS

The pleasures and possibilities of systematic and deliberate play had slowly emerged during the first half of the nineteenth century. However, an alarming decline in the health of sedentary city residents resulted in cries not so much for fun and games but rather a national commitment for physical fitness. Oliver Wendell Holmes, Sr., M.D. (1809-1894) and Thomas Wentworth Higginson (1823-1911) took up the challenge as a part of their long, varied, and illustrious careers. Dr. Holmes once startled members of the Massachusetts Medical Society by pointing out that "if the whole materia medica, as now used, could be sunk to the bottom of the sea, it would be all the better for mankind,—and all the worse for the fishes." The lovable, yet acid-tongued Holmes described college students of his day as "soft-muscled, pasty-complexioned youth." The robust life of the English gentleman, Holmes noted was superior to "the vegetative life of the American." The famous "Autocrat of the Breakfast Table" was a puny but energetic athletic enthusiast who declared that any kind of sport "is better than this white-blooded degeneration to which we all tend." Holmes rowed on and walked along the Charles River in Boston; he lamented the physical imperfections of his own New England intellectuals.

I am satisfied that such a set of black-coated, stiff-jointed, soft-muscled, paste-complexioned youth as we can boast in our Atlantic cities never before sprang from loins of Anglo-Saxon lineage ... and as for any great athletic feat performed by a gentleman in these latitudes, society would drop a man who should run round the Common in five minutes.[14]

The brilliant Holmes—physician, writer, poet, iconoclast—admired the athlete while at the same time poked fun at outworn clerical traditions. If only the clergy might learn the art of self-defense, he said, better sermons and less church militants would result. Ill-nature and indigestion might very well disappear after "a bout with the gloves," observed Dr. Holmes. One day he almost entered the ring with the champion "Benicia Boy," but thought better of it. Holmes continued to support the delights of exercise and their applicability to all levels of fitness. "You can row easily and gently all day," he reminded readers, or "you can row yourself blind and black in the face in ten minutes, just as you like." The poet in Holmes described the intoxicating delight, the rare joy of rowing on some sweet June morning, "when the river and bay are smooth as a sheet of beryl-green silk, and I run along ripping it up with my knife-edged shell of a boat, ..."[15] Holmes' totally disarming literary style, so lacking in sermonizing and so pointed to public issues, must have influenced many.

One of the most arresting series of writings on the subject of health, fitness, and sport came from the pen of Thomas Wentworth Higginson. Like Holmes, Higginson's ancestors were descendants of the earliest Massachusetts Puritans. The brilliant scholar, Higginson, physically vigorous and deeply introspective, graduated from the Harvard Divinity School in 1847, and launched a controversial career in which antislavery, temperance, women's suffrage, and other social reform, became an absolute passion for the youthful preacher. A strong admirer of Emerson and Thoreau, Higginson began a series of articles urging Americans to rediscover the joys of rugged, outdoor recreation. Higginson's fame as a professional writer began impressively with the fifth issue of the new *Atlantic Monthly*. The startling success of the periodical was due to the distinguished circle of contributors, including Emerson, Thoreau, Hawthorne, Whittier, Holmes, Longfellow, Mrs. Stowe, and Higginson. His first *Atlantic* essay appeared in March, 1858. It was called "Saints, and Their Bodies," and proposed the simple theme that physical and spiritual health were related. America's vigor and growth during the period were tempered by Higginson's observation that individual and national success are contingent on physical health, and, unfortunately, Americans were rapidly losing this priceless heritage. Higginson's pen

Oliver Wendell Holmes was wise not to fight "Benicia Boy" Heenan (left) who fought to a draw with British champ, Tom Sayers, in 1860.

also contributed a panegyric on "Physical Courage," a "Letter to a Dyspeptic," "The Murder of the Innocents," "Barbarism and Civilization," and on the eve of the Civil War, a contribution titled simply, "Gymnastics." Presenting a fresh and surprisingly modern view of an aspect of psychosomatic medicine, Higginson urged his readers to dwell on the fun and relaxation intrinsic in such an experience. "If it does you good, you will enjoy it; and if you enjoy it, it will do you good." He suggested that "not one-tenth part of the requisite amount has yet been said of athletic exercises as a prescription for this community."[16]

Higginson's crusade against America's physical decline, plus the outcry of other significant writers, was beginning to have an effect. Higginson's small gems on the subject of sport did not go unnoticed. He practiced his preachings and loved pedestrian diversions and long sessions of rowing and sailing. This uncommon American was the embodiment of the Greek athletic ideal with a modern flavor of transcendentalism and puritanism added. Higginson loved walking, swimming, boating, skating, riding, and fishing. "Outdoor life," says one of his biographers, "was no less important to him than the world of books and music." Thomas Wentworth Higginson was a pioneering physical culturist. In many ways his life was the embodiment of the classic scholar-athlete. He should be remembered not only for his vast literary accomplishments but also as a man who made significant contributions to America's sports scene and the new physical education.[17]

SPORTING RAMIFICATIONS OF THE THIRD GREAT AWAKENING

The idea that every activity had to be utilitarian persisted through the nineteenth century. In the midst of an American religious revival from 1857 to 1859, the concept of recreation and leisure was both deplored and defended by traditional and liberal clergymen. The first and second great religious revivals had, to a great degree, helped Americans free themselves from a preoccupation with sin, to make this world for the converted, no longer a vale of tears—to transcend gloom, to look for and work toward the Kingdom of Heaven on Earth. The third "Great Awakening" of 1857 called attention to the growing secularization of the Sabbath, the "bottomless materialism and worldliness" through which American pilgrims must pass, and the alarming deterioration of spiritual and physical health. The national disorientation on the eve of the Civil War prompted clergymen to call for either a revival of Puritan disciplines or a sidling in the direction of liberality and imaginative use of leisure time. The year 1851 saw the formation of the American Young Men's Christian

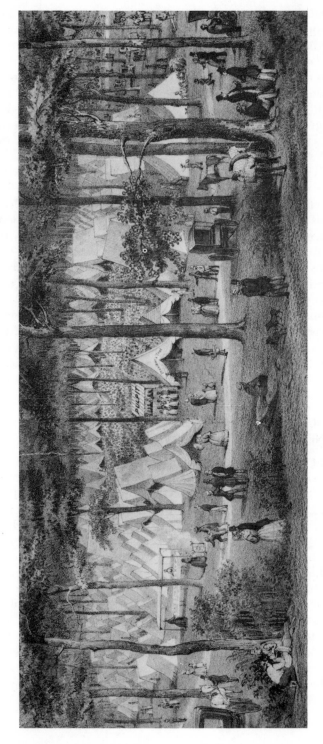

Camp meetings were part of the Third Awakening, which sanctioned re-creation but not amusements. (Courtesy of Library of Congress.)

Association—one of the first evidences of the social gospel and its commitment for wholesome urban amusements. Several years earlier, Frederic W. Sawyer's *A Plea for Amusements* called for a national mandate for "the lighter graces and pleasures of life." The staid Congregationalist *New Englander and Yale Review* printed a fifteen-page attack on Sawyer's use of the terms "amusements" and "recreation" as synonymous. The singular end of recreation, it stated, was the restoration of body and spirit in order to more effectively fulfill life's work. Amusements, on the other hand, have but selfish gratification and pleasure as primitive goals.[18] Man's chief end must be to glorify God. Small diversions had to find a place between Sunday worship and devotion to business through the long work week. In the same vein, the prominent Congregationalist preacher, Henry Ward Beecher, in his *Seven Lectures to Young Men*, stressed moral and ethical conduct rather than vain public amusements. "Is it safe," he said, "to accustom yourself to such tremendous excitement as that of [horse] racing?" His emphasis on ethical behavior rather than spiritual dedication contributed to the secularization of American Protestantism without losing the puritanical attitude toward amusements.

The years before the Civil War were especially disruptive. Leading journals despaired of what seemed innumerable signs of America's disintegration, politically, morally, and physically. *Democratic Review, Knickerbocker, Ladies' Repository, Harper's Monthly, Atlantic Monthly,* and the *North American Review* all talked about the nation's venerable foes—mammon, passion, corruption, physical weakness, and ill health. One of the most remarkable attacks on these foes (and others) appeared in a thirty-seven page tirade called "Young America; Its Health and Social Life," and was published in *The Presbyterian Quarterly Review* of March, 1856. The Reverend Sydney Smith was obsessed with the idea that many of mankind's mental and moral derangements were caused by poor health—the results of a lack of exercise and recreation. His quote from a contemporary *New York Times* article that "the Anglo-American nation of the United States is in danger of becoming physically contemptible" prompted a review of our Puritan heritage—of retaining its great qualities and revising its views of fun and games. We must exercise for health, he said, but beyond that "the duty of exercise is to be laid aside, and some pleasurable motive is to excite . . . it." Puritan and Christian virtues were consistently defended by Reverend Smith, as long as the Church made provision for recreation, game playing, and the "spirit" of healthful exercises. He frequently implored pagan historians to aid his cause.

Where are our Olympic games? And where is our substitute for them? Exercise, in the American mind, seems to be connected with vice, and only allowable when business or labor, to make money, requires it. It is a Herculean task to get a little exercise, and public sentiment puts down every thing like the amusements that lead to it. It is perilous to a respectable man to hunt, shoot, fish, or drive handsome horses. Cricket-Clubs and boat-clubs are discouraged by a dead weight of public opinion, and keeping a boat or yacht is considered a doubtful propriety. Skating and swimming for men are more and more discouraged, and even boys playing in the streets are watched with a jealous eye.[19]

Like most zealots, Reverend Smith exaggerated. Too many from the ranks of the clergy, the medical profession, and the literati had called for a more expansive view of leisure and recreational practices. The rise of sport had, in actuality, already begun. But for the trauma of the Civil War and its lingering after effects, these new attitudes might have manifested themselves far more dramatically and sooner. The decade of the 1850s was one in which thoughtful men and women looked carefully at their country. The fair-minded ones saw a nation unique and bursting with greatness. Yet profound shortcomings were evident everywhere. Just one of them was an increasing clamor for diversionary recreational activities in order to somehow balance the frenetic tempo of a people hurling themselves into a near fatal struggle.

PRELUDE TO THE RISE OF ORGANIZED SPORT

Down to the eve of the fall of Fort Sumter, Americans of the Middle Period enjoyed a sense of economic security rarely duplicated in modern history. On a hygienic and political basis, however, the years just before the Civil War were disruptive and filled with what Professor Roy Franklin Nichols called "the stress of hyperemotionalism." Explosive forces were at work, in part generated by the nation's phenomenal growth process. Between 1800 and 1860, the rural population of this country quadrupled, but the number of townspeople increased twenty-four times. The burgeoning cities had absolutely no organized provision for recreational practices among the masses. Untidy professional sports entertainment did exist, and drew impressive crowds, while the still sleeping giant of college athletics and physical education was, with several exceptions, informal, spontaneous play, rather than consciously organized programs. But the air fairly crackled with suggestions for vigorous sporting exercise, concern for physical health, and proposals for the reduction of mental and emotional tensions. The recurring appeals of educators, physicians, health advocates, journalists, sport enthusiasts, and certain theologians during the antebellum years brought into clearer focus the conception of mind-body relationship. Increasingly "Americans were aierted to the threat against their physical and mental powers that came with the confinements of the home and school and the more sedentary habits of the city."[20] The fruition of some of these ideas took place a generation later during the apex of the century's technological revolution. A society wedded to increasing mechanization needed sport and leisure opportunities. Provocatively, Betts also pointed out that "sport in the nineteenth-century America was as much a product of industrialization as it was an antidote to it."[21]

Most Americans of the Middle Period were conditioned to think in terms of change and to fix their minds upon the future. They saw civilization on the march. Personal and community ills demanded change and received attention. The rising interest in sport and physical culture during the 1850s took place in response to this national psychology. A growing fertile economic and social climate at mid-century merged with the decline of rigid Calvinism and the appearance of a more secular society. Massive sporting and recreational diversions seemed imminent. Thoughtful pioneers of the period, enamored of physical vigor, thought it as much a man's duty to take proper care of his body as it was to cultivate his reason. The student editor of the April, 1858 *Harvard Magazine* challenged his classmates with the question, "Will a kind fortune ever bring the day when the first scholar of his class can also claim the high honor of being the stoutest oarsman of the College?" *Harper's Weekly*, on August 1, 1857, pointed out that college life in New England needed far greater doses of physical training. "That game of football, which we are happy to say is not yet extinct, ought to be a matter of as much concern as the Greek or mathematical prize." Boat races and cricket matches, concluded the editorial, deserve at least as much attention as "all the prize poems or the orations on Lafayette that are produced in half a century." The push was on. Of course, for a long time to come, most would indulge in sporting pastimes while looking over their shoulder. Conventional morality was to influence the direction of mass leisure for decades. Fundamentalist attitudes, it has been noted:

> served to hold in check the growth of obscene and degrading pleasures, and it also dictated that time spent in the pursuit of fun should be confined to things that were constructive . . . involvement in sport was viewed as productive, in that participation resulted in improvement in physical and moral well-being. . . . Another stimulus resulted from the emergence of a concept of sport that provided it with inherent goodness. Once acquired, sport had the capacity to thrive in almost any environment.[22]

In the 1850s, the ideal of purposeful work was strong and would remain an American central theme for another hundred years when, ironically, it was joined by a national compulsion to have fun. For most antebellum Americans with a Puritan tradition, sport and fun activities were explained, in part, as a necessary prelude to more vigorous work. And they may not have been far wrong. The untrammeled surge of sport in the United States was slow in coming but when it did, as happens so often, it asked no quarter and became one of the nation's dominent social institutions. Joseph Strutt and Foster Rhea Dulles, both writers of sport history, have pointed out that what a nation does with its leisure is often times just as significant as how it either maintains itself economically or governs itself. The great difficulty comes in knowing the mind of man, for history is more than an organized chronicle of events. The concept of sport and leisure has changed because of what has occurred in the minds of men. Sport and recreation exist in their peculiar form today because of the mind of modern man. The historian, then, "is concerned with thoughts alone; with their outward expression in events he is concerned only by the way, in so far as these reveal to him the thoughts of which he is in search." The sporting history of America from 1607 to the Civil War, thus, is an attempt to understand what mind has done in the past. It is a near impossible task and thus a most challenging game and contest.

REFERENCES

1. Charles Francis Adams, Jr., *An Autobiography* (Boston: Houghton Mifflin Co., 1916), p. 18.

2. Arthur C. Cole, Our Sporting Grandfathers—The Cult of Athletics at Its Source, *Atlantic Monthly*, CL (July, 1932), p. 88.

3. William Rotch Wister, *Some Reminiscences of Cricket in Philadelphia before 1861* (Philadelphia: Allen, Lane & Scott, 1904).

4. Guy M. Lewis, America's First Intercollegiate Sport: The Regattas from 1852 to 1875, *Research Quarterly*, XXXVIII (December, 1967), pp. 637-647.

5. Charles Kingsley, *Alton Locke*, I (New York: J. F. Taylor and Co., 1899), pp. 311-312.

6. William Blaikie, American Bodies, *Harper's Weekly*, XXVII (December, 1883), p. 770.

7. Arthur Charles Cole, *The Irrepressible Conflict 1850-1865*, Vol. VII of *A History of American Life*, ed. Arthur M. Schlesinger and Dixon Ryan Fox (12 vols.; New York: Macmillan Co., 1934), p. 187.

8. How to Be Healthy, *American Agriculturalist*, XII (July 12, 1854), pp. 283-284.

9. Bayard Taylor in R. C. Beatty, *Bayard Taylor—Laureate of the Gilded Age* (Norman, Oklahoma: University of Oklahoma Press, 1936), p. 152.

10. Charles Astor Bristed, *The Upper Ten Thousand* (New York: Stringer and Townsend; 1853), pp. 19-20.

11. Charles Astor Bristed, *Five Years in an English University*. Vol. II (New York: G. P. Putnam, 1852), pp. 22-23.

12. Edward Everett, *Orations and Speeches on Various Occasions*, Vol. III (Boston: Little, Brown & Co., 1859), p. 407.

13. Edward Everett Hale, *Public Amusements for Poor and Rich* (Boston: Phillips, Sampson and Co., 1857), p. 21.

14. Oliver Wendell Holmes, Sr., The Autocrat of the Breakfast-Table, *Atlantic Monthly*, I (May, 1858), p. 881.

15. Holmes, *The Autocrat of the Breakfast-Table* (New York: Heritage Press, 1955), p. 151.

16. Thomas Wentworth Higginson, Gymnastics, *Atlantic Monthly*, VII (March, 1861), pp. 283-302.

17. John A. Lucas, Thomas Wentworth Higginson—Early Apostle of Health and Fitness, *Journal of Health, Physical Education and Recreation*, 42 (February, 1971), pp. 30-33.

18. Amusements, review of *A Plea for Amusements* by Frederic W. Sawyer in the *New Englander and Yale Review*, IX (August, 1851), pp. 345-359.

19. Young America; Its Health and Social Life, review of *A Memoir of the Reverend Sydney Smith*, by his daughter, Lady Holland, in *The Presbyterian Quarterly Review*, IV (March, 1856), p. 668.

20. John R. Betts, Mind and Body in American Thought, *Journal of American History*, LIV (March, 1968), p. 805.

21. John R. Betts, The Technological Revolution and the Rise of Sport, 1850-1900, *Mississippi Valley Historical Review*, 40 (September, 1953), p. 255.

22. Guy Lewis, Sport, Youth Culture, and Conventional Morality (paper presented at the American Historical Association, New York City, December, 1971), p. 18.

23. R. G. Collingwood, Human Nature and Human History, *Proceedings* of the British Academy, 1936, p. 111.

Part II.

American Sport in Transition

CHAPTER 9
Organized Sport in an Urban America

As the decade of the 1850s closed, it saw the birth of Theodore Roosevelt, probably the greatest sports-loving president in American history. Baseball was for the first time called the "Great American Game." Some of the nation's outstanding literary men at mid-century called for a transformation in sporting habits—a cry for healthful physical activity. At the same time a popular journal summoned colleges to make football as great a concern as Greek or mathematics, and the Harvard College newspaper editor encouraged the brightest scholars to take up the oar and physically stroke for the Harvard crew. The concluding years of the 1850s were all that and more, for the 1850s might be said to be the watershed between the unorganized sport of the colonial and early national period and the rise of organized sport which has dominated since. In the period from the mid-nineteenth century to the early years of the twentieth century rural pastimes gave way to business oriented, urban sport. This was the period of transition in American sport—an era concluded by the strenuous sporting era of the early 1900s made popular by President Theodore Roosevelt.

The process of transforming sport in America was a gradual one, for the forces of urbanization and industrialization, which were most responsible for the changes, were themselves evolving in the nineteenth century. Change is what most historians are concerned with; thus while many of the spontaneous sporting activities of another era continued to be popular with masses of people, the trend was moving toward commercial sports which would appeal to the various classes of urban dwellers. Americans from colonial times had been self-sufficient in many ways. They had, to a great extent, grown their own food, made their own clothing, built their own homes, and provided their own sporting activities. With the rise of industrialization and urbanization in the nineteenth century, people became interdependent in most aspects of life including their leisure pursuits. That is, when Americans began to crowd into cities the sports in which they participated actively or vicariously changed from activities of their own making, like sporadic barn raisings, wrestling matches, or cockfights, to organized spectacles like professional baseball games, bicycle and auto races, or college athletic contests.

The difference between traditional rural pastimes and the new order of organized sport was often more a change in intensity than a difference in the kind of sports in which Americans participated. Large superstructures developed with the proliferation of sporting activities in an attempt to better serve those who had an interest; spectators and participants as well as sport organizers and businessmen. With a general rise in sporting interest came the desire to compete and determine who or what team was best. Standard rules were needed as competition and rivalries increased. Thus local, regional, and national associations were constructed to legislate and enforce the rules and administer the various sports. In organized sport the participants often became secondary considerations when making rules and schedules, administering programs, or luring the spectators to the contests. The natural tendencies to set up power structures and to rule over the sporting structures and the commercial drive for increased wealth often took precedence. This can be seen in activities which will be discussed later such as the development of college sports from student-run activities to college controlled commercial enterprises; baseball owners taking control of professional baseball teams from players who had ruled the first league; amateur organizations, like the Amateur Athletic Union, fighting for control of the athletic lives of amateur sportsmen; and shrewd businessmen using such activities as six-day running or cycling contests to satiate the public's interest in sport and profit from the commercial enterprises.

Most of the sports which were organized in the nineteenth century—by drawing up standardized rules, forming national associations, creating competitive units, and drawing large numbers of participants and spectators—were popular sports a century later. A list of sports which were effectively organized in the 1800s shows the variety that were developed in the age of sport in transition: archery, baseball, basketball, bicycling, billiards, bowling, boxing, canoeing, coaching (horse drawn), cricket, croquet, cross country running, curling, fencing, football, golf, gymnastics, handball, harness and horseracing, ice hockey, ice skating, lacrosse, polo, pedestrianism (long distance running), roller skating, rowing, rugby, sailing, shooting, skiing, soccer, squash, steeplechasing, swimming, tennis, track and field, trap shooting, volleyball, water polo, wrestling, and yachting.[1]

INDUSTRIALIZATION, URBANIZATION, AND THE TECHNOLOGICAL IMPACT ON SPORT

A rising industrial America which was fast creating an urban dominated society brought about the pressure for organized sport. Cities from the time of ancient Athens, Alexandria, and Rome to the time of London, Paris, and New York have been the centers of change. The change was no less true regarding sport than that of fashion, art, or commerce. Urban America in the latter half of the nineteenth century means essentially the North Atlantic and North Central States area. In 1890, for instance, over 80 percent of all city dwellers in America were found in these two areas; two of every three New Yorkers and four of every five in Massachusetts were city folk.[2] We can conclude that organized sport was a phenomena dominated by the urban areas east of the Mississippi and north of the Ohio Rivers.

Limiting as well as liberating aspects of city life helped determine the nature of sport found there. It has been said that in cities wealth accumulates and men decay. That may not be axiomatic, but it is true that the greater wealth was often made and the quality of life showed a greater disparity in the city than in the country. The unquestioned increase in wealth resulting from industrial production contributed to organized sport through the sponsorship of teams and leagues and for the increased means by which more people could buy their entertainment. Sport became more commercial and spectator oriented. With increased wealth in cities came an increase in leisure time to enjoy it. Wealth and leisure time were liberating forces on urban sport development. The amount of space in a city, however, was a limiting factor. Because of the lack of open space, the city lent itself to spectator oriented sport where people would often purchase their sporting entertainment rather than participate actively in it. This, during the nineteenth century, limited organized sport to the upper and middle classes to a great extent, for the lower economic classes could not afford the commercialized sports, though the traditional interest in sport may have existed within the masses.

In the cities, then, where various sports like horse racing, professional running and bicycle racing, baseball, boxing, and football became popular, one could not have expected the average laborer to have strongly supported the growth of organized sport. An unskilled laborer living in America between the Civil War and 1900 earned between $1.00 and $2.00 per day.[3] The chance of masses of laborers paying 50¢ to see a major league baseball game or a dollar admittance fee to attend a professional running contest is rather remote. Furthermore most organized sports were held on weekdays and Saturdays. Laborers working ten to twelve hours per day, including all day Saturday, precluded mass attendance at spectator events. Sunday, a day when workers might have attended sport events if money were available, was generally restricted by the many state blue laws which forbade most commercial entertainments. Activities on Sundays were so restricted that in Pennsylvania the Philadelphia Centennial Exposition of 1876 was closed on the Sabbath.[4] For the urban poor, recreational pursuits were more often found in saloons than in organized sport.[5]

The middle and upper classes were far more prone to support and finance organized sport than were the lower classes. Businessmen and professionals could better afford the cost of a seat at a college football game or the membership fee of an athletic club. A shop owner or a real estate broker was more likely to have time available to spend an afternoon at the race track or baseball game than was a factory worker. In addition it was necessary for the growth of organized sport that the rising middle and upper classes provide capital for the support of teams, facilities, and an organizational structure. There were businessmen who contributed to this aspect of sport for the prestige that it gained them; others for the profit that it produced. Some did so for the love of sport. There were individual politicians who promoted sport for the political influence that was generated.[6] It should be noted that it was private individuals, not urban governments, who built the base for organized sport.

City governments generally neglected provisions for the amusement and leisure time pursuits of their constituents. This was natural because of the individualistic tradition in America and the pervasive nineteenth century belief in a laissez faire, or no government control, policy. Most organized sports were developed by those who had the money, for they had the means to support them. If there is a twentieth century belief held by some that sport is used as an opiate of the masses, it is a twentieth century (or ancient Roman) concept, not one of the nineteenth century. There is little evidence that private individuals or government officials provided recreation or sport for the masses to hold them in check. There is little record of companies organizing company recreation programs or sport teams in the 1800s, though it is true that George Pullman, the railroad magnate, may have had this in mind when he built a company town in the 1880s.

George Pullman began construction of a 4,000 acre company town in 1880 on the southern outskirts of Chicago. The $8 million town of Pullman provided playgrounds and athletic facilities for the contentment of the laborers housed there. The Pullman Athletic Association, controlled primarily by Pullman officials, organized the town's sports such as boating regattas and ice skating on Lake Calumet, track and field events, cricket and baseball games, and a bicycle race spectacle from Chicago, finishing at Pullman 16 miles away. This annual event drew as many as 15,000 spectators.[7] Yet, the use of sport by city officials or businessmen to satisfy or tranquilize workers was a rarity until the twentieth century. It was unusual to find even a city willing to build a public playground, while few wealthy businessmen could see the advantage of a benevolent attitude toward recreational pursuits. The quality of life for American workers was not the concern of most of the new business elite. The attitude of one New York employer was probably more common. He wrote that he had only one rule for his laboring force: "If a workman sticks up his head, hit it."[8] Production, not concern for the quality of life, was the key to nineteenth century growth in America, and that same concern was a key to the growth of organized sport.

America became the world's leading industrial producer by the 1880s from a position as seventh industrial nation a little over a generation before. This industrial growth, often at the expense of the laboring class, was nevertheless a major force in the development of organized sport. Through industrialization, urban people received much of their wealth and leisure time, and because of industrialization new technology was developed—all of which contributed to organized sport.[9]

Developments in technology in the fields of communications and transportation were probably the most significant to the development of structured sport for it was instant communications and rapid transportation which allowed those who were interested to learn about sporting competition results or to journey to the site of the events.

The railroad was of prime importance. By 1850, the railroad was fast becoming the major means of transportation in the United States when twenty years before there had been only 23 miles of rails in the entire nation. By 1880, over 90,000 miles of railroads covered the nation, and when America entered World War I, it had a maximum rail mileage of a quarter million miles.[10] Despite the fact that the Civil War was a great catalyst to industrialization and railroad building, by 1860 the northern industrial area of America was tied together by rail from Boston, New York, and Philadelphia to Chicago, Detroit, and St. Louis. Chicago was only a two day ride from New York. The rapid means of transportation meant much to such activities as horse racing, professional baseball, college sports, or to any team desiring intercity competition. Prior to railroads only steamboats or horse power could transport participants or masses of spectators to sporting events. With the rail it became more convenient to go on barnstorming tours with thoroughbred horses or harness racers. The rail was the stimulus to the first intercollegiate contest in America, a crew meet between Harvard and Yale in 1852 on Lake Winnipesaukee, New Hampshire, made possible by a rail line desiring to attract vacationers to the northeast vacationlands.[11] The first all-professional baseball team, the Cincinnati Red Stockings, toured from Maine to California in 1869, a trip made practicable by rail transportation and the opening of the first transcontinental railroad in that year. Only through the network of rail lines was it possible for the National League to organize in 1876 and play baseball games between such distant teams as the Boston Red Stockings and the Forest Citys of Rockford, Illinois.

There was often a close relationship between railroad entrepreneurs and organizers of sports, and it was only natural. Businessmen of both groups could see that each benefited the other. Railroad owners knew that if their lines went to the site of a spectator sport or amusement area the increased travel would mean increased profits. Sport promoters courted the favor of railroadmen and street car owners to service their facilities. For example, when the Athletic Association of Tulane University built a football field along the famous St. Charles Avenue in 1895, a railroad company financed a 2,000 seat grandstand with the thought that it would increase the number of passengers on its line.[12] When streetcars became popular after 1870, first as horse drawn and electric after about 1890, there were often complex political and economic battles to control the lines, and it was common for organized sport to become intricately involved.[13]

Sport was both a beneficiary of, as well as a stimulant to, the improved communications technology of the industrial revolution. Instantaneous news became possible after the invention of the telegraph in the 1840s. Only a half decade later the results of the Tom Hyer-Yankee Sullivan 1849 boxing championship were wired to New York from the site in Maryland. Later the telegraph sent long reports across the nation about horse races, yachting events, baseball games, prize fights, and other sporting contests including the celebrated steam boat race between the "Natchez" and the "Robert E. Lee" in 1870.[14] Only the year before, the Atlantic Cable carried the results of the first international crew meet between Harvard and Oxford University crews following their race on the Thames River in London which ended in the British upholding the "supremacy of the seas."[15]

Technological advances in telegraphy combined with new methods of printing stimulated interest in sport. Cheaper printing processes and the increased literacy which resulted from free public education, contributed to the publication of newspapers with sensational news

Athletic facilities were often serviced by the railroads. (Courtesy of Library of Congress.)

which often catered to the whims of sport interests of the masses. Though the separate sport page did not come into existence until the 1880s and 1890s, there were regular, lengthy accounts of sporting events from before mid-century as evidenced by James Gordon Bennett's New York *Herald* founded in the 1840s and others which followed.[16] By the turn of the century a British observer and member of the British Parliament, James Bryce, wrote that in America there was a "passion for looking on at and reading about athletic sports. . . . It occupies the minds of not only the youth at universities, but also of their parents and of the general public," pervading nearly all classes.[17] That this passion for sport had spread to the masses was noteworthy to an upperclass individual like Bryce, who indicated that in the greatest of all sporting nations, England, large scale interest in sport was limited to the upper classes only. A less stratified class structure was evidenced in America by its newspapers which had played a role in the spreading sport interest to the masses.

Technology influenced sport in ways other than communications and transportation. The development of mass production of a plethora of sporting equipment, the invention of the pneumatic tire, the still camera and motion picture, and the incandescent light bulb all aided sporting interests. The invention of the bicycle and later the automobile added another dimension of speed and excitement to the American sporting impulse by the end of the nineteenth century. Improvements in such items as the stop watch, ball bearings and shock absorbers, the rubber bound golf ball, and artificial ice gave evidence that industrial technology added to the growing gospel of organized sport in America.[18]

THE CIVIL WAR AND ORGANIZED SPORT

The great catalyst for industrialization and thus urbanization was the Civil War. America in 1860 was to a great extent an undeveloped country. The war created a strong domestic market for goods and greatly increased industrial output. The factory system reigned supreme by the time of Appomatox, and the national government favored the industrial system over agrarian interests, especially those of the old planter south.[19] Out of the industrial and urban north came the push for organized sport.

The Civil War contributed directly or indirectly to sport in several important ways. First, the exigencies of the war created a need for trained military officers. This pressured the federal government to provide for the support of colleges in the states to train military personnel. The Morrill Act of 1862 created land grant colleges which were to be supported by the sale of large land grants given to the states from the public domain. Each land grant college had a military officer program. That in itself was not a prime factor in the growth of sport in colleges. What was significant was that the war prodded the federal government into promoting educational institutions which were designed to serve middle America by offering a liberal and practical education for an enlarged number of citizens.[20] The idea of government sponsored higher education for the masses eventually brought vast numbers of young men (and later women) to colleges. The same land grant colleges, with strong state interests, expanded rapidly and became the leaders of big-time college athletics by the twentieth century. Land grant colleges such as Ohio State, Louisiana State, Penn State, California, Maryland, Massachusetts, and Wisconsin were important in promoting and stimulating organized sport.

The Civil War also created another piece of legislation which furthered the nationalization of sport. In 1864, with the South still at war and unable to oppose federal legislation designed to further northern industrial interests, the federal government passed a bill to build the first transcontinental railroad linking the east with the west. By 1869 the golden spike had been driven connecting the two ends of the railway. Within four months the first all-professional baseball team, the Cincinnati Red Stockings, traveled the length of it to play a series of games in California. Future land grants in the 1870s and 1880s to other private rail companies did much to tie together the various sections of the country and to provide the vehicle for the promotion of organized sport whether it be baseball, boxing, or horse racing.

The Civil War promoted a desire for organized sport, although when the war began the effect upon the growth of sport was negative. While the war raged, newly organized baseball teams disbanded, yacht clubs ceased racing, horse racing was greatly reduced, the German-American gymnastic organizations (Turnvereins) collapsed as their members joined the war effort, and the few eastern colleges which had intercollegiate athletics reduced their scheduling of baseball and rowing events. That, however, was short lived and minimal in its long term effect. The war, more importantly, brought together millions of young men, north and south alike, many of whom had not previously been involved playing on organized teams or observing them. The outstanding example of the war's effect upon a sport was that of baseball. Prior to the war baseball had been played by the youth of America, north and to some extent south, but the impact of its being played and watched by thousands of troops, like the 40,000 who watched a New York regiment play on Christmas Day, 1862, influenced others to take up the game. New York soldiers may have been more influential than most, for the game and rules were best established in New York. Soldiers returning home on leave or

Soldiers boxed as one of the many diversions of the Civil War. (Courtesy of Library of Congress.)

after discharge spread the game across the nation, often introducing the standardized rules of the New York game. One young man so influenced was Albert Spalding, a youth of thirteen years of age when he was introduced to baseball by a war veteran in his home town of Rockford, Illinois.[21] Spalding eventually became a premier pitcher, later owner of the Chicago White Stockings, and business baron in athletic equipment. There were numerous other examples. In the two years following the Civil War it was rare to find a town of any size without an organized team seeking competition with other towns.

What was true of baseball was to a lesser extent true with other sports. Young men were exposed to a variety of athletic activities in search of exciting diversions while in encampment. Boxing and wrestling, fencing and hunting, swimming and fishing, and soccer-football and horse racing were among the sporting activities which found adherents during the many lulls in action.[22] With the end of the war a sporting mania surged through the nation. Amateur baseball began nearly everywhere with professional baseball ready to tap the general spectator interest. Athletic clubs were formed in major cities which could support them. Boating and yachting clubs began to serve the wealthy. Horse racing was revived. Harness racing at agricultural fairs took on new significance. The rapid rise of intercollegiate sport introduced a new type of social life to college students throughout America. Even some religious organizations broke with tradition when they introduced physical activities in their programs as did the Young Men's Christian Association when it built a gymnasium in New York City in 1869.[23]

The Civil War was not the sole cause for the push toward organized sport, but it was an important catalytic agent. A generation after the war, historian Albert B. Hart believed that "the Civil War gave a singular impetus to field sports of all kinds."[24] The war had stimulated the national economy and was a principal force in the move toward industrialization. The secession of the south had allowed forces favorable to industrialization to push through federal legislation giving it added impetus. In addition the war had placed an emphasis upon physical strength as well as bringing together men with the opportunity to organize many sporting activities. It was not unexpected that veterans returning home would desire a peace time outlet for some of the excitement they had found in war. Wars have another stimulating effect upon sport in general, and the Civil War was no exception. As wars have the tendency to break down moral codes, in the case of the Civil War it helped to put a crack in the long standing, church founded, opposition to organized sporting activities and recreational pursuits including the traditional strong opposition to Sunday sports.

THE DECLINE OF RELIGIOUS OPPOSITION TO SPORT

The opposition to Sabbath sports and to religious disapproval of many sports in America could, of course, be traced to Puritan New Englanders. Their belief in keeping Sunday holy and conviction that immoderate sporting activities any other time were at least perilous to the soul if not actually a sin, became part of the American ethos.

Fishing was a Civil War recreation of many soldiers. (Courtesy of Library of Congress.)

There was a time in the latter 1700s, around the time of the American Revolution and the European deistic enlightenment, when some of the old traditions seemed in jeopardy. The religious Second Awakening, however, kindled the moralistic fire which again questioned the place of physical activity and sport. It was not until the second half of the nineteenth century that a liberalizing of religious views regarding sport made much headway. Even then it was a slow process.

Religious leaders of most faiths discussed the nature of sports and amusements from mid-century until the 1900s, generally with strong reservations regarding their worth. An insightful writer commenting in *The Christian Examiner* in 1830, noted the influence of colonial Puritanism when he stated that society "is much more strict with regard to the sins of amusements, than with regard to the sins of business."[25] Religious authorities often tried to differentiate between those who pursued sporting amusements for pleasure and those who sought a restoration or re-creation of the body to further the work of the world. The latter amusements were sanctioned while the pursuit of pleasure was questioned. "Amusement is not legitimate," a writer commented in an 1870 Congregational magazine, "unless sooner or later [it is] subservient to labor."[26] Washington Gladden, a leading clergyman and social reformer of the late nineteenth century, told how he questioned his own conversion as a twelve year old because he believed it involved giving up baseball.[27] Eleanor Roosevelt, as a youngster in New York in the 1890s, was discouraged from participating in sports, especially on Sunday when no games were allowed, not even croquet, a policy set by her strict grandfather.[28]

Religious opposition to recreation and sport, though, was softening. Henry Ward Beecher, minister and son of the Puritan-like Lyman Beecher, believed that even ministers should exercise freely. He stated that the sport despicable to most clergymen, billiards, was a good amusement.[29] Beecher would have been impressed by one of the characters depicted by Moses Coit Tyler in his delightful, 1869 novel, *The Brawnville Papers*. Reverend Bland was a true "Muscular Christian" who could "out-walk, out-run, out-jump, out-skate, out-swim, out-fish, out-hunt, and out-preach any other man for twenty miles around." In contrast Tyler's Deacon Snipp believed that nothing could be more scandalous than for a "minister of the meek and lowly Jesus to be noted for being the best ball player in the county."[30] By the 1890s a publication of the Methodist Episcopal Church asserted that if amusing young people would aid in saving them then it was worthy work of the church.[31] This was a far different attitude than that of a Methodist Church school which in 1872 stated that its students would indulge in nothing which the world called play.[32]

Churches and other religious organizations began to see the value of using sport to further their goals. Y.M.C.A.'s were some of the first to do this shortly after mid-century, believing that it was better to have young men participating in sporting activities under Christian auspices than to have them wander away and "drink of stolen and forbidden waters to the peril of their souls."[33] Building gymnasia, sponsoring athletic activities, and training leaders for this work were all accomplished before the century ended. Much of the impetus for this work could be traced to the British who were not only the greatest sporting people of the nineteenth century but who were the first modern people to consciously use sport for religious and moral goals.

THE PERVASIVE ENGLISH INFLUENCE

The English were a pervasive influence in the change of American attitudes toward sport, and they did much to stimulate organized sport in America in the latter half of the nineteenth century. As organized sport has been closely associated with the industrial revolution it is no surprise that England was the premier sporting nation. England was the first industrial nation in the world, preceding the United States by more than a generation. The English led the Americans in organized sport in a similar way. Nearly every sport in which Americans participated was first popularized in the British Isles; from baseball to billiards, football to field hockey, and tennis to track and field. England in the 1700s had rather well organized horse racing and had introduced the modern world to a set of rules for prize fighting. The English had boating clubs and cricket teams by the early 1800s, and its schools had developed written rules for both soccer and rugby by the 1840s. By mid-century the English private schools had accepted the belief that athletics were a positive force in educating youth while English publications had captured the American sporting reader's attention.

Writing in 1859, the editors of the New York based *Harper's Weekly* predicted that in another twenty years, "no doubt our people will be as devoted to athletic exercises as the English."[34] A year later another American looked longingly toward the British after reading a novel by Thomas Hughes about life at the English Public School at Rugby. "It makes one's nerves tingle," he wrote, "to read in 'Tom Brown's School-days' of the great game of Rugby."[35] The popularity of the book and the theme of "Muscular Christianity" arose out of the British Public Schools, privately run institutions of the British upper classes. The Rugby School, under headmaster Thomas Arnold from 1828-1842, is credited with fostering the belief that vigorous physical sports under proper leadership develop strong Christian character in youth, and leaders in adult life. To many Americans, who had for generations questioned in a religious vein the place of sport in education or even in a leisure setting, this English belief gave some justification for accepting the natural tendencies of youth to organize

The English influence was clear in cricket and most other American sports.

its sporting activities. An Englishman writing in the late 1860s felt that as a result of the "Muscular Christianity" movement, English youth had modeled a new religion which "enjoins its disciples above all things to fear God, and run a mile in four minutes and a half."[36] This pervasive athleticism which developed in England must surely have influenced the building of gymnasia in Y.M.C.A.'s and later in churches, stimulated the acceptance of athletics in American schools and colleges, and led to the concept still enunciated by many that athletics build character.

Americans did not solely borrow from the English, for they also looked to Continental Europe; but they almost invariably tested their progress and accomplishments against those of the English. England was the supreme athletic nation of the nineteenth century, and Americans judged their athletic success in terms of the British.[37] As late as 1900 an American writer compared English athletics with that of America, admitting that the British were stronger and more athletic than Americans. "I doubt if the day will ever come," wrote a sport enthusiast, "when we shall feel able to challenge 'all England' with an 'all American' team."[38] By then, however, Americans had gone through much of the transition to organized sport and many American athletes were equal to, some better than, their English cousins.

THE IMMIGRANT INFLUENCE

Before 1900 another force pushing America toward organized sport was the large number of foreigners coming to the states. They brought with them their own sporting pastimes, often carrying with them different mores regarding Sunday pleasures. They joined with native Americans as they flocked to the cities to organize urban amusements. About 10 million immigrants came to America between 1820 and 1880. In the next two decades another nine million arrived, and from 1900 until the First World War 12 million more landed. Two of the most significant immigrant groups in sport came from the British Isles, the Irish and the Scots. In addition continental Europe including the German influence was noteworthy prior to 1900.

The Irish were the most important immigrant group coming to America in the 1820s, 1830s, and 1840s. The Irish were for the most part of the lower social and economic classes. Their sport reflected their social environment. The most significant contribution was in boxing. As if fighting out of their social stigma, a number of young Irishmen took to pugilism. By the mid-1800s most boxing enthusiasts had heard of the big four boxers, all Irish: "Yankee" Sullivan, Tom Hyer, John Heenan, and John Morrissey, who later became a New York politician and sports promoter. By the 1880s and 1890s the top fighters in America were generally Irish (or blacks when they were allowed to compete). John L. Sullivan, probably the most famous American sport hero of the nineteenth century, fought another Irishman, Paddy Ryan, for the heavyweight championship in 1882. Sullivan retained the title for a decade until beaten by still another Irishman, James J. Corbett. It was Sullivan who fought the last bareknuckle heavyweight championship in 1889 when he outlasted Jake Kilrain in a 75-round contest of over two hours' duration. Vachel Lindsay caught the essence of the fight when he wrote:

I heard a battle trumpet sound.
Nigh New Orleans
Upon an emerald plain
John L. Sullivan
The strong boy
of Boston
Fought seventy-five red rounds with Jake Kilrain.[39]

Sullivan being world's champion may have done more to raise the esteem of the Irish than any other individual. The Irish had fought for their rights in Ireland against outsiders for centuries. The new immigrants were fighting literally and figuratively for respect in their adopted homeland. Sullivan was their hero, and he became the hero of many other Americans as well.

The Scots from the northern part of the British Isles and from Northern Ireland (Scotch-Irish) did not produce an athletic hero in America as noteworthy as Sullivan, but they did introduce many Americans to track and field. The Scots, or Caledonians as the Ancient Romans called them, had their own traditional games in the homeland. The games which we might call track and field were characterized by such activities as foot races, the hammer throw, shot putting, pole vaulting, the hop-step-and-jump, and tossing the caber (heaving a heavy wooden pole). These activities were brought to America with Scottish and Scotch-Irish emigres in the eighteenth and nineteenth centuries. Those of Scottish heritage formed social groups as early as the 1830s and 1840s at which time they played the customary games, called Caledonian games. In 1853, the Boston Caledonian Club was formed, and three years later, the New York Caledonian Club. Others soon followed. Each held its own Caledonian games. The New York Scots held their athletic events at Jones' Wood, a common site of New York City amusements.[40]

By the mid-1880s Caledonian Clubs and games had spread to such diverse places as Germantown, Pennsylvania; Fishkill, New York; Cleveland, Ohio; Richmond, Virginia; Lake Lindon, Michigan; and Stockton, California.[41] Large crowds, as many as 25,000 in New York City, attended the games and festivities. The popularity of the games

Two Irish fighters, Sullivan and Kilrain, in the last bareknuckle heavyweight championship fight. (Courtesy of Library of Congress.)

The winter sport of curling, introduced to the United States in the 1880s, was a Scottish contribution.

had no small influence on the development of organized amateur track and field in the United States. When the first important athletic club was formed in the United States, the New York Athletic Club, it was not surprising that in 1868 it contested the Caledonian Club of New York in its first track and field competition. Five years later the first intercollegiate track meeting was held in conjunction with the Saratoga Intercollegiate Regatta. The sole event, the two mile run, was won by a McGill University student and member of the Montreal Caledonian Club.[42] Track and field in addition to the winter ice sport of curling, and golf, which was developed in Caledonia and introduced into the United States in the 1880s, were Scottish contributions to American sport.

Still another immigrant group with sporting customs, the Germans, came to America by the thousands following the 1848 Revolution and its aftermath. So great was their influx to areas in the United States that entire cities became dominated by their presence. Cities like Cincinnati, St. Louis, and Milwaukee began to conform to aspects of the German culture. Three of their sporting customs appear to stand out: their emphasis upon gymnastics, their enjoyment of bowling, and their desire to enjoy Sunday sports.

German people had a tradition in gymnastics dating to the eighteenth century. It was Frederick Ludwig Jahn, though, who popularized gymnastic activity in what he called the Turnverein, an organization of turners or gymnasts. Jahn, early in the 1800s during the German (Prussian) encounters with the French Emperor, Napoleon, had formed the Turnverein in an attempt to develop sturdy youth who could repel future aggressors. Though this activity later got Jahn into political difficulty with the government, the idea of physical fitness and national welfare was rekindled and became an integral part of the school systems of the German states by the 1840s. Following the 1848 Revolution in Europe thousands of German immigrants arrived in America bringing their gymnastics with them. Turnvereins were organized in numerous American cities in the last half of the nineteenth century, and they joined together to sponsor national turnfests periodically. In addition, the German-American Turners promoted physical education in the late 1800s by actively campaigning for the inclusion of gymnastics in the public schools.[43]

The German immigrants' sport tradition such as bowling on Sundays did much to undermine the custom of restricting sport on Sundays. Nowhere was there a clearer breakdown of the Puritan Sabbath than in the urban areas highly populated by the throngs of immigrants, like the Germans, from continental Europe. The resulting continental Sabbath was more than a day for the worship of God—it was a day for enjoyable pastimes like those practiced in the old country. New York City felt the thrust of the new continental Sabbath as did other cities. Jones' Wood in that city became a Sunday center for German immigrants "toiling earnestly to experience amusements." There one could participate in bowling, billiards, and gymnastics, or try his luck at the shooting galleries. If one desired to be amused by others he could watch the professional tight rope artist or imbibe at the beer concession of Jones' Wood, which it was noted by one writer as reigning with "supremest power."[44] Similar occurrences in other cities gave clear evidence that the Sabbath was no longer solely for the solemn contemplation of the godly life. Immigration and the new industrial order had brought change to the nineteenth century city, a change which would be felt by rural America in the twentieth century.

The National Turnfest of German-Americans as celebrated in 1869.

The contribution of immigrants to American sport was not limited to the Irish, Scots, and Germans alone. The most noticeable, perhaps, were the Swedish and other Scandanavian people. The Swedes by the 1880s and 1890s assisted the physical education movement in America through a health and educational system of formal, light gymnastics. Never greatly popular with men, Swedish gymnastics did gain some following by women physical educators. In the twentieth century some of their activities were incorporated into competitive gymnastics. The Scandanavian people, the Finns, Norwegians, and Swedes, brought with them a love of winter sports including skiing, ski-jumping, and snow shoeing, all of which were introduced in America before the twentieth century.

While immigrants gave much to the American sporting scene, sport contributed intangibly to the assimilation of foreigners, a process probably more pronounced in the twentieth century than in the years before. With the rise of organized sport came its ritualization. Foreigners of the divergent cultures could share in American sport both as participant and as spectator. At sporting contests, first or second generation Americans could identify with many of the traditional American values so greatly mirrored in American sport. The drive of Americans, the impatience with mediocrity, the compulsion to win, the belief in progress and hope for the future, the demand for leadership and cooperation, the worship of the individual hero, and the outpouring of national spirit—all could be found in the ritualized organized sport of the late nineteenth and early twentieth centuries. Sport, more than some areas of society, may have served as a democratizing agent for the masses of immigrants who came to America from the 1850s to the time of World War I. In sport, where the emphasis was placed upon winning, it was often more important to be good than to be of a certain nationality, religion, or social class. For some new Americans, there could be the assimilation and acceptance in society through competence on a football field, baseball diamond, or in a boxing ring. Sport contributed to the Americanization of the immigrant almost as if there were a reciprocation for the contributions immigrants made to sport in America.

We find in the period of transition in sport from the mid-nineteenth century to the early 1900s that various forces led to the need and desire to organize sport. The throngs of people moving to urban America in a rising industrial and technological society demanded a new kind of sport fitted to urban needs. The Civil War had provided much of the impetus to industrialization and to an interest in sport. The decline of religious opposition to sport and the continued English influence allowed for a surge of sporting interest which was intensified by the mass emigration from Europe and the

British Isles. By the early twentieth century the situation was ripe for the sporting explosion which resulted, especially so in the period following the First World War. The sporting impulse was a product of many forces. As we will see none was likely more important than that produced by the new wealth produced in industrial-urban America.

REFERENCES

1. See the following books for greater detail on many of these sports: John A. Krout, *Annals of American Sport*, (New Haven: Yale University Press, 1929); Foster R. Dulles, (*A History of Recreation: America Learns to Play*, 2nd ed., (New York: Appleton-Century-Crofts, 1965); John R. Betts, *America's Sporting Heritage: 1850-1950*, (Reading, Mass.: Addison-Wesley, 1974); John Durant and Otto Bettmann, *Pictorial History of American Sports*, (New York: A. S. Barnes, 1952); Robert B. Weaver, *Amusements and Sports in American Life*, (Chicago: The University of Chicago Press, 1939); and Herbert Manchester, *Four Centuries of Sport in America (1490-1890)*, (New York: The Derrydale Press, 1931).

2. John A. Garraty, *The New Commonwealth, 1877-1890* (New York: Harper & Row, 1968), p. 180, and Arthur M. Schlesinger, *The Rise of the City, 1878-1898* (New York: Macmillan, 1933), p. 68.

3. Thomas C. Cochran and William Miller, *The Age of Enterprise: A Social History of Industrial America* (New York: Harper & Row, 1961), p. 234; Garraty, *The New Commonwealth*, p. 131; and Allan Nevins, *The Emergence of Modern America, 1865-1878* (New York: Macmillan, 1927), p. 70.

4. Nevins, *Emergence of Modern America*, pp. 212, 307.

5. Pleasures of the Poor, *Independent*, LII (26 April 1900), pp. 1023-1025.

6. Steven Riess, The Baseball Magnate and Urban Politics in the Progressive Era, 1895-1920, *Journal of Sport History*, I (Spring, 1974), pp. 41-62.

7. Almont Lindsey, *The Pullman Strike* (Chicago: University of Chicago Press, 1942), pp. 38-56.

8. Robert H. Wiebe, *The Search for Order, 1877-1920* (New York: Hill & Wang, 1967), p. 38.

9. For a well documented account of technology and sport read John R. Betts, "The Technological Revolution and the Rise of Sport, 1850-1900," *Mississippi Valley Historical Review*, XL (September 1953), pp. 231-256.

10. Mark Sullivan, *Our Times, The United States, 1900-1925*, Vol. II (New York: Charles Scribner's Sons, 1930), p. 257.

11. James M. Whiton, The First Intercollegiate Regatta (1852), *Outlook*, LXVIII (June 1901), pp. 286-289.

12. Dale A. Somers, *The Rise of Sports in New Orleans, 1850-1900*, (Baton Rouge: Louisiana State University Press, 1972), p. 255.

13. Riess, Baseball Magnate and Urban Politics, pp. 43, 45, 55.

14. Betts, Technological Revolution and the Rise of Sport, pp. 231-256.

15. Joseph J. Mathews, First Harvard-Oxford Boat Race, *New England Quarterly*, XXXIII (March 1960), pp. 74-82.

16. John R. Betts, Sporting Journalism in Nineteenth-Century America, *American Quarterly*, V (Spring 1953), pp. 39-56.

17. James Bryce, America Revisited: The Changes of a Quarter-Century, *Outlook*, LXXIX (25 March 1905), pp. 738-739.

18. Betts, Technological Revolution and the Rise of Sport, pp. 231-256.

19. Louis M. Hacker, *The Triumph of American Capitalism* (New York: Simon & Schuster, 1940), pp. 251-256.

20. Edward D. Eddy, Jr., *Colleges for Our Land and Time* (New York: Harper & Brothers, 1956), pp. 38-39.

21. Albert Spalding, *America's National Game* (New York: American Sports Publishing Co., 1911), p. 97.

22. David S. Crockett, Sports and Recreational Practices of Union and Confederate Soldiers, *Research Quarterly*, XXXII (October 1961), pp. 335-347.

23. John R. Betts, Home Front, Battle Field, and Sport During the Civil War, *Research Quarterly*, XLII (May 1971), p. 131.

24. A. B. Hart, The Status of Athletics in American Colleges, *Atlantic Monthly*, LXVI (1890), p. 65.

25. O. Dewey, Fashionable Amusements, *The Christian Examiner*, VIII (May 1830), p. 201.

26. W. De L. Love, Amusements and Education of the Sensibilities, *Congregational Review*, X (1870), p. 238.

27. Washington Gladden, Christianity and Popular Amusements, *Century Magazine*, XXIX (January 1885), p. 385.

28. Joseph P. Lash, *Eleanor and Franklin* (New York: W. W. Norton, 1971), p. 67.

29. Mr. Beecher on Amusements, *Frank Leslie's Illustrated*, XLVI (22 February 1879), p. 450.

30. Moses Coit Tyler, *The Brawnville Papers* (Boston: Fields, Osgood & Co., 1869), p. 30.

31. Foster R. Dulles, *A History of Recreation*, p. 205.

32. Stuart Chase, Play, in Charles A. Beard (ed.), *Whither Mankind* (New York: Longsman Green & Co., 1928), p. 334.

33. Amusements, *New Englander*, XXVI (July 1867), pp. 419-420.

34. The Cricket Mania, *Harper's Weekly*, III (15 October 1859), p. 658.

35. John Sweet, A Plea for Amusements and Physical Culture, *The Bookseller*, I (September-November 1860), p. 132.

36. Athletics, *Every Saturday*, VII (24 April 1869), p. 535.

37. Between 1850 and 1900, the Americans began to challenge the supremacy of British athletics. First John Stevens beat the British in a yacht race and captured the so-called America's Cup in 1851. Harvard challenged and lost a crew race against Oxford University in 1869. There were numerous other United States-English contests including cricket matches, horse races, pedestrian events, and in 1895 the United States won all 11 events of the U.S.-English track meet.

38. William Patten (ed.), *The Book of Sports* (New York: J. F. Taylor & Co., 1901), p. 8.

39. Vachel Lindsay, John L. Sullivan, the Strong Boy of Boston, in his *Collected Poems* (New York: Macmillan, 1946), p. 93.

40. Gerald Redmond, *The Caledonian Games in Nineteenth-Century America* (Rutherford, N.J.: Fairleigh Dickenson University Press, 1971), pp. 36-41.

41. *Ibid*., pp. 43-45.

42. *Ibid*., p. 82.

43. Fred E. Leonard and George B. Affleck, *The History of Physical Education* (Philadelphia: Lea & Febiger, 1947), pp. 294-314.

44. Sunday in Jones' Wood, *Harper's Weekly*, III (5 November 1859), pp. 707-708.

CHAPTER 10
Sport and the Social Set

Out of the industrial growth of the last half of the nineteenth century came a new elite class created by industrial wealth, the "nouveau riche." Sport and aristocracy had always been drawn together. The epic poet Homer had written of the upper class Greeks who ran foot races, wrestled, and raced their chariots while laying seige upon Troy a millennium and more before the birth of Christ. The Roman emperors held their gladiatorial combats; the Medieval knights had their tourneys and jousts; and the English kings gave out edicts to preserve hunting lands for use by the aristocracy only. In a similar way the American capitalistic aristocracy of wealth became the vanguard of conspicuous leisure and sport during the Gilded Age following the Civil War.

It may have been natural in a society which claimed an equal opportunity for all, that those who made the most of their opportunity, the "nouveau riche," should be the logical leaders of society and of its sporting leisure. This upper class created the prestige needed to give organized sport an important place in the social life of the nation. Eventually most of the sports popularized by the upper class were the sports which became popular with all classes. In sport as in other aspects of culture those who are not rich stand admiringly close to those who are. Once the rich man took up sport, the common man soon developed an interest, becoming a spectator or participant if his pocket book could support it, and if sufficient leisure time could be found. Even some working class men could save 50¢ for a major league baseball game. The pari-mutuel betting in horse racing was one method the less wealthy could gain the same thrill of betting that the rich man received, even if it were only a $2.00 wager. The poor man, however, could never be closely associated with polo or yachting—truly rich men's sports.

The upper class which stimulated sport in America was primarily the aristocracy of wealth, not that of birth, talents, or virtues. It was not the aristocracy of British tradition or that which developed during the American Colonial experience, but one built upon the materialistic standards of the new industrial age. To this new aristocracy of wealth the visible badge of a man's wealth could be found in the conspicuous display of his fashionable wife, his yacht, or his horses, though it was not limited to them. Social standing for the newly created industrial rich who lacked hereditary wealth or recognized talents could be most readily acquired by a display of his riches creating an economically won social position.

Upper class society which had been composed of merchants, planters, statesmen, clergy, lawyers, and physicians[1] had been more restrained in its sporting activity in colonial times and in the early national period. Not only had religious feeling tempered his display of sport, but the long tradition of the British sporting society and the concept of the gentleman sportsman was important to him. With the winning of independence, the belief in equality, and the trend toward egalitarianism growing out of the late eighteenth century, the aristocrats of "talents, birth, virtues, services, [and] sacrifices," as John Adams called them, were gradually replaced.[2] In their place came the steamship owners, rail tycoons, and steel manufacturers who were products of the laissez faire capitalism of the industrial nineteenth century. The new plutocrats felt little guilt in the wasteful leisure of sport as they felt little guilt in their practices in the competitive business world. It was survival of the fittest in business and conspicuous consumption in the sports of the wealthiest.

George J. Gould, son of the rail magnate, Jay Gould, could build a Lakewood, New Jersey house with an elliptical staircase of marble and bronze, surrounded by Italian sunken gardens, and graced with a quarter-million dollar sporting palestra which included a "tanbark hippodrome, shooting galley, and Turkish and Russian baths." Cornelius K. Vanderbilt could build a 2000 ton yacht, with a saloon furnished with rosewood upholstered with green plush, which cost $1500.00 a day to operate.[3] James Gordon Bennett, Jr., owner of the New York *Herald*, could spend an estimated $30 to $40 million on his sporting pastimes and social climbing in a lifetime. Few of the new rich took the advice of an 1870s writer who warned Americans that one should not estimate success by possession; that what a man is is more important than what he has.[4] This apparently little concerned the nineteenth century socially conscious sportsman.

The new rich in the period between the Civil War and World War I who had some leisure and plenty of money displayed their talents in a variety of sporting pastimes. They dominated horse racing; made fox hunting into a showcase of social regalia; contributed to the fashionableness of billiards, croquet, hunting and riflery, archery, tennis, golf, football, and coaching; introduced polo and the horse show to America; gave yachting an international flavor; parroted the English in innumerable ways, including the development of fashionable clubs; and gave the world the country club with all its sporting ramifications. Nothing was more important to the "nouveau riche" than yachting and horse racing.

THE RICH ON WATER

The most expensive sport known to the nineteenth century upper class was undoubtedly yachting. Beginning in the early 1800s, following the lead of the English, some American merchants were sailing their own pleasure yachts. By the 1830s and 1840s larger numbers of prosperous businessmen along the Atlantic coast began to experience the glory of sailing. The New York Yacht Club in 1844 was the first of its kind to be organized in America, but soon after there were yachting organizations on every major body of water across the land—even Oshkosh, Wisconsin had its own yacht club by 1870. Yacht clubs generally preceded city athletic clubs and were founded nearly a half century before country clubs and the ubiquitous golf courses of the twentieth century. All three became the domain of fashionable society. The yacht club, then, became a nineteenth century prototype of conspicuous sporting consumption with membership meaning a social position for merchants, manufacturers, and professionals. There were hundreds of yacht clubs formed after the New York Yacht Club, but none was more important.

The New York Yacht Club was formed on board John C. Stevens' yacht in mid-summer, 1844. The Stevens family fortune could well support Stevens' yachting interests for most of its wealth had been made in the transportation developments, primarily steamboats, of the early 1800s. Stevens and a small, select group, which included ownership of only nine yachts, built a one room club house in 1845 at Elysian Fields, Hoboken, New Jersey, where the New York Knickerbocker amateur baseball club was developing organized baseball in the same year. Each year the club held races off the New York coast. In 1851, a syndicate was formed of New York Yacht Club members to build an ocean going yacht which would be sailed to England to compete against the best England had to offer.

The result of this venture was a $30,000 yacht, the *America*, a 101 foot schooner with an 81 foot foremast. The *America* was guest of the Royal Yacht Squadron, the fleet of the long established club of British yachtsmen. Though John C. Stevens, commander of the *America*, desired to race his yacht against any British yacht for a side bet of from $5.00 to $50,000, the only offers he received were a challenge by a British schooner for a 100 pound race and a chance to race against the Royal Yacht Squadron for a 100 guinea ($500) cup around the Isle of Wight, off the southern coast of England. The latter proved vitally important to yachting history for when Commander Stevens won against 15 British yachts, he took home with him what was called the America's Cup.

The America's Cup was kept by Stevens as his trophy for conquering the British. Six years later the cup was given to the New York Yacht Club as a challenge cup. There were, however, no international challenges for the trophy until after the Civil War. Following the war several events occurred which led to a challenge for the cup. In 1866, three Americans, led by James Gordon Bennett, Jr., sailed in the first transatlantic race, between New York and England, creating interest in both countries. Bennett, four years later, pitted his yacht, *Dauntless*, against James Ashbury's *Cambria* of the Royal Yacht Club of England. This transatlantic race, won by Ashbury, led to increased British confidence and the first challenge for the America's cup. The New York Yacht Club using rules similar to the 1851 event allowed its yacht club fleet of 17 to race against the single challenger. The British challenge was easily thrown back as *Cambria* came in 10th out of the 18 yachts. In the century which followed the initial 1870 defense of the America's Cup, a score of other challengers from England, Canada, Scotland, and Australia have been thwarted in their attempts to take home the valued trophy.[5]

The America's Cup, of which there were 7 races in the 1870s and 1880s, was easily the most prestigious of the many yachting races in America. With it came an increase in yacht clubs. As it became socially more desirable for the wealthy to join yacht clubs, the nature of yachting changed. While most of the early members sailed their own yachts, increased membership for social prestige brought in numerous wealthy men who were ignorant of yachting and who hired professional sailors to man their yachts. As the craze for yachting expanded there was a broader range of wealth as well as skill in sailing. These two factors caused a demand for smaller boats to sail. The smaller sailboats were more suited to the novice sailor as well as to the pocketbook—especially for those who wanted to pretend their wealth, but could not afford the seaworthy yachts such as those of J. Pierpont Morgan, William Rockefeller, James Gordon Bennett, Jr., or Cornelius Vanderbilt.

The most prestigious watering place in America was Newport, Rhode Island. It was here that society dominated the social sporting season each summer with yachting being one of the important activities. An old-line member of the social elite, Mrs. John King Van Rensselaer, with some contempt for the new rich, reminisced about the Newport harbor in the late 1800s which "shone with the sails and white hulls of hundreds of yachts."[6] The antebellum society of Charleston, South Carolina had made Newport fashionable. The Civil War had virtually destroyed the established elite of the south, and the industrial rich of New York, led by the likes of Mrs. August Belmont, took their place. The silvergilts or goldfish, as they were called by those who disdained or envied them, brought sailing to a prominent place. The luxury yachts were only part of the "wasteful extravagance" which included polo matches, country clubs, tennis tournaments, and horse shows. Only sport, other than social consciousness, drew the Newport summer colony together and the social pageantry of sailing made it the social capital of society.[7] By the turn of the century sailing and yachting at Newport and other watering areas were an important preserve of the well-to-do, and the English visitor, James Muirhead, could write in his *The Land of Contrasts* that "sailing is tremendously popular at all American seaside resorts."[8]

SOCIETY AT THE RACES

While yachting had been the leading water sport it was horse racing, the sport of kings, with which society felt most at home on land. American horse racing, like yachting, had been transplanted from English soil. Unlike the water sport of the nineteenth century, thoroughbred or flat racing could trace its history to the previous century and before, being heavily influenced by developments in the Southern elite, especially that of Virginia. As the first of American organized sports, horse racing had its jockey clubs in the 1700s and by the early 1800s spectators at racing events in the tens of thousands were reported.[9] Race Week in various cities in the South especially, drew the notables of society such as William Randolph, General Wade Hampton, and George Washington before the Revolutionary War. In the two generations following independence, horse racing intensified as great intersectional, north vs. south, contests were held at the Long Island Union Course and elsewhere.

Interest in horse racing declined somewhat in the north in the 1840s and 1850s and the center of the sport shifted from New York to New Orleans. There it stayed until the 1860s when the Civil War erupted. Most of the flat racing, in the north and south, was done at distances of 3 or 4 miles, and there were generally multiple heats. For a horse to race 4 miles, rest for thirty minutes, and then race two more heats of 4 miles each within an hour was a common practice. "Bottom" or endurance was just as important as speed. The famous 1823

Eclipse-Sir Henry race, in which there were side bets of $20,000, was a race of 4 miles with three heats. A generation later little had changed when a group of Georgia turfmen challenged English turfmen to a $100,000 a side race of the best of three 4-mile heats.[10]

The Civil War obviously interferred with racing, but it was not entirely discontinued in either the south or the north. In Lexington, Kentucky two or three meetings were held each year during the war except in 1862 when the army was camped at the track. It seemed to matter little whether Lexington was under confederate or union control for the races continued. New Orleans, too, continued racing after it was taken by Union forces in 1862.[11] In the north there were enough horses and interest in racing in the midst of the conflict for William R. Travers and others in the prestigious New York Jockey Club to construct a race course at the socially elite resort at Saratoga Springs, New York. These examples may have been more the exception than the rule for in the south nearly all available horses were conscripted for the cavalry. Complete dedication to the war effort could not countenance the frivolity of racing. Horses, too, were scarce in the north though dedication to the war did not preclude all sports of the wealthy.[12]

A victorious north allowed a number of carpetbaggers to confiscate the southern stock of horses. This fact combined with the wealth created in the north by the war produced a resurgence in horse racing immediately following Appomatox. The "nouveau riche" came to support racing for social standing and for profit. Wealthy industrialists and horse racing promoters joined forces to fashion new tracks and create stables to improve the breed of thoroughbred horses. This influx of the new rich into racing transformed flat racing to a great extent from a sport dominated by a gentry class, often southern, to a commercial sport looking for profits. One of the major changes accompanying this displacement in leadership which led to greater spectator interest was the movement away from the distance races with heats to shorter mile or mile and one-half races. American sport was again following the British lead with the result that most distance races run in heats died by the end of the 1870s.[13]

Racing in the New York City area with its expanding society class showed the most significant signs of growth. The success of the fashionable Saratoga race course which opened in 1863 helped persuade Leonard W. Jerome, a wealthy Wall Street broker, that thoroughbred racing should be part of New York City and society. He and August Belmont, a prominent New York banker, formed the American Jockey Club and with their leadership the Club purchased over 200 acres in Westchester County, north of New York City as the site for Jerome Park. Opening in 1866, Jerome Park with seating for over 7,000 spectators ushered in a new era of thoroughbred racing, one dominated by the social prestige of the newly rich capitalists.[13] During the generation following the Civil War the wealthy who patronized the turf included such notables as William C. Whitney, John Hay Whitney, W. Averell Harriman, Marshall Field, Cornelius Vanderbilt, August Belmont, William R. Travers, Leonard Jerome, and Pierre Lorillard.

Pierre Lorillard was a good example of the influence of social position on horse racing and breeding. Lorillard became involved in 1873 when he bought land which he named the Rancocas Farm in Jobstown, New Jersey. Here he raised thoroughbreds which he raced throughout the United States and in England. In the 1880s, Lorillard sold his race horses to devote time to the development of Tuxedo Park, society's most fashionable showcase of upper class community living. He later reestablished his stud farm and finally retired from racing in 1900, but not before being instrumental in changing the control and rules of thoroughbred racing in America. Through Lorillard's influence a racing Board of Control was established in 1891 by the owners of race courses to license jockeys and trainers, and to control and improve racing in general. Because of protests from the various racing stables, a new organization was finally established in the 1890s, the Jockey Club, which represented both race track owners and stables. The Jockey Club from then on dominated racing rules, appointed officials, licensed jockeys and trainers, and set dates of meetings at race courses. Lorillard, the tobacco industrialist and socialite, had contributed much to the development of thoroughbred racing in America.[14] It was another indication that for an important part of the American upper social class, sport was what made life worth living.

ATHLETIC CLUBS AND THE PROMOTION OF AMATEUR ATHLETICS

For those in society whose life was made worth living by sport, it eventually became a must to belong to an athletic club. As in most aspects of upper class society, New York City took the lead in the development of the athletic club. This seems quite logical for it was in cities that clubs and associations (lodges, fraternal orders, unions) first became important, and New York was the fastest growing urban area in the late 1800s. Clubs, like athletic clubs, appeared to fill a need in providing a meaningful social structure, giving a feeling of self importance and of belonging, something which had been weakened by the push toward urbanization and the growth of the impersonal factory system.

The New York Athletic Club was one of the first and almost immediately became the most important athletic club in America. It was founded in 1868 by three athletes who were vitally interested in athletic competition and records, but who were little concerned with developing a social club or using athletics as a vehicle for gaining social prestige. Patterned after the London Athletic Club of England, the NYAC rented space for a gymnasium and included boxing as an important pastime. Track and field was its first important outdoor sport, though, strangely, it organized an indoor track meet as its first sponsored activity. The first indoor track meet in American history in November of 1868 pitted the NYAC against the well-organized Scottish Caledonian Club of New York. The site was an uncompleted skating rink. Two thousand spectators saw one of the NYAC founders, Bill Curtis, run in spiked shoes borrowed from an English friend, and as an added attraction the fans marvelled at the riding of a French velocipede, forerunner of the high wheel bicycle popularized in the 1870s and 1880s. Track and field, like that sponsored by the NYAC, has been the backbone of amateur athletics since the 1870s. The NYAC, in addition to gymnasium work and track and field, promoted rowing early in its history when it built a boat house on the Harlem River.[15]

Athletic clubs were a logical outgrowth of organized sport for they provided physical outlets for young urban men. In the decades of the 1870s and 1880s numerous athletic clubs were opened not only in New York City but elsewhere throughout the United States. Within a couple of decades most cities of 25,000 or more had athletic clubs. While it was common for athletic clubs to be middle class in origin, there was a tendency for the "nouveau riche" to be attracted to clubs which displayed the competitiveness and virility which they found in their own business and professional world.

The NYAC was a good example. Started by three young athletes, John Babcock, Bill Curtis, and Harry Buermeyer, the NYAC charged a moderate $10.00 initiation fee and annual dues. Desiring to make the club more socially acceptable its second president, Colonel William Van Wyck, began to proselytize new members from the social register of New York. His big catch was William R. Travers, a wealthy stockbroker who was prominent in yachting as well as the New York Jockey Club and who had founded the New York Racquet Court Club in 1875 (later the Racquet and Tennis Club).[16] With Travers and other socially conscious members in the fold, the nature of the NYAC began to change. Not only was Travers elected president, but the club became more exclusive by setting a membership quota, raising its initiation fee and annual dues, and building a costly social club house. This so outraged some of the older members who were only interested in athletics that two of the founders, Curtis and Buermeyer, resigned.[17] One bitter athlete in the 1880s, Frederick Jansson, attacked the movement to make athletic clubs vehicles of the social elite.

Said he:

> The social element in clubs is like dry rot and eats into the vitals of athletic clubs and soon causes them to fail in the purpose for which they were organized. . . . It is like an octopus that squeezes the life-blood out of the organization by burdening it with debt. Palatial club houses are erected at great cost, and money is spent in adorning them that, if used to beautify athletic grounds and improve tracks, would cause wide-spread interest in athletic sports and further the development of the wind and muscles of American youth. . . . The youths who participate in health-giving competitions, as a rule, cannot afford the expense of membership to the so-called athletic clubs and so they retire in favor of the wealthy young man whose sole claim to athletic distinction is his connection with a "high toned" club.[18]

The New York Athletic Club, like others infused with the wealthy social membership, began to use athletics for the social prestige it could gain from its members. While some of the social elite were top-flight performers, most were not. One method of achieving social prestige through athletic prowess used by the socially elite club members was to sponsor outstanding athletes in amateur sports like track and field. The desire to win and the pursuit of success which the new rich had experienced in business was apparently carried over into sport. Athletic clubs began to hire the best athletes, including collegians, by offering them free initiation and remitting dues, granting them free room and board, and giving them valuable prizes including cash. This prostitution of amateur athletics led to bitter quarrels between competing athletic clubs and to the formation of the Amateur Athletic Union by clubs who favored stricter rule enforcement.[19]

The emergence of the AAU and the fight over amateur athletic control is worthy of recounting, for the AAU has to a great extent dominated amateur sport in America since its origin and would probably be supreme today had not it been challenged for power by the college sport establishment since the early 1900s. Prior to the formation of the AAU in 1888, the most powerful amateur organization in the United States was the National Association of Amateur Athletes of America formed a decade before by and solely for athletic clubs. The NYAC rules became the standard for the NAAAA. This body functioned for eastern athletic clubs from 1879 until the late 1880s when internal squabbles and opposition of the NYAC led to its demise. The NYAC withdrew from the NAAAA and was followed by a number of other athletic clubs. The Manhattan AC, chief antagonist to the NYAC for athletic honors and social esteem in the east, attempted to keep the NAAAA alive.

To challenge the NAAAA, the NYAC and the the Athletic Club of the Schuylkill Navy in Philadelphia along with 13 other clubs formed the Amateur Athletic Union. To help destroy the older organization the AAU decreed that:

> Any amateur competing in any open athletic games in the United States under the rules approved by the National Association, will be debarred from competing in any games held by the rules of the A.A.U.[20]

The wealthy members of the AAU began to offer lucrative prizes worth as much as a quarter of an average laborer's yearly salary for winners of track and field competitions. Athletic clubs bid for recognized athletic talent helping further to debase the concept of amateurism with their hypocritical policies. Only because the clubs were backed by the industrial wealthy could they act so blatantly in quest for athletic power. Following a year long fight Abraham G. Mills, member of the NYAC and AAU, former president of the National League in baseball, and wealthy New York businessman, reached agreement with the NAAAA with the result that the NAAAA was dissolved and its former members joined the AAU.[21]

The wealthy athletic clubs and the dominating athletic ruling body, the AAU, had joined hands and were to continue to jointly support amateur athletics into the twentieth century. Men of wealth maintained their control over both the important athletic clubs and the AAU. This combination gave support to the physically talented, but as Janssen had noted, caused many of those who desired physical exercise in athletic clubs to forego the expensive diversion.

With the wealth needed to draw athletic talent the NYAC decided to test the British in the first important international track meet by challenging the London Athletic Club. A series of communications between the two athletic clubs in early 1895 brought about an agreement to meet at New York's Manhattan Field on the last day of summer that year. Both clubs began recruiting nationally for the best amateur talent available. In America this recruiting specifically broke the rules of the AAU. Fortunately, for the success of the Americans, the president of the AAU was William B. Curtis who had been a founder of the NYAC. Curtis allowed the club to recruit athletes to run under its colors who were not members and who were enlisted solely for this one performance. Nationalistic desires to best the English, whipped up by the American (Monroe Doctrine) concern over the tense British-Venezuela boundary dispute of the midsummer of 1895, prevailed over the ideals of amateur athletics. In essence an American team was gathered together, financed by the NYAC, to contest for eleven events mutually agreed upon by the British and Americans. From the first event, 880 yard run, to the final result, the 3 mile run, the Americans were supreme, winning in between three dashes, the mile run, shot put, hammer throw, 120 yard high hurdles, and the high and long jump. Socially elite NYAC members were present among the 10,000 spectators including August Belmont and John Jacob Astor, artist Charles Dana Gibson, long time AAU leader, James Sullivan, and rising politician and New York City Police Commissioner, Theodore Roosevelt watched the events in 98°F heat. None was hotter than Montagu Shearman, leader of the English team, whose bitter remarks said something about the importance in 1895 of Americans winning this international athletic contest: "The machinery of the New York Athletic Club with its free training stables—I mean tables—was ready to train anybody with ability."[22] Bitter but true.

Only a little more than a half year later Athens, Greece hosted the first games of the Modern Olympics. This time the NYAC took scant interest in the international competition, and though they were the wealthiest athletic club in America they sponsored no athletes to what were then considered relatively unimportant games. Only through the efforts of Princeton University history professor, William M. Sloane, some Princeton athletes, and the backing and representation from the Boston Athletic Club did the United States have representatives in Athens. Not one American athlete who had competed in the world record breaking NYAC-London AC meet participated in the auspicious April games in Greece. Yet Americans won 9 of the 12 track events, though the performances were considerably inferior to those in New York half a year before. The winning high jump in New York had been 6' 5 5/8''; at Athens it was 5' 11 1/4''. The 16 pound shot put was thrown 43' 5'' in New York and only 36' 2'' in Athens. The long jump was 22' 6'' in New York and only 20' 9 3/4'' at the first Olympics. Similar differences were found in running events where, for instance, the New York mile was run over 33 seconds faster than the equivalent distance at the Olympics.[23]

These two events, the New York meet and the first Olympics, and numerous lesser amateur athletic events had been made possible through the sponsorship or backing of athletic clubs like those of the NYAC and the Boston AC. The move to enlist socially prominent and wealthy patrons into the athletic clubs had changed the nature of the clubs and had provided the financial backing and prestige to successfully promote highly competitive, world class athletics. At the same time certain aspects of amateur sport were being prostituted to financial considerations and national and political purposes.

THE ELITIST COUNTRY CLUBS

The society members of the "nouveau riche" had dominated the water sports, were leaders of the sport of kings, came to dominate the highest levels of certain amateur sports, and, in addition, formed the

The 1896 American Olympic team in Athens with the sole Greek victor dressed in his native costume.

surburban phenomenon of country clubs. Country clubs were in some ways an antidote to the loss of country living in an urban America, and in other ways were an antidote for the need for social interaction for those living in the new suburban America. Prior to the development of suburbs and country clubs, urban society leaders often joined city social clubs. Whether city social clubs, urban athletic clubs, or surburban country clubs, club life served a need for belonging and expressing self-importance within a meaningful social structure which had been weakened by the rise of an impersonal, mass produced, industrial-urban society. Like much of American life, clubs were a manifestation of British class society and served to keep a gentlemanly tradition in a mass culture.

Urban club life in America existed in the first half of the nineteenth century, but its rapid growth occurred following the Civil War. According to one writer at the close of the war, clubs represented "every interest from the highest art to the lowest sport."[24] It was the social club in which males could get away from the rigors of business, isolate themselves from the lower classes, and be completely segregated from women, who were not allowed to step inside most club house doors. The clubs were based principally upon achievement rather than heredity.[25] The achievement motive was important. The wives and children of wealthy members often spent their summers at some fashionable watering place such as Newport or Saratoga, while the men remained at home working at their businesses and relaxing at their clubs.[26] The clubs thrived in the summer.

The concept of social clubs expanded as sport became more important to the "nouveau riche." In addition to athletic clubs which sponsored a variety of sports, many specialty clubs sponsored individual activities such as archery, bicycling, bowling, coaching, cricket, croquet, curling, fishing, hunting, lacrosse, polo, riding, riflery, rowing, squash rackets, tennis, walking, and yachting. Many of these clubs desired to build facilities in the country, away from the din of the city. In 1882, a country club, generally recognized as the first country club in America, was established on the outskirts of Boston in Brookline. The New York Athletic Club built a country club on Travers Island in 1886. A multitude of others followed in the next generation as nearly every city and even small towns established country clubs.

The country club without peer was undoubtedly that built in 1885 by Pierre Lorillard, III, the tobacco millionaire. Lorillard owned 7,000 acres of Orange County, New York, northwest of New York City. He and his friends used it for fishing and hunting. Lorillard decided to enclose 5,000 acres with a fence and develop it with modern roads and a sewer and water system. He sold lots and called it Tuxedo Park, the showcase of all country clubs. Tuxedo Park became the place for society's best to build their country mansions which they called "cottages." A gigantic club house was the center of attraction with a lake for those who desired water sports. The club contained glass enclosed verandas, numerous fire places, magnificent stairways, a theater, ball room, billard room, and dinning room. Outdoor sports were featured. In addition to hunting and fishing, provisions were made for ice skating, ice-boating, sleigh riding, and tobagganing on a mile long electrically lighted slide. The sports of pigeon shooting and steeplechasing were provided for members. A race track was included, and a golf course was constructed in 1889.[27] This was, according to a number of socially elite of New York, country living at its best.

The country club in the twentieth century generally has been associated with golf, but it originated in the nineteenth century generally around activities of horsemanship. Fox hunting, steeplechasing, polo, horse shows, or coaching were often the common element of the early country clubs.[28] The Brookline Club, which for years has been noted as a golf club, was first a horse racing center. It was not long, however, before golf became the main activity at Brookline and for most country clubs.

Golf in America did not become popular with the "nouveau riche" until the 1890s even though the sport had been introduced in colonial

Country clubs were first built around activities of the horse; here fox hunting in Southern Pines, North Carolina, in the early 1900s. (Courtesy of Library of Congress.)

times by the Dutch and Scotch emigres. The game remained popular in Scotland, generally considered the country of its origin, and in England. Two events favorable to the advancement of golf occurred in the 1880s. Joseph M. Fox, a member of Philadelphia's Merion Cricket Club, journeyed to England for a cricket match and then to Scotland to observe golf at the famous St. Andrews course. He learned the game and soon brought equipment and a love of the game to America. Fox began playing golf at his summer estate in Foxburg in Western Pennsylvania, establishing an eight-hole course. In 1887, he built his second course which exists as the oldest golf course in continuous use in the United States. That same year, John Reid, a Scot living outside of New York City in Yonkers, asked a friend to bring back some golf clubs and balls from a journey to Scotland. The next spring Reid introduced the game to his friends. Within the year they organized the St. Andrews Golf Club of Yonkers, named after the famous club in Scotland. The course was a 6 hole layout on a cow pasture. Other golf clubs were soon organized. By 1894 there was enough enthusiasm for golf in the east that a tournament at St. Andrews was called—open to all golfers and known as the United States Open. Late in the year the United States Golfing Association was formed to adopt rules and regulations and to conduct championships. The following year a championship was held for women at the Meadow Brook course on Long Island. By 1900 there were over 1,000 golf clubs in America, showing the rapid growth of another sport of society people.[29]

Golf soon became the central activity of many country clubs whose members had social status, sufficient money, and some free time. Golf as a social recreation was aided by the Saturday half-holiday which was becoming more accepted while the strict Sabbath was losing its hold upon urban America. As one observer noted, golf and the country club "promises to be the safety-valve of an over worked nation."[30] But it was a safety-valve for only the upper segment of society. A critic of the American social scene used golf as the illustration and hit into what she believed to be the hypocrisy of wealth on the one hand and deprivation on the other:

> The golf links lie so near the mill
> That almost every day
> The laboring children can look out
> And see the men at play.[31]

Wealthy men and women in increasing numbers began joining country clubs. After having cut their way into society, they often sliced their way around the golf links. As one country club observer remarked: "The nation is beginning to find as much fascination in driving a golf-ball as in driving a bargain."[32] It was true that by the early 1900s, work ethic America was seeing some value in playing even if that play was often as serious as work itself. Golf seemed to give a segment of society a feeling of individual accomplishment in a nation that was becoming increasingly regimented. That may have been its real appeal to many of the country club set.

Golf, like so many sports made popular by the wealthy classes, did not remain solely a prerogative of the upper classes. Public golf courses of the twentieth century allowed middle America to play. Even then golf continued to be often scorned as being effete.[33] By World War I there were possibly a million golfers in America. President Taft had made it more popular just prior to the war as he teed off regularly in the mornings rather than working at the White House. When an American, twenty-year-old Francis Ouimet, defeated the two English stars Harry Vardon and Ted Ray in the 1913 United States Open, a new stimulus was given the sport. Three years later the Professional Golfers' Association was created by millionaire Rodman Wanamaker, and the movement toward a game for middle America was given an additional thrust. The erosion of golf toward mass play had only begun while golf remained primarily a game for the well-to-do.

JAMES GORDON BENNETT, JR., THE ECCENTRIC SPORTSMAN

No member of society's best contributed more to the development of sport in America than did James Gordon Bennett, Jr., hereditary owner of the New York *Herald*. No member of society was more eccentric in work or in sporting life than the son of the founder of one of the most important newspapers of the last half of the nineteenth century. His father, James Gordon Bennett, Sr., a Scottish immigrant, had built the most profitable newspaper in America in part by denouncing the leaders of society and building mass appeal for the *Herald*. Because of his denunciation of the New York society he was a social outcast. The enormous wealth he created in the newspaper business, which was claimed to be the third largest assured income in America after Commodore Vanderbilt and William B. Astor, provided Bennett, Jr. with the gilded money needed to successfully invade New York's social set and to be prominent in sport.[34]

In 1857, at the age of sixteen, Bennett, Jr. owned a 77-ton yacht and with it became the youngest member ever admitted to the New York Yacht Club. From then until the early 1900s when he was promoting the sports of auto racing and aviation, he was constantly newsworthy as a result of his sporting interests. For a half century he promoted and participated in both amateur and professional sports. He sailed throughout the world in his yacht, provided hounds to rejuvenate fox hunting in Virginia, hosted a tennis tourney at the fashionable Newport, Rhode Island resort, hunted with royalty at Versailles in France, contributed to the Olympic movement of Pierre de Coubertin, supported professional pedestrian matches, joined the prestigious Jockey Club, and introduced polo to America. In addition he provided championship cups in the promotion of intercollegiate crew and track. His idiosyncracies led him to naked drives through the country side in his coach and four, and he created the sport of "Bennetting" which he introduced when he deliberately broke up girls' school promenades by riding his horse between the two-by-two strolling and frightened girls.

His greatest love was yachting which was his passion from an early age. While his mother brought him up in Parisian society, his father, usually living in New York, indulged him by buying his teen age son the sailing sloop, *Rebecca*. Shortly thereafter he was elected a member of the New York Yacht Club when the fleet was on its annual cruise in 1857. He was soon a champion sailor though his ethics were not always the highest. In 1858 he cut across the treacherous Plum Gut during a race around Long Island, but was disqualified because the race agreement said that Plum Gut was too great a risk to sail through. The next year at the age of eighteen he challenged a schooner to a 154 mile race for a $500 a side bet which he lost.[35] When the Civil War broke out the twenty-year-old Bennett volunteered his new 160 ton yacht, *Henrietta*, to the northern effort, and he was commissioned as a Lieutenant, serving for about a year before he and the navy had a mutual separation. Bennett's erratic behavior was not suited to the military chain of command.

James Gordon Bennett, Jr., as photographed by Matthew Brady after the Civil War.

Bennett had free reign when the Civil War was over. In 1866, when the rest of the nation was accepting baseball as the National Game, Bennett gained national attention by challenging two other yachts to the first transatlantic yacht race. Bennett, who within three years was to sponsor Henry Morton Stanley's search for David Livingston in the African jungles, bet $30,000 against two other $30,000 side bets that he could cross the Atlantic first. On December 11, 1866, Bennett in his *Henrietta*, Pierre Lorillard, Jr., in his *Vesta*, and George Frank Osgood in his *Fleetwing* set sail on a 3,000 mile race from Staten Island, New York to the Isle of Wight in England. The event generated the greatest interest in sailing since the beginning of the America's Cup race in 1851. On Christmas Day, almost fourteen days later, James Gordon Bennett, Jr. arrived first at the Isle of Wight. The dramatic nature of the race, in which six of the *Fleetwing* crew were swept to their deaths in a storm, gave added stature to Bennett who soon became the Vice-Commander and then Commander of the New York Yacht Club before he was thirty years old.[26] In addition it stimulated interest in yachting which led to the resumption of the America's Cup race in 1870.

Eventually Bennett went to the more luxurious steam sailing when he built the *Namouna* in the early 1880s. In 1900 he built the most palatial steamer of the time, the *Lysistrata*. This ship cost $625,000 and required a crew of 100 to man it. Each of the three decks had a suite of rooms for Bennett himself, plus ample quarters for guests. Its Turkish bath was only outdone in extravagence by the padded stall quarters for an Alderney cow which provided those on board with fresh milk and cream.[37]

Though sailing was his love, Bennett's sporting interest ranged as wide as his yachts took him. On one visit to England he saw the game of polo being played by English army officers who had brought the game to England in the 1860s from its colony, India. Bennett decided that the game should be introduced in America.[37] In 1876 he brought a polo playing English army captain and equipment to the States. He and his friends sent to Texas for a train car load of cow ponies, took lessons at the Dickel Riding Academy in New York where they played the first game of polo in America, and continued to play matches at Jerome Park, home of thoroughbred racing in New York. Shortly thereafter Bennett and several friends founded the Westchester Polo Club and built a clubhouse.[38] That summer Bennett was playing polo at the Newport polo grounds before the fashionables.[39]

Amateur track and professional long distance running were coming into fashion in the 1870s. Bennett gave his support and even indulged a bit himself. Just a few days short of his thirty-third birthday James Bennett and attorney John Whipple, both members of the exclusive Union Club of New York, had a $3,000 a side walking contest from Bennett's home on 38th street to Jerome Park, the site of horse races, over 10 miles away. With an estimated $50,000 bet on the contest and with Whipple favored, they set out at 7:00 a.m. on a rainy spring day in 1874. Bennett, dressed in a light blue shirt, light tweed coat, dark pants, and a white jockey cap, quickly took the lead. One hour, forty-six minutes, and fifty-five seconds later—time seemed to be important in this new industrial age—Bennett crossed the finish line and collected his money, but more importantly, prestige.[41]

A few days later Bennett was present at the start of the famous pedestrian Edward Payson Weston's attempt to break 500 miles in a "go-as-you-please" six-day pedestrian race.[42] It was not uncommon for Bennett to run the last few laps with the contestants at these

James Gordon Bennett, Jr., introduced polo to America in 1876. He is
seen in the center of action.

pedestrian meets as he did in this race. His interest was backed by his
money for he was known to financially support certain world class
pedestrians like Daniel O'Leary.[43] Bennett also helped to promote the
first American intercollegiate track meet which was held in conjunction with the fashionable intercollegiate rowing regatta held at Lake
Saratoga, New York. In 1873 he gave the victory cup for the winner
of the only track event, the 2 mile run. Later he contributed other
prizes as the event grew in size.[44]

Promotion of both amateur and professional sports continued for
Bennett, but after 1877 he spent his life living in voluntary exile in
Paris where he placed greater emphasis on sporting indulgence than
promotion. Bennett, who was highly eccentric, brought about his exit
from America by creating an indiscretionary scene in mixed Victorian
company by relieving himself into a roaring fireplace at his fiancée's
New Year's Day party. The engagement was broken, Bennett was
later physically beaten and humiliated by his fiancée's brother, and a
duel was carried out before he left an America whose social best now
shunned him.[45] Though he seldom returned to the United States,
Bennett kept close watch over the sporting scene, and his New York
Herald continued to report developments in the world of sport. James
Gordon Bennett, Jr. had arrived at the right time, being born of the
"nouveau riche." He grew up at the time organized sport was being

established and he, like many of the new rich, used sport as a means of climbing the social ladder. He was not alone in this, but he was a unique individual in American sporting history.

THE BEGINNING OF THE DECLINE OF THE SPORTING ELITE

In the early years of the twentieth century a member of the idle rich wrote:

> We are the rich; we own America; we got it, God knows how; but we intend to keep it if we can by throwing all the tremendous weight of support, our influence, our money, our political connections, our purchased senators, our hungry Congressmen, and our public-speaking demagogues into the scale against any legislation, any political platforms and presidential campaign, that threatens the integrity of our estate.[46]

Already there was a strong reaction in America to the plutocracy which was essentially governing the country. With it there was opposition to the same monied group which had for a generation and more been flouting its wealth through a conspicuous display of riches including those found in sport. Leaders of the social gospel movement in religion condemned their actions while favoring methods of helping those less fortunate in society. Politicians began pushing for more equality in society while advocating such schemes as graduated income taxes and inheritance taxes. Writers of the early 1900s attacked many of the wealthy elite and their corruption of the democratic process. These same "muckrakers" took some of the gilt edge off what Mrs. John King Van Rensselaer called the "silvergilts and goldfish," the established aristocratic name for the "nouveau riche."[47] Frederick Townsend Martin acknowledged what was happening to his own class of idle rich stating sadly that "when the nineteenth century closed, America worshipped great wealth. It sanctified its possessors. It deified the hundred-millionaire. In five years' time America has learned to hate great wealth."[48]

Thorstein Veblen, an eminent sociologist and economist, had been a leader of the assault upon the new rich in his 1899 volume, *The Theory of the Leisure Class.* Veblen theorized that after the historic struggle for necessities had been gained, a struggle for wealth was carried on for emulation and honor.[49] A conspicuous leisure or abstention from ordinary labor resulted which led to characteristic occupations of the leisured class such as government, war, devout observances, and sport.[50] It was in sport that Veblen saw the greatest amount of conspicuous consumption, the dry rot of a vibrant, advancing society. Conspicuous leisure and conspicuous consumption were to be condemned according to Veblen. As sport represented both, he attacked sport as well as the leisure class. "Sports are substantially of a predatory, social disintegrating effect," said Veblen. Furthermore he believed that the addiction to sport in the form of participation, sentiment, and moral support was a characteristic of the leisure class and was shared in common with lower class delinquents.[51] This addiction to sport, in Veblen's view, "in a peculiar degree marks an arrested development of man's moral nature."[52]

The rise of wealth in middle America probably did more to take the focus in sport away from the idle rich than did Veblen's biting remarks. The stimulation which the new rich had given to sport in the period after the Civil War had created an interest in sport in the masses. Not all sports of the rich were to become popular with all segments of society. There is little question, though, that such sports as horse racing, water sports, archery, tennis, golf, riflery, bicycling, and billiards were popularized first by the upper social class, later to be taken up by those socially and economically below them. The influence of the social elite had declined by World War I and would continue to do so, but not before its dominance had been strongly felt.

REFERENCES

1. Dixon Wecter, *The Saga of American Society* (New York: C. Scribner's Sons, 1937), p. 204.

2. *Ibid.*, p. 108.

3. *Ibid.*, pp. 132, 139.

4. C. D. Warner, Aspects of American Life, *Atlantic Monthly*, XLIII (1879), p. 9.

5. John H. Illingworth, *Twenty Challenges for the America's Cup* (New York: St. Martin's Press, 1969), pp. 11-19; Edwin P. Hoyt, *The Defenders* (New York: A. S. Barnes, 1969). 11-25; and Don C. Seitz, *The James Gordon Bennetts* (Indianapolis: Bobbs-Merrill, 1928), pp. 253-258.

6. Mrs. John King Van Rensselaer, *The Social Ladder* (New York: Henry Holt, 1924), pp. 241-242.

7. Wecter, *Saga of American Society*, pp. 455, 457.

8. James F. Muirhead, *The Land of Contrasts: A Briton's View of His American Kin* (Boston: Lamson, Wolffe, 1898), p. 122.

9. Refer to Chapters 5 and 7 *in this text*.

10. *Spirit of the Times*, February 20, 1858, p. 8.

11. Dale A. Somers, *The Rise of Sports in New Orleans, 1850-1900.* (Baton Rouge: Louisiana State University Press, 1972), pp. 77-78.

12. Charles E. Trevathan, *The American Thoroughbred* (New York: Macmillan, 1905), pp. 365-369.

13. John A. Krout, *Annuals of American Sport*, Vol. XV of *Pageant of America* (New Haven, Conn.: Yale University Press, 1929), p. 36; Trevathan, *American Thoroughbred*, pp. 330-331; and Allan Nevins, *The Emergency of Modern America, 1865-1878*, Vol. VIII of *A History of American Life* (New York: Macmillan, 1927), p. 219.

14. Frank G. Griswold, *Race Horses and Racing, Recollections* (Norwood, Mass.: Privately Printed, ca. 1925), pp. 29, 42-43.

15. S. Conant Foster, The New York Athletic Club, *Outing*, IV (September 1884), pp. 403-415; Duncan Edwards, Life at the Athletic Clubs, *Scribner's Monthly*, XVIII (July 1895), pp. 4-23: and Bob Considine and Fred G. Jarvis, *The First Hundred Years: A Portrait of the NYAC* (London: Collier-Macmillan, 1969), pp. 9-12.

16. Athletics in America, *The Saturday Review*, LVIII (October 11, 1884), p. 464.

17. Foster, The New York Athletic Club, pp. 410-411.

18. Considine, *The First Hundred Years*, pp. 18, 26.

19. Charles P. Sawyer, Amateur Track and Field Athletics, *Scribner's Magazine*, VII (June 1890), 775-782; and Edwards, Life at the Athletic Clubs, p. 9.

20. Daniel J. Ferris, The A.A.U. is Formed, *The Amateur Athlete*, IX (December 1938), p. 5.

21. *Ibid.*, pp. 35, 38.

22. John A. Lucas, The First Great International Track Meet, *Sports Illustrated*, XXXVII (October 23, 1972, Midwest ed.), pp. M6-M8.

23. Richard D. Mandell, First American Olympians, *Sports Illustrated*, XXXIII (August 3, 1970), pp. E5-E8; and John Kiernan and Arthur Daley, *The Story of the Olympic Games* (Philadelphia: J. B. Lippincott, 1948), pp. 18-30.

24. C. A. Bristed, Club Life, *Nation*, I (July 6, 1865), p. 12.

25. Wecter, *Saga of American Society*, pp. 253-254.

26. E. S. Nadal, Clubs in London and America, *Scribner's Monthly*, IX (1891), p. 298.

27. Ripley Hitchcock, Country Club Life, *Chautauquan*, IX (1889), pp. 601-603.

28. Edward S. Martin, Country Clubs and Hunt Clubs in America, *Scribner's Magazine*, XVIII (1895), pp. 302-321; Nadal, Clubs in London and America, p. 302.; and Caspar W. Whitney, Evolution of the Country Club, *Harper's Magazine*, X (December 1894), pp. 16-33.

29. Gustov Kobbé, The Country Club and Its Influence on American Social Life, *Outlook*, LXVIII (1901), pp. 253-266.

30. *Ibid.*, p. 256.

31. A poem by Sarah N. Cleghorn as quoted by Walter Lord, *The Good Years, From 1900 to the First World War* (New York: Harper & Brothers, 1960), p. 320.

32. Kobbé, The Country Club, p. 255.

33. Mark Sullivan, *Our Times, The United States 1900-1925*, VI vols. (New York: Charles Scribner's Sons, 1925), I, p. 63.

34. Seitz, *The James Gordon Bennetts*, p. 218.

35. *Ibid.*, pp. 251-252.

36. J. D. Jerold Kelley, *American Yachts: Their Clubs and Races* (New York: Charles Scribner's Sons, 1884), pp. 20-32.

37. Seitz, *The James Gordon Bennetts*, p. 261.

38. Richard O'Connor, *The Scandalous Mr. Bennett* (Garden City, N.Y.: Doubleday, 1962), pp. 51-52.

39. E. Willard Roby, The Beginnings of American Polo, *Outing*, XL (1902), p. 318.

40. *Spirit of the Times*, September 16, 1876, p. 152.

41. *New York Times*, A Walking Match, May 6, 1874, p. 8; and *New York Daily Tribune*, May 6, 1874, p. 8.

42. *New York Times*, May 11, 1874, p. 8.

43 *Ibid.*, March 24, 1878, p. 1.

44. Gerald Redmond, *The Caledonian Games in Nineteenth-Century America* (Rutherford, N.J.: Fairleigh Dickinson University Press, 1971), pp. 81, 85, 97-98.

45. O'Connor, *The Scandalous Mr. Bennett*, pp. 137-143.

46. John Frederick Martin, *Passing of the Idle Rich* (Garden City, N.Y.: Doubleday, Page & Co., 1911), p. 149.

47. Van Rensselaer, *The Social Ladder*, p. 202.

48. Martin, *Passing of the Idle Rich*, p. 111.

49. Thorstein Veblen, *The Theory of the Leisure Class* (New York: The Modern Library, 1934), p. 25.

50. *Ibid.*, pp. 38-40.

51. *Ibid.*, p. 269, 271.

52. *Ibid.*, p. 256. The Polish exile, Adam G. de Gurowski saw in the mid-1800s that Americans attached "more value to outward distinctions than to inner worth of an individual. . . ." He wrote that "the love of show and of shining, of keeping up external appearances, and of thus winning consideration, is carried by the Americans to a degree unusual in Europe. . . . See de Gurowski, "Customs, Manners, Habits, etc." in Carl Bode, *Mid-Century American Life in the 1850s* (Carbondale: Southern Illinois University Press, 1972), p. 6. One might attribute this showy materialism to America's historic lack of an aristocratic class. With a less structured class system, it took skill or show to stand out, not noble birth. Show was the quickest way to be noticed and to attain status.

CHAPTER 11

The National Pastime:
A Game for the Masses

As much as society dictated the sporting tastes, it was the masses who created the sporting symbol of America; baseball, the national pastime. For the entire period from the Civil War until after World War I no other sport dominated the sport scene as did baseball. Mark Twain called it the "symbol" of America. The masses took it as their game, a symbol of exuberant, individualistic, and driving spirit. It mattered little that it had British origins or that socially conscious urbanites first organized it in America; the masses of Americans thought of it as their game, and one native to America.

Like so many games played in the United States, baseball's origins are shrouded in the British past. In Britain among the games of bat and ball that were played from Medieval times was rounders, the forerunner of baseball. The first known written rules of baseball are found in a 1744 British book of etiquette, *A Pretty Little Pocket Book*, which went through 11 editions from 1744 to 1790. In America it was first published in 1762 and it contained a little ditty titled, "Base-Ball."

> The Ball once struck off
> Away flies the Boy
> To the next destin'd Post
> And then Home with Joy.[1]

More than a half-century before, this game and others had been criticized by a member of the British Puritan ministry for he had "seen Morris-dancing, cudgel-playing, baseball, and cricket, and many other sports on the Lord's Day."[2] Baseball, then, had British antecedents. As Britain was already playing bat and ball games such as rounders, one old cat, stoolball, and baseball, we need not concern ourselves at this point with disproving the erroneous belief still held by some that baseball is of American origin.

There is some evidence that a form of baseball was being played in America toward the end of the Colonial period. The first recorded game, if it can be called that, occurred during the Revolutionary War when one of George Washington's Valley Forge troopers recorded in his journal that he had "exercised in the afternoon in the intervals played at base." Following the war a student at Princeton College, who obviously lacked the skills which demanded much practice, reported in his diary: "A fine day, play baste ball in the campus but am beaten for I miss both catching and striking the ball."[3]

In the early 1800s baseball, with no established written rules, was becoming more popular. It is clear that rules existed for it would have been impossible otherwise for Thurlow Weed and more than 40 other men between the ages of eighteen and forty to have played baseball every afternoon during the 1825 ball playing season in Rochester, New York. Weed, who became a noted New York politician, gives us no details in his reminiscences of this game other than that it was played on an 8- or 10-acre ball ground.[4] Others have left reminiscences of their ball playing days in the early decades of the 1800s including one who wrote in the 1850s that for two decades "baseball has been a *popular game* wherever I have lived" and was almost always the game played after a barn or house raising in the rural districts of New York.[5]

Written rules of the game of baseball (or rounders as it was often called because one "rounded" the bases) are described in an 1829 English children's book, *The Boy's Own Book*, which was also published in Boston. The book described rounders in which a pitched ball made of soft material was struck by bat or hand. Once the ball was struck the players ran the bases in a clockwise direction and were put out by being hit with the ball between bases on the diamond shaped field. Three missed swings (or strikes) was also out, and when the whole team (no specified number) had batted the other side took its place. These were the simple rules of rounders. Five years later Robin Carver plagiarized *The Boy's Own Book* and issued his *The Book of Sports* in which he changed the name of rounders to base, the rules being the same as rounders. Before the decade of the 1830s had ended another book, *The Boy's Book of Sports* was printed and the game was called base ball with the players being required to run the bases in a counter-clock motion similar to the practice today.[6] It is obvious that Abner Doubleday, as will be seen later, did not invent baseball in 1839. It was already played by children and adults with some semblance of rules, with both play and rules having their roots in England, the place of origin of most American sports.

Base-ball as played on the Boston Commons in the 1830s before the Doubleday myth was developed.

THE KNICKERBOCKERS AND THE POPULARITY OF BASEBALL

Baseball, though it was popular, was only played in an unorganized manner by the 1840s as were nearly all sports in the United States at that time. It was in the forties that form and well organized rules were given baseball by the socially conscious New York Knickerbockers, a group of upper middle class New York City professionals and businessmen. The Knickerbockers, being a social club, began playing baseball on certain afternoons during the summer of 1842 at the Elysian Fields in Hoboken, New Jersey, a surburban summer resort. As a relaxation and recreation this activity served the club well for the next few years. In 1845, one of the Knickerbocker members, Alexander Cartwright, decided that the rules of baseball should be codified and a regular baseball organization should be formed.[7]

The rules which Cartwright developed became the basis for organized baseball in America. Many of the rules would be readily recognized today. The Knickerbockers played on a field with the four bases 90 feet apart. There were 9 players with each player in a definite position, the pitcher being in the middle of the diamond shaped infield, 45 feet from the batter. There were three outs per inning with the batters hitting in rotation. Rather than the old practice of hitting the player with the ball to put him out (soaking), the player was to be tagged or forced out by having the ball reach the base before the runner. These rules, with little modification, have remained as the basis of baseball.

Some of the rules have changed from those of the original Knickerbockers. At first 21 runs (then called "aces") constituted a game, not 9 innings. Under the original Cartwright rules an out would result if the ball was caught on the first bounce as well as for a fly ball. In addition the pitcher had to toss the ball underhand with an unbent elbow, similar to the game of softball today. Lastly, though there was no rule to govern it, no one wore gloves which of course made fielding more difficult and led to teams achieving the necessary 21 runs in a relatively short period of time.

Had the nature of baseball differed the Knickerbocker Club might have been successful in its attempt to keep baseball an exclusive, amateur sport out of reach of the masses. The character of the game, however, presaged any exclusiveness which the organizers of baseball may have desired. To keep a sport from the masses one of three conditions has to exist: its cost must be prohibitive, it must take more time than laborers can devote to it, or it must occupy space to which masses do not have access. Baseball was one of the least expensive sports to participate in, requiring only a bat and ball. Though the time limitation was a factor some workers in the 1850s were willing to get up at dawn to play a game before work, or to participate only on weekends. The space limitation was not as significant in the 1850s as it might have been in urban America a half-century later. As a result most young men could find an open space or a park to use if they desired to play. So the Knickerbocker team, from 1845 to 1860, composed of 17 merchants, 12 clerks, 4 professional men, 2 insurance men, 1 bank teller, 1 hatter, 1 cooperage owner, 1 stationer, 1 United States Marshall, 1 "Segar" dealer, and several "gentlemen," could not keep baseball part of an exclusive domain.[8] Baseball, unlike the more costly sports such as horse racing, polo, yachting, tennis, and golf, soon became popular with men of all means.

The popularity of baseball can be attributed to several factors. More than one American reflecting on the times believed that the excitement of baseball as played in the mid-nineteenth century made it the most popular of all sports. Thomas Wentworth Higginson, preacher, reformer, and litterateur, wrote in 1858 that baseball was a game "whose briskness and unceasing activity are perhaps more congenial . . . to our national character, than the comparative deliberations of cricket."[9] Another shrewd observer, Mark Twain, later called baseball the "very symbol, the outward and visable expression, of the drive and push and rush and struggle of the raging, tearing, booming nineteenth century!"[10] Similar sentiment was expressed by the most important sporting journal of its day, *The Spirit of the Times*, when it stated that baseball "is a pastime that best suits the temperament of our people."[11] When *Harper's Weekly* asked in 1859 whether baseball was really "our national game" a reader replied that it was not only popular and organized in the cities, but that it was commonly played in the then western states of Ohio, Indiana, and Michigan though it was not well organized. He noted a phenomonon among public school children that baseball was "the game" during recess and noon hour, a popular event a century and more later.[12]

AMATEUR BASEBALL AND THE DESIRE TO WIN

As the United States neared the Civil War, baseball appeared to be gaining what *The Spirit of the Times* claimed for it in the 1850s, that is, status as the national game. It had spread from New York City, which had about 50 organized teams in 1856, to major urban areas such as Cleveland, Chicago, New Orleans, and San Francisco. Everywhere, before the Civil conflict, it was solely an amateur game, but only because it had not yet been exploited for its commercial values. There was nothing particularly moral or pure about baseball because its players were not being paid to participate. It may well be that the only sports which can be kept purely amateur are those which are either aristocratic (for the participants do not need to be concerned about their finances as they play) or those which are not generally attractive to spectators. Because organized amateur baseball was thriving in the 1850s an amateur association was formed in 1857 composed of the baseball clubs of New York and vicinity. Fourteen clubs were represented in the original meeting called by the Knickerbockers and three others. The next year they officially named the organization the National Association of Base Ball Players and counted among their numbers 22 of the more than 50 New York area teams.[13] The NABBP created two rules associated with the amateur spirit. One stated that no player could be paid; the other that no player or official could bet on the games.

Unfortunately for amateur baseball neither rule was successfully upheld for long, and it was primarily the interest generated in the game among the masses which led to gambling and more importantly to the paying of players. As early as 1858 a crowd of about 2000 paid 50¢ admission each to see a baseball game at the New York Fashion Race Course. Two years later 15,000 paid to see two Brooklyn teams compete. The betting instinct in the American culture which had been

The gentlemanly New York Knickerbockers remained amateur, but professionals began to dominate in the 1860s. (Courtesy of National Baseball Hall of Fame and Museum.)

exhibited in colonial times in horse races and cockfights, found its way into the new national pastime. With the increasing interest generated among the city dwellers there was a greater desire to produce winners. Winning in turn would increase spectators and gate receipts. Rivalries created in the new Association, intensified by a gambling interest in the outcome of key games, led to occasional high tension, controversies, and eventual riots among players, umpires, and fans.[14]

For most of the clubs it became more important to win than to be gentlemen sportsmen as the original Knickerbockers had proposed. Winning, fierce competition, and the commercial aspect of baseball reflected the dominant values of the new laissez faire capitalism which was becoming apparent in America at mid-century. Though the rules of the Amateur Association strictly forbade payment of players there is evidence that certain players, especially pitchers, were being paid on the side for playing for certain teams. Not only was this covert professionalism in existence, but the players were regularly dividing the gate receipts, a sure sign of professional, as opposed to amateur, status. By 1863 the NABBP recognized that professional players existed in their organization.[15] Winning had become the dominating feature of the game, leading to the downfall of amateur baseball as the leading force in the direction baseball would move. Only the Civil War, and then only for a few short years, would slow the movement toward bringing about the first all-professional team.

THE CIVIL WAR IMPACT UPON BASEBALL

No single event helped more to promote baseball as a game of the masses than did the Civil War. Even though organized baseball was played in major urban areas before the firing upon Fort Sumter there were millions of Americans who had never seen a systematic game using the basic New York rules. Both the horror and boredom of war contributed to the spread of the game. It is likely that a large percentage of the estimated eight million soldiers, north and south, had played some form of baseball before their entry into the conflict. As the war progressed the need for recreational relief from the strain of conflict or the need for activity after long periods of inactivity led the young men to pursue the sport of baseball. Soldiers from Kansas or Wisconsin or Ohio were often in contact with those from places like New York which had a number of soldiers who had played on organized teams. At one camp there were an estimated 40,000 army spectators at a Christmas Day game in 1862 between two picked nines of their comrades.[16] Many troopers, keeping diaries and writing memoirs, reported playing baseball during their war years. Men on furlough brought the organized game with them as they returned home. Albert G. Spalding, then thirteen years of age and soon to be a famous pitcher, was taught how to play baseball in Rockford, Illinois in

Baseball was played during the Civil War even by Union soldiers in a Confederate prison camp in Salisbury, North Carolina. (Courtesy of I. N. Phelps Stokes Collection, Prints Division, New York Public Library, Astor, Lenox and Tilden Foundations.)

1863 by a wounded returning veteran. Even in some prison camps baseball games were reported and the only known illustration of baseball being played during the war showed the excitement of a game played by Union prisoners at Salisbury, North Carolina in the early days of the war.

Many soldiers, then, were introduced to the New York style of baseball in the years between the firing on Fort Sumter and the collapse of the Confederacy. The mustering out of the hundreds of thousands of veterans in 1865 and 1866 helped to intensify the development of baseball which would likely have grown even without the impetus of war. In the west as in the east the two years following the Civil War saw a phenomenal growth of organized city teams and college nines. The "Frontier Baseball Club" of Leavenworth, Kansas chartered a team in 1867 which was composed primarily of Civil War veterans.[17] A number of the 1867 state champions in Wisconsin, hailing from Beloit, were army returnees.[18] In Minnesota, which had been a state for less than a decade, there was no less enthusiasm for baseball. Teams were promoted by individuals and by communities so that one newspaper in 1867 reported that "the game of Base Ball has become so much the style that nearly every village and hamlet has its club, and to be a member of the first nine is now looked upon as being nearly as honorable a position as a seat in the legislature."[19] In the same year the *Spirit of the Times* said that it had "become the rage with all classes and conditions."[20] Western newspapers as well as those in the east were calling baseball a "truly American game."[21] Indeed it was. The *New York Times* reported that "there is scarcely a village throughout the country which does not contain one or more associations devoted to the exposition of the beauties of our national game."[22]

PROFESSIONAL BASEBALL BECOMES RECOGNIZED

The National Association of Base Ball Players, which had been somewhat quieted by the war, continued to be the leading force in rules and organization. But the movement toward the professionalization of the game, begun in the early 1860s, continued as teams composed of both amateurs and professionals competed in hotly contested games before larger and larger crowds. The increasing number of spectators (spending as much as 25¢ admission or one-fourth of a laborer's average daily wage) demanded higher performance and winning teams. Outstanding players from the lower and middle economic classes were lured by the larger gate receipts and promises of making good money in baseball. It was becoming more common for players to offer their services to the highest bidder in the form of a share of the gate receipts, a political job like those offered in New York City or in the United States Treasury Department in Washington, D.C., cash payments, or eventually a straight salary. Outright salaries were reported by several New York teams, and there were a number of other similar reports by the end of the 1860s.[23] Thus when the Cincinnati Red Stockings signed all of their players to professional contracts in 1869, they were only making official what a number of other teams were already pursuing, that is, professional baseball.

The Cincinnati Red Stockings had been organized shortly after the Civil War and had been defeated badly in 1867 by a touring Washington Nationals team. Prodded by this defeat and by competition from another local Cincinnati team, a young lawyer, Aaron Champion, decided to hire an outstanding team. He first contracted Harry Wright, a talented player and even more gifted manager and organizer, who began hiring professionals in 1868 and completed an all-professional team the next year. In 1869 the Cincinnati Reds, with a ten man payroll of $9,300, set out to challenge all comers for one-third of the gate receipts. The Red Stockings went on their historic crosscountry barnstorming tour in which they defeated 56 teams without losing a game. In their journey they played before an estimated 200,000 spectators and tested out the newly built transcontinental railroad that allowed them to play as far west as San Francisco.[24] Not until 1870 was the Cincinnati team defeated, and then it took 11 innings for the Brooklyn Atlantics to stop them, 8 to 7, before 9,000 fans who had each paid 50¢ admission. Each Brooklyn player was paid $364, equivalent to an average yearly laborer's wage in 1870. If that payment were based upon a major league schedule a century later, it would have been equivalent to a yearly salary of well over $50,000.

The influence of the professional and successful Cincinnati team was electric upon the development of professional baseball. The amateur National Association of Base Ball Players soon lost control of its more or less aristocratic attempt to keep players from being paid to perform. The masses had won in their desire to see highly skilled, winning teams which demanded that those players not prosperous enough to support themselves while playing baseball should be paid for their skills. Early in 1871 the National Association of Professional Base Ball Players was born and with it came teams from New York City, Philadelphia, Washington, D.C., Boston, Cleveland, Chicago, Fort Wayne, Rockford, Illinois, and Troy, New York. Cincinnati, which had started the all-professional team idea, fell victim of the bidding for player talent as their best players "jumped" to other teams.

The NAPBBP took essential control of organized baseball in 1871,

The first all-professional team was the Cincinnati Red Stockings of 1869.

and professional baseball has-continued in that capacity for over a century, setting rules and standards. (This has been quite unlike football which has for the most part been a college dominated game.) The control and guidance of the NAPBBP, however, was at best tenuous for no sooner had the first major baseball league been set up than it ran into difficulties which jeopardized its existence. The NAPBBP was organized by the players primarily, unlike any of the major professional sports today. Though financial support came from club owners, the owners were more interested in public esteem than in business profits. Players had freedom of contract and mobility in baseball's first major league.

Player contracts and mobility were important to the demise of the league which existed only five years. By allowing a player to sign a contract with the highest bidding club, the richest team was able to field the strongest team. It so happened that the Boston Red Stockings, who stole the Cincinnati name and signed its best players, was able to dominate the league. It won the pennant four years in the five-year existence as the best players "revolved" to the club. The club paid salaries averaging about $2,000 per man, five times the average laborer's income in the mid-1870s. In athletics if there is continual uneven competition the competitive situation breaks down as the financial support for the weaker teams fails. A league like the NAPBBP, which allowed the competitive edge to pass to Boston with a 71 win, 8 loss record in 1875 and with the Brooklyn Atlantics winning only two of 44 games, was bound to collapse.[25] The NAPBBP needed some means of binding players to one club, but the player dominated league failed to use the reserve clause techniques of later professional leagues.

Though the "revolving" of talent to the rich clubs was probably the major cause of the NAPBBP failure, there were other reasons for the demise of the first major league. Individual teams scheduled their own games and playing dates, and as a result some teams played many more games than their opponents while there was a constant battle to choose advantageous opponents and playing dates. Umpires, using a British tradition, were unpaid. They were picked by the home team which led to constant bickering because the American game of baseball played by the masses lacked the British upper class amateur notion of sportsmanship and fair play. In addition professional baseball was ripe for gambling and the bribing of players which led to the lack of confidence in the NAPBBP. "Hippodroming" was the name used for throwing of games for money, a term derived from the fixing of horse races, a problem common then as now in the sport of racing. That bribing of players found its way into baseball is probably not surprising for public and private graft and corruption after the

Civil War is legendary and sport has often been found to reflect many of the values of society. These problems combined with the lack of stability caused by teams entering the league for an entry fee of $10 and dropping out as easily led to its collapse in 1875.[26]

THE NATIONAL LEAGUE IS BORN

Professional baseball did not die with the NAPBBP, but player dominance did. When a socially conscious and profit motivated Chicago businessman, William A. Hulbert, gained control of the Chicago team of the NAPBBP in 1875 he decided to organize baseball on the basis of capital (club dominance) rather than labor (player dominance). He proceeded to get the clubs of St. Louis, Louisville, and Cincinnati along with his own Chicago club to represent the Western clubs and then persuaded four teams from Boston, New York, Philadelphia, and Hartford to form the Eastern clubs with the purpose of joining a new league, the National League of Professional Baseball Clubs. The National League was finalized in early 1876 with the players relegated to positions inferior to the club owners, a turnabout from the previous major league. With club owners in command baseball soon developed conditions similar to those produced in industrial America where the workers became subservient to and exploited by management. Yet this is seemingly what was needed to bring order to organized professional baseball. It was a monopoly, then as now, but it was competitive within that monopoly.

The order which the National League desired was seen in its original constitution. Following the business ethics of the time, the League set up strict worker rules and blacklisted any player who violated the constitution, playing rules, or his contract. Player contracts were sent to the league office to prevent "jumping" or "revolving" to other clubs during the season. This, though, did not check a player at the end of the season from negotiating a higher salaried contract with any of the other seven National League teams.[27] The reserve rule which bound a player to one team was only a few years away.

To further insure a more orderly league it was decided to allow only clubs from cities of 75,000 or more population to enter the League. To insure quality control two negative votes of League members would prevent a new club from receiving a franchise. Territorial rights were also drawn up to prevent one club from being set up in the proximity of another. Desiring to prevent some of the disorder of scheduling which plagued the NAPBBP, a 70-game schedule was decided upon in which all clubs played 10 games with each of the others. With an orderly, profit motivated business operation in mind, the League founders wanted to attract a good class of spectator and raise the moral image of professional baseball. In forbidding Sunday baseball they decided that consideration for the lingering belief in a Puritan Sabbath outweighed the profits which Sunday baseball might have brought to some cities which had no Blue Laws. By informally agreeing to a relatively high 50¢ admission price there may have been another thought as important as the revenue; that a high price might keep out the trouble makers, uncouth individuals, vulgar masses, or the "hoi polloi." Even if unruly fans did get in, the umpires, who were now being paid, could ask the police to remove them.[28] Nothing could have raised the image of baseball more than the attempt to do away with gambling and hippodroming. Betting on club grounds was forbidden, and more importantly the League took steps to prevent the throwing of games. Situations had previously occurred in which two teams traveled across the country and acted like chief rivals, but threw games with impunity to keep the series close and insure larger crowds. The National League attempted to squelch this fraudulent competition by preventing teams from playing in any but their home towns. It seemed to be a necessary measure to preserve the integrity of the proclaimed national game.[29]

The National League had created the basis for an enduring professional sport through owner management rather than player control as they pursued primarily monopolistic rather than laissez faire attitudes toward rules and regulations. At the same time they created an outward mien of morally sound practices. After surviving the first five years of existence in the depression ridden 1870s, most of the clubs became more profitable businesses as baseball reached unprecedented heights of popularity in the 1880s. The National League did not go unchallenged as rival leagues sought profit and prestige in the 1880s and 1890s, but in each case the interlopers were beaten back in classic business struggles of the new industrial America.

As baseball became more and more a big business, it had to solve constant financial problems. Bankrupt franchises were primarily responsible for the large number of teams, 22, which were in the National League at various times from 1876 to the early 1900s. Such unlikely sites as Troy, New York; Worcester, Massachusetts; Hartford, Connecticut; and Indianapolis, Indiana were National League cities at various times. Sometimes rival major leagues, such as the American Association in the 1880s, the Union Association in 1884, and the Players League in 1890, competed for players and spectators cutting into expected revenues. Furthermore the long standing National League rule forbidding Sunday baseball affected those cities which had no Blue Laws and which had large populations of Germans who liked to drink beer. Moral suasions of the League may have cost certain franchises their existence. Some could have been made profitable by tapping the urban labor class who had little time other than Sunday to see the professional game. Indeed Sunday ball was such a lure to Cincinnati in the early 1880s that it was expelled from the league for scheduling games on the Sabbath. St. Louis dropped out of the league in 1877 when permission was not granted for scheduling League games on Sunday, a policy which was changed by the early 1900s.[30] What the League was doing was little different from other areas of society, for a number of New England industrialists a generation before would only hire and retain factory workers who attended church on Sunday, and the Philadelphia Centennial Exposition of 1876 was never open on a Sunday.[31] All of this may indicate what a reforming writer noted in 1830. He said that American society "is much more strict with regard to the sins of amusement, than with regard to the sins of business."[32] Yet the sins of business in baseball as in the new industrial society were strong forces in the development of the professional game of baseball. When baseball became a business, as it did in the 1870s, it developed the undemocratic and authoritarian methods of the business world which it considered necessary for its survival. Of most importance for baseball's existence was the "reserve clause" which helped to reduce salaries and kept players in voluntary servitude to one club.

THE RESERVE CLAUSE AND BONDAGE IN BASEBALL

If baseball was casting back the values of American society in the generation before the twentieth century, it was probably seen most clearly in the reserve clause which was created by the National League in 1879. The gravest threat to professional baseball, as with most business, was financial failure. Were the National League to have remained a free competitive system in which each club struggled to survive by hiring the best players, then the clubs would have bid each other into debt. Eventually the competitors, the baseball clubs, sought ways to end the cutthroat practices which led to extremely high salaries and players "revolving" to the richest clubs. Through the reserve clause, competition was reduced; wage agreements replaced wage wars. By abandoning the laissez faire, free competitive system the club owners sought to divide the business among the former competitors in a way similar to that of other industrialists who formed trade associations, pooling agreements, and later trusts, all of which were intended to bring about stability and increased profits. In this way the National League had created territorial rights and within a few years had developed the reserve clause in player contracts.

The reserve clause gave a baseball owner a permanent option on a player's services. When a player signed his contract he was in effect agreeing to permanent, voluntary bondage to that team, which has been called a "vestige of the preindustrial peonage system. . . ."[33] If a player wanted to continue playing major league baseball, he was required to play with the original team unless he was traded, sold, or given his outright release.

At first, in 1879, the National League agreed to allow 5 players on each club to be reserved so that at the end of the season the top stars of a team could not seek employment at higher salaries with other clubs. Originally the reserve clause was more of a power play to prevent Chicago, the richest club, from gaining a corner on the league's best talent. Four years later the two major leagues, the American Association and the National League, agreed to raise the total reserved players to 11, nearly an entire club at that time. This all seemed logical to the club owners for they knew that their profits depended upon rather equal competition among the clubs to insure spectator interest, and that salaries could be kept lower by reducing the bargaining position of the players. Furthermore, with reserve clause contracts the owners could, at times, make enormous profits by selling the contract to another team.[34] No clearer exploitation of labor by management could be found in the world of sport in the nineteenth century.

Even John Ward, a player and baseball radical of the 1880s and 1890s, agreed that the reserve rule "more than anything placed base-ball on the basis of a permanent business investment."[35] Ward was a rare ball player in the nineteenth century for he attended college, at Penn State, before playing professional baseball. While starring for the New York Giants he attended Columbia where he received a law degree with honors. He was a celebrity of sorts, married a noted actress, hobnobbed with some of New York society members, and was repeatedly asked to be part of baseball management. Yet, with all that, he led the fight for player's rights. In 1885, at the time of a rising union movement among American laborers, Ward organized The Brotherhood of Professional Base Ball Players. Within a year the Brotherhood had members from each of the National League clubs, and they were ready to attack the reserve clause, blacklisting practices, and the salary ceiling which the League had adopted. Beginning in 1887 the Brotherhood met with League officials in an attempt to reach accord on the player grievances. The League politely listened, but made little effort to modify the all-important reserve rule. With the leadership of Ward, the Brotherhood revolted and formed its own league, the Players League, in direct opposition to the National League.[36]

A true labor-management conflict was born. The business dominated National League immediately charged the player group with creating anarchy, a common ploy when labor strife was imminent.

John Montgomery Ward organized the first baseball union, The Brotherhood of Professional Base Ball Players, in the 1880s. (Courtesy of National Baseball Hall of Fame and Museum.)

After a year in which both leagues operated with fraudulent attendance figures, blackmail, bribes, and charges and recriminations, both leagues lost large amounts of money and the Player League folded. The National League, which had rescinded its ceiling on salaries and changed its reserve clause during the heated 1890 season, reverted to its monopolistic ways as soon as the Players League was crushed. In the National League struggle for survival, any competition among member clubs for profits was subordinated to cooperation to prevent the financially weaker clubs from going bankrupt. Individualism had succumbed to combination, and when the Players League died in 1890, there was a decade of baseball monopoly in which the capitalists punished the players by lowering salaries over 30 percent while increasing their own profits.[37] The reserve clause was to be challenged generation after generation, though unsuccessfully, into the late twentieth century, and it took about eighty years for an effective player organization to be founded which would once again challenge the club owners.

BASEBALL AND NATIONALISM: THE DOUBLEDAY MYTH

Organized professional baseball had survived its early existence partially through the leadership given by the club owners who made it fiscally sound through tough labor practices. The game, whether professional or amateur, was assuredly the most popular sport in America for the last half of the nineteenth century. In the years between the organizing of baseball by Alexander Cartwright and the New York Knickerbockers and the beginning of the twentieth century, the United States had fought a Civil War and preserved the Union. The nation's people had crossed the continent creating a massive frontier society before effectively settling the area. America had begun its swift move to the city and had become the number one industrial nation in the world. The country was big, it was powerful, its influence was spreading worldwide, and there was some justification to boast about the nation and its institutions.

Baseball was a national institution and as such there was a stirring of emotions about its national origins in the 1880s especially after Albert Spalding, who was approaching a monopoly in the sporting goods business, sent a team of all-stars on an exhibition tour around the world in 1889. At a celebration banquet at the famous Delmonico's restaurant, National League president Abraham Mills noted that baseball was of American, not British, origin.[38] It was to be expected that a young nation feeling pride and patriotism would welcome such a statement for its national game.

The statement by Mills did not go unchallenged. Henry Chadwick, a sports writer, sometimes called the father of American baseball, claimed in 1901, as did James Steele three years later, that baseball was of British origin, derived from the game of rounders.[39] Albert Spalding, though, caught up in the nationalistic spirit of the times, called for the formation of a commission to once and for all settle the question of the origin of baseball. Seven prominent men were chosen, including two United States senators, giving the commission respectability. Meanwhile the work of the committee was carried out by the chairman, Abraham Mills, a past president of the National League. After three years of collecting testimony, primarily in the form of reminiscences, the commission reported that baseball was of American origin and had been devised in 1839 by Abner Doubleday of Cooperstown, New York. The sole evidence came from the testimony

Henry Chadwick, "Father of American Baseball," challenged the Doubleday myth without success. (Courtesy of National Baseball Hall of Fame and Museum.)

of an octegenarian who recalled that sixty-eight years before, Abner Doubleday had improved town ball by limiting the number of players, creating definite teams, and placing the pitcher in the middle of the four bases set out in a diamond shape.[40] It mattered little to the commission members that Doubleday was not in Cooperstown in 1839 for they did not check to find out that he was training to be a military officer at West Point. This training led him to a military life and an honored position, for Doubleday claimed that he "aimed the first gun on our side in reply to the attack on Fort Sumter. . . ,"[41] and later commanded a division in the battles of Antietam and Gettysburg. It was during the war that Abraham Mills first met Doubleday; later they became friends. So it was Mills who, using a single piece of reminiscing evidence, consecrated the origin of baseball upon the head of a nationally known Civil War general at a time of chauvinistic nationalism as America felt the rushes of international power at the turn of the century. No wonder the myth caught the imagination of Americans and persisted decades later. There is still a pervasive myth that the Cooperstown Baseball Hall of Fame was built where baseball was developed. Let us praise Doubleday, if we must, for having aimed the first northern gun, but credit the British for first playing a form of baseball which became "simply glorified rounders."[42] If honor is needed give kudos to the New York Knickerbockers and

Alexander Cartwright for organizing the game and forming baseball into a sport which eventually became a game for mass participation and spectator enjoyment.

REFERENCES

1. Robert W. Henderson, *Ball, Bat and Bishop* (New York: Rockport Press, 1947), p. 135.
2. *Ibid.*, p. 132.
3. *Ibid.*, p. 136.
4. Thurlow Weed, *Autobiography* (Boston: Houghton, Mifflin, 1883), p. 202.
5. F. H. Guiwits, Letter to the Editor, *Harper's Weekly*, III (November 5, 1859), p. 707.
6. Henderson, Ball, Bat and Bishop, pp. 144-160.
7. Henry Chadwick, Old Time Baseball, *Outing*, XXXVIII (July 1901), p. 420.
8. Harold Seymour, *Baseball: The Early Years* (New York: Oxford University Press, 1960), p. 16.
9. Thomas Wentworth Higginson, Saints and Their Bodies, *Atlantic Monthly*, I (March 1858), p. 593.
10. Samuel L. Clemens, *Mark Twain's Speeches* (New York: Harper & Brothers, 1923), p. 145.
11. *Spirit of the Times*, May 4, 1867, p. 150, as quoted in John R. Betts, Organized Sport in Industrial America, Ph.D. dissertation, Columbia University, 1951, p. 72.
12. The Cricket Mania, *Harper's Weekly*, III (October 15, 1859), p. 658; and F. H. Guiwits, Letter to the Editor, *Harper's Weekly*, III (November 5, 1859), p. 707.
13. *Spirit of the Times*, March 20, 1858, p. 65.
14. Seymour, *Baseball: The Early Years*, pp. 29-30.
15. David Q. Voigt, *American Baseball: From Gentleman's Sport to the Commissioner System* (Norman: University of Oklahoma Press, 1966), pp. 15-18.
16. *Ibid.*, p. 11.
17. Harold C. Evans, Baseball in Kansas, 1867-1940, *Kansas Historical Quarterly*, IX (May 1940), p. 175.
18. Charles McKenny (ed.), *Educational History of Wisconsin* (Chicago: The Delmont Co., Pub., 1912), p. 369.
19. Cecil O. Monroe, The Rise of Baseball in Minnesota, *Minnesota History*, XIX (June 1938), p. 181.
20. *Spirit of the Times*, May 4, 1867, p. 150.
21. *Grant County* [Wisconsin] *Witness*, October 4, 1866, p.3.
22. *New York Times*, April 15, 1867, p. 8.
23. Seymour, *Baseball: The Early Years*, pp. 47-56.
24. *Ibid.*, pp. 56-57.
25. *Ibid.*, p. 75.
26. David Q. Voigt, Baseball's Lost Centennial, *Journal of Popular Culture*, V (Summer 1971), p. 62.
27. Voigt, *American Baseball*, p. 64.
28. *Ibid.*, pp. 64-65.
29. *Spirit of the Times*, February 12, 1876, p. 12.
30. Seymour, *Baseball: The Early Years*, pp. 93, 135.
31. Thomas C. Cochran and William Miller, *The Age of Enterprise: A Social History of Industrial America* (New York: Harper & Row, 1961), p. 20; and Allan Nevins, *The Emergence of Modern America, 1865-1878* (New York: Macmillan, 1927), p. 307.
32. O. Dewey, Fashionable Amusements, *The Christian Examiner*, VIII (May 1830), p. 201.
33. Max Lerner, *America as a Civilization* (New York: Simon and Schuster, 1957), p. 815.
34. Seymour, *Baseball: The Early Years*, pp. 104-110.
35. John Montgomery Ward, Notes of a Base-Ballist, *Lippincott's Monthly Magazine*, XXXVIII (August 1886), p. 215.

36. John Montgomery Ward, *Base-Ball: How to Become a Player* (Philadelphia: The Penn Pub. Co., 1890), pp. 29-32; and Voigt, *American Baseball*, pp. 154-160.

37. Seymour, *Baseball: The Early Years*, pp. 265-274.

38. *Ibid.*, p. 9.

39. Chadwick, Old Time Baseball, p. 420; and James L. Steele, How the National Game Developed, *Outing*, XLIV (June 1904), p. 333.

40. Henderson, *Ball, Bat and Bishop*, pp. 184-188.

41. Abner Doubleday, I Aimed the First Gun, *Battles and Leaders of the Civil War*, edited by Ned Bradford (New York: Appleton-Century-Crofts, 1956), p. 8.

42. James F. Muirhead, *The Land of Contrasts* (London: Lamson, Wolffe & Co., 1898), p. 111.

CHAPTER 12

College Sport and the Extracurriculum

The rise of intercollegiate athletics is one of the most unique features of the development of organized sport in America. It had British origins to be sure, but nowhere in the world did it become such a dominating feature of student life as it did in American colleges. In the year 1850, the place of sport on college campuses was minimal and nowhere did intercollegiate sport exist. In a half century it was the most important social function of private and public colleges across the land. The period from the mid-nineteenth century to the early 1900s was, as with organized sport in general, the period of transition from unorganized participation within colleges to highly organized intercollegiate competition. To understand how this phenomenon took place and how students alone directed it, it is helpful to gain an insight into college life in the mid-1800s.

COLLEGE LIFE IN THE MID-1800s

The picture of a mid-nineteenth century college was strikingly different from that of a century or even a half century later. Nearly all colleges were church affiliated. Most of the approximately 180 colleges at the time of the Civil War were liberal arts institutions emphasizing the classical studies of Greek and Latin. The more practical studies such as applied sciences or modern languages were not found in the curriculum. Students had to take a set course of studies as the elective system had not been inaugurated. For a nation which was moving into the urban-industrial age the colleges were slow to change their traditional role of preparing individuals for the ministry, law, and the scholarly life. The colleges, whose presidents were overwhelmingly clergymen, continued to pursue a policy of paternalism which produced a rigid system of controls over student life. School officials acting "in loco parentis" produced a set of forbidden activities for all students. A list of prohibited activities in many of these all-male colleges included no drinking, no smoking, no dancing, no card playing, and no absence from campus without presidential approval. In addition, compulsory chapel was demanded as often as 14 times each week as well as compulsory study hours enforced by tutors. For a new country based upon freedom of the individual and for a nation moving from an agrarian economy to an industrial one there was a logical student attitude of defiance toward the regimented life and the unchanging curriculum.

The rejection of the status quo took both a negative and a positive form. First, students in numerous colleges in the early to middle 1800s rebelled against their colleges with such defiant acts as disrupting classes, obstructing compulsory chapel services, burning down college buildings, and physically attacking tutors, professors, and college presidents. These acts of insolence and destruction have been recounted in most college histories. Also chronicled has been the development of a positive reaction to the paternalism of college authorities, the extracurriculum.

The nineteenth century found students creating their own activities to compensate for that part of life which the college administration did not provide. The extracurriculum, which began as a supplement to the unchanging classical curriculum, eventually became the primary concern for many students. Some of the earliest organizations were the literary societies which were formed to discuss and debate current, some would say relevant, literature which had been lacking in the curriculum. Fraternities, too, began to be part of the life of colleges by the mid-1800s, offering an escape from the regimen of daily recitation in the classroom and prayer meetings in the chapel. Oratorical and debating societies developed in the latter 1800s in most colleges as did musical groups and college newspapers. Athletics in the colleges were another avenue for release from the intellectual climate of a classical education. Eventually organized sport came to dominate the extracurriculum.

Sporting contests were not new to college students in the second half of the nineteenth century; only the development of intercollegiate contests was an innovation. College men even in colonial times had spent some idle hours playing such various games as baseball, soccer-football, cricket, wrestling, field hockey, and horse racing—all in a rather unorganized manner. In the mid-1700s aristocratic youth attending William and Mary College in Virginia were fond of horse racing and betting as was society in the colonial south. College authorities, however, saw this as being at cross purposes with the goal of the institution and banned students from keeping horses or "making races, or in backing, or abetting, those made by others."[1] In the north, students at Harvard College in the 1750s, and probably before, played some kind of baseball and football. John Adams, a future president, recorded that as freshmen at Harvard they were required by upperclassmen to provide "batts, balls, and foot balls for use of the students. . . ."[2] Yale, one of seven colleges in America in 1765, permitted its students to punt a football, but forbade them to scrimmage at their game which resembled soccer.[3] Dartmouth, a strict Congregational college, had stringent rules against sporting diversions when it was founded. In the 1770s its students were cautioned against childish recreations: "Whereby their diversions may be turned from that which is purile, such as playing with balls, bowls and other ways of diversion as have necessarily been gone into by students in other places for want of an opportunity to exercise themselves to that which is more useful and better calculated to answer all the great and ends proposed."[4] At Princeton students who had been playing bandy (field hockey) saw their game banned by college authorities in 1787 for being "low and unbecoming gentlemen and scholars."[5] Somehow the Presbyterian authorities had not banned baseball for it had been played a year earlier. A Princeton student of questionable athletic skills recorded in his diary: "A Fine day, play baste ball in the campus but am beaten for I miss both catching and striking the ball."[6] It can be seen, then, that athletic contests were known to college men in the eighteenth century though they were not well organized and often the college authorities looked with a jaundiced eye upon the activities.

THE DEVELOPMENT OF CLASS STRUGGLES

The more-or-less spontaneous sporting contests continued into the nineteenth century when they became slightly more structured with the introduction of class against class struggles. Inter-class contests, often called rushes or class scraps, became a fixed part of most college extracurricula in the nineteenth century and often did not die out until well into the twentieth century. At Harvard and Yale and some lesser known institutions these class struggles erupted on the first Monday of the fall term, called "Bloody Monday."*

Bloody Monday became a tradition at Harvard after its introduction sometime in the early 1800s. Its origin seems to be surrounded by a kind of initiation ceremony of new freshmen into college life. The Bloody Monday event pitted the freshman class of possibly 100

---

*The name "Bloody Monday" was likely coined some time after 1860 though, of course, the same type of rough activity existed well before.

members against the sophomores in a game which resembled soccer and was called by its English name, football. With the tradition firmly established by the 1840s a Harvard sophomore recorded that "the great annual battle between the Sophs and the Fresh came off at the beginning of the term,—we 'licked' them 'all hollow' of course."[7] He retold what John Adams had noted a century before that the freshmen were required to furnish the football, a cost which amounted to about $30 for the year. Tradition in sport, as in all aspects of society, dies slowly. A decade later, in the 1850s, another Harvard sophomore participating in the Bloody Monday contest has given us a feeling for this traditional symbolic sacrifice:

> It was an animated scene, the Delta was quite full say three hundred and upwards on the field, and as the parties rushed from this side to that, now battling desperately contended for every foot, I might add with every foot, then as the ball flew yards over their heads to one side or the other running at full speed to gain it first, it gave one an idea of a real battle with its charges, retreatings and desperate rallies, and too when near the bounds the 'forlorn hope' was not wanting to send it back again over the head of the seeming certain victors. The moon was quite high before we left off playing, so it was a beautiful scene. After the games we formed one huge ring, sang Auld Lang Syne, hurrahed and broke. The Sophs however in double column formed and joined hands rushed across the Delta knocking over all before who would not flee, and to *us* it was jolly fun as we cleared everyone from the front. Thus ended the great contest and praiseworthy victory of the Class of '57.[8]

Though it was a sophomore-freshman battle the seniors and juniors looking on at the festivities at times joined in the fray, and it was not uncommon for a junior-freshmen vs. senior-sophomore contest to result.

Bloody Monday-type confrontations were not isolated events; rather they set the stage for other interclass battles throughout the year taking various forms in different colleges. For instance bandy or field hockey was more popular than football in some institutions and was played north and south. At Trinity College, now Duke University, mid-nineteenth century students engaged in a bandy game in which about 20 players on a side with "big clubs bent round at the lower end" would rush after victory with uplifted clubs swinging right and left, hands being hurt, limbs bruised, shins cracked, and heads struck. According to one observer "it was exciting, it was fun and the weak timid boy was not in it."[9] In addition to bandy and football, baseball in a primitive form, remained a popular pastime, while students on a number of campuses participated in cricket and wrestling.[10]

Generally the faculty and president were not overly concerned with these class scraps, though now and then incidents arose for which they

Harvard's Bloody Monday class battle, as drawn by Winslow Homer in 1857.

felt action must be taken to uphold the dignity of their institutions. As Princeton officials in the 1780s had condemned the student games as "low and unbecoming gentlemen and scholars" so too did Yale officials become involved for they passed a law in 1822 which prohibited "hand or foot ball in the college building or in the college yard" with the penalty being a 50 cent fine or suspension or dismissal from college.[11] Some colleges, rather than taking either a laissez faire or a disapproving attitude, even supported exercise through student games. Henry Wadsworth Longfellow, attending Bowdoin College in the mid-1820s, observed that the college authorities induced students to play a game of ball now and then as an antidote to a rash of sickness on campus. A rage for play resulted, according to Longfellow, with a "thorough-going reformation from inactivity and torpitude."[12] Later, this same reasoning was used to justify intercollegiate athletics. For much of the 1800s, however, college officials generally had no policy toward these extracurricular games, did little to improve or control the occasional athletic activities, and only in times of crisis did they act. Then, without looking deeply into the nature of the action, they might ban the game and with that forget the incident. A few years later the same activity might again be seen played while the faculty and president maintained a laissez faire attitude toward the games.

BEGINNINGS OF INTERCOLLEGIATE PLAY

The development of class games in colleges was a gradual process, much more so than the transition to intercollegiate play which occurred within a generation. This was logical, for colleges in the colonial and early American period were isolated institutions being kept apart by a lack of ready communication or transportation system. Until the railroad came into prominence in the east by the mid-1800s there was no easy way for colleges to expand from interclass games to intercollegiate contests even if the competitive desire existed. Harvard and Yale who participated in the first American intercollegiate contest, a crew meet in 1852, could only have done so with the help of rail transportation. The first intercollegiate baseball contest in 1859 between Amherst and Williams, two Massachusetts colleges, would have been extremely difficult to schedule without train service to connect the institutions, separated by only about 50 miles. Similarly Rutgers and Princeton, who played the first intercollegiate football (soccer) game in 1869, were able to do so because of the railroad which made a difficult 20 mile journey into an easy one.

Both the railroad and intercollegiate athletics had British origins. In technology and in athletics, as in many other aspects of social and economic life, the Americans followed where the British led. The

Industrial Revolution which began in England in the late eighteenth century was seen in America a generation later. The same thing occurred in intercollegiate sport for the two major educational institutions in England, Oxford and Cambridge, had competed in both cricket and rowing in the late 1820s. A generation later the two New England colleges, Harvard and Yale, began the tradition of intercollegiate play in America.

In 1843, Yale students began a boating club. The precedent for collegiate boat clubs had been set by Oxford in 1815 and by Cambridge a decade later. In the United States the first boating clubs, though not collegiate, had been formed on the eastern seaboard in the 1830s especially in the New York area. These were as much social organizations as athletic clubs. When the boating clubs were started at Yale and at Harvard a year later they were also primarily social clubs. Rowing was an enjoyable activity for the club members and competition, at first, was more incidental than purposeful. However, with the help of technology and a mind toward profit making this was all changed nine years before the Civil War.

A member of the Yale crew was riding on the Boston, Concord, and Montreal Railroad on a June day in 1852 when he struck up a conversation with an acquaintance, the Superintendent of the line, James N. Elkins. Elkins was looking for ways to promote his new line which went into the heart of New Hampshire vacationland. He suggested to James Whiton, a Yale junior, that an ideal location for a crew race, which could be viewed from an observation train, would be the calm water of the Winnipesaukee River as it entered New Hampshire's largest body of water, Lake Winnipesaukee. "If you will get up a regatta on the Lake between Yale and Harvard," Elkins said, "I will pay all the bills."[13] Whiton, pleased with the terms, soon contacted a friend of his on the Harvard crew and the offer of a regatta was accepted. For the owner of the railroad, the first intercollegiate contest in America was entirely a commercial venture. The Yale and Harvard crew members, though, did not consider it as such. They thought of it as a "jolly lark" which provided them with an eight-day, all-expense paid vacation on Lake Winnipesaukee thanks to an enterprising businessman. The venture, which was intended to be the harbinger of vacationland travel to New Hampshire, became the auspicious beginnings of intercollegiate sport. The event brought only about 1000 spectators including one presidential candidate, Franklin Pierce, who was campaigning that August in his home state. Those few in attendance saw the Harvard crew of eight defeat two Yale boats in a 2 mile race rowed in about fourteen minutes. A reporter for the New York *Tribune* predicted that intercollegiate sport would "make little stir in the busy world."[14]

CREW: A 'JOLLY LARK' TO SERIOUS WINNING

Intercollegiate athletics in the form of rowing did not immediately make a "stir in the busy world," but it was not long in coming. If a contest meant little to the performers—as did that first rowing contest on Lake Winnipesaukee—it was not likely to cause much excitement among the college student body or general public. Even though Harvard won the initial contest it was not overly important to either crew or to the students of the institutions involved. Only the Yale faculty appeared concerned; they banned contests with Harvard for the next two years. Within three years, though, another Yale-Harvard meeting was scheduled. There seemed to be no visible preparations or training for this meeting, nor did there seem to be a great need to win the contest or to uphold the prestige of the colleges involved. Yet, for the first time, though far from the last, a question of eligibility was raised. Yale believed that the Harvard coxswain, who had previously graduated from Harvard, should not be allowed to participate. Yale really had no one with whom to register an official complaint as the completely student-run contest had no well formulated rules or eligibility standards. Had there been no feeling for the necessity to win, the question of eligibility would not likely have arisen. Institutional pride associated with success in winning was only beginning to appear.

Late in the decade before the Civil War, two other colleges, Trinity in Hartford, Connecticut and Brown in Providence, Rhode Island, joined Harvard and Yale to form the College Union Regatta. The first regatta was cancelled because a Yale crew member accidentally drowned shortly before the scheduled event. The next year, 1859, enthusiasm for the regatta ran high among crew members, students, and the public. A Yale reporter acknowledged the importance of winning when he wrote that the Yale crew was "running faster, eating more and rawer food, which we hope will not be all in vain." It was. Harvard won before an estimated 15,000 to 20,000 spectators at Lake Quinsigamond, near Worcester, Massachusetts. The next day another regatta was held, sponsored by the city of Worcester. This time, with a prize of $100 for first place, Yale was victorious. With the event receiving over three front page columns in James Gordon Bennett's New York *Herald*, interest was being generated for future regattas.[15] Because of the commercialization of college athletics through profit seeking organizations like newspapers and railroads it was little wonder that it was difficult to differentiate between amateur sport and playing for financial stakes. It was clear that victory was becoming more meaningful to a greater number of people.

The following year as the nation approached civil strife so too did

Harvard and Yale. In the regatta, held again at Worcester, Yale claimed that Harvard fouled them. Without waiting for the decision regarding the foul, Harvard fans began celebrating their victory by tearing down doors and signs and proceeded to build a huge victory bonfire which resulted in physical battles with the local police. Later the Yale faculty again decided to ban future contests with Harvard. The rivalry was by now so important that, while the Civil War raged, Yale students got the faculty to revoke the ban. In addition Yale undergraduates raised $1000 toward the purchase of a boat house. With a small amount of alumni support and a promisory note for over $3000 from two Yale professors they built the facility. Civil War or not, Yale was readying itself for the next encounter with Harvard. With the outcome of the Civil War in doubt, the Harvard-Yale rivalry was resumed once again in 1864. To make sure its preparation was more sound than Harvard's, Yale hired its first professional coach, and for the first time defeated Harvard in a dual meet. "No friendly hands met," wrote a newspaperman, "at the close of the conflict."[16] For Harvard and Yale it had been a rather short trip from their first "jolly lark" meeting in 1852 to open hostility in 1864. A decade later when numerous colleges were contesting for supremacy at the nationally prestigious Saratoga Intercollegiate Regatta, a college professor caught the sense of the desire to win which by then had swept the colleges into fevered unrestraint: "The crews of thirteen colleges," he wrote, "long and carefully trained for the approaching struggle, wrestled together there and then as if for life or death, for the recognized mastery of the oar, in that one supreme moment of decision."[17] The pervading feeling of the necessity to win dominated intercollegiate athletics from an early time.

STUDENT LEADERSHIP: THE CAPTAIN AND THE ATHLETIC ASSOCIATION

The high degree of competitive spirit with a desire for conquest had been developed early in crew, but it was also seen in baseball by the 1860s and football by the 1870s. This phenomenon had been achieved almost completely by student leadership. "Neither the faculties nor other critics assisted in building the structure of college athletics," stated Walter Camp, the leading figure in college athletics in the nineteenth century, "it is a structure which students unaided have built. . . ."[18] And so it was.

Baseball, the rising amateur sport in the 1850s, was to be first played intercollegiately in 1859 when Williams played Amherst. It was not until after the Civil War that college teams across the nation formed teams and sought out competition. Most colleges in the late 1860s and early 1870s formed teams. If they did not play other

Baseball thrived in colleges while cricket languished.

colleges, they were quite sure to compete against town teams, athletic clubs, or local high schools. By this time baseball had no peer for student interest generally, and only crew, in a few eastern colleges, gathered more attention for selected competitive events. Cricket, which was first played intercollegiately by Haverford College and the University of Pennsylvania in 1864, never received the athletic attention which baseball generated. While cricket languished, baseball generally thrived. Interest was so great at Brown College at one point in the 1870s that 5 members of the football team withdrew to play on the baseball squad with the resultant cancellation of a football game with Harvard.[19] At Dartmouth support for baseball was so enthusiastic that even the faculty voted to allow the baseball team to take a four day leave of absence in 1871 for a baseball trip.[20] Harvard College's baseball team the previous year had made a tour playing professional as well as amateur teams as far west as Milwaukee and Chicago. They won most of their games and nearly defeated the great Cincinnati Red Stockings.[21] No less was the interest in baseball in the west where most institutions organized baseball teams shortly after the Civil War. A good example of this was a Wisconsin teacher training institution, Platteville Normal School, which formed a team composed partly of Civil War veterans and was playing outside competition less than a year after the school was founded in 1866.[22] Farther west the University of California was playing baseball with outside competition in the mid-1870s.[23] Similar development was taking place in the south. At the University of Georgia three college teams sprang into existence in 1867, and one team journeyed from Athens to Augusta, about 100 miles away, for a game. They lost 61 to 21, not an unusually high scoring game which was played with bare hands and under-handed pitching.[24] These examples were common occurrences as students organized their sport following the war. They bought a few bats and balls and played on any vacant lot or field of the college, often on a cow pasture as did Cornell. In one Cornell game, according to a newspaper account, the "main feature of the game occurred in the seventh inning, when the visitors' captain slid into what he thought was third base."[25] Such were the tribulations of a low cost, student sponsored sport.

Football, too, was a phenomenon of student cultivation. Football in America was a copy of British soccer and in terms of intercollegiate play was a post-Civil War development. It is one of the few sports to have evolved primarily on the college campus. This kicking game was first played at the intercollegiate level when, following the beginning of a baseball rivalry between Princeton and Rutgers, the two schools got together on a football field in 1869. There were no established rules like those found in baseball, and the team captains at the first game and later games spent considerable time before matches deter-mining what rules they would follow. Not until Rugby football was introduced in the 1870s, and only after it became Americanized with important rule changes, did it become a popular spectator as well as participant sport on college campuses. That story will be told later.

Track and field, the fifth intercollegiate sport after crew, baseball, cricket, and football, was first established as a small component of the Intercollegiate Crew Regatta held at Saratoga, New York in the mid-1870s. To promote track in colleges, James Gordon Bennett, Jr. of the New York *Herald* put up a challenge cup for a 2 mile race as part of the Saratoga celebration in 1873. Three men, one each from Cornell, Amherst, and McGill College in Canada competed with the result that a Canadian became the first winner of a United States intercollegiate track contest. The next year there were 5 events including a 100 yard dash, 120 yard high hurdles, mile and 3 mile runs, and a 7 mile walk. The following year an entire day was devoted to track and field at the Saratoga regatta. A short time later the oldest college amateur association still existing was formed, the Intercol-legiate Association of Amateur Athletes of America (IC4A), and again it was entirely through student initiative.[26]

Whether it was crew, baseball, football, or track, the leading figure of each sport was the elected captain of the team. The captain became the dominant person on all teams, though he was more indispensable to a sport demanding team play and subordination like football than to the more individualistic sport like track and field. If a team was formed one year, it usually elected a captain for the succeeding year.

It was the captain's task to ensure the continuance of the organization the following year. The captain, who was usually an outstanding player with some leadership qualities, was given the task of organizing practice, developing plays or strategy, determining the starting team, and setting the training rules for the squad. When athletics began to dominate the extracurriculum in the last quarter of the century, it was the captain who became the campus hero. This was only logical for the captain was in most respects the "coach" of the team, and, if he had success in winning and gaining prestige for his institution, much of the team's success was almost certainly a result of his leadership. The captain as school hero was considerly different from the campus leader of a half-century before who was noted for his "speech-making, debating, or fine writing."[27] Athletic brawn and savvy had conquered over the eloquent intellectual or as a noted historian stated in 1890: the muscular student-athlete did away with the caricature of the college student as one who was a "stoop-shouldered, long-haired grind."[28]

As intercollegiate teams began playing larger schedules while spending more money on travel, training tables (specially prepared food), and costly uniforms, it became apparent that financial support was needed. The athletic association filled this need. Nearly every college in America formed an athletic association in the generation between 1870 and 1900 for the purpose of financial and moral support of the college team or teams. At times a college might have separate football or baseball associations, but generally the students would combine their support in one large athletic association. There would usually be yearly dues to belong which combined with income taken in from fund raising drives helped to support college athletics. Members of the athletic association also provided manpower in the administration of athletic contests whose gate receipts were a major source of revenue. As important as the athletic associations and their officers were for the financial support of teams, they usually possessed little power. The principal power remained with the teams. The team (be it baseball, football, track, or crew) chose its captain, and either the captain or the team elected an athletic manager who was in charge of the athletic purse strings and usually the scheduling of games.[29]

Large numbers of students in most colleges did join their athletic association. In fact if they did not choose to belong there was strong social pressure to do so. Newspapers, which sprang up on college campuses at about the same time as athletics, constantly harangued students to support the athletic effort by trying out for the team or support it financially by joining the association. The athletic association at Syracuse University, organized in 1876, was probably typical of others begun in the east at this time for it purchased athletic supplies, took care of the athletic grounds, and generally financed the athletic program.[30] When the students of the University of Pennsylvania organized one of the country's earliest athletic associations in 1873 it received no administrative encouragement or faculty support.[31] Two decades later when an institution such as Illinois State Normal School formed its first one, it had the support of the faculty.[32] Administrations and faculties were often vigorously encouraging athletics by the 1890s and it was not uncommon for faculty members to be active members of the associations.

THE ATHLETIC EXTRACURRICULUM BY THE EARLY 1900s

Intercollegiate athletics, which dominated the extracurricula by the turn of the century, were not restricted to four major sports. A

Lacrosse was played intercollegiately in the east by the 1880s.

number of minor sports had by then come into existence on many campuses. Besides the four major sports of baseball, crew, football, and track and field, there were numerous team, individual, and dual sports in the growing athletic extracurriculum after 1880. Lacrosse, the pervasive North American Indian team game, was introduced in American colleges after the game had been formalized with written rules in Ontario, Canada in the mid-1800s and after athletic clubs had begun to play it in New York state. By the early 1880s Harvard, Princeton, New York University, and Columbia had teams and had formed the Intercollegiate Lacrosse Association.[33]

Another team sport, cricket, the popular British pastime, never really became popular with Americans. A few colleges had teams which generally played city cricket clubs. Haverford College in Pennsylvania in the 1830s made the first concerted effort to organize the game in colleges, and in 1864 defeated the University of Pennsylvania in the first intercollegiate cricket match in America.[34] With some lapses in interest it continued to support the game though collegians and Americans in general evidently believed that cricket lacked the vigor and unceasing energy which other games offered them. With Haverford and the University of Pennsylvania leading the way in the 1880s, the center of cricket enthusiasm was in the Philadelphia region, but as a writer at that time noted only "a languid interest in the game is maintained."[35]

As cricket was languishing, hare and hound racing or paper chasing came into being. The hare and hound race was a predecessor to the sport of cross-country running, and like most American sports was of British origin. The race involved a group of "hounds" chasing one or two "hares" who, carrying bags of small paper scraps which they scattered as scent for the hounds, were given a lead of possibly one-half mile. The object, of course, was for the "hounds" to catch or sight the "hares" in a proposed one-to-two hour chase over the country side. Harvard evidently first introduced this sport in the colleges in 1879, though only on an intramural or club basis.[36] A little over a decade later, in 1890, the first intercollegiate cross-country race was run between the University of Pennsylvania and Cornell with a well-defined course and no paper chasers.[37]

Two winter team sports, basketball and ice hockey, grew out of the athletic developments of the 1890s. Ice hockey had been a popular game in Canada for a number of years. In 1895 a student from Montreal studying at Johns Hopkins in Baltimore formed a hockey club and challenged a Canadian team to a contest. Yale and Harvard, too, formed teams, and soon after other eastern colleges followed suit. The sport was sporadic for ice skating rinks and playing talent were sparce, but an intercollegiate hockey league was consumated with

Hare and Hound cross country races were first introduced by Harvard in 1879.

Brown, Columbia, and Princeton along with Harvard and Yale as charter members.[38] Ice hockey did not become the dominating winter sport—that honor was eventually won by basketball.

Basketball is one of the few sports of United States origin and is rarer still for it was invented to serve a specific purpose. With the development of football as the dominating sport in the fall and baseball in the spring, there was a concern at the Springfield, Massachusetts, YMCA Training School that a sport be developed using natural activities which would serve as an enjoyable, vigorous, gymnasium sport in the winter months. There was a thirst for an indoor activity that would replace formal German and Swedish gymnastics which had come to dominate American physical education programs. In the fall of 1891 an instructor at the Springfield YMCA Training School, James Naismith, took the challenge of Luther Gulick, head of the Physical Training department and a leader in progressive physical education thought. Gulick asked that Naismith attempt to create a game based upon natural movements of man. Naismith experimented with various games and finally invented basketball with the ingenious idea that in an indoor setting a ball be tossed in an arc rather than driven through a goal. Basketball did help to overthrow formal gymnastics with the introduction of a natural type sport, but more than that, the game of basketball caught the imagination of college men and women who began to form teams and seek outside competition. Women began to play the game intercollegiately as soon as did men (see Chapter 15) and in some ways may have slowed slightly the development for men, for no small element at first believed the game was too feminine for intercollegiate play. Yet, the game grew amazingly fast. By 1900 teams had been formed across the nation, especially after the leading collegiate athletic power in the nation, Yale, had taken a tour as far west as Wisconsin in 1896. Before World War I, basketball had come to dominate the winter athletic scene in colleges (and also schools) and probably became the second most important sport in colleges next to football.

In addition to the minor team sports, college students began to introduce dual and individual sports to the extracurriculum. Tennis may have become the most popular. Lawn tennis was brought to America in 1874 after Mary Outerbridge had seen British troops playing it at their Atlantic Ocean island base, Bermuda. Within two years a United States tourney was held in Nahant, Massachusetts. College men soon began setting aside space on grassy lawns to play the game which was becoming fashionable in society's upper class. Not long afterwards, in 1883, Trinity, Brown, Amherst, and Yale formed the Intercollegiate Lawn Tennis Association, and it occurred only two years after the United States Lawn Tennis Association had been set up to standardize rules, balls, and court size.[38] Even with the growth of tennis, college students would compare tennis with their favorite sports of football and baseball and think of tennis as something less than a manly, virile sport. Especially was that argument used if an athlete, who was good enough to make one of the major teams and uphold the prestige of the college, chose to play the less prestigious sport of tennis.

The sport of fencing had a small collegiate following by the 1890s. Fencing had been a popular pastime in Germany, France, and Italy during the 1800s. The growth of physical education in colleges in the late 1800s with its European flavor, especially that of German gymnastics, found fencing as part of college physical activities. With the seed for the development of fencing teams planted, intercollegiate competition began in 1894 when Harvard and Columbia met. Soon an intercollegiate Fencing Association was established which included in addition to Harvard and Columbia, Cornell, Yale, Pennsylvania, Princeton, and the two service academies at West Point and Annapolis. In a short time national meets found champions being decided in foil, épeé, and saber competitions.

At about the same time, swimming competition was beginning at eastern institutions. In 1896 the first intercollegiate meet took place with Columbia, Pennsylvania, and Yale competing. One of the major reasons for the relatively slow development of swimming was the lack of facilities. Smaller institutions often could not afford the added expense of costly swimming pools. Important growth in swimming awaited a later period.

With the numerous athletic sports coming into existence on college campuses, the extracurriculum was challenging the curriculum for students' interest, time, and efforts. The president of Princeton, Woodrow Wilson, believed that the extracurriculum dominated the curriculum in the early 1900s. "The side shows," he wrote, "are so numerous, so diverting,—so important, if you will—that they have swallowed up the circus, and those who perform in the main tent must often whistle for their audiences, discouraged and humilated."[40] To many students the side shows were what made college a valuable experience. The type of student going to college had changed in the half century after 1850. The average student was no longer primarily interested in one of the traditional professions, the ministry, the law, or the academic life. With the rise of industrialization, urbanization, and the business world, one of the important aspects of college life was the development of social graces. It was important for a future leader in the business world to know people, probably more important to financial success than knowing how to translate Homer's *Iliad* or recite the *Odes* of Horace. The extracurriculum was almost certain to be more stimulating to the average undergraduate than attending compulsory chapel service.

Not a few college officials were questioning the value of athletics in the college. As early as 1876 the president of the University of Wisconsin, John Bascom, declared that if college athletics were needed "as amusement, we should hire a few persons, as we do clowns, to set themselves apart to do this work."[41] Not long after a Princeton undergraduate told a professor that he had "come to Princeton to play football, not study," a statement that shocked Princeton's president, McCosh.[42] Startled or even horrified as some educators were at the expanded athletic extracurriculum, more and more college faculty members were beginning to not only tolerate athletics but to support them. As a Yale mathematics professor said in the mid-1880s: "Truth is not to prevail by the dry light of intellect alone, but through the agency of good, wise, and strong men."[42] Eventually the faculty attempted to take the student run athletic programs and place them under what they believed was sounder educational control.

REFERENCES

1. Edward D. Neill, Journal of the Meeting of the Presidents and Masters of William and Mary, *William and Mary Quarterly*, II (July 1893), p. 55.

2. Page Smith, *John Adams* 2 vols. (Garden City, N.Y.: Doubleday, 1962), I, p. 20.

3. Jennie Holliman, *American Sports (1785-1835)* (Durham, N.C.: Seeman Press, 1931), p. 69.

4. Leon B. Richardson, *History of Dartmouth College* 2 vols. (Hanover, N.H.: Dartmouth College Publications, 1932), I, p. 106.

5. Henry D. Sheldon, *Student Life and Customs* (New York: D. Appleton and Co., 1901), p. 147.

6. Robert Henderson, *Ball, Bat and Bishop* (New York: Rockport Press, 1947), p. 136.

7. Thomas Chase, Harvard '48, letter to Horace Davis, October 21, 1845, in A Sophomore in 1845, *Harvard Graduates' Magazine*, IX (December 1900), pp. 203-206; and Thomas Cushing, Undergraduate Life Sixty Years Ago, *Harvard Graduates' Magazine*, I (1893), p. 556.

8. Amos T. French (ed.), *Exeter and Harvard Eighty Years Ago: Journals and Letters of F. O. French, '57* (Chester, N.H.: Privately printed, 1932), p. 71.

9. Nora C. Chaffin, *Trinity College, 1839-1892: The Beginnings of Duke University* (Durham, N.C.: Duke University Press, 1950), p. 208.

10. Richardson, *History of Dartmouth College*, Vol. I, p. 381, Vol. II, pp. 493-494; William H. S. Damerest, *History of Rutgers College* (New Brunswick, N.J.: Rutgers College, 1924), p. 314; Edward P. Cheyney, *History of the University of Pennsylvania, 1740-1940* (Philadelphia: University of Pennsylvania Press, 1940), p. 313; Kent Sagendorph, *Michigan, The Story of the University* (New York: E. P. Dutton & Co., 1948), p. 110; Thomas Cushing, "Almost a Riot," *Harvard Graduates' Magazine*, VIII (September 1894), pp. 17-18; and William R. Wister, *Some Reminiscences of Cricket in Philadelphia Before 1861* (Philadelphia: Allen, Lane & Scott, 1904), pp. 6-17.

11. Holliman, *American Sports*, p. 70; and Lowell H. Harrison, Rowdies, Riots, and Rebellions, *American History Illustrated*, VII (June 1972), pp. 18-29.

12. Louis C. Hatch, *The History of Bowdoin College* (Portland, Me.: Loring, Short & Harmon, 1927), p. 342.

13. James Whiton, The First Harvard-Yale Regatta (1852), *Outlook*, LXVIII (June 1901), pp. 286-289.

14. Guy M. Lewis, America's First Intercollegiate Sport: The Regattas from 1852 to 1875, *Research Quarterly*, XXXVIII (December 1967), p. 639. Even though 1852 was the first intercollegiate meeting in crew, there had been outside competition in crew before 1852. In 1846, for instance, Harvard had rowed against and beat a Boston crew. See *Spirit of the Times*, August 13, 1859, p. 317.

15. Lewis, *Ibid.*, pp. 640-641: *Spirit of the Times*, August 6, 1859, p. 308; and George S. Mumford, Rowing at Harvard, *The H Book of Harvard Athletics, 1852-1922*, ed. by John A. Blanchard (Cambridge: Harvard Varsity Club, 1923), pp. 20-40.

16. Lewis, *Ibid.*, pp. 641-642.

17. B. W. Dwight, Intercollegiate College Regattas, Hurdle-Races, and Prize Contests, *New Englander*, XXXV (1876), p. 253.

18. Walter C. Camp, College Athletics, *New Englander*, XLIV (January 1885), p. 139.

19. *Spirit of the Times*, October 25, 1879, p. 299.

20. Richardson, *History of Dartmouth College*, II, p. 563.

21. Henry Chadwick, Baseball in the Colleges, *Outing*, XII (August 1888), pp. 407-408.

22. Ronald A. Smith, From Normal School to State University: A History of the Wisconsin State University Conference, Ph.D. dissertation, University of Wisconsin, 1969, pp. 1-3.

23. William W. Ferrier, *Origin and Development of the University of California* (Berkeley: The Sather Gate Book Shop, 1930), p. 623.

24. E. Merton Coulter, *College Life in the Old South* (Athens: The University of Georgia Press, 1928), p. 268.

25. Morris Bishop, *A History of Cornell* (Ithaca, N.Y.: Cornell University Press, 1962), p. 133.

26. Jack A. Weierhausen, The History of the Development of Track and Field Athletics in the United States, M.A. thesis, Stanford University, 1941, pp. 11-13; and Ellery H. Clark, "Track Athletics" in Blanchard, *The H Book of Harvard Athletics*, pp. 463-465.

27. Francis A. Walker, College Athletics, *Harvard Graduates' Magazine*, II (September 1893), p. 3.

28. Albert Bushnell Hart, The Status of Athletics in American Colleges, *Atlantic Monthly*, LXVI (July 1890), p. 65.

29. Sheldon, *Student Life and Customs*, p. 245.

30. William F. Galpin, *Syracuse University*, 2 vols. (Syracuse: Syracuse University Press, 1952-1960), p. 160.

31. Cheyney, *University of Pennsylvania*, p. 314.

32. Donald E. Garrett, A History of Intercollegiate Athletic Program at Illinois State Normal University, M.S. thesis, Illinois State Normal University, 1959, p. 20.

33. Michael M. Fleischer, A History of the Eastern Collegiate Athletic Conference, Ed.D. dissertation, Teachers College, Columbia University, 1959, pp. 5-9.

34. Wister, *Some Reminiscences of Cricket*, pp. 6-17; George W. Orton (ed.), *A History of Athletics at Pennsylvania, 1873-1896* (Philadelphia: The Athletic Association of the University of Pennsylvania, ca. 1896), p. 162; and Horace M. Lippincott, *Early Philadelphia: Its People, Life and Progress* (Philadelphia: J. B. Lippincott, 1917), p. 223.

35. A. M. F. Davis, College Athletics, *Atlantic Monthly*, LI (1883), pp. 679-680.

36. *Spirit of the Times*, November 22, 1879, p. 384.

37. History of Cross Country Running, Paper in John Lucas File, The Pennsylvania State University.

38. John A. Krout, *Annals of American Sport* (New Haven, Conn.: Yale University Press, 1929), pp. 272-273.

39. Fleischer, Eastern Collegiate Athletic Conference, pp. 3-6; and Joanne Davenport, The History and Interpretation of Amateurism in the United States Lawn Tennis Association, 1881-1966, Ph.D. dissertation, Ohio State University, 1966, pp. 20-37.

40. Woodrow Wilson, What Is a College For? *Scribner's Magazine*, XLVI (November 1909), p. 577.

41. John Bascom, The Seat of Sin, Baccalaureate Sermon, June 18, 1876, University of Wisconsin, *John Bascom Papers*, University of Wisconsin Memorial Library Archives.

42. Thomas J. Wertenbaker, *Princeton 1746-1896* (Princeton: Princeton University Press, 1946), p. 329.

43. E. L. Richards, College Athletics, *Popular Science Monthly*, XXIV (March 1884), p. 597.

CHAPTER 13

College Athletics: From Student to Faculty Control

The British had given America its sporting traditions in society in general and in college in particular. Yet, there was little British precedent for the system of highly commercialized sport which developed in American educational institutions with their acceptance of the professional coach and college men being paid directly or indirectly to perform athletic feats. It did, though, reflect many values held by Americans. It has been seen that commercial and professional aspects of college sport were not the "raison d'etre" when students first formed teams and sought outside competition. Nevertheless it developed early; the seeking of professional athletic guidance and financial and other gain through sport was common practice by 1900. Students who had started it all were to forfeit their control partly because they were unable to effectively control athletic growth and partly because there were others who wanted to control college athletics for purposes in variance with those of the students. By the early 1900s students had lost effective control of this most important aspect of the extracurriculum.

WINNING, COACHING, AND RECRUITING

"The English," wrote a knowledgeable American observer in 1900, "seem to play more for the love of sport and less for a desire to beat somebody than their American cousins."[1] The Americans had a long tradition of winning: the early colonists had won their struggle for survival against the mother country, the people pushing westward had beaten the Indians and subdued the continent from east to west, and the abundant natural resources had been conquered and their use had produced the wealthiest nation on earth. All this had been accomplished, according to popular thought, by hard work and

210

perseverance. The Puritan work ethic had become an American work ethic and it carried over into athletics. Success in athletics was synonymous with the word victory. To be victorious, to conquer, to win, became the end-all of competitive athletics. This was probably not peculiar to Americans, but the means to achieve victory, both fair and foul, were exploited with greater vigor than by the leading sporting nation in the world, England.

The emphasis upon winning, what opponents of athletics termed winning-at-all-costs, led to inducing promising prep school and high school athletes to matriculate at a particular college: recruiting, which in a later era became a full time professional position. The quest for victory also led to the hiring of professional coaches who could generally train and lead a team more successfully than could student captains. The desire to outdo the opposition also demanded costly equipment, training tables, first class travel accommodations, and scouting or what was at first called spying on the opposition. All these crept into the student controlled games. To pay for these added expenses students were expected to join the athletic association and make private subscriptions to support the team; the alumni was asked for support; and gate receipts, the eventual primary financial source, came into being. In order to attract large crowds to bring in revenue needed to support the teams, it became necessary to win. Thus the cycle to attract the finest players, the best coach, and whatever else was thought necessary was predicated upon the belief that only winning was important.

America, which lacked a dominating gentleman class, also lacked the restraining influence found in gentleman's sport. Of this, one Englishman wrote shortly after the turn of the century: "The winning of a game being the only end that an American player has in view, he subordinated every other consideration . . . ,"[2] something which he noted was not true of an Oxford University athlete. James Muirhead, a British traveler, questioned the emphasis upon winning in American college sport believing that "the desire to win must be very strictly subordinated to the sense of honour and fair play."[3] These were common statements coming from the upper social class in England, indicating that Americans took their sport seriously in terms of winning and that they did not have the British sense of sportsmanship that had been developed in the upper class "public" schools of England and the colleges of Oxford and Cambridge.

Despite foreign comments criticizing aspects of the American college sport scene, the movement toward greater stress and need for winning continued. Action bringing about the professional coach in the latter 1800s did not change the emphasis upon winning, it only intensified it. Walter Camp, the leading figure in college sport at the time, noted the difference between the captain's control of athletics as opposed to control by a professional coach. "The captain usually desires to win that one year, no matter at what expense. The coach sometimes, particularly if he is to continue assisting his college," noted Camp in the early 1890s, "had the desire to win that year coupled with a hope of developing good material for further victories."[4] A decade later an observer of the collegiate scene emphasized the same point: "Players like to win," he wrote, "but head coaches and especially paid coaches, *had* to win."[5] For some institutions the hiring of a professional coach solved the problem of how to produce a winner, but in so doing created other problems. One of these was the intensified recruiting of athletes.

Long before professional coaches entered the scene, students were engaged in recruiting of talented prep and high school players. This was occurring as early as the 1870s and 1880s.[6] Albert Bushnell Hart, the Harvard historian, described the athletic recruits as "the few young men who become regular members of the college in order to develop and exhibit their skill as athletes."[7] Athletes were often flattered and given promises of social favor if they would attend a certain college. Generally it was up to the team manager, captain, or an athletic association officer to search out the best talent available. Before eligibility rules it was common for the larger colleges to seek out athletes from the small colleges to play for them. Fielding H. Yost, noted University of Michigan coach in the first three decades of the twentieth century, recounted his undergraduate experience at West Virginia when he was hired by Lafayette College to play against the University of Pennsylvania in a crucial game of unbeaten teams. Shortly after the game Yost "transferred" back to West Virginia.[8] Sometimes former college graduates who had starred in athletics were given instructorships on a college faculty and continued to compete in intercollegiate athletics. Another method of recruiting was to register the athlete as a "special" student as Syracuse University had done as early as 1873 when they hired some Irish boys to row on their crew while placing them in an analytical drafting "special" course.[9] There were also outright financial inducements for athletes to participate. One outstanding example was the captain of Yale's football team, James Hogan, who was twenty-seven years old at the turn of the century when he began his intercollegiate career. He occupied a suite of rooms at Yale's most luxurious dormitory and was given his meals at the University Club. His tuition was paid and he was given by Yale a $100 a year scholarship. He and two others were additionally given the privilege of selling game programs from which they received the entire profits. Furthermore, Hogan was appointed agent for the American Tobacco Company and received a commission on every

Fielding H. Yost of West Virginia played in a crucial game for Lafayette. (Courtesy of University of West Virginia Library.)

package of cigarettes sold in New Haven. If that wasn't enough for this "amateur" collegian, Hogan was given a ten-day vacation trip to Cuba during the school term after the football season was successfully completed.[10]

It should be pointed out that recruiting for extracurricular activities did not begin with athletics. When debating societies were the primary extracurricular activity prior to the introduction of intercollegiate athletics, there was intense recruiting of sub-freshmen from preparatory schools to gain pledges to join certain debating societies. That students would continue this policy when athletics became a dominating activity was not unexpected and was indicative of the strong competitive spirit in America.

When professional coaching became more commonplace, the recruiting of athletes could become more systematized and the year-to-year continuity could be better maintained. Eventually the student recruiting program was placed in the hands of the professional coach and the paid athletic staff (with the help of loyal alumni) who had more time and a financial incentive to bring athletic talent to an institution.

Athletics on college campuses became the scene of a type of professionalization of pure amateurism as defined by the British. They had defined amateurism as the love of sport with no thought of remuneration. The hiring of professional coaches and the proselytizing of athletes to attend college to create a winner became the norm and was a major reason why outside forces came to control the student sports.

ATHLETIC EVILS AND BENEFITS: THE CONCERN OF THE FACULTY

To the amateur sportsman who critically viewed college athletics, professionalism was only one evil aspect. Four other major areas were held up to ridicule: (1) the financial or commercial side of athletics, (2) the question of sportsmanship in athletics, (3) other values held by the athletes, and (4) the relation of athletics to the entire student body.

A number of observers, often faculty members, felt that the student run sporting contests at major institutions were becoming highly commercial affairs with increasing gate receipts allowing for expensive uniforms, an increased number of games, costly training tables, and an extravagent amount spent on travel accommodations, in addition to the cost of professional coaching and recruiting. Besides the questionable accounting procedures used by most student athletic managers, the inherent work ethic of many college professors could not countenance what was considered misspent finances as well as time. At a number of smaller instituions the lack of money for athletics was at least as great a concern. At many institutions athletic programs were constantly in debt, with the school faculty and administration being continually embarrassed by the financial irresponsibility of the students who were in charge. For both extravagant reasons and for penurious circumstances school authorities began to believe that the primary student extracurricular activity was in need of direction by older, more responsible individuals.

If finances raised the ire of some observers, the questions centered around the meaning of sport and sportsmanship were also raised. The charge of breaking the spirit of the rules, if not the letter of the rules, was often heard. This was more strongly felt when home teams procured their own officials who were often biased toward the home team. The question of the ethics of spying on future opponents to find out their type of plays or their strengths and weaknesses was to some an immoral act. Having practices behind closed doors was questioned as unbecoming an educational institution. More often than not the game of football became the sport commonly accused of being unsportsmanlike for it was a gladiatorial-type sport in which the charge of brutality and winning-at-all-costs was heard from the 1880s until World War I. There were those who saw the lack of sportsmanship as a justification for greater controls.

Athletic values, then, such as sportsmanship, were being questioned. As athletics began to dominate student thought by the end of the 1800s, faculty members, especially, asked if athletics should be

EDUCATION.   IS THERE NO MIDDLE COURSE?

considered by students as being more important than study. The amount of time for practicing each day and the number of away games was deterring a number of athletes from the pursuit of knowledge. Furthermore, the emphasis upon athletics led to newspaper notoriety and a glorification of the athlete, heaping upon him praise and fame. This, it was noted, created a false college standard and a corresponding decline in intellectual efforts. To those critics it was clear that athletics must be controlled (if not abolished) if athletics were not to dominate collegiate life.

Athletics were involving non-athletes more and more so that discussions on the college campus were often centered around the baseball "nine," the football "eleven," or the crew "eight." To a college professor who was used to the pursuit or dissemination of knowledge it was difficult to empathize with students who were caught up in the spectator hysteria brought about by the big games between rival institutions. There were also concerns about the gambling and drunkenness apparent at many collegiate contests. To such observers only by taking control and passing rules, limiting schedules, and making athletics a subordinate part of college life could order be restored.

If only the evil side of athletics had been exposed, they would surely have been abolished by college faculties or the presidents. As much as the evils were deplored there was wide agreement that athletics had been a welcome addition to collegiate life in the nineteenth century. It was common in the 1880s and 1890s for those who had experienced the pre-athletic era to compare it with the new college era dominated by athletics. Almost invariably college authorities favored the latter.

One point stressed over and over was that athletics were a positive force in the promotion of college discipline; that they had been a major factor in curbing student disorders. "During the past fifteen years one can not fail to be struck by the decreasing number of really great disorders" wrote a Yale professor in 1884 as he praised the influence of athletics.[11] Charles K. Adams, writing in 1890 shortly before becoming president of the University of Wisconsin, reflected upon the morally uplifting effect of athletics upon student behavior. "It would be curious to know just how much the improved order in our colleges in the last twenty-five years is due to athletic sport. That they have had not a little influence in that direction," wrote Adams, "there is no reason whatever to doubt."[12] It was commonly believed that athletics provided the outlet for students' "superabundant animal energy" which had previously found vent in town-gown fights and student rebellions on campus.

This was likely true just as was the argument that athletics did much to change the college student from a mid-nineteenth century stoop-shouldered, sickly, long-haired grind to a more healthy, robust, and virile character whom some claimed to be an example of Muscular Christianity. It was probably a more common belief that national character rather than Christian character was being developed on the athletic field—a kind of courage, self-reliance, and subordination of self to a common cause. This was important to those who felt American men were becoming effeminate—a prevalent belief—and lacked the qualities necessary for progress and world influence.

Along with the belief that better discipline and increased health and robustness were positive results of athletics, numerous people saw the development of a college "esprit de corps" once athletics became an important social force. Whereas class loyalties had been the important unifying element in colleges for most of the 1800s, intercollegiate athletics had become the organization which students could rally around and show their allegiance. Larger enrollments and more emphasis upon greater course selection under the new elective system tended to dissipate the unity which classes had once developed. Furthermore the unity which had been brought about by the collective opposition to a paternalistically controlled classical education and compulsory chapel attendance had run its course by the end of the century. The new spirit engendered by athletics was welcomed—and welcomed most by institutional leaders who were anxious to create viable institutions which would attract new students, increase institutional esteem, and further the goals of educational institutions caught in an era of business expansion that furthered the belief that bigness and greatness were synonymous.

ATHLETICS, INSTITUTIONAL PRESTIGE, AND COLLEGE ADVERTISING

"Do you know, Mr. Bolton," President Witherspoon of Atwater College said to the star Atwater football player, "this craze for pugilistic sports is demoralizing our institutions."

"Oh I hardly think so," replied Billy Bolton. "Do you know I never heard of Atwater until it scored against Cornell two years ago?"

"Oh, my dear young friend, you too, are possessed of this madness," rejoined the president. "Well, come along, Mr. Larrabee (the football coach), I suppose we shall have to give the team whatever it wants."[13]

George Ade in his popular, satirical play, "The College Widow," caught the athletic spirit of the times in the early 1900s. He pictured athletics with all its apparent evils as dominating collegiate thought, but at the same time realizing its great popularity among students, alumni, and the public at large as it brought recognition to institutions of higher learning. College administrators, more than the faculties, appreciated this fact. College presidents, in tune with the materialistic, business dominated times, were becoming more pragmatic than moralistic in their approach to college leadership. College administrations, with a concern for survival, were constantly in quest for private and public support. The desire for popular support led college presidents to advertise their institutions in any way they could. Scouring the country they went on speaking tours; they went to the state legislators to summon money and other support; they allied themselves with the influential—often the rising business class who were becoming members of the college ruling bodies, the boards of trustees. No other advertising medium had a greater hold upon the populace than did athletics.

When "Siwash College" or the state university won an important athletic contest, people everywhere could read about it in the newspapers and glory in the recognition it brought to their locale and institution. People generally had no idea what was occurring in the college philosophy or geology class, but they could easily relate to the institution through a visible athletic program. Presidents knew this and began supporting and using athletics to promote their institutions. Keen observers had noted this long ago; one being Henry S. Canby, who believed that it was a "crude confusion of the methods of business with the aims of education that drove many a college president to justify professional sports by their advertising value."[14]

The fact that college presidents used athletics to advertise their institutions was a national phenomenon by 1900; it started in the 1870s. In 1873 it would have appeared that President Andrew D. White of Cornell was not thinking of the advertising value of athletics when he responded to a University of Michigan football challenge with an outright rejection. "I will not," White telegraphed forcefully, "permit thirty men to travel four hundred miles merely to agitate a bag of wind."[15] Yet, two years later when Cornell's varsity and freshman crews won the important intercollegiate regatta at Saratoga he wired his winning crews: "The University-chimes are ringing, flag flying and cannons firing. Present hearty congratulations to both the victorious crews."[16] Shortly thereafter, recognizing that the victories did more to publicize Cornell than if the trustees had spent $100,000, he agreed that the College should absorb the $1,100 debt of the Cornell crew and charge it to college advertising. Only the year before when Columbia had won the same regatta President Barnard told his crew that winning the regatta had "done more to make Columbia known than all your predecessors because little was known about Columbia one month ago but today wherever the telegraph cable extends, the existence of Columbia College is known and respected."[17]

When the University of Chicago opened in 1891, one of President

Harper's first thoughts was to publicize his John D. Rockefeller financed institution through winning teams. To pursue this aim he hired as coach a former all-American football player from Yale, who was also probably good enough to pitch for a major league baseball team, Amos Alonzo Stagg. Harper made an offer to Stagg stating in a letter that he was most heartily in favor of athletics. He wanted Stagg "to develop teams which we can send around the country and knock out all the colleges. We will give them a palace car and a vacation too."[18] Stagg accepted the offer which made him the first professional athletic coach with a professorial rank. President Harper gave his athletic teams both financial and moral support. During one game in the 1890s Chicago was losing a football game to the University of Wisconsin at half time, 12 to 0. Into the dressing room walked President Harper, and he delivered a stirring speech to the Chicago players. "Boys, Mr. Rockefeller has just announced a gift of $3,000,000 to the University," the President declared. "He believed that the University is to be great. The way you played in the first half leads me to wonder whether we really have the spirit of greatness in ambition. I wish you would make up your minds to win this game and show that we do have it."[19] Chicago won 22 to 12.

President Harper was not unique in using athletics for promotional or institutional purposes. In 1888 the presidents of Trinity College (now Duke University) in North Carolina and Miami College of Ohio organized football teams in their respective institutions to help publicize their schools. After defeating the University of North Carolina, President Crowell, who had coached the Trinity team, said that the victory over North Carolina "gave the College an indefinable prestige of a general but most effective kind."[20] President Warfield at Miami of Ohio may have been the first college president to incur an injury while playing for a college team. He hurt his knee in a December football game, the same year he organized the team. Warfield had insisted that all able-bodied men at Miami play on the team; a means, in part, to publicize the institution.[21]

Whether it was President McCosh of Princeton recruiting students for his college by mentioning Princeton victories over Harvard and Yale or whether it was the University of California sending its track team to tour the east as it did in 1895, institutions were pursuing their goals in part by taking advantage of the publicity successful athletic programs could generate.[22] In the midwest when Indiana University first won the state football championship in 1899 it was noted that "everything that was connected with our university became suddenly alive with interest to the people of the state."[23] Similarly at the University of Oklahoma when Vernon L. Parrington (later a noted historian) joined the English department in 1897 he became the football coach with a desire to win and bring recognition to the institution. At Colorado College, President Slocum believed that his institution could "never gain the recognition that it deserves until it has a winning football team."[24] With similar feelings existing in the minds of numerous college administrators across the nation it created sufficient motivation for college authorities to begin to direct what had once been solely student affairs.

Not all college presidents favored advertising their institutions through athletics though they generally did not speak out loudly for fear of losing enrollment, public support, or alumni backing. One president felt that he could speak out; he was Charles W. Eliot, foremost educator in America, who headed Harvard College from 1869 to 1909. Eliot had rowed on one of Harvard's early crews in the 1850s and was not opposed to athletics. In fact in his inaugural address upon becoming president of his alma mater he called for achieving excellence in athletics. After a generation as president he became disillusioned with the dominating nature of athletics and sought ways to keep it in educational perspective. He denied that athletic wins and losses affected prestige and enrollment. After carrying out his own study of wins and losses of Harvard, Princeton, and Yale and accounting for institutional growth over the years, he concluded that American colleges should "satisfy themselves that success in athletics is not indispensable to college growth. . . ."[25] He then filed the report and other athletic statements in a file titled "publicity." At the same time that he was publicly denigrating the effect of athletic publicity on an institution's prestige, he was involved in awarding a George Emerson Lowell scholarship to a mere "C" student, "Home run" Frantz, who was said to be "the greatest college first baseman of his time."[26] When questioned about this possibly hypocritical action regarding a prestigious scholastic honor award, Eliot replied that Harvard's ruling body (the Corporation) "accepted the trust and proposes to execute it."[27] Harvard was able to remain a prestigious institution though usually losing to Yale and Princeton in important athletic events. Even those losses must have played somewhat upon Eliot's mind for he kept an athletic quip from the *Saturday Evening Post* in his possession:

> As Burrett Wendell once remarked, with as much truth as humor, Yale was founded fifty years after Harvard to counteract its radical tendencies, and has kept a half century behind ever since, until, at last, it has taken to beating Harvard in athletics.[28]

There may have been more truth in it than Eliot wanted to believe.

Despite the statements of Eliot and those in lesser positions who usually did not speak out, college presidents came increasingly to accept athletics as an integral part of the college and something which created in the public mind a viable institution. Support for institutions of higher learning would come from people who could identify with the institution. College athletics, especially football, helped to create this identity. Even if a college president was opposed to intercollegiate athletics, he would find it hard to publicly condemn them for he would be losing public support and good will which athletics had helped to create. Rather than condemn the evils of athletics, a number of shrewd presidents did all they could to promote athletics and especially winning athletics. They could do this in a number of ways such as attending games and congratulating victorious teams; speaking at various functions and creating the image of an institution with a vigorous athletic program; asking the board of trustees for athletic facilities and accepting funds from the alumni for the same; providing monies for athletic teams; granting scholarships to students who were athletes; and hiring coaches who were often euphemistically called directors of physical training. With these involvements, students increasingly saw their control over the athletic programs dissipating.

FACULTY CONTROL IN INSTITUTIONS AND IN CONFERENCES

As educators began to accept athletics as an integral part of collegiate life, if not actually in the curriculum, they began to feel that they should exert greater control over its negative aspects. "Some of our faculties," wrote one observer in 1885, "are showing a laudable desire to regulate supposed excesses. . . ."[29] Previously there had been a period of a generation in which most faculties felt that they had neither the time nor the inclination to form and hold to a consistent athletic policy. The prior inclination to have either a hands-off, laissez faire policy or to be wholly prohibitive evolved to one of providing general guidelines and certain restrictions over the athletic program. The 1880s saw the first important faculty guidelines as they related to the time, place, and number of intercollegiate games which teams would be permitted.[30] With the growth of athletics and the resulting controversies it became increasingly difficult for an entire faculty to attempt to control athletics.

Harvard appears to be the first college to have formed an athletic committee of faculty members. Prior to 1882 Harvard's faculty had imposed only one important regulation over athletics stating that no contests should take place at Harvard except on Saturdays or after 4:00 p.m. on weekdays. In the spring of 1882 the faculty became alarmed over the number of baseball games being played away from Cambridge and struck a standing athletic committee of three faculty members, including the director of the gymnasium, to look into the athletic situation. The committee restricted student athletics by prohibiting them from playing professionals as the baseball team had previously done; limiting games to Saturday except by special permission; requiring a physical examination for every athlete; and demanding the final say on any coaching assignment. The students, though not liking the rules, acquiesced. Soon the faculty committee expanded its powers by firing the baseball coach. It further refused to give the crew reason why it could not hire a specific crew coach and placed sufficient pressure on the college newspaper staff to prevent it from publishing letters favorable to the student's point of view. Soon after that it prohibited football because of alleged brutality.[31] A faculty committee did indeed mean loss of student power.

By 1885 the Harvard faculty expanded the athletic committee to five members including the gymnasium director, a physician, an alumnus, and two student athletic leaders. By this time the committee was recommending faculty control over a proposed athletic conference rather than student control which had existed in previous athletic leagues. With numerous problems besieging Harvard athletics in the 1880s and with the Committee of Athletics of the Harvard Board of Overseers recommending that all intercollegiate contests be abolished, the faculty formed a new nine member athletic committee in 1888. It consisted of three faculty, three alumni, and three students and was given supervision and control of the whole athletic program.[32] This was eventually the prototype of athletic control seen in many eastern colleges, with faculty, and students, as well as alumni represented.[33]

By 1900 there were essentially three types of college athletic control. One was the centralized system founded by Harvard which saw a combination of faculty, alumni, and student control. A second type was the older form of student control with little faculty interfer-

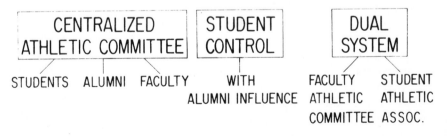

TYPES OF COLLEGE
ATHLETIC CONTROL BY 1900

ence. This was seen at Yale, Princeton, and the University of Virginia, though there was often a strong alumni influence. A third type, which was often found in the midwest and south, was a dual plan in which there was a faculty athletic committee which usually set guidelines and prohibitory legislation while the athletic association comprised mostly of students administered the program.[33] At the end of the nineteenth century there were few programs which had complete student control. If there were not strong faculty or administrative restrictions, there was alumni influence.[34]

The alumni, even before they gained an official voice on many of the college athletic committees, had acquired some control over athletic programs. Generally this was with the blessing of student athletes and the school athletic associations. An alumnus was often asked to help coach one of the teams for part of the season. Additionally, the financial indebtedness of a team, as often happened, required alumni support. This frequently meant that the alumni would contribute financially to the program if they could control the purse strings. As a result it became common for the student athletic manager to lose much of his power to a graduate treasurer or an alumni athletic manager. This occurred at Harvard, Dartmouth, Penn State, Wisconsin, Missouri, and numerous other institutions by the late 1800s and early 1900s.[35] In some cases, but not most, the alumni gained almost absolute control of the athletic program.

Student power was further dissipated in the late 1800s and especially in the next century when intercollegiate conferences were formed. The earliest intercollegiate associations had been organized solely by students who sought standardized rules and continuity in the scheduling of events in a specific sport. The 1858 College Rowing Association consisting of Harvard, Yale, Brown, and Trinity started it all. By 1880 there were additional associations or leagues formed in crew, baseball, football, and track and field. Student representation continued for some time, but some colleges felt it was advantageous to send former athletes from their institutions to represent them. Walter Camp was likely the first graduate to become a member of such an association when, following graduation, he continued to be Yale's representative to the Intercollegiate Football Association in the early 1880s.

The most important change, though, was the formation of conferences by college administrators of certain institutions with a resultant faculty control over all forms of athletics. Most important of all conferences of this type was the Intercollegiate Conference of Faculty Representatives formed in 1895; later known as the Western Conference or the Big Ten. Led by President Waldo of Purdue, a group of large midwestern institutions including Chicago, Illinois, Michigan,

Minnesota, Northwestern, Purdue, and Wisconsin decided to place athletics under greater faculty control than had previously existed anywhere. The Conference immediately ruled that only bona fide undergraduates who were not delinquent in their studies could participate. Further, no athlete could receive gifts or any type of remuneration, nor could professionals or coaches participate as had previously occurred. In addition a transfer student could not play immediately but had to wait a half year before competing. But most importantly, the Conference was to be ruled by faculty representatives.[36] While in practice this was not always clearly the case, the precedent for faculty control of an athletic conference was set. Other institutions began to look to the Big Ten for their guiding principles.

It is apparent that the last two decades of the nineteenth century saw diminishing student power in athletics. In individual institutions, faculty and sometimes alumni interests seized power which had formerly belonged to students alone. When conferences governing many sports among specified institutions came into existence they were often specifically to be run by faculty appointed representatives. It had plainly been an expedient method of attemping to curb abuses in the intercollegiate games, not an attempt to make athletics an educational experience. There still were college leaders who opposed sanctioning faculty control. One was President Hadley of Yale who, refusing to send a faculty representative to a 1902 intercollegiate athletic conference, stated:

> We believe that the responsibility for carrying out the measures intended to promote honorable athletics must of necessity fall upon the shoulders of academic public sentiment, graduate and undergraduate, and that action of a faculty which is construed as assuming the responsibility tends to weaken its force in places where it really belongs.[37]

Student influence continued well into the twentieth century, eventually relinquishing its power to professional coaches, athletic directors, faculty, graduates, national associations, and even boards of trustees, state legislatures, and at times commercial enterprises.

THE PLACE OF COLLEGE ATHLETICS BY WORLD WAR I

By World War I, from the pioneering colleges in the east to those that followed in the midwest, south, and far west, athletics were firmly established. The basic pattern had been set and the benefits as well as evils revealed. Because of laissez faire development of intercollegiate athletics, in which students had to devise policies which would produce money for their continuance, commercialized rather than educational activities developed. Had college authorities and others who supported colleges believed that athletics could be valuable educational entities in institutions of higher learning, then the provisions for financing them could have come through regular educational channels. This was not the case and the students organized and ran their own programs, commercializing them for reasons of survival as well as for the glamour of highly organized sport. When colleges eventually took control of the student games, they did so retaining the commercial aspects, continuing for years the policy of keeping athletics outside the curriculum. The centuries old antagonism to things of the flesh as opposed to things of the mind and spirit retarded the movement to bring athletics into educational focus. It was much easier to rationalize other extracurricular activities such as music, drama, or journalism as being part of the educational curriculum than athletics. Even when athletics were made part of the curriculum of many colleges by the 1920s and 1930s, it was done more for pragmatic reasons of control of abuses than because it was thought to contribute to a well-rounded education.

The open faculty hostility which had been a constant threat to the development of highly organized college athletics had dissipated to a great extent by World War I. The faculty may have yielded to stronger voices such as administrators, alumni, students, or the public, or it may have been that faculties came to accept athletics and some of the educational abuses which went with them. According to an educational historian, E. E. Slosson, who was opposed to intercollegiate athletics at the time:

> University presidents, with few exceptions, express approval of intercollegiate contests, alumni give them enthusiastic support, students vent their displeasure upon any who presume to question their value, and the outside world encourages and applauds, but in every university there is a considerable, and I believe, an increasing number of the instructing staff who are profoundly dissatisfied with the athletic conditions of to-day, though they are not always free to express their opinions on the subject.[38]

When strong opposition to athletics developed within faculties, great pressures from without were brought to bear by those who felt that athletics were symbolic and gave identity to their institutions. Creation of identity, a feeling of togetherness or esprit de corps was a strong characteristic of college athletics. A Princeton professor poignantly pointed out in the mid-1880s that esprit de corps is "good for the student and good for the college . . . , of course, it may be carried, like patriotism, to a foolish and unjust excess."[39] By 1915, college spirit was a national phenomenon, not just found in eastern colleges. Much of the devotion college graduates and the general public gave to colleges was kindled or intensified by the clearest, outward identifying factor of the college—athletics. When Lawrence Lowell was inaugurated as Harvard's president in 1909, he spoke of athletics and of their place in the college. He said that the exaggerated prominence given to athletics was not because students believed that the physical was more important than the mental, but "it is due rather to the fact that such contests offer to students the one common interest, the only striking occasion for a display of college solidarity."[40]

What was probably most important in holding the student body together was the development of the ritual which surrounded athletics. As athletics grew, the traditions surrounding them became more pronounced. The mass meetings, bon fires, spirited orations, organized cheers, and college songs, as well as the college colors, marching bands, homecoming, and the "big game" had become traditional at most colleges by World War I. Like the flag for the nation, athletics became the rallying point for college loyalties. An English professor at the University of Wisconsin, J. F. A. Pyre, who had been an athlete in the 1890s and had also coached, stated it well:

> It is a mistake to suppose that the extravagant enthusiasm lavished upon athletics by students and the alumni implies a proportionate over-estimate of their intrinsic worth. It is a mistake that arises from a puritanic failure to appreciate the significance of a ritual. That "esprit de corps" amongst the undergraduates and graduates of a school that we call "school spirit" requires a rallying point or occasion for demonstration. Athletic contests and rivalries are convenient and pleasurable occasions for its manifestations.[41]

Thus Pyre had hit upon probably the most important aspect of college athletics for they are "a tradition that fuses together all the forces of an institution in enthusiastic social consent."[42] They were no longer just student games. The students had lost their controlling power, but it was their games which had joined together undergraduate, alumni, administration, the public, and often the faculty.

REFERENCES

1. Henry D. Sheldon, *Student Life and Customs* (New York: D. Appleton and Co., 1901, p. 53.

2. T. Cook, Some Tendencies of Modern Sport, *Quarterly Review*, CXCIX (January 1904), pp. 141, 150.

3. James F. Muirhead, *The Land of Contrasts: A Briton's View of His American Kin* (Boston: Lamson, Wolffe and Co., 1898), p. 107.

4. Walter Camp, Football in 1893: Its Lessons and Its Results, *Harper's Weekly*, XXXVIII (February 3, 1894), p. 117.

5. Frank S. Butterworth, Honesty in Football, *Outing*, XLV (November 1904), p. 141.

6. William F. Galpin, *Syracuse University*, 2 vols. (Syracuse: University Press, 1952-1960), I, p. 152.

7. Albert Bushnell Hart, The Status of Athletics in American Colleges, *Atlantic Monthly*, LXVI (July 1890), p. 65.

8. John R. Behee, *Fielding Yost's Legacy to the University of Michigan* (Ann Arbor, Mich.: privately printed, 1971), p. 21.

9. Galpin, *Syracuse University*, I, p. 152.

10. Henry B. Needham, The College Athlete, *McClure's Magazine*, XXV (June 1905), p. 124.

11. E. L. Richards, College Athletics, *Popular Science Monthly*, XXIV (February 1884), p. 452.

12. Charles K. Adams, Moral Aspect of College Life, *Forum*, VIII (February 1890), p. 674.

13. George Ade, *The College Widow*. (New York: Samuel French, 1924), p. 36.

14. Henry S. Canby, *Alma Mater: The Gothic Age of the American College* (New York: Farrar and Rinehart, 1936), p. 236. See also: Laurence R. Veysey, *The Emergence of the American University* (Chicago: The University of Chicago Press, 1965), pp. 1-16; George P. Schmidt, *The Liberal Arts College* (New Brunswick, N.J.: Rutgers University Press, 1957), pp. 199-202; John S. Brubacher and Willis Rudy, *Higher Education in Transition* (New York: Harper and Brothers, 1958), p. 127; and Guy M. Lewis, Sport and the Making of American Higher Education: The Early Years, 1783-1875, National College Physical Education Association for Men, *Proceedings* (1971), pp. 208-213.

15. Morris Bishop, *A History of Cornell* (Ithaca, N.Y.: Cornell University Press, 1962), p. 136; Walter P. Rogers, *Andrew White and the Modern University* (Ithaca: Cornell University Press, 1942), p. 142; and Kent Sagendorph, *Michigan, The Story of the University* (New York: E. P. Dutton, 1948), p. 150.

16. B. W. Dwight, Intercollegiate College Regattas, Hurdle-Races, and Prize Contests, *New Englander*, XXXV (1876), p. 255.

17. Guy M. Lewis, America's First Intercollegiate Sport: The Regattas From 1852 to 1875, *Research Quarterly*, XXXVIII (December 1967), pp. 644-645.

18. Richard J. Storr, *Harper's University: The Beginnings* (Chicago: The University of Chicago Press, 1966), p. 179.

19. Amos A. Stagg and Wesley W. Stout, *Touchdown!* (New York: Longmans, Green and Co., 1927), p. 203.

20. Nora C. Chaffin, *Trinity College, 1839-1892: The Beginnings of Duke University* (Durham, N.C.: Duke University Press, 1950), pp. 443-446.

21. Walter Havighurst, *The Miami Years 1809-1959* (New York: Putnam, 1958), p. 150.

22. George P. Schmidt, The Liberal Arts College (New Brunswick, N.J.: Rutgers University Press, 1957), p. 200; and William W. Ferrier, *Origin and Development of the University of California* (Berkeley: The Sather Gate Book Shop, 1930), p. 625.

23. James A. Woodburn, *History of Indiana University: 1820-1902*, 2 vols. (Bloomington: Indiana University, 1940), I, p. 448.

24. Guy M. Lewis, The American Intercollegiate Football Spectacle, 1869-1917, Ph.D. dissertation, University of Maryland, 1964, pp. 177, 181.

25. The President's Report, *The Harvard Crimson*, XL (January 29, 1902), pp. 1-2, in *President's Papers, Charles W. Eliot*, Box 109, Folder 132, Harvard University Archives.

26. John A. Blanchard (ed.), *The H Book of Harvard Athletics, 1852-1869* (Cambridge: Harvard University Press, 1923), p. 222.

27. Ira N. Hollis, Chairman of the Athletic Committee, letter to Charles W. Eliot, January 16, 1903, in *President's Papers, Charles W. Eliot*, Box 110, Folder 143, Harvard University Archives.

28. John Corbon, Which College for the Boy? *Saturday Evening Post* (September 21, 1907), pp. 10-11, in *President's Papers, Charles W. Eliot*, Box 239, Harvard University Archives.

29. Alfred L. Ripley, Gentlemanliness in College Athletics, *New Englander*, XLIV (January 1885), p. 141.

30. Albert B. Hart, The Status of Athletics in American Colleges, *Atlantic Monthly*, LXVI (July 1890), pp. 63-71; and Augustus Hemenway, *et al.*, (The Committee on Physical Training, Athletic Sports, and Sanitary Condition of Buildings), Important Suggestions in Athletics, *Harvard Graduates' Magazine*, VI (December 1897), pp. 191-196.

31. Athletic Committee Minutes, Harvard University Archives, September 27, 1882; December 19, 1884; January 10, 1885; and October 8, 1885.

32. *Ibid.*, October 8, 1885; December 14, 1886; and November 1888, a Special Report of A. B. Hart.

33. Sheldon, *Student Life and Customs*, pp. 246, 249.

34. George W. Pepper, Faculty and Alumni Control of College Athletics, National Education Association *Proceedings*, (1894), pp. 808-815.

35. Leon B. Richardson, *History of Dartmouth College*, 2 vols. (Hanover, N.H.: Dartmough College Publications, 1932) II, p. 724; Wayland Dunaway, *History of the Pennsylvania State College* (State College: The Pennsylvania State College, 1946), p. 454; Edward S. Jordan, "Buying Football Victories," *Collier's*, XXXVI (November 18, 1905), p. 22; and Jonas Viles, *The University of Missouri* (Columbia; University of Missouri Press, 1939), p. 260.

36. Carl D. Voltmer, *A Brief History of the Intercollegiate Conference of Faculty Representatives with Special Consideration of Athletic Problems* (Menasha, Wis.: George Banta Publishing Co., 1935), pp. 5-8.

37. Caspar Whitney, The Guiding Hand of Faculty in College Sport, *Outing*, XL (July 1902), p. 497.

38. Edwin E. Slosson, *Great American Universities* (New York: Macmillan, 1910), p. 503.

39. C. A. Young, College Athletic Sports, *Forum*, II (October 1886), pp. 144-145.

40. Lawrence A. Lowell, President Lowell's Inaugural Address, October 6, 1909, in S. E. Morison (ed.), *The Development of Harvard University, 1869-1929* (Cambridge: Harvard University Press, 1930), p. lxxx.

41. J. F. A. Pyre, *Wisconsin* (New York: Oxford University Press, 1920), p. 329.

42. *Ibid*.

CHAPTER 14

Football: The Dominating College Sport

"Uninteresting things will never run riot; it is the interesting and fascinating affairs which have the greatest capacity for evil as well as for good."[1] This was said about basketball in 1895 shortly after its invention, but it could not have been a truer statement at the time had it been directed at the most important of all college sports, football. No sport came to dominate college athletics as did football. It was football which had the greatest influence in turning college athletics from student to faculty control; it created the dominant figure of the professional coach and the demise of the student captain; it attracted the alumni to the alma mater; it created a visible college to large masses of the public; it commercialized intercollegiate sport; and it brought about highly organized and consumer oriented spectator sport on the college campuses across the nation. Football has dominated most athletic programs by consuming the largest amount of money and creating the greatest revenues, while at the same time generating the most institutional prestige through winning teams. It has likewise produced most of the problems which have arisen in college sports, and because of these problems it has led to the most powerful college athletic agency, the National Collegiate Athletic Association.

THE BEGINNINGS OF THE COLLEGE GAME

It started rather innocently—young men kicking a leather covered animal bladder on the college green, usually class against class. Sometimes they would chase the ball for two or three hours each afternoon or evening during the fall or spring. Football was a simple game as there was no running with the ball; generally only kicking with the feet or batting with the hand, attempting to propel it over a fence or beyond a goal. Catching an opponent on the shin with a well-directed kick was nearly as common as kicking the ball. With from 10 to 70 on a side all could not pursue the ball so the weaker players, or younger, were generally sent to defend the goals. Football was a game primarily for the younger college men. To see fourteen, fifteen, or sixteen year olds playing was common, for college students in the early and mid-1800s were much younger on the average than twentieth century collegians. Thomas Wentworth Higginson recalled being the only senior playing at Harvard in 1841 at the age of seventeen. He pictured "the growing exhilaration as one drew near the 'Delta' on autumn evenings, while the game was in progress,—the joyous shouts, the thud of the ball, the sweet smell of the crushed grass." Higginson recalled "the taking of sides, the anxious choice of a position, the wary defense, the magnificent 'rush.' It seemed a game for men and giants," he said, "rather than for boys."[2]

At about the same time that American college students were playing this rather unorganized game, the British were beginning to develop a systematic game in the English Public (private) Schools, especially at Eton and Rugby. The upper class English Public Schools had been playing a rough, kicking game of football for years with the unwritten rules varying from school to school. In the period from the 1840s to the 1860s most of the Public Schools reduced their rules to written form. At the Rugby School they provided for running with the ball, therefore the name rugby football. Although most football histories trace running with the ball to an 1823 game when Rugby student William Webb-Ellis was said to have picked up the ball and run with it, there is no reliable evidence for this probable myth. Like American nationalistic attempts in the late 1800s and early 1900s to "prove" that baseball was originated in America, the Webb-Ellis myth was perpetuated by a committee of old Rugbians in the 1890s attempting to convince everyone that its form of football had indeed been originated at the Rugby School. At the highly aristocratic Eton School, running with the ball or touching it with the hands was expressly forbidden. This was a response to the Rugby School students, whom they believed were their social inferiors and therefore should not be setting precedents, even in football rules. We thus find the origins of association football (soccer) and Rugby football (running and kicking over a cross bar) arising in the English Public Schools.[3]

By the 1860s and early 1870s some eastern American college students began writing rules for football by using the British models and adding some of their own traditions. Most of the colleges playing the game by 1870 used the soccer-type, Etonian game with no tackling and no running with the ball. When the first intercollegiate soccer football game was played between Rutgers and Princeton in 1869 it was this type of game which prevailed.

Princeton and Rutgers were not entirely new rivals when they met for the first time on the football field; the two institutions had previously played baseball against each other. The Princeton football players, with an enthusiastic following of students, arrived by train at Rutgers on a Saturday morning in early November, 1869. By twentieth century standards their seriousness in competing against Rutgers would be questioned. Arriving before noon, the players strolled around New Brunswick stopping off in a local emporium to play billiards. The two teams arrived at the playing field shortly before the 3:00 p.m. starting time and proceeded to remove their top hats, coats, and vests in preparation for the encounter. The captains, on whom most attention was focused, discussed the rules which would be used. Though the two schools were physically less than 20 miles apart, the accepted rules differed significantly in some points. The Princeton captain agreed to give up the practice of free kicks whereby a player could catch the ball in the air and freely kick it toward the opponent's goal. It was decided that the ball could be advanced by kicking or batting it with a closed fist; no tripping or holding would be permitted; and the team getting six scores by advancing the ball through the 8 paces wide goals would be the victor. A Rutgers school reporter summed up the play of the two 25 man squads while accounting for the 6 to 4 Rutgers' victory:

> Princeton had the most muscle, but didn't kick very well, and wanted organization. They evidently don't like to kick the ball on the ground. Our men, on the other hand, though comparatively weak, ran well, and kicked well throughout. But the great point

Rutgers beat Princeton in the first intercollegiate foot-ball (soccer) game, 6 goals to 4, in 1869. (Courtesy of Rutgers University.)

was their organization, for which great praise is due to the captain Leggett, '72. The right men were always in the right place.[4]

Following the game the two teams capped the day by eating a roast game dinner, delivering impromptu speeches, and singing college songs together. One week later a return match was held at Princeton with Princeton rules. An 8 to 0 victory resulted for the home team. A third game was cancelled when faculty members of both institutions decided that too much attention was being given to these contests.[5]

The unrefined game of soccer football was played not only at Princeton and Rutgers, but also at Yale and Columbia. Intercollegiate games involving these four institutions took place between 1870 and 1873. The game, noted for kicking and "babying" the ball with the hand as interference formed ahead, might have become the proclaimed college game had not Harvard University gone its own way.

THE RUGBY GAME: GENESIS OF AMERICAN FOOTBALL

Harvard in the early 1870s was playing a type of football called the Boston game. It had more in common with rugby than with soccer. One fundamental principle of the Boston game allowed a player to pick up the ball, run with it, or throw it as long as he was pursued by an adversary. Strangely, if the opponent stopped pursuing, the runner had to kick the ball from that point. A player could also hold another to prevent him from getting the ball which was unlike the game of the other colleges. When Yale called a meeting of Harvard, Columbia, Princeton, Rutgers, and Yale in 1873 to form an intercollegiate association in order to codify the rules, Harvard students refused to attend because they knew that their form of football would be abandoned by the other four teams.[6] By refusing to join an association devoted to soccer football Harvard chose to develop its own game at the expense of intercollegiate competition with Yale, Columbia, Princeton, or Rutgers.

In the spring of 1874, McGill University of Montreal challenged Harvard to two football matches, one to be played under Harvard's rules and one with rugby rules. It was agreed that both games would be played in Cambridge; the first, under Harvard rules, on May 13, 1874. It was won easily by Harvard before about 500 spectators who paid 50¢ each to provide a fund to entertain the McGill men. The second game was more important, for the Harvard team tied McGill and found that rugby was enjoyable. When the Harvard team was invited to McGill the following fall, the first match at rugby was won by Harvard and with that win Harvard never returned to its own Boston game. After Harvard played Tufts College in the spring of 1875 in the first intercollegiate rugby game between colleges in the

Harvard traveled to McGill for a return game of rugby and thereupon introduced a new type of football to America.

United States, Harvard and Yale agreed to play a match at New Haven with modified rugby rules the following fall. Harvard won the game rather easily, something they were not to do again until 1890.

The game of rugby between the two most influential colleges in America was far more important than the 1869 Rutgers-Princeton soccer game, for it was rugby, not soccer, from which American football was developed. Following the Yale defeat of Harvard in an 1876 rugby football game, Princeton accepted rugby football and called a meeting of the Intercollegiate Football Association at which time modified rugby rules were adopted. They further decided to arrange a championship game between Yale and Princeton and thus began the first of a series of Thanksgiving Day games between eastern powers in football. Yale won the first before about 1,000 spectators in Hoboken, New Jersey.[7] From that time forward important colleges played rugby football which was soon modified into American football.

The Americanization of football occurred within a half dozen years under the leadership of Yale, Princeton, and Harvard. There were four major rule changes entwined around the intense American desire to win which transformed British rugby into American football. In rugby no person could lead interference for the ball carrier. Both Yale and Princeton in the late 1870s developed a method of protecting or guarding the runner by sending a player at each side, though not in advance, of the ball carrier.[8] This was the forerunner of modern interference in which blockers form ahead of the runner.

A second innovation, adopted in 1880, was a change in the method of putting the ball in play. In rugby the play began with a scrummage whereby the ball was placed between two rush-lines with no clear separation between teams. The ball was worked out of this scrummage with the foot, usually backward, where a back could pick it up and run or kick it forward or pass it back to a teammate who could advance it. A preplanned play was difficult because one was not sure which team would receive the ball, nor what direction the ball would come out of the scrum. Walter Camp, Yale's football captain and representative to the football rules committee, devised a method for retention of the ball by one team. This became known as the scrimmage, replacing the scrummage. The team in possession of the ball could have one person put the ball in play by snapping it back with his foot to a quarter back who would pass the ball to a runner behind him.[9] Eventually the snapper-back used his hands to pass the ball to the quarterback, becoming known as the center. Ball possession was of utmost importance under the scrimmage system of play.

A third major change resulted from misuse of the ball possession rule which had no provision for surrendering the ball. Under this rule a team could keep the ball an entire half without the opposition even once having control. A weaker team could thus gain a tie by never relinquishing the ball. Princeton used this tactic, called the "block game," in the 1880 Thanksgiving Day championship game against Yale. The Princeton captain directed his team not to kick or pass the ball. Since they did not lose the ball by fumbling the entire second half, they were able to preserve a scoreless tie and retain the championship they had won the previous year.[10] Following another year when the "block game" was used to the advantage of a weaker team, the rules committee established that a team must make 5 yards (or lose 10 yards) in three attempts (downs) or forfeit the ball. This feature, along with the scrimmage for putting the ball into play, was notable in transforming English rugby into American football.

A fourth important change was the method of scoring. Under original Rugby rules (1876) four touchdowns by crossing the opponent's goal were equal to a goal kicked from the field (field goal) or one kicked after a touchdown (extra point). It obviously favored a strong kicking game. In 1883, numerical scoring was added giving more weight to a touchdown, though not nearly as much as that given a field goal. The scoring system was 5 points for a field goal, 4 points for a goal following a touchdown, 2 points for a touchdown, and 1 point for a safety (downing an opponent with the ball behind his goal line). By the late 1880s, touchdowns were increased in value to 4 points, while extra points were reduced to 2 points, the same as a safety. By 1897 the emphasis upon running had increased the value of a touchdown to 5 points, an extra point was reduced to 1 point, while field goals and safeties remained as before.[11] Seven years later the field goal was reduced to 4 points and finally in 1909 to 3 points, while the touchdown was awarded 6 points in 1912.[12] The nature of the game had turned from an emphasis on kicking to one of running, a further Americanization of football.

SPECTATORS, FINANCES, AND THE THANKSGIVING DAY GAME

The American brand of English rugby began to attract spectators especially among the Big Three—Yale, Princeton, and Harvard. As early as 1883 it was predicted that football might well usurp the popularity of baseball as the favorite sport in American colleges.[13] Before the turn of the century this had been more-or-less accomplished not only in the eastern colleges but nationally. Students had been quick to see the commercial possibilities of increased spectators by charging admission for the support of the game. In 1873, 500 spectators attended the Yale-Rutgers football game with each team receiving only $90 as its share of the gate receipts. Twenty

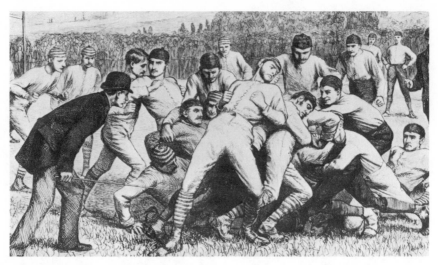

After this Yale and Princeton game in 1879, Thanksgiving Day games brought increasingly larger gate receipts.

years later Yale and Princeton each received $13,000 from gate receipts of a Thanksgiving Day game.[14] That was a great deal of money for any one aspect of college life in that period.

Athletic income at Yale from the 1880s to the early 1900s shows one aspect of the growth of football at the nation's most powerful football college in those years. During one year in the early 1880s Yale's athletic income from all sports was approximately $18,000. Only about $2,800 came from football receipts while baseball and crew incomes were over $7,000 each and lacrosse grossed slightly less than $600.[15] Early in the next decade income from just football was consistently over $50,000. A decade later, in 1903, Yale's football income reached $106,000. That figure represented one-eighth of the total gross income of Yale University or an equivalent of the combined budgets of Yale's law, divinity, and medical schools.[16] In comparison, Harvard's football receipts went from $11,000 in 1890 to $72,000 in 1904.[17] Expenses at Yale generally reflected receipts, though an excess of income resulted over the years.

The example of Yale gives only one picture of the meteoric rise of football in the last decade of the nineteenth century. While football was becoming the number one college extracurricular attraction in other colleges, it was not nearly as successful financially as it was at Yale. For example, in the first year of football at the University of Chicago in 1892, Amos Alonzo Stagg's team took in $732 in 13 games while spending $100 less. Harvard in the same year received $16,000 and expended nearly $18,000 for football.[18] Probably a majority of colleges organized football teams between 1887 and 1894. For most of them the financial situation was tenuous, but the game was not. As a result, schemes for supporting college's most favored game were numerous.

Football teams, as well as other athletic teams, depended primarily upon gate receipts for their financial support. Athletic associations often contributed part of their dues and monies from special fund raising activities, such as sponsoring dances and minstrel shows, for the support of teams. Another method of fund raising was through student subscriptions in which members of the student body were asked to contribute to the welfare of the team. Strong social pressures were brought to bear on individuals in some institutions resulting in something like a patriotic duty to fund the team. Yale raised about $10,000 from its 1000 student body to support athletics in 1881.[19] A decade later Harvard raised over $10,000 a year by this method.[20] In some institutions faculty members contributed to the football team. There were cases of faculties buying uniforms for the team. In one Wisconsin teacher training institution the faculty in the early 1900s was levied a 2½ percent assessment on one month's salary for athletics.[21] By the early 1900s mandatory student fees were commonly used to support football and other sports. Alumni contributions, also, began to be received especially in the private colleges. College boards of trustees through much of this period had generally supported athletics by providing fields and other facilities. As pressure for winning football teams mounted in the last decades of the nineteenth century and the first decades of the twentieth century, trustees began to contribute to athletics in other ways, such as providing athletic scholarships or supporting paid coaches, though they were often titled college physical directors. Even business concerns began to support college athletics. First, there were subsidies for teams for travel by transportation companies or by hotel owners. In fact, President Eliot of Harvard criticized this practice as early as the 1880s charging that it contributed to the furtherance of commercialization of college athletics.[22] Later, businesses were to underwrite football expenses at some colleges while providing athletic grants-in-aid to skilled football players.[23]

Almost every college in America attempted to bring in added revenue by sponsoring or playing in a Thanksgiving Day football game. Thanksgiving Day became not only the best day financially for most teams, but the annual Thanksgiving Day game became the most important single event on the college athletic scene. This was due to a large extent to the importance which Yale, Princeton, and Harvard placed on their championship games each Thanksgiving. Colleges nationally tended to pattern their activities after the leading Big

Three. Yale and Princeton had played the first of the annual affairs in 1876 before about 1000 spectators. About 10,000 watched the festivities five years later when it was first played in New York City. When Harvard and Yale met in New York in 1887, attendance reached 23,000.[24]

When the nouveau riche in New York City made the annual Thanksgiving Day game the kick-off of their social season, it gave added social significance to the event. By the 1890s, the game held in New York City's Polo Grounds and the Manhattan Field had changed from just a sporting event to a social spectacle. Some people even rented horse drawn coaches one year in advance so that they could arrive in time and in full view of those who admired social distinctions. One reporter, more interested in society's show than in Yale's winning performance, noted that Mrs. William C. Whitney sat conspicuously in her box seat "trimmed profusely in Yale colors and beautifully decorated with a bevy of young girls. The silvery frost of the wintry atmosphere which settled upon the box framework was strangely similar to the glistening shades of her hair, and her café au lait broadcloth, with garnet and sable trimmings, made a' la Russian and royally fitted, enhanced her appearance."[25] Box seat tickets for the game were sold for $150. Thousands of dollars, probably hundreds of thousands, were bet on each game. A four hour parade up Fifth Avenue allowed thousands, who were not among the sellout 30,000 or 40,000 at the game, to see the football heroes riding in tally-ho's as if they were on their way to a coronation. Even church services on Thanksgiving Day were let out early for the event.[26]

With the prestige and notoriety emerging from the annual game in New York City the tradition soon spread nationally. The University of Illinois newspaper looking to the east for leadership wrote the following after its first Thanksgiving Day game in 1890: "There is no reason why the game should not be as popular as it is in the East."[27] In the same year the University of Missouri played its first Thanksgiving Day game.[28] Even a normal school in Wisconsin in 1894 caught the spirit of the occasion when it completed its first season undefeated by traveling to Dubuque, Iowa, on Thanksgiving Day and beating its high school team.[29] The *Chicago Tribune* in the mid-1890s estimated that 5,000 games were played on Thanksgiving Day involving 120,000 players.[30] One of those games was played indoors in the Chicago Coliseum. That first American indoor football game, played between the University of Chicago and the University of Michigan brought in over $10,000 in gate receipts, nearly twice as much as Chicago grossed the entire season two years before.[31]

This increase in revenue from one game alarmed some who believed that the commercial aspect of football, along with gambling, corrupted the intercollegiate game. One such critic was President Warfield of Lafayette College in Pennsylvania whose own school was becoming a football power capable of defeating the nation's best teams. Warfield pointed out that one Thanksgiving game involving big time teams brought in revenue greater than the total expenditure of a college supporting 25 professors and educating 300 college men. Possibly looking at his own college which was playing before thousands on Thanksgiving, Warfield wrote that the extravagance of the leading colleges "communicates itself to the smaller colleges and leads them dishonestly to contract bills for athletic supplies which they can never pay."[32]

Despite protests like that of Warfield, Thanksgiving Day games attracted even greater popularity in the early 1900s. At the same time, the critics of football became more numerous as they attacked the brutal nature of the game. An outgrowth of this attack which threatened the existence of football was the passage of the Big Ten Conference rule prohibiting the annual Thanksgiving Day game as one method of deemphasizing football. A number of other colleges followed suit. The extravaganza on Thanksgiving Day did not die out, but there is evidence that the peak period of its popularity had been reached. Football continued to grow, but not before a sporting crisis in the late 1800s and early 1900s thoroughly shook the foundations of the game.

THE DEVELOPMENT OF MASS PLAYS AND THE CHARGE OF BRUTALITY

The combative nature of football, which created much of its excitement and an increasing public interest, led to denunciations of the sport beginning in about 1880 and increasing in tempo into the early 1900s. The charges against football varied from that of an emphasis upon commercialization and hiring of professional coaches to gambling, drunkenness, and mass hysteria whipped up by the intense athletic spirit. No charge, however, was heard more often than the accusation that football was a violent, brutal sport. The outcry against brutality arose in part because of the great number of injuries which resulted from aggressive play by players who wore little protective equipment. There were no helmets, although the primitive nose guard and ear protectors were first being worn. Of more importance in the charges of brutality than the injuries received was the means used in bringing about the injuries. That there was a great deal of unsportsmanlike play associated with American athletics, such as slugging and kicking, can hardly be denied. Brutality and the eventual reform movement were to change the nature of football and the control over the sport.

Primitive nose, mouth, and ear guards were used in the 1890s.

Beginning in the mid-1880s the first important charges of brutality were being sounded. Even then there seemed to be more important considerations. President Eliot of Harvard in justifying manly athletics said that "effeminacy and luxury are even worse evils than brutality."[33] A decade later, though, when charges of brutality were more intense, Eliot was so distraught over the foul and violent developments in football that he called it "unfit for college use."[34] What appeared to be excessive slugging in football was probably magnified by the sound of legal striking upon the chests of the canvas jacket clad athletes as well as by the many spectators who did not understand the nature of the game.

American football, with its unique development of rules such as the line of scrimmage and emphasis upon running to gain a certain number of yards in a limited number of plays, became a game of mass momentum plays. By the 1890s eastern colleges had produced such plays as the V formation, the flying wedge, and the tandem-tackle back, all of which directed an assemblage of players at one point of the opponent's defense. The flying wedge was probably the most unique football play ever invented. Certainly it was one of the most danger-ous. It was a play devised for the team putting the ball into play at the start of each half of the game. The rules allowed the team which was kicking-off to either kick to the opponent or merely touch the ball with the foot, pick it up, and pass it back to a teammate who could run with it. The Harvard coach, Lorin DeLand, ingeniously thought of using the latter kick-off method by having one man over the ball with the other 10 players divided into two groups about 25 yards behind the ball. The man over the ball signaled the two groups who converged on the ball with tremendous momentum, creating a flying "V" or wedge formation. When Harvard first used the flying wedge against Yale in 1892, it resulted in a Harvard gain to Yale's 25 yard line. Ingenious or not, it led to more injuries as it was the ultimate in mass momentum plays. It was abolished within two years.

Other forms of mass plays continued, while unethical actions and flagrant violations persisted. A keen observer of the college football scene tried to draw it into perspective. "The spirit of the American youth, as of the American man," the editor of *Nation* wrote, "is to win, to 'get there,' by fair means or foul; and the lack of moral scruple which pervades the struggles of the business world meets with

Football play looked brutal, but many justified it saying that it developed manly character (Princeton vs. Yale—1890).

temptations equally irresistible in the miniature contests of the football field."[35] Most people did not see as clearly that football and other sports were a reflection of the larger society. Lack of "moral scruples" led to Marquette College in Milwaukee dropping football because of a slugging outburst in one of its games in 1897.[36] Far more important nationally was the decision by the state legislature in Georgia that same year to outlaw football following the death of a University of Georgia player in a game with the University of Virginia. Only a veto by the governor, following a plea by the dead boy's mother not to sign the bill, saved football in Georgia.[37] More than one southern college abandoned the game, while other states including Indiana and Nebraska considered prohibiting the game which some compared to gladiatorial battles found in the ancient Roman arena.[38] Those who did could well have used the example of a Yale player who dipped his football jacket in a pool of blood at a slaughter house to make himself appear "more business like."[39]

Charges of brutality continued into the early years of the twentieth century while athletic "muckrakers" had a field day with the charges. One of these writers quoted the dean of the Divinity School of the University of Chicago as stating that football "is a social obsession—a boy-killing, education-prostituting, gladiatorial sport."[40] Deaths and injuries mounted as did opposition to mass plays. One death in particular, that of a Union College player in a game with New York University, helped precipitate a marked change in football and was a major event in bringing about the 1905-06 football crisis.

REFORM AND THE FOOTBALL CRISIS OF 1905-06

The 1905 college football season was not particularly more brutal than previous years. The athletic "muckrakers" may have been more vocal than in the past, but the major difference was that influential people began to take action. Even before the Union College player died as a result of a football injury during that season, the President of the United States, Theodore Roosevelt, became involved.

Teddy Roosevelt was the leading spokesman for the strenuous life in American society (see Chapter 17). Roosevelt was a Harvard graduate (1880), and he kept an interest in Harvard athletics through his early political career. This continued after he became president in 1901. His interest in football was greater than that of any president before and probably even greater than any twentieth century president including Richard Nixon in the late 1960s and early 1970s. Both presidents were masters at using football for political ends. During the 1905 football season the headmaster of Groton Preparatory School, Endicott Peabody, asked Roosevelt to draw together the football coaches of the Big Three, Harvard, Yale, and Princeton, to persuade them to set an example for honesty and sportsmanship in the playing of football. Peabody believed that if the leaders would set the moral tone other schools and colleges would follow.[41] Within a couple of weeks Roosevelt hosted the White House Conference on Football with coaches, faculty, and alumni representatives from the Big Three. The three colleges pledged themselves to carry out both the letter and the spirit of the football rules.

Roosevelt, a master of political timing, made headlines for attempting to bring about saner athletics at the time the athletic reforming "muckrakers" were making the ethics of football a national issue. He had, as one historian has noted, the ability to transform "important contributions into dramatic, personal victories."[42] In 1905, he glorified the reform movement in football by calling the most prestigious colleges together. Without changing the nature of the game in any important way, Roosevelt was given public accolades which brought about in the public mind the thought that he had saved football by reforming it. He had neither reformed, nor saved it though he was to keep involved in it.

There is little question that Roosevelt had made the game more visible by using the office of the presidency. The reforming of it, however, came principally from the efforts of the Chancellor of New York University, Henry McCracken, who pushed for a national meeting to either reform or abolish football. It had been football at McCracken's institution which had caused the death of a Union football player during their last game in 1905. McCracken almost immediately invited college presidents in the east to a meeting in early December. The small group of colleges which met decided to form a new rules committee for football and to invite institutions nationally to meet at the end of the month.

Over 60 colleges sent representatives to the New York meeting. The old rules committee, dominated by Yale's Walter Camp and eastern football powers, did not attend. They were meeting in Philadelphia and chose not to recognize the new organization that was to become the National Collegiate Athletic Association. In early January, with a behind-the-scenes push by Roosevelt, the two groups met in independent sessions at a New York hotel.[43] The Harvard representative to the old rules committee made a calculated move when he left that committee and joined the new national group. Shortly thereafter the two groups exchanged notes and met together.

This January meeting resulted in legislation which reformed the game. Rule changes allowed football to take on much of its present form; thus allowing it to remain the number one college sport and to eventually become the most popular professional spectator sport. Of most importance was the decision, against the desire of Walter Camp, to introduce the forward pass in football. The rugby football tradition to only pass backwards was broken. Only the decision to penalize incomplete passes prevented it from earlier becoming a tool to open up the game and prevent the brutalizing mass plays which typified the game in the early 1900s. In another move to prevent mass plays it was decided that the team with the ball must make 10 yards (rather than 5 yards) in 3 plays or lose possession of the ball. It was hoped that adding twice the distance would bring about runs around the ends of the line of scrimmage rather than smashes into the middle of the line. The new rules also required 6 offensive men (increased to 7 several years later) to be on the line of scrimmage rather than having them mass behind the line. The major thought at the meeting had obviously been one of reform rather than abolition.

Meanwhile an abolition movement was underway that, if a few key institutions had been successful in abandoning football, might have carried the nation. Some important, but not leading, schools in athletics did drop football. Included in the list were Columbia, Union, Northwestern, Stanford, and California. Numerous schools considered similar action including Harvard whose liberal arts faculty desired to see an end to the game. At the same time there was a movement in the Western Conference (Big Ten) to end football. Northwestern was the sole institution to suspend football when it voted to not play for five years though football was reinstated in two

Deaths and charges of brutality caused some colleges to drop football.

years.[44] Of more importance to the national scene was the decision of the Big Ten to organize a meeting of conference members in January, 1906. President Angell of Michigan had called the meeting at the urging of the President of the University of Wisconsin. Wisconsin's faculty was pressing for a two year suspension of Big Ten intercollegiate football games.[45] Wrote a law professor at Wisconsin to his institution's faculty representative to the Big Ten, historian Frederick Jackson Turner:

> Don't abandon us on this foot-ball proposition. With your help we can wipe it out once for all. If we temporize now, when things are in their present shape, we shall be right back where we were in a few months, and the faculty will enjoy the contempt of everybody for having wanted to do right but not dared to.[46]

The Angell Conference of the Big Ten did not suspend or abolish football, but it voted to suspend football for two years unless the individual institutions agreed to modify the existing rules. The meeting resulted in adoption of some radical changes for the leading athletic conference in the nation. Coaches were to be employed by the trustees of the institutions at the recommendation of the faculties, and they were to be members of the faculty. Freshmen and graduate students were to be made ineligible for intercollegiate competition. The football season was to be limited to 5 games, ending before Thanksgiving. Admission charges for football games could be no more than 50 cents in order to cut down the commercial aspect of football. Pre-season football practice and the training table were forbidden. Finally, the financial management of athletics, previously under student control, was to be placed in the hands of the university faculties.[47]

The reforms which grew out of the 1905-06 football crisis did indeed change the nature of football and intercollegiate athletics. The formation of a new national rules committee, which was the beginning of the NCAA, gave some power to a central administrative office. In the generations which followed, the NCAA gained considerable power to not only administer, but legislate and adjudicate for intercollegiate athletics. The football crisis also was a factor in the steady loss of student control over athletics as evidenced by the Big Ten regulations. The 1905-06 events were a turning point in bringing about rule changes which not only were intended to make the game less brutal, but more importantly opened up the game creating greater interest as a popular spectacle.

THE FOOTBALL SPECTACLE BY 1917

Football survived the crisis of the early 1900s with only a change in the form of play. The fundamental role of football as a spectacle with its commercial and professional aspects remained and even intensified. The reform had little changed the ethics of the game. Progressive leaders in education had found that reforming football was as difficult as reforming society, for in football as in society it was not easy to have an ethical game if those carrying out the rules were unethical. In football being ethical was most difficult because so much emphasis was placed on winning. To the player it was felt necessary to win because of individual and institutional prestige, while the stigma attached to being a loser was to be avoided. To many alumni winning in football was paramount, for it was the most visible symbol of a virile institution; one was always sure of the final score of a football game while one was never sure of the academic score of one institution in relation to another. To the college presidents there was a widespread belief that success in football meant greater institutional, as well as personal, recognition. This in turn would bring in larger enrollment and public and private support. To the professional coach, winning in football was essential—his job depended upon it.

The professional coach by 1917 had achieved recognition and had wrested nearly all of the control over the team from the previously all-powerful captain. The captain was now mostly a figurehead. Coaching had become a well paid position in numbers of colleges by World War I. Whereas the coach in the 1890s was often paid a couple hundred dollars by the athletic association to coach football, by the early 1900s a few thousand dollars was more common. Glenn "Pop" Warner was paid $34 a week by Georgia to coach the 1895 football team. Cornell hired him for $800 for the 1898 season. The next year Carlisle raised the ante to $1200 for the fall season. Pittsburgh gave him a salary in 1915 of $4,500. Later he was to earn $20,000 at Stanford.[48] When Harvard hired its first professional football coach, William Reid, in 1905 they paid him "only" $3,500, slightly less than an average full professor's salary at Harvard. The athletic committee had agreed to hold the figure at $3,500 for they felt that it would be wrong to pay the football coach more than that received by any professor on campus. The committee agreed to allow Harvard graduates to add an additional salary so that the football coach's salary approached that of the president of Harvard.[49] Fielding Yost was brought in as football coach at Michigan in 1901 from Nebraska where he had earned a $500 salary. Michigan paid him $2,300 plus living expenses, equivalent to a full professor's salary though he worked only during the fall of the year. By 1908 he was earning $4,000 and double that a decade later.[50] At Penn State football coaches were paid variously $45 in 1902, $1,500 in 1908, and $14,500 by the 1920s.[51] When coaches like "Pop" Warner, William Reid, and Fielding Yost were paid higher salaries than most full professors, one could indeed say that football and the coaches' position on the college campus was considered a revered and vital one.

Thousands were turning out to see highly trained teams compete. A 5,000 or even 20,000 seat stadium for most of the larger colleges and universities was considered insufficient even though it might seat 3, 5, or 10 times the number of students and faculty in the institution. Football belonged as much to the public as it did to the institution. Most colleges were proud of this fact and did what they could to accommodate the public's wishes. Building permanent concrete stadia was part of that. Even though the 1920s was the stadium building decade of the twentieth century, it began well before that. Harvard, finding a loyal and affluent alumni, decided to erect a Roman sized stadium with Greek columns. It seated 38,000 when completed in 1903. A decade later Yale completed a 67,000 seat bowl placed so that one walked down into the nearly $1,000,000 structure. Other institutions generally had wooden stadia which could seat as many as 46,000 such as the one at the University of Michigan. In the midwest it was envied for some time, long enough to carry into another period following World War I when the auto brought the stadium closer to the masses and the masses brought concrete stadia to the public institutions.

As the period of intercollegiate athletics between the Civil War and World War I came to a close it was clear that college athletics had reached an early stage of maturity with football leading the way. A survey by the NCAA at that time indicated that 150 colleges were spending a combined total of over $1,000,000 on athletics each year, a sizable amount then. Harvard was spending $160,000 for inter- and intracollegiate athletics, while it was reported that half of the students at the University of Wisconsin were participating in the athletic program. Nationally, an average of $59 was spent on each varsity athlete, while the east led by spending an average $170 per athlete—much on the one sport of football.[52] College football had matured in many ways by World War I. It would grow profoundly in the decades which followed, but the direction, the evils, and the benefits were well established by the second decade of the twentieth century.

REFERENCES

1. Luther Gulick, Basket Ball, *Physical Education*, IV (November 1895), p. 120.

2. Thomas Wentworth Higginson, Harvard Athletic Exercises Thirty Years Ago, [Harvard] *Advocate*, June 12, 1874, as quoted in John A. Blanchard (ed.), *The H Book of Harvard Athletics, 1852-1922*. (Cambridge: Harvard University Press, 1923), p. 316.

3. E. G. Dunning, Football in Its Early Stages, *History Today*, XIII (December 1963), pp. 838-847.

4. Richard P. McCormick, *Rutgers: A Bicentennial History* (New Brunswick, N.J.:

Rutgers University Press, 1966), p. 13. For a more complete history see Larry Pitt, *Football at Rutgers* (New Brunswick, N.J.: Rutgers University, 1972), pp. 3-23.

5. Thomas J. Wertenbaker, *Princeton 1746-1896* (Princeton: Princeton University Press, 1946), p. 326; and Park H. Davis, *Football: The American Intercollegiate Game* (New York: Charles Scribner's Sons, 1911), p. 50.

6. Henry R. Grant, captain of the Harvard University Foot Ball Club, letter to the Secretary of the Yale Football Association, October 11, 1873, in the John A. Blanchard (ed.), *The H Book of Harvard Athletics*, pp. 356-357.

7. Guy M. Lewis, The American Intercollegiate Football Spectacle, 1869-1917, Ph.D. dissertation, University of Maryland, 1964, p. 30.

8. Davis, *Football: The American Intercollegiate Game*, p. 73.

9. Blanchard (ed.), *The H Book of Harvard Athletics*, p. 378.

10. Davis, *Football, The American Intercollegiate Game*, p. 77.

11. *Ibid.*, p. 489.

12. *Ibid.*, p. 499; and A. M. Weyand, *American Football: Its History and Development* (New York: D. Appleton & Co., 1926), p. 252.

13. Andrew M. F. Davis, College Athletics, *Atlantic Monthly*, LI (1883), p. 682.

14. William H. S. Damerest, *History of Rutgers College* (New Brunswick, N.J.: Rutgers College, 1924), p. 430; and Leon B. Richardson, *History of Dartmouth College* (Hanover, N.H.: Dartmouth College Publications, 1932), II, p. 641.

15. E. L. Richards, College Athletics, *Popular Science Monthly*, XXIV (March 1884), p. 591.

16. Clarence Deming, The Money Power in College Athletics, *Outlook* LXXX (July 1905), p. 570.

17. Harvard Athletic Accounts in the *Presidents' Papers, Charles W. Eliot*, Box 202, Athletics, in the Harvard University Archives.

18. Amos A. Stagg and Wesley W. Stout, *Touchdown!* (New York: Longmans, Green and Co., 1927), p. 190; and Harvard Athletic Accounts, in the *Presidents' Papers, Charles W. Eliot*, Box 202, Athletics in the Harvard University Archives.

19. Richards, College Athletics, p. 597.

20. Harvard Athletic Accounts, *Presidents' Papers, Charles W. Eliot*, Box 202, Athletics, in the Harvard University Archives.

21. Ronald A. Smith, From Normal School to State University: A History of the Wisconsin State University Conference, Ph.D. dissertation, University of Wisconsin, 1969, p. 55.

22. Dudley A. Sargent, Evils of the Professional Tendencies of Modern Athletics, *Journal of Social Science*, XX (1885), p. 90.

23. Thomas C. Cochran and William Miller, *The Age of Enterprise: A Social History of Industrial America*. (New York: Harper & Row, 1961), pp. 340-341.

24. Lewis, The American Intercollegiate Football Spectacle, pp. 40, 52, 55.

25. *New York Herald*, November 25, 1892, as quoted in Lewis, *ibid.*, p. 119.

26. Richard Harding Davis, The Thanksgiving-Day Game, *Harper's Weekly*, XXXVII (December 9, 1893), pp. 1170-1171.

27. Robert Ebert (ed.), *An Illini Century: One Hundred Years of Campus Life* (Urbana: University of Illinois Press, 1967), p. 41.

28. Jonas Viles, *The University of Missouri* (Columbia: University of Missouri Press, 1939), p. 242.

29. *Grant County* [Wisconsin] *Witness*, December 5, 1894, p. 5.

30. *Chicago Tribune*, November 29, 1896, as stated in John R. Betts, "Organized Sport in Industrial America," Ph.D. dissertation, Columbia University, 1951, p. 249.

31. Stagg and Stout, *Touchdown!*, pp. 190, 205.

32. Ethelbert D. Warfield, Are Foot-Ball Games Educative or Brutalizing? *Forum*, XX (January 1894), p. 653.

33. John Hays Gardiner, *Harvard* (New York: Oxford University Press, American Branch, 1914), p. 59.

34. Charles W. Eliot, President Eliot's Report, *Harvard Graduates' Magazine*, III (March 1895), p. 369.

35. The Future of Football, *The Nation*, LI (November 20, 1890), p. 395.

36. *The* [Milwaukee] *Sentinel*, October 26, 1897, p. 6.

37. Lewis, The American Intercollegiate Football Spectacle, pp. 176-177.

38. James F. Muirhead, *The Land of Contrasts* (London: Lamson, Wollfe & Co., 1898), p. 115, 117; and Paul Bourget, American Pleasures, in his *Outre-Mer: Impressions of America* (New York: Charles Scribner, 1895), p. 329.

39. Richard Harding Davis, A Day With the Yale Team, *Harper's Weekly*, XXXVII (November 10, 1893), p. 1110.

40. Football Reform by Abolition, *The Nation*, LXXXI (November 30, 1905), p. 437.

41. Endicott Peabody, letter to Theodore Roosevelt, September 21, 1905, *Theodore Roosevelt Collection*, Letters Received, Vol. 97, Library of Congress, in Lewis, The American Intercollegiate Football Spectacle, pp. 223-224.

42. Robert H. Wiebe, *The Search for Order: 1877-1920* (New York: Hill & Wang, 1967), p. 192.

43. Guy M. Lewis, Theodore Roosevelt's Role in the 1905 Football Controversy, *Research Quarterly*, XL (December 1969), p. 723.

44. Walter Paulison, *The Tale of the Wildcats* (n.p.: privately printed, 1951), p. 132.

45. Merle Curti and Vernon C. Carstensen, *The University of Wisconsin: A History 1848-1925* (Madison: University of Wisconsin Press, 1949), II, pp. 536-538.

46. Howard Smith, University of Wisconsin College of Law, letter to Frederick Jackson Turner, University of Wisconsin Athletic Faculty Representative, March 21, 1906, *Frederick Jackson Turner Papers*, Wis/Mss/AL, Box 2, Athletics, State Historical Society of Wisconsin Archives.

47. The [Chicago] *Sunday Record-Herald*, January 21, 1906, Part 2, p. 1, in the *Frederick Jackson Turner File*, Series 5/21/5, Box 1, University of Wisconsin Archives.

48. Lewis, The American Intercollegiate Football Spectacle, pp. 163-164.

49. R. B. Merriman, Proceedings of the Athletic Committee, *Harvard Graduates' Magazine*, XIII (June 1905), pp. 630-631; and Archibald C. Coolidge, Professional Coaches, *Harvard Graduates' Magazine*, XIV (March 1906), pp. 392-395.

50. John R. Beehe, *Fielding Yost's Legacy to the University of Michigan* (Ann Arbor, Mich.: privately printed, 1971), pp. 26, 45, 51.

51. Wayland Dunaway, *History of The Pennsylvania State College* (State College: The Pennsylvania State College, 1946), p. 465.

52. H. Shindle Wingert, Report of the Committee on Sports, *American Physical Education Review*, XIX (1914), pp. 352-369.

CHAPTER 15

From Corsets to Bloomers—Women in Sport

The story of women in sport from the mid-nineteenth century to the early 1900s tells much of the social status of women in the period. For women it was a time of being placed upon a pedestal to be admired while being kept in a kind of bondage. The pedestal was never entirely toppled, but the social, political, and economic bondage was shaken by the end of the period. Women even participated in sport, though for most it was at a social cost and with great difficulty. In the half-century women began to participate in croquet, archery, tennis, golf, bicycling, and other sports which boded well for greater equality in sport and other aspects of social life in the twentieth century.

THE PLACE OF WOMEN IN THE NINETEENTH CENTURY

Tradition in Western culture has put women in an inferior place. One need look no further than the most important piece of Western literature, the Bible, for rationalizing a role of subjugation of women. The Apostle Paul wrote:

Let the woman learn in silence with all subjection.
But I suffer not a woman to teach, nor to usurp authority over man, but to be in silence.
For Adam was first formed, then Eve.
And Adam was not deceived, but the woman being deceived was in transgression [in sin].
Notwithstanding she shall be saved in childbearing, if they continue in faith and charity and holiness with sobriety.[1]

The place of women was obviously in the home, to be subservient to men, and to bear children while being the upholders of morality in society.

The Biblical injunction fit nicely into the mid-nineteenth century Victorian era which demanded obedience of women, especially those who were married. Middle class women in the more urban areas soon learned the rules of the game which subjected them to a molded existence, one in which indulgence was substituted for justice. Women were accorded recognition by their display of dress and etiquette rather than through more substantial contributions. A women's righter, Amelia Bloomer, asked at mid-century: "What is woman? Is she a slave? Is she a mere toy? Is she formed, like a piece of fine porcelain, to be placed upon the shelf to be looked at?"[2] Believing that middle and upper class urban women were too pure and delicate for the men's competitive world, in which making money was the major preoccupation, women became the recipients of that money by being adorned with visible symbols of their husbands' successes. The major goal of a young woman was to seek out and secure a husband, thus adapting herself to the masculine stereotype of the ideal woman, more-or-less like that pictured by Amelia Bloomer.

Besides this obvious social inferiority, women in the nineteenth century were politically and legally inferior. In most states during the 1800s women could not vote or hold office. Men generally refused to allow women to take part in any public capacity except in minor roles. Two examples occurred in the early Victorian period which emphasize this point. Early women's righters were often associated with the movement to abolish slavery. At a Connecticut anti-slavery society meeting in 1840 the chauvinistic chairman resigned in protest after a women's righter was given permission to address the meeting. Said the indignant chairman before he stormed off the platform: "I will not consent to have women lord it over men in public assemblies. It is enough for women to rule at home. It is women's business to take care of children in the nursery. . . . I am a man, I will not submit to it."[3] In the same year 8 women delegates to the World's Anti-Slavery Convention in Victorian England were denied admission because of their sex. Included among those rejected were Lucretia Mott and Elizabeth Cady Stanton who were to struggle for women's rights for the remainder of the century. Women, in addition to playing minor roles or being rejected from the political arena, could not, in most states, own property once they married, nor could they have legal responsibility for their children. Women, furthermore, could not sue or make contracts, nor could they retain their own wages which legally belonged to the husband.

Most women became resigned to their inferior station, trusting in God and the belief that a better life lay ahead. Even Catharine Beecher, a mid-century educational reformer, accepted her position. Catharine was the daughter of Lyman Beecher noted Congregational minister, sister of Harriett Beecher Stowe the author of *Uncle Tom's Cabin*, and sister of Henry Ward Beecher, possibly the best known minister of the nineteenth century. She voiced an opinion which dominated her age for it accepted the inequality between the sexes. "Heaven has appointed to one sex the superior, and to the other the subordinate station," wrote Miss Beecher. "It is therefore as much for the dignity as it is for the interest of females, in all respects to conform to the duties in this relation. As it is as much a duty as it is for the child to fulfill similar relations to parents, or subjects to rulers."[4] Womanhood had as its central virtues submissiveness, domesticity, purity, and piety. An early women's righter, Elizabeth Cady Stanton, believed that women accepted their degraded state because they could see no way of escaping from it. She likened women's bondage to that of the Negro slave. The woman, Stanton said, also "sighs and groans in her chains; and lives but in the hope of better things to come. She looks to heaven; whilst the more philosophical slave sets out for Canada."[5]

It is difficult to conceive of an 1800s sports' minded woman considering the Victorian restraints placed upon middle class females. Her place was in the home; her demeanor was one of delicacy and submissiveness; her role was as the upholder of morals and decency, and her position was degraded by raising her upon a pedestal rather than allowing her to enter the mainstream of American life. Feminist, Frances Cobbe, wrote in 1870 that women would never participate in sports and amusements until they began participating in meaningful work. "Not one lady in five hundred past girlhood," she claimed, "cares for any game or sport . . . as men care for these things."[6] Frances Cobbe was writing at the point in time, the post-Civil War era, when the industrial revolution was creating jobs which women would begin to fill. Industrialization, probably more than any other force brought women into the economic mainstream and indirectly led them to a more involved role in sport in American society.

WOMEN AND INDUSTRIALISM

In the early 1800s, before the dynamic impact of industrialism, if a woman in an urban area desired to work she was greatly limited to a few vocations such as domestic service, the cotton mills of New England, and teaching, though even teaching was male dominated. The industrial revolution, with its technological advances, opened up many new areas of work for both men and women. The Victorian characterization of women as "tender mothers, angels of mercy, and keepers of morals"[7] directed that women should concentrate their efforts in humanitarian directions—teaching and social work. These were less lucrative positions, and men generally allowed them to take these jobs. Women, though, expanded their job opportunities in the latter 1800s to include such employment as typists, bookkeepers, telephone operators, librarians, journalists, nurses, doctors, lawyers, and artists. The number of women workers grew from 2½ million in 1880 to 5 million in 1900.[8]

Even though it took an exceptionally bright and determined woman to enter areas dominated by men, progress was begun toward creating meaningful work and a place for women outside the home. This change brought about a greater independence for women—an independence needed if sport was to have a meaningful place in the lives of the dominated sex. With expanded freedom brought about by the increase of wealth and leisure of urban women, women began to expand their interests into the larger areas of social life while coming to assert their rights to greater equality. Nowhere was this seen more clearly than with the upper middle class and upper class women. For the upper income classes, money and cheap immigrant labor made it possible to pay servants for tasks which had previously kept women at home. The new found freedom was to influence women's role in sport.

WOMEN'S INVOLVEMENT IN SPORT

The popular writer Anne O'Hagan was enthusiastic, possibly overly so, when she said at the beginning of the twentieth century that "with the single exception of the improvement in the legal status of women, their entrance into the realm of sports is the most cheering thing that has happened to them in the century just past."[9] There was a striking difference between the acceptability of sport for women in the early years of the twentieth century and that found a half century before. Yet, the mores of the Victorian era were so strong that the struggle for the social freedom to participate in sport was far from achieved by World War I. Generally only those who braved social scorn and the stigma attached to the athletic girl participated in sport.

The pervasive attitudes of those opposed to vigorous activity for women was strong for the entire period of transition of women in sport from the 1850s and before to the second decade of the twentieth century. In the first year of the reign of Queen Victoria of England (1837) a book was written on exercises for women. The writer, a male, condemned horseback riding because he believed it produced an "unnatural consolidation of the bones of the lower part of the body, ensuring a frightful impediment to future functions, which need not here be dwelt on. . . ."[10] At the end of the reign of Victoria (1901) vigorous activity for women was still condemned for similar reasons.

In a melodramatic outburst a writer with a Victorian flare offered the thought that many a young girl:

> is battered and forever crippled in the breakers of puberty; if it cross these unharmed and is not dashed to pieces on the rocks of childbirth, it may still ground on the ever-recurring shallows of menstruation, and lastly, upon the final bar of the menopause ere protection is found in the unruffled waters of the harbor beyond the reach of sexual storms.[11]

The common opposition to sport for women because of its believed negative effects upon sexuality and childbirth was enough to keep many from participating. There were other reasons.

In many people's minds sports were virile activities suited only for men. For a woman to participate in a masculine sport would be to unsex herself. Added to this was the belief held by both men and women that females were biologically weaker as well as emotionally and physiologically frailer: They could not take the strain of physical exertion and certainly not competition. Combining these prevalent views with the nearly universal conviction that woman's place was in the home was sufficient cause for a languishing physical life for women.

With these strong physiological and sociological pressures opposing women's entry into sport and recreation, it was remarkable that the subdued sex was able to break out of its Victorian imposed physical apathy. The beginnings appeared shortly after the Civil War and became more marked as the century closed. A croquet craze swept the country in 1866 spreading to most small towns even in the sparsely settled west.[12] Groups in towns even formed teams, becoming proficient enough with the mallet to "roquet" opponents far from the next wicket. When a small midwestern town, Delavan in rural Wisconsin, put together a team it challenged a neighboring town 20 miles distant.[13] The popularity of croquet brought women and men together in a sporting pastime while serving a more important social function. Here was a sporting activity in which it was socially acceptable for women to participate. The lackadaisical nature of the game allowed women to participate in full hoop skirts dragging on the ground and required no more physical effort than that needed to push a stroller from the nursery to the park. Lamented a feminist: "Shall the croquet lawn be set forth as the 'earthly paradise' of the modern Eve?"[14] For some it had and continued to be into the twentieth century at which time croquet still "had not given way to golf."[15]

In the generation between 1860 and 1900, however, other sports had made an impact on some women. Archery, a sport first popularized in England, was one. Participated in primarily by the well-to-do in the 1860s and 1870s it, too, required no undue exertion

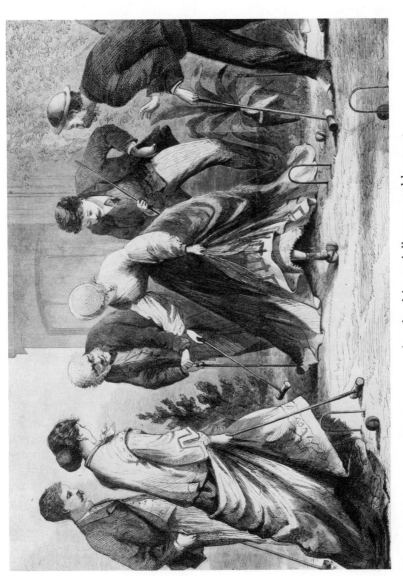

The croquet craze got some women involved in socially acceptable sport.

and was found to be socially acceptable. Women even participated in the first national archery tournament in 1879 though they shot fewer arrows and at a shorter distance than did the men.[16] Lawn tennis was another sport which was accepted socially for women. Lawn tennis was introduced by a woman, Mary Outerbridge, in 1874, after she had seen the British playing tennis on the island of Bermuda. Tennis, far different from that found a century later, was a gentle game in which men and women could be found patting the ball gently back and forth across a sagging net. Ladies had merely to lift their trailing skirts slightly with one hand while they lightly stroked the ball over the net. As many as three or four partners might be on one side of the net, and the act of running after the ball was considered unladylike. When playing outdoors, women were seen donning hats to shade their eyes while wearing veils over their faces to protect themselves from the sun's rays and preserving their fashionable lily-white complexions.

Women in the last generation of the nineteenth century were seen participating more frequently than in the past in such sports as horseback riding, bowling, yachting, canoeing, roller skating, and swimming. The sport, though, which had the greatest influence upon women's participation was bicycling.

Lawn tennis became a fashionable women's sport soon after its introduction in 1874.

THE BICYCLE AND DRESS REFORM

Bicycling, like all the other sports, was far from a woman's activity solely. It was, like the rest, primarily a man's sport, but the social impact was likely greatest for women. A primitive form of the bicycle, which had no pedals so that the rider used his feet to propel it, had been invented in the early 1800s in both Germany and France. By mid-century gears and pedals were developed in Europe. There had been a short craze in the United States for bicycling, or velocipede riding as it was called, shortly after the Civil War. Yet, bicycle riding did not prosper until after the high wheel bicycle was exhibited at the Philadelphia Centennial Exposition in 1876. Riding the high wheeler was almost entirely a preserve of wealthy men.[17] It was considered too dangerous, which it undoubtedly was, for women who, wearing

An 1819 velocipede before the advent of pedals.

extensive and cumberson outerwear, had to climb atop a precarious high wheeler and jeopardize life and limb. Thus when the League of American Wheelmen was organized from a group of 29 bicycle clubs meeting at the Newport resort in 1880, it was a fashionable male organization.

For women enthusiasts in the 1880s the tricycle, an expensive plaything, became socially acceptable. The fact that Queen Victoria's daughter had ridden one was a decided factor in giving it prestige. "We have been educated from infancy to consider Queen Victoria a model mother" commented a lady journalist in the mid-eighties. "Therefore, when the cable flashed over that her daughter had taken a turn on the tricycle, we felt a national glow of emulation."[18] At least the wealthy did, for a tricycle cost $200 to $300, almost as much as an average laborer's yearly earnings. Enough individuals, however, had the necessary income to purchase tricycles, and with the increasing numbers in New York City the Ladies' Tricycle Club was formed in 1884.[19]

Not until the low wheel or safety bicycle was introduced in the late 1880s and early 1890s did bicycling become popular with women. Even then it was far from being free of social scorn. With larger numbers of women braving social custom in the 1890s it was reported by one woman medical doctor who favored physical activity for women, that while tennis was socially acceptable, bicycling had not yet achieved that status.[20] To ride a bicycle was in many ways a challenge to Victorian mores for it created freedom and independence for women where none was sanctioned; it demanded physical exertion when it was thought women could not physiologically stand the strain; and it required radical attire where modesty and conservative clothing was the custom. The women who braved the stigma attached to the athletic girl and rode bicycles helped to break the generations-old beliefs that the urban middle class woman's place was in the home where she was to be displayed, but under a prescribed layer of clothes. It was likely that the late nineteenth century drive for greater equality for women was a stimulus to increased sporting activity for women. It was, though, a reciprocal action. When a few women started riding their bicycles it, in all probability, opened up greater freedoms for women in general. This was seen best in the freedom of dress.

Nineteenth century women were bound to convention in many ways. They were literally bound into their clothing. With customary clothing it was almost impossible for a woman to ride a bicycle or do any other extended physical exertion. First, she had a long trailing skirt in which it was difficult to pedal or to keep the skirt out of the moving parts. More important, perhaps, were her undergarments, especially the corset. Women were tied from bust to hip in a

When the high wheeler was replaced by the safety bicycle, women began to take up bicycling.

constricting garment which attempted to create a wasp-like waist where nature intended none. For a woman to have a 15 or 18 inch waist was not unusual. By constricting the viscera into the area occupied by the lungs, there was little room for breathing. Acts of fainting by nineteenth century women were as much a function of the physiology of oxygen deprivation as they were of social custom. Oliver Wendell Holmes' mid-century poem, "My Aunt," was still apropo at the century's end:

> They braced my Aunt against a board,
>   To make her straight and tall;
> They laced her up, they starved her down,
>   To make her light and small;
> They pinched her feet, they singed her hair,
>   They screwed it up with pins;
> Oh! never mortal suffered more
>   In penance for her sins.[21]

The necessity to loosen or remove the corset while riding, to unlace her as Holmes said, contributed to women's freedom. Outward dress reform, however, was more visible in its effect. Dress reform had been discussed for much of the nineteenth century with little result. When the short skirt and turkish trouser costume was introduced in about 1850 it became a newspaper sensation though the number who wore it was miniscule. Bloomers, the costume was called, after Amelia Bloomer, a woman's righter who did not invent but who wore the bifurcated costume for a number of years.[22] Only when the safety bicycle became popular in the 1890s did women begin wearing divided skirts, knickerbockers, or bloomers in any significant numbers. To this, writer Mrs. Reginald de Koven commented that it was nearly impossible to overestimate the role of the bicycle in the matter of women's dress and social reform. "To men, rich and poor," she wrote, "the bicycle is an unmixed blessing; but to women it is deliverance, revolution, [and] salvation."[23] A writer for *Scribner's*

The bloomer costume was popularized by women bicyclists.

Monthly believed that in the two years of the bicycle craze, 1894 and 1895, it had "given to all American womankind the liberty of dress for which the reformers have been sighing for generations."[24] It hardly did all that the most lavish praisers attributed to it, but the change was felt. This did not prevent those who scorned the new found freedom in dress and sport from speaking out. The chief of the Chicago Detective Department questioned women's bicycling as well as their attire when he replied to a Methodist minister that "a large number of our female bicyclists wear shorter dresses than the laws of morality and decency permit. . . ."[25] That was undoubtedly the majority view of Americans, but majorities seldom are the precipitators of social change.

The bicycle, for men and women, had had an important influence in the nation. It had brought numbers of people into a healthy leisure activity and had provided a cheap means of transportation. The bicycle lobby had done much to improve roads, a factor in the growth of the automobile industry after 1900. For women it was even more important as bicycling was noteworthy in bringing about greater sexual equality. The census bureau seemed to indicate the significance of the bicycle when it reported in 1900 "that few articles ever used by man have created so great a revolution in social conditions as the bicycle."[26]

THE COLLEGE EDUCATED WOMAN AND SPORT

For a woman to ride a bicycle in 1890 was no more a challenge to society's mores than for a woman to attend college a generation before. In the 1850s almost no girl attended college—this at a time when only about 1 percent of males attended college. The small number of females who attended college for the next half century had far more influence in sport, as in politics, than their numbers. For females attending women's colleges as well as women attending coeducational institutions it was a crusade to prove that women were equal in mental ability and worthy of an education similar to that obtained by men. A prevalent belief was that women were not equal mentally, that they would break down both emotionally and physically if they had to do college level work.

College education for women was part of the nineteenth century women's rights movement, and those who formed women's colleges or were associated with women in coeducational institutions believed that women must be physically active and healthy if they were to succeed at intellectual efforts. Almost every college in which women attended had a program of physical activity for them. Often that activity was as passive as daily two-by-two promenades of a mile or so. A number of institutions set up gymnastic programs such as the

Swedish system using light weights and movements. Nearly every institution by the 1890s had a sports program.

College women, by participating in sports, were helping to break down the stereotyped image of women as "taper-fingered, narrow-chested, lily-cheeked girls."[27] They began to participate in a variety of activities including archery, bowling, boating including 8 oared crews, baseball, track and field, horseback riding, skating, swimming, ice hockey, golf, tennis, and basketball. An 1860s Vassar graduate recalled her baseball playing days in Poughkeepsie, New York and the college girls' anti-social sporting ways:

> The public, so far as it knew of our playing, was shocked, but in our retired grounds, and protected from observation even in these grounds by sheltering trees, we continued to play in spite of public censorship.[28]

At the University of Nebraska in the 1890s young women in physical education were required to wear bloomers. They were, according to one observer, "overcome with shame, although no man, not even a janitor was allowed to enter while the girls were there; most of the new girls were so shy, even before others of their own sex and age, that they could not take a step, but sank down in a heap on the gymnasium floor, huddling together and refusing, almost to tears, to take part." Within a week, it was said, these girls "exulted in their new freedom."[29] It may have been the desire for greater freedom that drew women to sport or it is possible that greater social freedom allowed women to more fully enjoy sporting activities. In any event a girl pole vaulting, like the Nebraska girl in the early 1900s, would not have occurred a half century earlier. Neither would a girls' intercollegiate athletic contest have been possible in the mid-1800s as it was around 1900.

An important change occurred between mid-century and 1900 in women's college athletics. If croquet introduced women to outdoor sport in the 1860s and tennis and bicycling made it more fashionable for women to exercise in the 1890s, it was basketball which became the acclaimed game of college women across the nation within one decade of its origin in 1891. The game, developed for men in the Springfield, Massachusetts YMCA, was introduced to college women first at nearby Smith College by Senda Berenson. The men's rules were modified by Berenson soon after the first jump ball when a Smith girl dislocated her shoulder. But it was not the dislocation which most concerned Berenson. She felt that the men's rule which allowed one player to snatch the ball from an opponent led to roughness. The Victorian provision to prevent grabbing the ball from the opposition brought about the tendency for girls to just stand with the ball. Berenson then introduced the rule that a player could hold the ball no

A University of Nebraska woman pole-vaults in 1905—somewhat ahead of her times. (Courtesy of University of Nebraska Photo Archives.)

more than three seconds. Some enterprising player then decided to dribble the ball in between three second breaks so Berenson ruled that the ball could not be bounced more than three times. Finally, she divided the basketball court into three sections, requiring that players had to remain in one section and preventing the "star" player from dominating the game in all areas of the court. This latter rule was generally justified by other schools, not because it prevented an exceptionally talented player from dominating the game, but because it prevented players from exhausting themselves. At the time it was generally thought to be physiologically too taxing to run continuously from basket to basket and would lead to a physical collapse. These rules—no grabbing of the ball, three seconds to pass, three dribble limit, and a divided court—were the basis for twentieth century women's basketball until the 1960s when the game reverted basically to men's rules once again.[30]

Though there was no general agreement among women leaders regarding basketball rules for women, the game spread rapidly across the nation becoming the most important sport in schools and colleges. Interscholastic and intercollegiate games were common despite concern by a number of leaders who feared the evils which had already infected men's school and college sports. Elizabeth Burchenal, a leader of women's athletics in education, strongly opposed interschool competition and the coaching of girls by men. She saw no reason to imitate highly competitive men's sports, rather she favored "sports for sport's sake," an oft quoted phrase.[31] A desire to direct women's sport with sound educational outcomes under female leadership was heard over and over. It may have been stated best by a forceful woman physical educator who, when speaking before a mixed audience, spoke for her sex: "We are setting forth under our own sail, with women at the helm and women manning the whole craft."[32] Though the charge was stronger than the action which followed, it was an indication that not only was women's sport growing in educational institutions, but that women wanted to have a controlling voice over its direction. By World War I the struggle to liberate women in a sporting sense had only begun. The schools and colleges had contributed significantly to this emancipation.

WOMEN IN SPORT IN RETROSPECT

The degree of woman's emancipation in sport from mid-nineteenth to early twentieth century is difficult to appraise. To go from almost complete abstinence in the 1850s to participation in a score of sports by World War I seems to indicate a tremendous growth. Yet, a woman writer shortly after World War I could write that "athletics for girls have scarcely passed out of the stage of infancy. . . ."[33] The Victorian picture of the delicate female "worshipping at the shrine of the conventions" was still a strong force. The fact that forceful women were breaking out of this mold in a sporting sense was a reflection of the greater women's struggle for rights which culminated in the national right to vote shortly after the war. Most of the strides forward had occurred in urban areas or in educational institutions in the populated states. Rural and small town America continued to cling to nineteenth century conventions. The south, which had placed women higher on the pedestal than had any other section, was also slowest in freeing women in the sporting world. Other than riding of horses little other sport was socially sanctioned for the southern woman.[34]

The real revolution in mass sport participation by women was to wait until the last third of the twentieth century when the forces of civil rights and women's liberation made women's sport a respectable activity in a male dominated society. It is interesting that the women's struggle for greater equality has been associated in both the nineteenth and twentieth centuries with the struggle of blacks for equal rights. In the 1830s and 40s it was principally the women involved in the antislavery fight who became the leaders of the women's rights movement. More than a century later the women's liberation movement followed on the heals of the civil rights marches and laws which were passed in an attempt to give blacks equal rights. For both women and blacks it has been a long struggle for recognition in sport as in social life in general.

REFERENCES

1. Timothy I, 2:11-15, in the King James version of the *Bible*.

2. D. C. Bloomer, *Life and Writing of Amelia Bloomer* (Boston: Arena Publishing Co., 1895), p. 107.

3. Quoted in Page Smith, *Daughters of the Promised Land, Women in American History* (Boston: Little, Brown, 1970), p. 125.

4. Quoted in Arthur M. Schlesinger, *New Viewpoints in American History* (New York: Macmillan, 1922), p. 135.

5. Quoted in William O'Neill, *Everyone Was Brave* (Chicago: Quadrangle Books, 1969), p. 9.

6. Frances P. Cobbe, Ladies Amusements, *Every Saturday*, IX (1870), p. 101.

7. Robert Wiebe, *The Search for Order: 1877-1920* (New York: Hill & Wang, 1967), p. 122.

8. Arthur M. Schlesinger, *The Rise of the City, 1878-1898* (New York: Macmillan, 1933), p. 142.

9. Anne O'Hagan, The Athletic Girl, *Munsey's Magazine*, XXV (August 1901), p. 730.

10. Donald Walker, *Exercises for Women* (2nd ed., London: Thomas Hurst, 1837), p. 45.

11. George J. Engleman, The American Girl Today, *American Physical Education Review*, VI (March 1901), p. 29.

12. American Croquet, *Nation*, III (9 August 1866), pp. 113-115.

13. *The Whitewater* [Wisconsin] *Register*, 12 September 1872, p. 3.

14. Cobbe, Ladies' Amusements, p. 101.

15. Mark Sullivan, *Our Times, The United States 1900-1925* (New York: Charles Scribner's Sons, 1930), I, p. 26.

16. C. J. Longman and H. Walrond, *Archery* (New York: Frederick Ungar Publishing Co., 1967, (originally published in 1894), pp. 445-448; and E. G. Heath, *The Grey Goose Wing* (New York: New York Graphic Society, 1971), p. 202.

17. Henry J. Garrigues, Woman and the Bicycle, *Forum*, XX (January 1896), p. 579.

18. Mini C. Smith, Women as Cyclers, *Outing*, VI (May 1885), p. 318.

19. *Ibid.*

20. Mary T. Bissell, M.D., Athletics for City Girls, *Popular Science Monthly*, XLVI (December 1894), p. 149.

21. Moses Coit Tyler, *The Brawnville Papers* (Boston: Fields, Osgood, & Co., 1869), p. 193.

22. Bloomer, *Life and Writing of Amelia Bloomer*, pp. 66-69.

23. Mrs. Reginald de Koven, Bicycling for Women, *Cosmopolitan* XIX (August 1895), p. 386.

24. The Role of the Bicycle, *Scribner's Monthly*, XIX (June 1896), p. 783.

25. Morals of Wheelmen, *New York Times*, May 16, 1899, p. 1.

26. Axel Josephsson, Bicycles and Tricycles, *United States Census Reports*, X (1900), p. 329.

27. Our Sons, *Harper's Monthly*, XV (June 1858), p. 61.

28. Sophia E. Richardson, Tendencies in Athletics for Women in Colleges and Universities, *Popular Science Monthly*, L (February 1897), p. 517.

29. Sullivan, *Our Times*, II, pp. 191-192.

30. Ronald A. Smith, The Rise of Basketball for Women in Colleges, *Canadian Journal of History of Sport and Physical Education*, I (December 1970), pp. 18-36.

31. Elizabeth Burchenal, A Constructive Program for School Girls, *American Physical Education Review*, XXIV (1919), p. 273.

32. Agnes R. Wayman, Women's Athletics—All Uses—No Abuses, *American Physical Education Review*, XXIX (1924), p. 517.

33. Willystine Goodsell, *The Education of Women* (New York: Macmillan, 1923), p. 312.

34. Elizabeth C. Barney, The American Sportswoman, *Fortnightly Review*, LVI (August 1894), p. 271.

CHAPTER 16
The Nadir of Blacks in American Sport

The Civil War is the pivotal event in American sport history for it marks the watershed between unorganized and organized sport. It is, of course, the paramount episode in the history of blacks in America because it provided the official abolition of slavery. Freedom from slavery, however, did not mean acceptance in society, and this was borne out clearly in the realm of sport. The period between the Civil War and World War I was a scarred era for black participation in sport, especially during the years around the turn of the century, for it became nearly as difficult to participate in sport in a segregated America as it had been while in "chains." The period after the 1880s, when blacks were often legally and socially segregated in sport as in society, lends credence to the belief that this was the nadir of blacks in sport. As the period closed, by World War I, blacks had been effectively excluded from most white organized sport. The story is worth recounting for it provides the background necessary to better understand the breakthrough of blacks into the mainstream of sport following World War II; one of the important social changes in American life.

THE SPORTS OF BLACKS IN SLAVERY

The saga of blacks in sport supports those who claim that sport most often reflects the larger society. Negro slaves were used by their masters for sporting amusements; following freedom, blacks were given some opportunity to participate in sports; and by the end of the nineteenth century, when custom segregated and Jim Crow laws legally separated the races, blacks saw their chance to participate with whites in organized sport pass into oblivion. This may have been natural, but it was not inevitable.

Prior to the Civil War there is evidence indicating that blacks and whites participated and were spectators in sport together. At one of the key nineteenth century horse races, the South's Sir Henry vs. the North's Eclipse in 1823, a black is thought to have ridden Sir Henry. An account of a cockfight in the early national period in Virginia noted the arrival of "carriages, horses, and pedestrians, black and white, hastening to the point of attraction." The cock-pit was "surrounded by many genteel people, promiscuously mingled with the vulgar and debased."[1] During the Civil War two blacks fighting cocks before a group of officers of the north was a scene which would have been less likely to have occurred a half century later when the two races were more socially separated. As handlers of roosters in cockfights, blacks were involved directly with the sport. Similarly slaves became groomsmen and jockeys for plantation owners who enjoyed racing thoroughbreds.

Blacks were used by slave owners in boxing in a similar way. One owner might pit his best fighter against another plantation's strongest slave. One example was Tom Molyneux, a Virginia slave around 1800. It is believed that Molyneux was granted his freedom when he defeated a fighter from a neighboring plantation. After working as a dock hand in Baltimore and porter in New York City while continuing to box, Molyneux became a protegé of Bill Richmond, a well known black boxer of the period. Richmond took Molyneux to England where the fight game was best established. In England Molyneux defeated a number of white opponents, earning a match in December of 1810 with the reigning English Champion, Tom Cribb. Molyneux, packing 185 pounds on his 5'8½" frame, contested the Englishman Cribb in one of the first great heavyweight championships. In a fifty-five minute, 44 round fight to the finish, Molyneux was bloodied and defeated in this bareknuckled contest.[2]

Molyneux challenged Cribb for a return match and in doing so he raised the question of color. "As it is possible this letter may meet the public eye," Molyneux wrote, "I cannot omit the opportunity of expressing a confident hope that the circumstance of my being a different colour to that of a people amongst whom I have sought protection will not in any way operate to my prejudice."[3] The challenge was accepted by the 188 pound Cribb for a September meeting. Another bloody encounter resulted for the $10,000 purse. With Cribb bleeding from every organ, according to the London *Times*, Cribb struck Molyneux with a 9th round jaw-breaking punch, and the fight was terminated at the end of 11 rounds.[4] The challenge by blacks to white supremacy of the boxing heavyweights was not accepted for nearly another century. In that time many events occurred to radically change the position of blacks in a white dominated society.

BLACKS AND BASEBALL IN THE POST-CIVIL WAR ERA

Baseball serves well as an example of blacks in sport in the post-Civil War era. If blacks played baseball prior to emancipation it was probably as freedmen in the New York area in the 1850s or during the Civil War after they saw union or confederate troops playing the game. That baseball had mass appeal and showed rapid growth immediately following the Civil War is evidenced by Negro participation. In the late 1860s and early 1870s, blacks organized baseball teams in both the north and south, and in the north some blacks participated on predominately white teams.[5] Soon after the war, in 1867, the ruling amateur baseball organization, the National Association of Base Ball Players, decided to exclude all blacks from member teams and to exclude "any club which may be composed of one or more colored persons."[6] The NABBP which was attempting to keep its purely amateur game under gentlemanly control obviously did not consider any blacks of a class equal to itself. It was to be pure amateur and pure white. The NABBP reasoned that: "If colored clubs were admitted there would in all probability be some division of feeling, whereas, by excluding them no injury could result to anybody, and the possibility of any rupture being created on political grounds would be avoided."[7] This was entirely a view of northern origin for the NABBP was composed of only northern teams in 1867.

In professional baseball, where winning at times has dominated social or racial considerations, some blacks did participate. At the same time the first all-professional baseball team was formed in Cincinnati in 1869, a fifteen-year-old black was becoming proficient at the game. John "Bud" Fowler, born in Cooperstown, New York, site of the mythical origin of baseball, learned to play baseball in upstate New York. In 1872, when he was eighteen, he became a salaried player on the previously all-white New Castle, Pennsylvania baseball team, becoming the first black professional baseball player. He was the first of a score or more black players who played minor and major league baseball in the generation before the twentieth century when total exclusion of blacks from white-dominated baseball occurred.[8] Fowler continued to play for a quarter century, but never in the major leagues. When he was thirty-one years old a story in *Sporting Life* told something of the nature of a black man existing at odds with the society which was drawing a tighter color line in 1885. The story read:

Fowler, the crack colored second baseman, is still in Denver, Colo., disengaged. The poor fellow's skin is against him. With his splendid abilities he would long ago have been on some good club had his color been white instead of black. Those who know say there is no better second baseman in the country; he is besides a good batter and fine baserunner.[9]

Others found that integrating baseball was a Sisyphean task when the larger American society was moving in an opposite direction in the 1880s.

We find, however, that blacks first broke into the major leagues in the 1880s when Moses Fleetwood Walker and his brother Welday Walker became members of the Toledo Club of the American Association which then had major league status. It is worth noting that the Walker brothers had attended Oberlin College in Ohio, the first college in America to open its doors to blacks and to women.[10] Fleet Walker's reception in some of the American Association league cities was not as cordial as it had been at Oberlin College, a center of the abolition movement before the Civil War. One of the American Association franchises had been moved in the late summer of 1884 from Washington D.C. to Richmond, Virginia, the former capital of the confederacy. The Toledo manager received a threatening letter from Richmond racists. It read:

> We the undersigned do hereby warn you not to play Walker, the negro catcher, the evening that you play in Richmond, as we could mention the names of 75 determined men who have sworn to mob Walker if he comes on the ground in a suit. We hope you will listen to our words of warning, so that there will be no trouble; but if you do not there certainly will be. We only write to prevent much bloodshed, as you alone can prevent.[11]

Moses Fleetwood Walker (seated left) and Welday Walker (standing) were the first blacks to play in college baseball (Oberlin) in the 1870s. (Courtesy of Oberlin College.)

The Richmond fans need not have gone to all the trouble for Fleet Walker broke a rib while catching and was unable to travel to Richmond.

Following Walker there were 4 blacks playing professional baseball in 1886 in predominately white leagues. The next year there were at least 8. Stirrings of unrest among white players seemed to increase as more blacks entered baseball. A white member of the Syracuse, New York team of the International League refused to have his picture taken with his teammates, one of whom was a black. Later the International League voted not to approve any more contracts for blacks though the 5 black players in the league were allowed to remain on league teams.[12] Only a few days following the International League's decision to create its color bar, George Stovey, a talented black pitcher for the League's Newark club was scheduled to pitch in an exhibition game against the Chicago White Stockings of the National League. Adrian "Cap" Anson, probably the best known ball player of the nineteenth century, was the Chicago manager. Anson refused to field his team if Stovey were allowed to play. Stovey did not play, it was noted at the time, because he was "sick." Situations like this caused a Newark newspaper to question the discriminatory policies of baseball, bringing up points mouthed a century later. "If anywhere in the world the social barriers are broken down," the newspaper noted, "it is on the ball field. There many men of low birth and poor breeding are the idols of the rich and cultured; the best man is he who plays best."[13] The International League did not agree and instead consented to a quota system which allowed only 1 black player per team.

The same year Adrian Anson prevented the New York Giants from signing George Stovey to a contract, the last recognized black to have a chance to play major league baseball until Jackie Robinson played for the Brooklyn Dodgers in 1947.[14] The minor leagues were following suit. When the Ohio State League drew the color line, Welday Walker, the Negro from Oberlin College, protested with an eloquent plea. "There should be some broader cause—such as lack of ability, behavior, or intelligence—for barring a player," Walker wrote, "rather than his color. . . . I think ability and intelligence should be recognized first and last—at all times and by everyone—I ask the question again, why was the law permitting colored men to sign repealed. . . ?[15] Professional baseball by the 1890s had become an apologist for Jim Crow legislation.

JIM CROW IN AMERICAN SOCIETY

Jim Crow legislation, laws to segregate Negroes from Caucasians, was not first directed at sports like baseball though sport soon came under the aegis of white segregation laws and customs. Following the Civil War the Republican reconstruction policy freed the slaves, gave the blacks civil rights under the 14th Amendment, and the vote to males in the 15th Amendment. Military control enforced to some extent the carrying out of policy in the south where 90 percent of all blacks lived, three-quarters of whom lived in rural areas. One might have expected social segregation, if not legal separation, in sport in southern states. This was to some extent true, for baseball teams were usually all-black or all-white. Yet, black teams often played white teams. For nearly a quarter century after the Civil War Negro and white teams competed against each other in New Orleans. An 1887, black newspaper account of an interracial game, won by blacks, stated: "The playing of the colored club was far above the average ball playing and elicited hearty and generous applause from the large crowd in attendance, which was about evenly divided between white and colored."[16] This was at a time when the color line was beginning to be socially sanctioned in both north and south. By the 1890s interracial baseball had almost completely been eliminated in the south.

The question as to why this occurred in sport and in society in general is more difficult to explain. Many forces were at work between the Civil War and 1900 to bring about an effective separation of blacks from the rest of American society. In the first place freedom and political responsibility were thrust upon a people who were not prepared for their rights and responsibilities in a white dominated culture. It was not to be expected that the approximately four million blacks[17] who had been in a position of complete subordination and who were suddenly given power and importance, should be accepted on an equal basis with those who had dominated them for generations. The Black Codes, passed almost immediately after the Civil War by the white southern governments, indicated this antipathy to black freedom and a desire to legislate a system of social control to substitute for slavery.[18] As this southern white backlash occurred, northern Republicans created legislation intended to give blacks civil rights, but more importantly to insure continued Republican control of southern states. The black man was caught between the indignation of racist southern whites who became Democrats and the often exploitive northern Republicans. Eventually the Republicans deserted the Negro cause which had been much more politically than humanitarianly motivated.

The withdrawal of the last United States troops from the former confederate states following the Compromise of 1877 was part of the white's reconciliation of the two sections. By bringing about greater harmony between north and south, the Negro was sacrificed.[19]

Though there were federal and state laws to protect blacks, there was general agreement, north and south, to allow local and state authorities to acquiesce to the views of the white majorities. How similar this was to the National Association of Base Ball Players who in 1867 agreed to exclude Negroes, for as they said "by excluding them no injury could result to anybody. . . ."[20]

The deterioration of black rights with the reconciliation of the two sections was seen in the decisions of the United States Supreme Court in the latter 1800s. An 1883 Supreme Court decision declared the 1875 Civil Rights Bill unconstitutional stating that the 14th Amendment which prevented discrimination against individuals by states did not prevent discrimination by individual citizens. This accelerated the denial of "social rights" which was already in process through local and state segregation laws and in social customs.[21] The next decade's famous Plessy v. Ferguson case (1896) upheld "separate-but-equal" accommodations on railroads. But more importantly the Plessy decision legally sanctioned separation of schools by race. Two years later the Supreme Court upheld literacy tests and poll-tax qualifications for voting, policies devised to keep the Negro out of politics. These decisions legally acknowledged the inferior role of blacks in American society. In the Plessy decision Justice Henry Brown wrote of the blacks: "If one race be inferior to the other socially, the Constitution of the United States cannot put them upon the same plane. . . ."[22]

That white America believed in the inferiority of the black race is obvious to the most casual observer. Two important phenomena were occurring in the late 1800s to reinforce and intensify this belief in the inferiority of the black race or the superiority of the white race, more specifically the Anglo-Saxons. The first was the influence of Darwin's theory of evolution; the second was the push for territory outside of the continental United States, imperialism, and the subjection of non-white people by Caucasians.

Charles Darwin's theory of evolution as espoused in his *Origin of Species* (1859) was adapted to human society shortly thereafter by those believing in the theory of natural selection, the struggle for existence, and the survival of the fittest. These Social Darwinists, led by the Englishman Herbert Spencer and Yale University's William Graham Sumner, gave force to the belief that the white race through a process of the survival of the fittest came to dominate the world. Even white people with a humanitarian bent despaired at the situation of blacks on the evolutionary ladder, believing that crowded conditions in cities, poor health, and rising crime rates were indications that they were losing out in the struggle for existence. Even Justice Harlan, who wrote the dissenting opinion strongly condemning the 1896 Plessy, "separate but equal" decision, believed that "in prestige, in achievement, in education, in wealth and power the white race is the dominant race in the country."[23] The supposed liberal and progressive, Theodore Roosevelt wrote privately in the early 1900s that "as a race and in the mass" the blacks are "altogether inferior to the whites."[24] There were outright racists like Thomas Dixon, author of *The Leopard's Spots*, who believed that Negroes were permanent cripples in the evolutionary struggle for existence.[25] To further damage the picture of blacks, caricatures of Negroes in popular periodicals of the time portrayed them as lazy, foolish, and incapable of making wise decisions in addition to being a step down on the evolutionary ladder.

These attitudes of racial inferiority were heightened by the rise of imperialism toward the latter 1800s and early 1900s. While the nations of industrial Europe were carving up Africa and the Far East in the late 1800s, the United States, too, was flexing its international muscles. When the United States engaged in the Spanish-American War in 1898, it not only gained new territories in the Caribbean but also in the Pacific area. It was commonly believed that these non-white "backward" peoples were in need of being enlightened and shaped in the image of Anglo-Saxons—what the Englishman Rudyard Kipling called taking up the White Man's Burden. A clear superiority of the white man was proclaimed by noted people in government, business,

Popular periodicals carried caricatures of Negroes looking foolish while participating in sport.

and religion, and that feeling spread to the masses. A Congregationalist minister, Josiah Strong, believed that the Anglo-Saxon was "divinely commissioned to be, in a peculiar sense, his brother's keeper."[26] A Senator from Florida stated that wherever the Anglo-Saxon "has been placed side by side with people of other races he has ruled."[27] Thomas Dixon was satisfied that "God has raised up our race . . . to establish and maintain weaker races, as a trust for civilization, the principles of civil and religious Liberty and the forms of Constitutional Government."[28] No wonder blacks began to feel an increasing inferiority with numbers withdrawing, even when not forced, from the mainstream of American life including its sporting life.

In response to the increasing Jim Crowism occurring in American life, Negro leadership and the masses turned toward accomodation rather than protest. The dominant Negro leader of the late 1800s and early 1900s, Booker T. Washington, led the way toward accommodation with the whites. In his famous Atlanta Compromise speech in 1895, Washington held up his hand, fingers outstretched, to a mixed crowd of blacks and whites, proclaiming that "in all things that are purely social we can be as separate as the fingers. . . ." He believed that the masses of blacks by proving their worth "by production of our hands" was far more valuable than demanding either political or social rights.[29]

Accommodation when applied to sport meant a quiet withdrawal from white dominated sport by blacks—exit from major and minor leagues in baseball, loss of a dominating position as jockeys in horse racing; general exclusion from the upper class sports like golf and tennis; and an increasing difficulty gaining important matches in the lower class sport of boxing. What was left for blacks generally was participation of black against black and the formation of Negro leagues. At a less organized level it meant acceptance of the Jim Crow laws which called for separate (but almost never equal) playgrounds, public parks, swimming pools, and other recreational facilities. The first few decades of the twentieth century found such laws as those passed to provide separate entrances, exits, and ticket windows at recreational facilities; an Atlanta law prohibiting amateur baseball teams of different races from playing within two blocks of each other; a Texas law prohibiting "Caucasians" and "Africans" from boxing or wrestling against each other; an Oklahoma law forbidding blacks and whites from fishing together in the same boat; and a Birmingham, Alabama ordinance prohibiting the two races from playing dominoes or checkers together or in company.[30] Most blacks must have felt they needed to accommodate themselves to white society in order to survive.

BLACKS ON FOOT, ON THE BICYCLE, AND ON HORSEBACK

The exclusion of blacks from the mainstream of sporting and social life took place over several generations at an uneven pace. While there was exclusion of blacks from professional baseball toward the end of the 1800s and for the next half-century, there is evidence of blacks in the white organized sports of track, bicycling, and horse racing into the twentieth century, although it was on a limited basis.

In the 1870s professional long distance running races were drawing thousands of spectators. The contests, often six days in duration, were known as "go-as-you-please" events. The object was to run or walk as many miles as possible on an indoor track in six days beginning one minute after midnight on Monday morning (to eliminate running on the Sabbath) through the following Saturday. A common goal was 500 miles though an amazing record of 623¾ miles was covered in one six-day event by an Englishman, George Littlefield in the 1880s. At the height of the "go-as-you-please" pedestrian contests, Sir John Astley, an English sporting enthusiast and member of the British parliament, put up a large amount of prize money and a championship belt for a series of six-day pedestrian contests in London and in New York's Madison Square Garden. In the last of five challenges for the Sir Astley belt, run in 1879, a twenty-two-year-old Boston Negro, Frank Hart, was entered. One account of Hart said that "he is a negro, and so little known in New York City that many people thought his entry was intended as an insult to the other contestants, and even threatened to reject him from the list of starters."[31] While the winner, Charles Rowell of England, was covering 530 miles and collecting $26,000 in gate receipts and stake money, Frank Hart was not far behind in fourth place with 482½ miles with a share of the gate receipts worth $2,730. A popular sporting journal stated that the "Smoked Irishman" had a "beautiful style, modest cheerful behavior, and plucky performance [which] made him a great favorite, and he received more than his share of applause and floral tributes."[32] The next year Hart ran 566 miles in a similar event, a record distance at the time.[33] Professional long distance running began to die out in the 1880s and 1890s though it had little over-all effect upon blacks for there were so few participating. As professionalism in track withered away, amateur track and field became stronger in athletic clubs and colleges. Athletic clubs became class and race conscious with the result that few blacks were given opportunities to run as members of athletic clubs. In northern colleges some blacks found success in track as well as other sports like football and baseball.

With the advent of the bicycle and bicycle racing, professional long distance running died. The novelty of the bicycle and its greater speed created an attraction in organized bicycle races, amateur and professional. The amateur League of American Wheelmen, organized in 1880, came into existence as the color line began to be drawn nationally. Southern state affiliates of the League started to withdraw from the LAW in the early 1890s because of its policy of admitting black members. By 1894 the LAW inserted a whites only clause in its constitution in an effort to accommodate the white southerners. Wrote a LAW official rationalizing its position: "There is no question of our accepting the negro in preference to the white wheelman of the south. If it should be narrowed down to a question such as that, we should undoubtedly decide that we want our southern brothers in the league in preference to the negroes of the country."[34]

In professional bicycle racing a similar separation of blacks and whites took place. One outstanding exception, however, existed. Marshall "Major" Taylor, a black from Indianapolis, was the premier bicycle racer in America in the late 1890s, and he chose to fight the segregation policies in the cycling sport. Possibly because he was so outstanding and was thus an economic force by being a major drawing card to cycling events, "Major" Taylor was usually allowed to compete in otherwise all-white contests. While most black riders were cycling in an all-Negro league, Taylor chose to compete with whites for larger prize monies. In 1898, at the age of twenty, he won 21 times, came in second 13 and third 11 times—what the sports writers claimed to be the national cycling championship. The next year he repeated as champion finishing out of the top three places only twice. After a third year as the top bicycle racer in America, Taylor sailed for Europe to challenge the world's best cyclists. There in 1901 he defeated Edmond Jacquelin, the French champion as well as champions from other countries.[35]

A super athlete like Taylor was able for a time to break the grip of the rising tide of racial segregation at the turn of the century even though both the League of American Wheelmen and the National Racing Association forbade Negro membership. Taylor was unique in this respect. But then, even Booker T. Washington dined at the White House—once. This was a mistake according to President Theodore Roosevelt who confided that he would not be invited twice.

Unlike cycling in which few blacks became notable, an aspect of horse racing was dominated by blacks before they were eased out of prominence. Negroes were jockeys from colonial days when it was common for a southern plantation owner to use one of his slaves as jockey in challenge races. Throughout much of the 1800s, until after the Civil War, horse racing was generally in the hands of the old time elites who believed that the important aspect of successful horse racing was the blood lines of the horse, not who rode the horse. The owners raced for honor, not for pecuniary value.[36] Therefore jockeys were generally chosen from among the stable attendants, exercise boys, and trainers. Because those were menial tasks, it was often blacks who had those jobs.

By the 1880s and 1890s the "nouveau riche" began to dominate horse racing and to operate it as a business. As with other successful businessmen they looked to all aspects of horse racing in their desire to provide a winning combination. Thus the new rich were concerned with more than breeding lines in racing. The position of jockey became a vital and prestigious one, whereas previously the names of the jockeys were seldom noted. By the late 1800s, because of the tradition, there were numerous black jockeys. Their dominant position was short lived. With the prevailing belief in the superiority of Anglo-Saxons and the inferiority of blacks, in addition to the increasing segregation as a way of life in America, blacks were pushed back into the stable to engage in menial tasks, while whites began to ride the horses and take a large share of the increased prize money for the successful jockeys. In other words when the awards, both financial and prestigious, became attached to the jockey, Negroes were slowly removed from that position. Some notoriety, nevertheless, was first gained.

The general ignoring of jockeys, both black and white, was seen in an 1830 account of a horse race in Georgia. When the horse Eclipse fell, the jockey, a black, was killed. A white woman was quoted as she left the race track: "I declare, had it not been for that little accident, the sport would have been delightful."[37] Forty years later when the first Kentucky Derby was run at Churchill Downs, the names of the jockeys were not even listed in the program. The position of jockey was not considered of great enough import to be included. Of the 15 riders in that 1875 derby 14 were blacks including the winner, Oliver Lewis.[38]

The Kentucky Derby serves well to illustrate the demise of Negroes as jockeys. From 1875 through 1902 blacks were the winning riders in 13 races. Probably most outstanding was Isaac Murphy who won three times, a record eventually matched by Eddie Arcaro in the mid-twentieth century. When Murphy died in 1896, his estate was worth about $50,000. By this time race track owners and stable owners had formed a Board of Control to govern the sport and the prestigious Jockey Club of New York (1894) took control of licensing jockeys. The established black jockeys were allowed to remain, but racial restrictions limited the number of blacks admitted as jockeys. Eventually the color line was drawn completely and no Negro rode in the Kentucky Derby after 1911.[39]

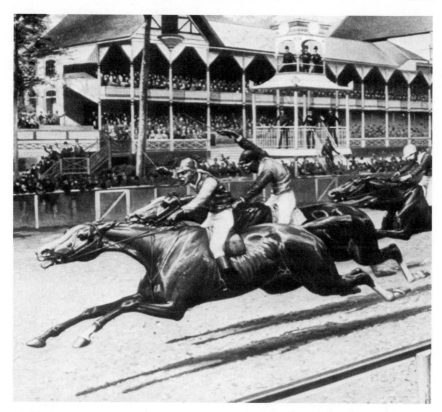

Black jockeys dominated racing until the color line was drawn by racist America. (Courtesy of Library of Congress.)

In the generation between the 1870s and the early 1900s a combination of racial reactions to blacks and an intensification of economic considerations removed blacks from racing. It has been estimated that jockeys in the 1870s earned about $5.00 for being a winning rider in a race. By the early 1900s it was reported that 8 black jockeys were each earning between $5,000 and $10,000 a year.[40] Within a decade there were almost no more Negro jockeys. The Jim Crow attitudes in America had removed blacks from another aspect of sport and society, one in which they had had a dominating position for a quarter century.

BOXING, JACK JOHNSON, AND THE NATIONAL MOOD

Boxing, essentially a lower class sport, was a logical choice as a last battle ground before Jim Crowism became supreme in sport in the early 1900s. While boxing as a sport in England and America had been influenced by elements of the upper class, it had generally been the lower classes who did the actual fighting. In America the lower class Irish and, to a lesser extent, Negroes had dominated boxing from the mid-nineteenth century.

Heavyweight boxers have always attracted the greatest attention. This was true in 1860 when the English champion Tom Sayers fought and drew with the Irish-American, John "Benicia Boy" Heenan. It was no less true in 1882 when John L. Sullivan defeated Paddy Ryan for the heavyweight championship. While Sullivan was champion for the next decade a number of black boxers were gaining impressive records—mostly boxing other Negroes. One was George Godfrey who was considered the black heavyweight champion of America in the mid-1880s. When he challenged John L. Sullivan for a match, Sullivan refused the challenge.[41] In 1892, the year Sullivan lost to James J. Corbett, Sullivan agreed to defend his title against all challengers except Negroes, the most promising of whom would have been Peter Jackson who had fought a 61 round draw with Corbett the year before.[42] No black was given a chance to win the prestigious heavyweight title against Corbett, Bob Fitzsimmons, or Jim Jeffries for the next decade. In 1895, the editor of the New York *Sun*, Charles A. Dana, wrote of the black challenge to white superiority at some lower weight classes in boxing:

> We are in the midst of a growing menace. The black man is rapidly forging to the front in athletics, especially in the field of fisticuffs. We are in the midst of a black rise against white superiority. Just at present we are safe from the humiliation of having a black man world's champion, but we had a pretty narrow escape. . . . But the menace is still with us.[43]

The "menace" did not come in the heavyweight division until Tommy Burns won the title shortly after the retirement of Jeffries as the undefeated champion of the world.

Jack Johnson became the first modern challenger for the heavyweight championship almost a hundred years after Tom Molyneux, a freed Virginia slave, had fought the English champion, Tom Cribb. It was not easy for Johnson to receive a chance to be world champion. He had literally to pursue Tommy Burns, the reigning champion, from New York to London, to Paris, back to London, and then to Sydney, Australia before Burns agreed to fight him. With the acceptance Johnson agreed to fight for $5,000 while Burns was to receive $35,000, win or lose. In addition the fight was refereed by Burns' manager, a concession Johnson said he made to insure getting a chance at the championship.[44] Johnson won easily on the day after Christmas, 1908, before a crowd of more than 20,000 Aussies.

A black man had been elevated to national prominence at a time when much of American society was expecting Negroes to be second

Jack Johnson became the first black heavyweight boxing champion in 1908. (Courtesy of Library of Congress.)

class citizens in a nation of legal and social segregation. It was appalling to some that a black was the symbolic physical master of the world. Almost immediately there was a call for a "White Hope" to defeat Johnson. Jack London, the writer, concluded his New York *Herald* account of the Burns-Johnson fight with the plea to the retired and undefeated heavyweight champion to do battle. "Jim Jeffries," he wrote, "must emerge from his alfalfa farm and remove the golden smile from Jack Johnson's face. Jeff, it's up to you."[45] Jeffries, himself, believed that "Burns had no right to fight Johnson for the heavyweight championship." He indicated that he would not be the "White Hope" and challenge the new black champion.[46] Others looked to previous champions Bob Fitzsimmons and James Corbett. Corbett said he was willing to meet Johnson "in order to bring the championship back to a white man," while Jeffries believed that either Corbett or Fitzsimmons could beat him.[47]

Johnson returned to the United States from Australia, fighting several lesser known boxers and retaining his world supremacy. At the same time he was widely seen with white women, thus breaking with the social conventions of the times. Among the white women who traveled with him were Belle Schreiber, described as a prostitute with class,[48] and later Etta Duryea, the ex-wife of Clarence Duryea of auto racing fame, whom he eventually married. So while a black man remained the symbolic strong man of the world, Johnson intensified white animosity toward him by breaking the rigid social custom.

The call for a "Great White Hope" became stronger, and increasingly pressure was brought to bear upon Jim Jeffries to regain the crown from which he had retired undefeated half a decade before. Finally Jeffries agreed to a $101,000 fight with 60 percent going to the winner. The July 4, 1910 fight was discussed in papers across the nation for a half year preceding the event. Much of it was racial in content. On the day of the fight Jeffries spoke for those who believed he was the "Great White Hope:"

> That portion of the white race that has been looking to me to defend its athletic superiority may feel assured that I am fit to do my very best.[49]

The thirty-five-year-old Jeffries probably did his best, but it was far short of what was needed to dethrone Jack Johnson whom many have said was the greatest heavyweight of all time. Johnson beat Jeffries into submission in 15 rounds.

The victory of a black man over the "Great White Hope" touched off celebrations by blacks in a number of cities and was also the cause of racial riots in which several people were killed. Johnson was a "persona non grata" to many white Americans. Organizations, under the aegis of Christian churches, worked doggedly to prohibit the showing of the Johnson-Jeffries fight films in American theaters. The Congress of the United States came to the aid of these reformers and made it a Federal crime to transport moving pictures of boxing matches in interstate commerce, while a number of state legislatures barred the showing of fight films.[50]

Jack Johnson was, perhaps, most disliked because of his relationships with and marriage to white women. Two years after the Jeffries fight, Johnson's first white wife, Etta Duryea, committed suicide. Shortly thereafter a nineteen-year-old white girl, Lucille Cameron, from Minneapolis asked Johnson for a job in his Chicago night club, the Café de Champion. Cameron's mother charged Johnson with the abduction of her daughter across a state border for immoral purposes, a federal crime under the 1910 Mann (White Slave) Act. Miss Cameron, however, would not substantiate the charges. In the meantime Belle Schreiber, a white prostitute with whom Johnson had previously lived and traveled, charged Johnson with a violation of the Mann Act claiming that she had been a victim of Johnson. So while a trial date for this charge was set for 1913, Johnson was acquitted of the charges filed by Lucille Cameron's mother. Out on bail of $32,000 pending his trial, Johnson and Miss Cameron were married. Even some blacks began turning away from Johnson. One was Booker T. Washington who spoke out during the controversy stating that: "Undoubtedly Johnson's actions are repudiated by the great majority of right-thinking people of the Negro race. . . ."[51] But the hue and cry came mostly from whites. Speaking at the annual state governors' meeting the governor of South Carolina called Johnson a "black brute. . . . If we can not protect our white women from black fiends, where is our boasted civilization?" In a bit of rightous male chauvinism and racial hatred he confirmed that:

> In the South we love our women, we hold them higher than all things else, and whenever anything steps between a Southern man and the defense and virtue of the women of his nation and his states, he will tear it down and walk over it in her defense regardless of what may be the consequences. . . .[52]

As a result of similar opposition to interracial marriage a number of states which had not already done so considered passing anti-miscengenation laws.

All of this occurred before the trial in 1913 at which time the jury brought a verdict of guilty. Johnson was sentenced to one year and a day in jail for violation of the Mann Act. While Johnson was granted a two weeks' stay of execution to take the case to the Circuit Court of Appeals he decided to slip bond and flee the country. This he did by a cloak-and-dagger episode in which he changed places with a member of a touring black baseball team and escaped to Canada and then to France. At this point we find a black man who did not respect Jim Crow laws being champion of what many considered a disreputable sport, married to a white woman, guilty of a federal crime, and fleeing from the law.

In Europe he boxed occasionally and traveled frequently giving boxing exhibitions and theatrical performances. When the nations of Europe fumbled their way into World War I in the summer of 1914, Johnson was in Russia performing in St. Petersburg. He quickly returned to France through Germany and then to England where national concerns were more important to England than was Jack Johnson. In late 1914, Johnson agreed to fight Jess Willard whom some were holding up as the new "White Hope." The match was eventually scheduled for Havana, Cuba in April, 1915. Johnson claimed in his autobiography that he threw the fight to the 6 foot 6 inch, 250 pound Willard in an attempt to reduce white hatred and thus be able to return to the United States without spending time in prison.[53] Fight films, though, would tend to substantiate those who believe that Willard landed a clean knockout punch in the 26th round under a boiling hot sun. A "Great White Hope" had finally been found.

Jack Johnson finally returned to the United States in 1920. He was not given leniency and served his one year and a day sentence at the federal penitentiary at Levenworth, Kansas. Johnson eventually came to be symbolic of the plight of blacks in the early decades of the twentieth century which found blacks practically eliminated from the mainstream of American sport. While the Negro was at his nadir in organized sport in the 1910s, three blacks were born: Jesse Owens, Joe Louis, and Jackie Robinson. They were a promise of things to come in another generation and of change in American society and in sport.

REFERENCES

1. Jane Carson, *Colonial Virginians at Play* (Charlottesville: The University Press of Virginia, 1965) p. 161.

2. Edwin B. Henderson, *The Black Athlete Emergence and Arrival* (New York: Publishers' Co., 1968), pp. 21-22; A. S. Young, *Negro Firsts in Sports* (Chicago: Johnson Publishing Co., 1963), pp. 21-22; and John P. Davis, The Negro in American Sports, *The American Negro Reference Book* (Englewood Cliffs, N.J.: Prentice-Hall, 1966), pp. 776-777.

3. London *Times*, December 25, 1810, p. 4 as quoted in Davis, Negro in American Sports, p. 778.

4. London *Times*, September 30, 1811, p. 3, *Ibid.*, p. 779.

5. Dale A. Somers, *The Rise of Sports in New Orleans, 1850-1900* (Baton Rouge: Louisiana State University Press, 1972), p. 120; and Robert Peterson, *Only the Ball Was White* (Englewood Cliffs, N.J.: Prentice Hall, 1970), pp. 16-18.

6. Peterson, *Ibid.*, pp. 16-17.

7. Harold Seymour, *Baseball: The Early Years* (New York: Oxford University Press, 1960), p. 421.

8. Peterson, *Only the Ball Was White*, p. 18.

9. As quoted in Peterson, *Ibid.*, pp. 21-22.

10. Carl F. Wittke, Oberlinian Was First Negro Player in Major Leagues, *Oberlin Alumni Bulletin* (First Quarter, 1946), p. 4; and Fleetwood Walker: The First Black Player in Major League Baseball," *Black Sports*, I (Nov.-Dec. 1971), pp. 48-49.

11. Peterson, *Only the Ball Was White*, p. 23.

12. *Ibid.*, p. 28.

13. *Ibid.*, p. 31.

14. Young, *Negro Firsts in Sports*, p. 56.

15. Peterson, *Only the Ball Was White*, p. 33.

16. *New Orleans Pelican*, May 28, 1887, as quoted in Somers, *Rise of Sports in New Orleans*, p. 120.

17. *Statistical History of the United States* (Fairfield, Conn: Fairfield Publishing Co., 1947), p. 9.

18. August Meier and Elliott M. Rudwick, *From Plantation to Ghetto* (New York: Hill and Wang, 1963), p. 138.

19. C. Vann Woodward, *The Strange Career of Jim Crow* (New York: Oxford University Press, 1966), pp. 52-53.

20. Seymour, *Baseball: The Early Years*, p. 42.

21. Rayford W. Logan, *The Betrayal of the Negro from Rutherford B. Hayes to Woodrow Wilson* (New York: Collier Books, 1965), p. 48.

22. Plessy v. Ferguson, May 18, 1896, in Rayford W. Logan, *The Negro in the United States* (Princeton, N.J.: D. Van Nostrand, 1957), p. 133.

23. Harlan's Dissenting Opinion in the Plessy Case, 1896, *Ibid.*, p. 134.

24. Seth M. Scheiner, President Theodore Roosevelt and the Negro, 1901-1908, in Richard Resh (ed.), *Black America* (Lexington, Mass: D. C. Heath, 1969), p. 26.

25. Maxwell Bloomfield, Dixon's The Leopard's Spots: A Study in Popular Racism, in Charles E. Wynes (ed.), *The Negro in the South Since 1865* (University, Ala.: University of Alabama Press, 1965), p. 96.

26. Thomas C. Cochran and William Miller, *The Age of Enterprise* (New York: Harper & Row, 1961), p. 204.

27. Logan, *Betrayal of the Negro*, p. 78.

28. Bloomfield, Dixon's The Leopard's Spots, p. 99.

29. Booker T. Washington's Atlanta 'Compromise' Address, September 18, 1895, in Logan, *Negro in the United States*, pp. 126-130.

30. Woodward, *Strange Career of Jim Crow*, p. 84.

31. *Spirit of the Times*, 4 October 1879, p. 232.

32. *Ibid.*

33. John A. Lucas, Pedestrianism and the Struggle for the Sir John Astley Belt, 1878-1879, *Research Quarterly*, XXXIX (October 1968), p. 594.

34. Somers, *Rise of Sports in New Orleans*, p. 223.

35. Marshall W. "Major" Taylor, *The Fastest Bicycle Rider in the World* (Battleboro, Vt.: Green-Stephen Press, 1972 Reprint), passim; Henderson, *The Black Athlete*, pp. 52-53; and Richard Mandell, "The Major Made It on a Bike," *Sports Illustrated*, XXXIV (12 April 1971), p. E7.

36. Charles E. Trevathan, *The American Thoroughbred* (New York: Macmillan, 1905), p. 21.

37. A. B. Longstreet, *Georgia Scenes* (New York: Sagamore Press 1957), p. 146. Originally published in 1835.

38. Young, *Negro Firsts in Sports*, pp. 50-51.

39. Davis, Negro in American Sports, pp. 790-793; and Young, *Ibid.*, pp. 52-53.

40. Davis, Negro in American Sports, pp. 792-793.

41. Jerome Zuckerman, G. Alan Stull, and Marvin H. Eyler, The Black Athlete in Post-Bellum 19th Century, *The Physical Educator*, XXIX (October 1972), p. 142.

42. Somers, *Rise of Sports in New Orleans*, p. 178.

43. Davis, Negro in American Sports, p. 780.

44. Jack A. Johnson, *Jack Johnson is a Dandy: An Autobiography* (New York: Chelsea House, 1969), pp. 155-164.

45. New York *Herald*, December 1908, as quoted in Finis Farr, *Black Champion* (New York: Charles Scribner's Sons, 1964), p. 62.

46. New York *Tribune*, December 27, 1908, p. 8.

47. *Ibid.*, January 2, 1909, p. 5 and January 5, 1909, p. 9.

48. Farr, *Black Champion*, p. 72.

49. *Ibid.*, p. 107.

50. *Ibid.*, pp. 132-134 and Davis, Negro in American Sports, p. 783.

51. As quoted by Al-Tony Gilmore, Jack Johnson and White Women: The National Impact, *Journal of Negro History*, LVIII (January 1973), p. 25. See also Gilmore's, *Bad Nigger! The National Impact of Jack Johnson* (Port Washington, N.Y.: Kennikat Press, 1974).

52. *Ibid.*, p. 31.

53. Johnson, *Jack Johnson*, pp. 100-102.

CHAPTER 17
Epilogue to Sport in Transition: Call for the Strenuous Life

As a new century dawned, the man who was to be the most dynamic leader of the first two decades of the twentieth century, Teddy Roosevelt, called for the strenuous life. He spoke for the confident and aggressive Americans in 1900 when he said that "in life, as in a football game, the principle to follow is: Hit the line hard; don't foul and don't shirk, but hit the line hard."[1] Within a year Roosevelt assumed the presidency from which he led his crusade for a more virile, manly life. Athletics were, by then, an important part of the American psyche, and Roosevelt was a shrewd enough politician to profit from the interest in sport—an interest that would have been lacking nearly a half century before at the time of Roosevelt's birth. By the time Teddy Roosevelt gave his clarion call for manly physical activities, sport had moved from a rather unorganized, principally provincial, and generally individualistic form in the 1850s to a more highly organized, often national, and spectator oriented structure.

The society which Roosevelt was to preside over was fast becoming the sport oriented culture known to most observers of the twentieth century. America of the pre-World War I era had become an industrial-urban society in which over 100,000 people would observe a national championship amateur baseball game just prior to the war. It was the same society in which vast numbers of its members awaited the outcome of a heavyweight championship bout pitting a black man, Jack Johnson, against a former champion, Jim Jeffries. A similar enthusiasm for sport brought out 80,000 spectators to see the first Indianapolis 500 mile auto race in 1911, while three years before, over 200,000 saw the Thanksgiving Day Automobile Club of America Grand Prize Race in Savannah, Georgia.[2] America's sport consciousness had made national events of the World Series between the

National and American professional baseball leagues in the first decade of the twentieth century. It, too, had made possible the collegiate Rose Bowl in football, national tournaments in tennis and golf as well as numerous other continental sporting events. Roosevelt was to use the nationalization of sport to further his goals which included creating a nation with vigor, drive, and world influence.

THE STRENUOUS LIFE AND MASCULINITY

The strenuous life became an important theme in the late 1800s and early 1900s as the American nation began to question its own masculinity. America had always emphasized the strenuous life, the struggle, competition, and drive for success. From the hard times of the first colonial settlements on the east coast, to the frontier experience, to the rise of the early industrial enterprises, there had been a need for the rugged individual, what was called the "masculine type." With the rise of cities and the corporate state there was a loss of individuality, something which had been an integral part of manhood. The decline of the frontier and the crowding of cities created what a number of observers called the threat of overcivilization—a softness that posed a threat of decay in American society.[3]

Others attributed the loss of a strenuous American life to the influence of women, who were beginning to play a larger role in society. When Charles W. Eliot, President of Harvard University, referred to football and said that "effeminacy and luxury are even worse evils than brutality," he was suggesting that vigorous sport must keep the nation from being dominated by feminine, thus what he considered weaker, qualities.[4] The lack of national virility was observed by the American novelist, Henry James. Through one of his characters, James wanted to save Americans "from the most damnable feminism. . . . The whole generation is womanized; the masculine tone is passing out of the world." James wanted to preserve "the masculine character, the ability to dare and endure, to know and yet not fear reality. . . ."[5] Psychologist G. Stanley Hall asked at the turn of the century whether man could devirilize himself and take on qualities of the other sex without "evincing either defective masculinity or else tending to induce feminism."[6] A Yale mathematics professor suggested that vigorous sports like football will lead to the "death of that effeminacy which is so rapidly undermining the American nation."[7]

Nowhere was the feminine influence seen more than in the nation's schools and teacher training institutions. Writing in 1901, the educator Charles De Garmo was alarmed that the vast majority of teachers were now females with the danger "of decay of virility."[8] He, like a host of other educators, called for active athletic programs in schools

Male dominated America criticized effeminacy at the same time it satirized athletic women.

to develop the characteristic of virility. While established colleges were wrestling with questions of professionalization and commercialization of athletics, small teacher training institutions were striving to infuse a greater masculine—thus athletic—element into theirs.[9]

In the liberal arts colleges and universities the issue of virility was also raised. The President of Notre Dame meant to have a virile institution and boosted football for his students saying he would rather incur "the danger of a broken collar-bone occasionally than to see them dedicated to croquet."[10] Football, the sport most often criticized for its brutality and commercial aspects was also most praised by defenders of sport for its fostering of manly virtues. An official of the University of Pennsylvania argued that football "contributed to the making of good, strong, manly fellows."[11] Even a professor who was strongly opposed to intercollegiate athletics remarked that exclusively male colleges often showed a tendency toward femininity.[12]

Teddy Roosevelt, too, spoke and wrote voluminously of the need for a rejuvenation of manliness. Not only that, but he acted the part. It had been Roosevelt who led his Rough Riders to victory in the Spanish-American War in 1898, and in the process helped to create an empire for the United States to oversee. Roosevelt emerged from the war as the leader of the strenuous life. He had, in fact, lived a strenuous life from his boyhood, when he had been a sickly asthmatic, through his college years at Harvard in the late 1870s when the cult of athleticism was being felt in the eastern cities and colleges. He continued in his adult years even spending several years as a rancher in the west. In 1893, while he was a reform member of the Civil Service Commission, he was concerned about the threat of an urban-industrial overcivilization. "No sweetness and delicacy," he

Teddy Roosevelt symbolized the strenuous life.

lectured, "no love for and appreciation of beauty in art or literature, no capacity for building up material prosperity, can possibly atone for lack of the great virile virtues."[13] As Vice President, only four days before President William McKinley was shot, he reiterated his desire for a strong, courageous, and virile nation. He reintroduced an old proverb to a midwestern state fair crowd when he said: "Speak softly and carry a big stick—you will go far," while claiming that "no prosperity and no glory can save a nation that is rotten at the heart."[14]

When he became president in 1901, Roosevelt, more than any other person, gave status to virile, manly sports in the pursuit of the strenuous life. He enjoyed riding, and many politicians who wanted his ear learned to mount a horse and to ride with him. He gave a boost to the popularity of tennis when he had a tennis court constructed enabling him to play matches with his aides at the White House. Once, he even took ju jitsu lessons in the privacy of the White House. When the game of college football was threatened by brutal play in the early 1900s, it was Roosevelt who spoke out against abolishing the game, believing that no college should "turn out mollycoddles instead of vigorous men. . . ."[15] At the same time President Eliot of Harvard College proposed dropping football at Harvard, Roosevelt wrote in private that Harvard would be "doing the baby act if she takes any such foolish course as President Eliot advises!" In 1907, on the same day that Roosevelt wrote a personal letter in which he wondered whether the Japanese navy might attack the American "Great White Fleet" which he had sent around the world as an American show of strength, he, in a lighter vein, chided his Secretary of Interior who had suggested that Harvard College might better substitute the women's college of Vassar for Yale on the football schedule.[16] Through his entire presidency he kept a keen interest and took a vigorous stance in strenuous sport, continuing after he left office in 1909 when he embarked upon a big game hunting expedition in Africa.

FROM LAISSEZ FAIRE SPORT TO GREATER CONTROL

The call for the strenuous life and for a reinvigorated masculinity appeared to be a reaction to a society which had begun to turn its back on rugged individualism. America was moving from a period of laissez faire individualism, in which private initiative prevailed and in which little governmental regulation existed, to a society which demanded greater governmental controls. Sport, like the larger society, was beginning to feel the demand for controls where few had existed before.

Laissez faire individualism had originally been a liberal nineteenth century doctrine which opposed governmental controls over people's lives, especially their economic lives. The principle followed was to allow the individual a great amount of freedom to pursue his own selfish interest which in the end would contribute, it was believed, to the general good. In this free competitive system the state would only act as a "passive policeman," protecting property and administering justice.[17] The nineteenth century belief in the laissez faire doctrine was reinforced by the introduction of Social Darwinism which was championed in America between the Civil War and 1900. Social Darwinism was a theory of human society based upon the Darwinian principles of the survival of the fittest in the evolution of animals. It was believed that if humans, the highest form of animal, were allowed individual freedom, the most fit would survive and mankind would move toward a higher state of being.

When laissez faire individualism and Social Darwinism were applied to the business world, whether it was producing steel or winning baseball teams, it meant a fierce struggle for existence and the survival of the fittest. The end result, when drawn to its ultimate, was the complete control of an industry by the most efficient company or the domination of one team in sports. Monopolies resulted.

Monopolies were created in industries such as steel, oil, railroads, and sporting goods in the late 1800s. The same thing began to happen in sport competition where the desire to win and dominate was just as great as in other areas of the business world. The very nature of sport demands competition. Uneven competition results in the collapse of losing teams and an ultimate failure of the competitive situation. To preserve the competitive state, sport promoters generally turned away from a laissez faire policy toward some form of controlled competition. There are some ready examples of this occurring in the late nineteenth and early twentieth centuries. In the first major league in baseball, the National Association of Professional Base Ball Players, 1871-1875, the league allowed the free movement of players to sign contracts with any team. The richest club, the Boston Red Stockings, acquired the largest number of quality ballplayers in this laissez faire situation. The result was four league

The Boston Red Stockings dominated the first major league by hiring the best players in a laissez faire situation.

championships in five years for the Boston team.[18] When the league collapsed in 1875, much of the blame for its demise was placed on its free competitive business policy which led to a near monopoly. The National League which began in 1876, soon found that it needed league governing control to prevent a similar occurrence. The reserve clause, restricting player movement, was the result three years later.

In amateur sports similar actions were taken to control the competitive situation. A prime example occurred in the 1870s and 1880s with athletic clubs in the east being the focal point. A major controversy arose over the concept of amateurism. The English had given an aristocratic meaning to amateurism in the nineteenth century when amateurs in rowing were defined as those rowers who did not work with their hands in their daily employment. In America, with a more egalitarian society rejecting such blatant patrician ideas but desiring to keep the lower "rabble" out of amateur athletics, athletic clubs began to define amateurs as those who did not compete for cash or pursue athletic exercise as a livelihood. Several abortive amateur associations were organized in the 1870s before the National Association of Amateur Athletes of America was formed in 1879. The NAAAA was formed primarily by the collective action of the leading, exclusive athletic clubs of the New York City area. It had been an attempt to prevent a laissez faire policy in amateur track and field, a sport which had had a history of concealed professionalism. Previously there had been a large degree of autonomy within the clubs to run their own affairs, and because of this the NAAAA had great difficulty settling cases of eligibility and violations of the amateur code. The desire to win, as in the desire to compete in a free business economy, led clubs to hire the best athletes as performers for the athletic clubs.[19] While the New York Athletic Club and the Manhattan Athletic Club warred over the domination of several sports in the 1880s, the NYAC withdrew from the NAAAA claiming that it was lax in its enforcement of the rules of amateurism.[20] The Amateur Athletic Union, formed in 1888 with NYAC leadership, was in many ways a rejection of laissez faire individualism in amateur athletics and a manifestation of the desire for greater collective control. The NYAC and the Manhattan AC continued to feud, but the AAU moved toward greater control over the affairs of the individual member clubs.

College sport reflected this same movement toward collective control. When colleges first began intercollegiate competition, there were no restrictions on the policies of individual colleges. Some students, like Walter Camp at Yale, played as many as six years of varsity competition. If a college desired to allow graduate students to play, as most eventually did, there was no restriction. It was common to recruit graduate students for their athletic reputations in the late

1800s. In the free system of athletics, the larger institutions recruited athletes from the smaller ones. Those who were recruited were often derogatorily referred to as "tramp" athletes. Fielding H. Yost was a good example. He was enticed away from West Virginia College to play football for Lafayette College only days before Lafayette broke the University of Pennsylvania's long winning streak in 1896. Under the laissez faire system a group of wealthy eastern schools, with the help of alumni, dominated intercollegiate athletics by recruiting better athletes and hiring quality professional coaches to produce winning teams. It became increasingly clear that if athletics were to survive, a system of common rules was needed. By the 1890s, leagues in various sports were being constructed. Conferences, like the Intercollegiate Conference of Faculty Representatives (Big Ten), were being formed to rule over a variety of sports. By the early 1900s a national controlling organization was formed, the National Collegiate Athletic Association. The NCAA set up regulations for the conduct of college sport when it was found that individual college actions had failed. Beginning with no enforcement powers, the NCAA by the mid-twentieth century had gained the right to punitive action though it seldom exercised that right.

In sport there had been a movement away from laissez faire individualism toward collective behavior. This occurred when the individual competing units saw that a failure to make joint efforts would lead to the ruin of the competitive situation. In the larger society laissez faire individualism began its slow demise when elected officials were prodded into passing governmental regulations to control the competitive economic system. Both actions occurred at the end of the nineteenth century as the nation moved into the Progressive period. The competitive spirit and individualism were not lost during the Progressive period dominated by Teddy Roosevelt, but the desire to see some regulations passed to regulate the competition was seen in sport and society.

THE SPORT'S HERO BY THE TWENTIETH CENTURY

The thread of the strenuous life and remaining individualism in American society was apparent in the development of the athletic hero by the early 1900s. A half-century before there was nothing resembling an athletic hero of major dimension. By the turn of the century athletic heroes were prevalent from the plethora of organized sports which had arisen.

The American hero, whether in sport or out, was a doer not necessarily a thinker—he was a practical person, not an intellectual. Americans could have made Thomas Jefferson into a national hero because of his eclectic mind and intellectual curiosity, but rather it chose George Washington who acted in heroic ways while producing few original thoughts. A century later the nation made a hero out of the dynamic Teddy Roosevelt, while granting little recognition to a world renowned intellectual such as Charles S. Peirce, the psychologist-philosopher. In America, by the nineteenth century, the hero was usually a person of the equalitarian society, not of the aristocracy: Americans preferred performance, not birth, as the true measure of a man.[21] Heroes were more often apt to act than think, and in America that quality was praised often.

The sport hero of the new era of organized sport fit well into the mold of American heroes. The hero was the man of action who appeared larger than life. Young people or old timers recounted the 1880s exploits of the great John L. Sullivan, and in so doing probably found some identity and ego satisfaction. Jack Johnson, who became an anti-hero to much of white America around 1910, was heroic to many blacks who were seemingly searching for someone who had a fearless quality with which to identify. In baseball the hero had developed somewhat earlier for baseball was the leading sport in the age of transition from unorganized to organized sport. Mike "King"

Ty Cobb symbolized the rugged individualist in his role as baseball hero. (Courtesy of National Baseball Hall of Fame and Museum.)

Kelly may have been baseball's nineteenth century hero for his dash
on the basepaths was symbolic of America's unbridled individualism.
The song, "Slide, Kelly, Slide," was only outdone by the famous
"Casey at the Bat." By World War I Ty Cobb, a fighting individualist,
had the hero's spotlight turned upon him, though by then there were
those who felt that his attitude to win-at-all-cost was unheroic.

It was not surprising that the self-made man in sport was among the
heroes of the age. Organized sport was a business like others in the
new capitalistic, industrial society which dominated the period.
Americans glorified the self-reliant, industrious and financially successful person. The same age created the mythical Horatio Alger who
grew up from rags to riches with a mixture of the work ethic and good
fortune. This type of hero remained in society and in sport in the
early 1900s, but a slightly different gallant figure began to emerge. In
fiction it appeared in the figure of Frank Merriwell.

Frank Merriwell, the intrepid character of Gilbert Patten, was the
athletic hero to thousands, nay millions of young people for a
generation from the mid-1890s. The Merriwell sagas, written under
the pen name Burt L. Standish, were geared to America's upward
striving middle class. Frank was a clean living, adventurous, wealthy,
educated, brave, and athletic all-American boy who had first attended
a private preparatory school and later became a student at the
foremost of American social and athletic institutions of higher learning, Yale University. The stories of Merriwell's exploits ran for twenty
years in the *Tip Top Weekly*, a 5¢ publication aimed at the youthful
reading audience, and they were grouped together in 15¢ books with
such likely titles as *Frank Merriwell at Yale* and *Frank Merriwell's
Dilemma*. Frank was inevitably faced with disaster; a sprained ankle or
some sinister force out to stop him and one of the Yale athletic teams
of which he was the star. Frank, however, overcame the obstacle to hit
a home run in the ninth inning, plunge for a touchdown in the last
moments of the Harvard contest, or nip an opponent at the tape in
the mile run.[22] Frank Merriwell was a real hero to many American
youth for he was successful and masculine, a fictitious but believable
character who was part of the strenuous life. He was intelligent,
morally upright, and a man of vigorous action. What middle class
Progressive could have asked for more for his child in a period when
the belief in the certainty of moral values and in human progress was
generally accepted?

THE LINGERING RURAL SPORTS

A person living in rural America at the turn of the century had his
own heroes; possibly Paul Bunyon who could plow half a state in a
morning or clear a field with one swing of his axe. If it were a sporting

hero, it could well be a trotting horse like "Maud S" whose picture might be seen hanging in the parlor or the living room of the farm house as one of numerous Currier and Ives lithographs. No one had to tell a rural American about masculinity and the strenuous life for the country "hayseed" lived it, and was skeptical of the life of a city "slicker." If many Americans were leaving the farm for the city, still half of all Americans were living in rural areas when the twentieth century began. As much as America had changed with the industrial revolution, much of agrarian life remained the same as it had been a half century before. There was still the same isolation that had existed before. Farmer's rural recreation, too, did not change greatly nor would it until the automobile, radio, and later television effectively permeated the rural areas.

Rural life had its sporting diversions, but it was sporadic, usually less commercialized, particularly on the Sabbath, than its urban counterpart. Traditional rural holidays were occasions to look forward to. July 4th was one of these festive events in which sport was often found. The main feature of the Independence Day celebration was a rousing patriotic oration, though the chance to socialize was probably the subtle motive for people gathering together. Following the morning grandiloquence there were the customary baseball games, wrestling matches, or horse shoe pitching contests in the afternoon. The 4th of July was at times the special occasion of the annual picnic of the Grange, a society promoting the interests of agriculture. When held as a separate holiday, it was another opportunity for isolated farmers to get together and enjoy social and recreational pursuits.

At no time was sport more popular with rural Americans than at fair time. Annual fairs for the promotion of agriculture were held by numerous township, county, and state agricultural societies from the mid-nineteenth century. The county and state fair became a tradition, and it was sport which was a major factor in drawing thousands to the fairgrounds. County fairs in the late 1800s and early 1900s featured baseball and football games, bicycle races, wheelbarrow and sack races, balloon ascensions, and aeroplane flights. The primary sport, however, from the mid-century until well into the twentieth century was harness racing.[23]

Harness racing, rather than throughbred racing on horseback, was justified by rural America on the grounds that racing was an integral part of the scientific breeding of road horses. Even people with a fundamentalist religion, who might have been expected to oppose racing on the grounds that it fostered gambling, could see the apparent logic that the testing of trotting and pacing horses[24] on the track would in the end bring about an improved breed of horse and add to the utility as roadsters for farmers. Once justified, state

Harness racing was a rural tradition. (Courtesy of Library of Congress.)

legislatures seldom restricted harness racing at the fairs. Great trotters and pacers travelled across the country and were featured at the various fairs: "Lady Suffolk," "Flora Temple," "Dexter," "Goldsmith," "Maid," "Dan Patch," and "Maud S" were equine heroes to many rural Americans in the last half of the nineteenth and early twentieth centuries.[25]

A good example of the influence of harness racing on agricultural fairs was seen at the Walworth County Fair in southern Wisconsin. Beginning in the early 1850s, fair officials built a trotting track at the county seat, Elkhorn, within five years of the founding of the fair. With crowds turning out to see the annual racing, an amphitheater was built in 1896 seating 4,000, at the time one of the largest grandstands in the United States on a half-mile track. The next year a champion, "Lone Pacer," helped bring a crowd of 60,000 to the fair over a three-day period. Several years later the state mile pacing record was set at two minutes and six seconds, and crowds were drawn from Illinois as well as Wisconsin on special excursion rail lines to see the harness racing.[26]

With the mass media today speeding the results of sporting events with regularity to both the rural and urban populace, it is probably difficult to imagine the excitement that was generated when recreation was limited to a few special occasions, such as county fairs, Grange picnics, and 4th of July celebrations. Though rural sport lingered behind that of urban America, it must have seemed to the farmer that it was part of the strenuous life of which Teddy Roosevelt spoke. As for Roosevelt, he probably sensed the agrarian desire for the strenuous life for he was speaking on national and moral strength at the Minnesota state fair when he called for speaking softly and carrying a big stick.

THE DIRECTION OF ORGANIZED SPORT BY THE EARLY TWENTIETH CENTURY

The forces contributing to the development of organized sport—urbanization, industrialization, advancing technology, a major war, the decline of religious opposition, and the immigrant influence combined with the pervasive English sporting tradition—occurred in the period from mid-nineteenth century until the start of World War I. Sport was still far from being the dominating interest of the masses of Americans that it became in the latter years of the twentieth century, but it had been organized, publicized, and commercialized. Much of what became more noticeable as the twentieth century progressed was in its youthful form. The direction of twentieth century sport was, though, clearly discernable.

It was evident by the early 1900s that the leadership in organized sport was to come from urban America. Sport had already become an urban spectacle, both amateur and professional, and it was often difficult to differentiate between the two as they were both imbued with commercial interests. It was equally manifest that sport was male dominated—nearly exclusively so for both spectator and participant although a ripple of female concern could be seen. Furthermore one could see the greater interest in team sports as opposed to individual sports. Baseball, the team game with unique opportunity for individualism, was supreme in the laissez faire nineteenth century. Football, at the college level, with its demands for cooperation or team work, was rising in importance more in tune with the less individualistic, industrial society of the twentieth century. Both sports were at the time considered dynamic and explosive, symbolic of the American society. Nearly all of the organized sports exhibited another American quality which emphasized winning, almost to the exclusion of any other quality. Those teams and those individuals who won were portrayed in heroic proportions: John L. Sullivan, the most notable sport hero of the nineteenth century; Jack Johnson, the boxing hero of the blacks; Ty Cobb, the symbol of dynamic baseball; and Jim Thorpe, the greatest football and track athlete of the early 1900s.

Barney Oldfield, driving Henry Ford's car, helped to make auto racing a dynamic sport by the early 1900s. (Courtesy of Library of Congress.)

That sport and sport heroes had permeated the educational institutions was probably reflective of the pragmatic and non-intellectual nature of the American educational system, while at the same time it mirrored the egalitarian nature of American higher education which was beginning to cater to the middle classes. Finally one could see the beginning of the use of sport for nationalistic purposes. Actions like those of the leaders of professional baseball who in the early 1900s proclaimed baseball to be of American origin and that of the United States Olympic team which refused to dip the American flag in respect to the King of England at the 1908 Olympics, focused attention on the proud and nationalistic tendencies of Americans in sport as in society. The direction that sport would take was reasonably clear by the early 1900s. The progress of organized sport during the age of sport in transition by the early years of the twentieth century gave a clue to the growth of sport which followed America's involvement in World War I and the prosperous decade which followed.

REFERENCES

1. Theodore Roosevelt, "The American Boy," in *The Works of Theodore Roosevelt*, Vol. XIII (New York: Charles Scribner's Sons, 1926), p. 407.

2. John R. Betts, Organized Sports in Industrial America, Ph.D. dissertation, Columbia University, 1951, p. 297.

3. For a discussion of the era of the strenuous life see Gerald F. Roberts, The Strenuous Life: The Cult of Manliness in the Era of Theodore Roosevelt, Ph.D. dissertation, Michigan State University, 1970.

4. John H. Gardiner, *Harvard* (New York: Oxford University Press, 1914), p. 59.

5. Henry James, *The Bostonians* (New York: Dial Press, 1945), p. 283.

6. G. Stanley Hall, Student Customs, *American Antiquarian Society Proceedings*, New Series, XIV (1900-1901), p. 92.

7. Eugene L. Richards, Intercollegiate Football, *New Englander*, XLV (December 1886), p. 1050.

8. Charles De Garmo (annotations) in John F. Herbert, *Outlines of Educational Doctrine* (New York: Macmillan, 1901), pp. 188-189.

9. Ronald A. Smith, From Normal School to State University: A History of the Wisconsin State University Conference, Ph.D. dissertation, University of Wisconsin, 1969, pp. 100-103.

10. Caspar Whitney, Is Football Worth While? *Collier's* XLIV (December 18, 1909), p. 25.

11. *Ibid.*, p. 13.

12. Edwin E. Slosson, *Great American Universities* (New York: Macmillan, 1910), p. 309.

13. Theodore Roosevelt, The Duties of American Citizenship, (1893), in *The Works of Theodore Roosevelt*, Vol. XIII (New York: Charles Scribner's Sons, 1926), p. 281.

14. Theodore Roosevelt, National Duty, (September 2, 1901 address at the Minnesota State Fair), *Ibid.*, p. 474.

15. Theodore Roosevelt, Athletics, Scholarship, and the Public Service, (February 23, 1907 address at the Harvard Union, Cambridge), *Ibid.*, p. 560.

16. President Theodore Roosevelt, letter to Edward Deshon Brandegee, March 7, 1906, in Elting E. Morison (ed.), *The Letters of Theodore Roosevelt*, Vol. V (Cambridge: Harvard University Press, 1952), p. 46; and Roosevelt, letter to Ralph D. Paine, November 19, 1907, *Ibid.*, p. 853.

17. Sidney Fine, *Laissez Faire and the General-Welfare State: A Study of Conflict in American Thought, 1865-1901* (Ann Arbor: University of Michigan, 1956), pp. 9, 30.

18. David Q. Voigt, *American Baseball*, Vol. I (Norman: University of Oklahoma Press, 1966), pp. 43, 52.

19. Duncan Edwards, Life at the Athletic Clubs, *Scribner's Magazine*, XVII (July 1895). pp. 4-23.

20. Charles P. Sawyer, Amateur Track and Field Athletics, *Scribner's Magazine*, VII (June 1890), p. 775.

21. Marshall Fishwick, *American Heroes Myth and Reality* (Washington, D.C.: Public Affairs Press, 1954), p. 157.

22. Stewart H. Holbrook, Frank Merriwell at Yale Again—and Again and Again, *American Heritage*, XII (June 1961), pp. 24-28, 78-81.

23. Wayne C. Neely, *The Agricultural Fair* (New York: Columbia University Press, 1935), pp. 107, 115, 190-212.

24. Trotters' and pacers' gaits differ. Pacers advance both legs on the same side at once. Trotters advance the fore and hind legs on different sides at once. Trotters and pacers do not differ greatly in speed attained.

25. John R. Betts, Agricultural Fairs and the Rise of Harness Racing *Agricultural History*, XXVII (April 1953), pp. 71-75.

26. "Hi, Ho, Come to the Fair," *Wisconsin, Then and Now*, XVII (August 1970), pp. 4-5, 8.

Part III.

Sport in Twentieth Century America

CHAPTER 18

Sport in the Golden 20s and After

"A new Golden Age of sport and outdoor amusements is admittedly with us," wrote a journalist of the early 1920s.[1] It was true, and that age had been ushered in by America's participation in the First World War. With the declaration of war on Germany in April of 1917, the United States Army and Navy enlisted sport figures, primarily from the colleges, to train military personnel for battle. Two former athletes and college athletic advisors, Joseph Raycroft of Princeton and Walter Camp of Yale, headed the army and navy athletic programs. By Armistice Day, a year and one-half later, about 5,000,000 servicemen had been trained at military camps which had fitness programs that included for the first time an emphasis upon sport. Many sports were played including wrestling, football, baseball, basketball, and volleyball, but it was boxing that received the most attention. Boxing was considered the foundation of bayonet training, necessary for the hand-to-hand trench combat on Europe's Western front.[2] No wonder, then that when the war was over, the popularity of boxing rose to new heights, while states, like New York, which had previously forbidden prizefighting sanctioned the sport.

THE INTER-ALLIED GAMES OF 1919

As the nation began to demobilize in 1919, the United States military decided that sport was to be a major means of occupying servicemen while they awaited discharge. Mass military games at the regimental level were to lead to a culminating extravaganza—a "Military Olympics" or the Inter-Allied Games. The Inter-Allied Games were significant in the promotion of sport in the 1920s for they directly involved the federal government in the sponsorship of competitive athletics at an international level, thus giving sport extensive exposure and promotion. The concept of the Inter-Allied Games was conceived shortly before the Armistice by the Director of Athletics of the American Expeditionary Forces in France, Elwood S. Brown, a YMCA official. He believed in the moral value of sports and thought that mass military sports should have their apex in an athletic meeting of all the allied nations of the Great War. "Such games," Brown assumed, "would focus the interest of the athletic world both in Europe and in America; would give a striking illustration of the place of athletics in the military training of the Allied Armies and would be of absorbing interest to great numbers of troops during the somewhat restless period waiting their return home."[3]

Within six months of the end of the war the Americans, with the cooperation of the French government, organized the games which represented 18 countries, involved 1,500 athletes, and included 24 sports. A 25,000-seat stadium on the outskirts of Paris, named in honor of General John J. Pershing, was built in two months. The contests, staged at Pershing Stadium, at Colombes Stadium—site of the 1900 Paris Olympics, and at other sites, drew an estimated half-million spectators. The games were publicized in the United States from Rhode Island to Oregon with the *Chicago Tribune* carrying nearly 100 articles on the "Military Olympics" in the week preceding the games. During the two weeks of the games the United States dominated as they won 12 of the 24 events including rifle and pistol shooting, basketball, boxing, prize jumping with horses, swimming, catch-as-catch-can wrestling, and the tug-of-war. Charles W. Paddock, the 1920s "fastest man in the world," won the 100 meter race and equaled the world's record in winning the 200 meter dash. Even a black man, Solomon Butler, competed and won the long jump for the Americans.[4] While the games did not open up white dominated athletics for American Negroes, they did reflect the significance of sport in American life. As one writer saw it, World War I had helped "stress a higher claim for sport. . . ."[5]

The Inter-Allied Games revealed the importance of sport to the American war effort. One can attribute the growth of American sport in the 1920s in part to the love of sport developed during the war. It was no accident that the newly formed American Legion organized its Junior Legion baseball program for youth in the 1920s. Similarly the war had an influence on the formation of Golden Gloves Boxing as well as college boxing; on the expansion of community recreation programs; and on the greatly expanded system of state laws requiring physical education in the schools which often saw sport a central part of the curriculum rather than traditional formal gymnastics. While wars generally have a positive influence on post-war sports, World War I appears to have stimulated the sport spirit even greater than did the Civil War a half century before.

POPULAR INDULGENCE IN 1920s SPORT

One must not get the impression that sport had not been popular before the First World War. Major league baseball had been commercialized and successful for two generations. Even amateur baseball drew an estimated 100,000 to its championship game in Cleveland in 1914. College football could draw a crowd of 75,000 filling Yale's stadium built in 1915. The entire nation appeared concerned about the outcome of the heavyweight boxing championship matches of 1910 and 1915. Auto racing was drawing crowds of over 100,000. Newspapers went to great expense to create their sports sections for the masses of readers. Yet, the popular indulgence in sport in the 1920s was a phenomenon of major proportion which eventually led to bitter criticism by a vocal minority.

The mass involvement in sport can probably best be seen in three sports: boxing and its rapid rise to fame and fortune; baseball and its recovery from the 1919 "Black Sox" scandal to the glory years of Babe Ruth; and college football and its emphasis on stadium building and the Saturday spectacle. This is not to say that other sports were not significant. Horse racing had its Man-of-War, winner of 20 of 21 races in only two seasons of racing, and Exterminator who won 50 of 100 starts in seven years, along with Earl Sande dominating as the best of the jockeys. Auto racing and especially the Indianapolis 500 mile race, begun in 1911, caught the imagination of many of those middle class Americans who were buying and driving their first cars. In tennis, Helen Wills won 8 Wimbledon titles in England and 7 United States championships before she retired in the 1930s. Bill Tilden was nearly unbeatable playing before thousands of spectators while vying for national acclaim at Forest Hills or battling the officials and the world's best players at Wimbledon. The golfing world, dominated by the businessmen-country club set, could glory in the professional feats of Walter Hagen or Gene Sarazen, and they could savor the wins of the best of them all—Bobby Jones who, as an amateur, thrilled the golfing aficionados when he capped his brilliant career by completing golf's Grand Slam in 1930, winning the British Amateur and British Open and the United States Amateur and Open. He then retired at age twenty-eight. Glenna Collett, who was reputed to have driven a golf ball over 300 yards at age eighteen, was the best of women golfers as she captured the U.S. Women's Amateur 6 times. No woman achieved the renown of Gertrude Ederle who was an Olympic triple medal winner in the 1924 Paris Olympics, but more importantly was the first woman, in 1926, to swim the English Channel. She did so, breaking the time of the fastest of the previous 5 male channel swimmers by two hours. Johnny Weissmuller by the end of the 1920s held every free-style swimming record from 100 yards to the half mile and won a total of 5 gold medals in the Olympics. Willie Hoppe dominated the

Bill Tilden dominated tennis with driving determination, as seen in the 1925 Forest Hills championship. (Courtesy of Library of Congress.)

billiard scene, Charlie Paddock was the world's fastest runner, Tommy Hitchcock ruled the polo field, and Gar Wood knew no peer in speedboat racing. Yet, no sports commanded the American attention as did professional boxing and baseball and college football. In no sports were the heroes more exalted.

Boxing and Jack Dempsey

On July 4, 1919, two days before the end of the Paris, Inter-Allied Games, Jack Dempsey, who had embarrassingly remained out of

World War I, fought and defeated the massive, 6 foot 7 inch heavyweight champion Jess Willard in the scorching heat of Toledo, Ohio. Dempsey's $27,500 share of the nearly half-million dollar gate was a pittance in relation to what he would earn in the next decade as the most popular boxer since John L. Sullivan. Teaming up with Tex Rickard, the promoter of the Jack Johnson–Jim Jeffries "Great White Hope" fight of 1910, they passed the million dollar mark for gate receipts for the first time when Dempsey knocked out Frenchman Georges Carpentier in 1921 before 80,000 in Jersey City. This was the first heavyweight fight to be broadcast on radio, and boxing helped to stimulate radio sales, reciprocating the promotion of boxing by radio in the 1920s. When an ex-marine of World War I, Gene Tunney, challenged Dempsey in 1926, over 120,000 fans paid to see what most thought would be another Dempsey knockout in Philadelphia's rain drenched Sesquicentennial Stadium. A hero to millions of boxing enthusiasts, the thoroughly defeated Dempsey was given a return match the next year with Tunney in Chicago's massive Soldier's Field.

The second Tunney-Dempsey match was perhaps the single most dynamic sports event in the post-World War I era. Jack Dempsey was a symbol of the American aggressive spirit. He would stalk his opponent in the ring accepting punishment as he delivered it. He was the picture of courage, tenacity, and was very much the frontier-type, saloon or dance hall fighter one might have found a generation earlier in Dempsey's native Colorado. Gene Tunney was born in more cosmopolitan New York City. He joined the marines in World

Jack Dempsey KOed Georges Carpentier before a national radio audience in 1921. (Courtesy of Library of Congress.)

War I and became the American Expeditionary Forces light heavyweight boxing champion. It may seem ironic that Dempsey, the evader of the military draft, achieved heroic proportions in the 20s. That Tunney never did might be explained by his being a "scientific" boxer rather than a street fighter of Dempsey's stature. But more importantly Tunney's seeming indifference to public acclaim combined with his love of books, including Shakespeare, and intellectual discussions in a period of anti-intellectualism in America, contributed to his lack of public appeal. Dempsey's fighting spirit more nearly typified the American experience.

Tunney was champion in 1927 when he met Dempsey in Chicago. Promotor Tex Rickard hoped to sell 150,000 tickets for the event with the prospects of a $3,000,000 gate. Ringside seats cost $40; those in the farthest reaches of the stadium sold at $5, an average daily wage in Henry Ford's assembly plants. Spectators sat as far as 200 yards and 313 rows from the boxing ring. Some of the more enterprising

Gene Tunney defeated Jack Dempsey twice, but Dempsey remained the hero. (Courtesy of Library of Congress.)

brought portable radios to listen to 1 of 7 Chicago stations broadcasting the match. Another 67 stations on the NBC network carried the event to an estimated 50 million Americans crowded around their receivers. Even some Englishmen heard the broadcast on short wave as announcer Graham McNamee called the 10 round contest. Many notables were among the 140,000 spectators. Former boxers Jim Corbett, Jim Jeffries, and Jack Johnson; actors and entertainers Douglas Fairbanks, Charlie Chaplin, Gloria Swanson, and George M. Cohan; baseball figures Commissioner Kenesaw Mountain Landis and Ty Cobb; businessmen Charles Schwab, Otto Kahn, Bernard Baruch, and Alfred Sloan, president of General Motors; and a host of governors and other politicians. Wrote the *New York Times*: "Out of the welter and turmoil and clamor of the 'fight of the ages' one clear fact stands out—that tonight Tex Rickard unveiled the most beautiful picture in the history of sport here or elsewhere."[7]

When challenger Dempsey entered the ring the fight fans let him know that he was their idol. When his name was announced the sound was deafening though there were thousands who favored Tunney. Tunney, feinting and jabbing, won 5 of the first 6 rounds. Then in the most famous round in ring history, the 7th, Dempsey plunged recklessly into Tunney and stunned the champion with a left to the jaw followed by 6 more crashing blows. Tunney "toppled like a fallen tree," the first knockdown of his career. Rather than moving directly to a neutral corner, Dempsey stood over Tunney waiting to batter him if he arose as he had done four years before in a controversial fight when he knocked out the Argentinian Louis Firpo as he began to arise from a knockdown. The referee did not begin the count until Dempsey moved to a neutral corner. Almost five seconds elapsed— the count then began. At the count of 9 Tunney arose and stayed away from the charging Dempsey until he was once again able to box effectively. By the 9th round Tunney was again in command, and he controlled the fight to the end winning a clear decision.[8]

The American public debated the question then and for the next generation: Could Tunney have prevented a knockout had the count started at the knockdown? Tunney was "quite sure" that he could have gotten up—the American public was not sure.[9] Had Dempsey won he would have been the first heavyweight champion to have regained the title. There was no third match though both boxers continued to fight the next year. Jack Dempsey evidently was concerned that he might precipitate an early blindness if he were exposed to the continual pounding about the eyes he received from Tunney. Tunney, after fighting one more fight, retired undefeated. The fight game did not revive greatly until Joe Louis became heavyweight champion in the late 1930s.

Baseball: Landis and Ruth

Baseball, not boxing, was still in name and in fact, the National Pastime when the First World War came to a close. In 1919, Ty Cobb won his 12th and last batting title though he was to play a decade longer, and Babe Ruth set the major league home run record of 29 and was soon traded from the Boston Red Sox to the New York Yankees. The same year saw the most famous scandal in sport history—the "Black Sox" scandal.

If wars tend to stimulate a resurgence of sport, they also are conducive to corruption in the aftermath. The "Black Sox" scandal was certainly not the first case of corruption in sport, nor the last, but it created the strongest reaction and directly influenced baseball's development. The summer of 1919 saw race riots in Chicago as well as the American League championship for the White Sox. Cincinnati, which had not won a championship since the 1880s, was not expected to defeat the Chicago team which had 29 and 23 game winners, Eddie Cicotte and Lefty Williams, and stars the stature of Joe Jackson and Eddie Collins. When Cincinnati won the 9 game series easily, it was rumored that gambling interests were involved. The rumors might have been muffled had not sports writer Hugh Fullerton pursued the question and exposed his findings. It took a year before a grand jury was formed, and finally in the summer of 1921 the conspiracy trial to throw the World Series began. Though 8 Chicago players, including Cicotte, Williams, and Jackson, confessed their involvement at the grand jury, the confessions disappeared before the trial and all 8 repudiated their involvement. The trial ended with a not guilty verdict.[10] Major league baseball, however, took the law into its own hands and convicted the 8 of throwing the World Series.

It was Federal District Judge Kenesaw Mountain Landis, Commissioner of Baseball, who banned the 8 from professional baseball for life. Landis became the first commissioner of baseball replacing a commission of three which had ruled since the early 1900s. He was given dictatorial powers in exchange for the integrity which his image was to give to baseball. Landis unilaterally fined and banned players, chastised certain team owners, and created arbitrary rules for the operation of baseball for a generation. The creation of the baseball commissioner after the scandal appears to have been part of the burden that baseball has borne for being considered almost sacred in American life. Baseball, it seemed, had to have the appearance of purity demanded of a national pastime. The commissioner as symbol of this purity has remained, however, with the death of Landis during World War II, the ultimate power was taken away.

While the name of Kenesaw Mountain Landis has faded with age, that of Babe Ruth has remained as the supreme figure in baseball, if

Kenesaw Mountain Landis gave baseball integrity following the 1919 "Black Sox" scandal. (Courtesy of National Baseball Hall of Fame and Museum.)

not of all sports. Landis gave baseball integrity; Ruth gave it flare. Baseball needed both. Until the 1920s, baseball had few challenges to its popularity. With the increased income and mobility of Americans after World War I, other sports such as college football, golf, boxing, and horse and auto racing began to thrive. Writers began to ask the question: Is baseball still the national pastime? Largely because of Ruth and the dynamics of the home run, baseball remained supreme.

Babe Ruth entered professional baseball in 1914 at the age of nineteen after spending most of his wayward youth in a Baltimore boys' school. He was quickly sold the same year by the Baltimore Orioles of the International League to the Boston Red Sox. Ruth soon starred as a pitcher helping lead the Red Sox to three pennants and World Series championships in 1915, 1916, and 1918 while setting a series record of pitching 29⅔ scoreless innings. Beginning to both pitch and play the outfield, Ruth first led the league in home runs in 1918 and set a record the next year. The New York Yankees then purchased Ruth who helped create the greatest dynasty in baseball history.

When Ruth hit 54 homers for the Yankees in 1920 followed by 60 seven years later, he set a new style of play which glorified power hitting. It replaced the "scientific" mode exemplified by Ty Cobb which called for the placement of hits, strategic bunting, and skillful base running.[11] The "Big Bang" style of Ruth brought spectators to the ball park and made Ruth the unparalleled folk-hero of the celebrity producing 20s. Not Jack Dempsey in boxing, Red Grange in football, Rudolph Valentino in movies, nor Charles A. Lindbergh in aviation could match the continuous adoration which Ruth received.

Ruth, like Dempsey, was an unlikely hero for he, too, was accused of being a "draft dodger" during World War I. The idealism of the First World War soon faded as did negative feelings toward Ruth as a non-participant in the war effort. Ruth was possibly more like the 1920s than any other public performer. His success was unquestioned. His salary, in a period when money stood for personal success, became the highest in baseball and stood at $80,000 in 1930. He also symbolized a nation bent on the enjoyment of life.[12] Ruth indulged in the pleasures of food, drink, and women as any hedonist of the Roaring Twenties might have desired. His nighttime escapades were legion. That he could live such a life and remain the dominating athlete that he was for twenty years was amazing. With Ruth, as with such American legendary figures as Daniel Boone, Davy Crockett, and Mike Fink, it was difficult to separate fact from fiction. What other American athlete could point his finger at the pitcher's mound in a rash of temper, hit a home run, and then become mythologized as having called for and on the next pitch hit a home run to center field,

The "Big Bang" home run style of baseball had a Babe Ruth trademark. (Courtesy of National Baseball Hall of Fame and Museum.)

the direction of his tempestuous signal? Only Babe Ruth, who accomplished this in 1932 with his last World Series home run.

Football and Red Grange

While baseball with Babe Ruth remained the sport of the masses in America, football—the college game—was its most serious challenger for popular acclaim. Football had dominated the extracurriculum of colleges since about 1890. The commercialization of the college game was seen in its hiring of professional coaches at salaries far greater than professors, in its building of stadiums seating tens of thousands, and in its expansion of intersectional competition. All of these elements existed when coach Knute Rockne's Notre Dame team beat Army 13-7 in 1924. Grantland Rice, superb writer for the *New York Herald Tribune*, set the scene in the most dramatic of the 1920s sports writing:

> *Outlined* against a blue-gray October sky, the Four Horsemen rode again. In dramatic lore they are known as Famine, Pestilence, Destruction and Death. These are only aliases. Their real names are Stuhldreher, Miller, Crowley and Layden. They formed the crest of the South Bend cyclone before which another fighting Army football team was swept over the precipice at the Polo Grounds yesterday afternoon as 55,000 spectators peered down on the bewildering panorama spread on the green plain below.[13]

The same day at the University of Illinois' newly dedicated stadium, Harold "Red" Grange exhibited the form which was to make him the most renowned football player of the period. Playing undefeated Michigan before 67,000 spectators, Red Grange took the opening kick off and wended his way 95 yards for a touchdown. Before the first quarter ended Grange dodged and sprinted for touchdowns of 66, 55, and 40 yards. In the second half he ran 15 yards and passed 23 more for two additional scores. In all he handled the ball 21 times and gained 402 yards.[14] The national notoriety given Grange for this game during his junior year helped make him "the most famous, most talked-of and written about, most photographed and most picturesque player that the game has ever produced. . . ."[15] The following year Grange's Illinois team played before 370,000 fans, over twice the number of spectators in attendance in 1924. Philadelphia's Franklin

Red Grange on his way to one of four first-quarter touchdowns against undefeated Michigan in 1924. (Courtesy of University of Illinois.)

Field held 65,000 when Grange gained 363 yards and scored 3 touchdowns while defeating the pride of the east, the University of Pennsylvania, 24-2—all on a mud-laden field. He completed his career before 85,500 at Ohio State University in the midst of a national controversy over his amateur status.

The public acclaim which went with Grange whenever he played carried enormous commercial value. Rumors that Grange was a professional abounded before his last game for the University of Illinois. One report said he was offered $40,000 to play 3 games with the New York Giants professional football team. Another indicated that he would be paid $120,000 a year to sell real estate in Florida. There was probably truth in the rumors for as soon as his last game was played Grange signed a contract with his manager, C. C. Pyle, who negotiated for him to play professional football with the Chicago Bears. When Grange went on a barnstorming tour with the Chicago team of the five-year-old National Football League, he probably did more for the fledgling professional game than any other individual. With a $10,000 guarantee for each of 30 games to be played, Grange's name brought tens of thousands to see professional football for the first time.[16] It also brought cries of despair from those who thought professional sport was a sordid occupation. Among them were his father, his coach, the Illinois athletic director, and the Big Ten Commissioner, John L. Griffith, who felt that Grange's turning professional would hurt the college game. While Grange became immediately rich, professional football had to wait its turn. It was estimated that Grange would earn a million dollars within six months after turning professional from his football exhibitions, a $300,000 movie contract, and numerous advertisements which used his name.[17] One cynic of professionalized sports, dissatisfied with commercial college sport and Grange's actions, called it exchanging "football ability into coin of the realm."[18] Football, like the other commercialized sports of the 1920s, had critics who used sport to condemn what they found wrong in American society.

THE CRITICS OF SPORT ARE HEARD

If the 1920s were a period of indulgence in sport and in the larger society by the majority, they were also the period of social criticism by the minority. The Twenties were ripe for critics who saw in sport and in other social institutions signs of decadence. Looking at the larger America, writers like H. L. Mencken, F. Scott Fitzgerald, T. S. Eliot, Upton Sinclair, and Sinclair Lewis, berated wealthy America which had lost its soul and was intellectually barren, while becoming mechanical, commercial, business oriented, and materialistic. They would note the slogan of President Coolidge that "the business of

America is business" and tie it to the Tea Pot Dome scandal which found oil magnates bribing government officials for special favors. They would see the hypocrisy of a nation voting to prohibit the production and sale of alcohol yet disobeying the law by the millions with the production of "bathtub" gin and the patronizing of the popular "speakeasies." They would cite the World War I slogan that the war was fought "to make the world safe for democracy" and look despairingly at the revived and growing Ku Klux Klan of five million members which was doing all it could to prevent Catholics, Jews, Blacks, and aliens from achieving the expected freedom of a democracy. They would, of course, conclude that the Black Sox scandal was emblematic of the world of sport which was materialistic and corrupted as was the rest of society.

College sport, though, far more than professional sport, took the brunt of the criticism. Professional sport had always been looked upon by a significant portion of the middle class as being a spurious vocation, not to be dignified by association with amateur sport. When sport in colleges, which claimed to be amateur, took on many of the vestiges of professional sport, it came under vicious attack. The assault upon the college sport establishment was not entirely new, but the volume was unprecedented. Excoriating college sport and American society, one social critic satirized the scene:

> The whole tendency of our times is toward quantity production of standardized materials: automobiles, tin spoons, army uniforms, boots. Then why not minds? This age does not like individuals. We want standard people: standardized minds, or else no minds. . . . Educationally, the stadium will be just our biggest success . . . reassuring for good citizenship and obedience to our finished institutions. . . .[19]

Upton Sinclair would have agreed with this. "The masters of Ancient Rome provided gladiatorial combats for the purpose of diverting the minds of the populace from the loss of their ancient liberties," wrote Sinclair, "and in the same way the masters of modern America provide gigantic struggles on the football field." Claiming that American colleges and their sports were dominated by the captains of industry and finance, he asserted that athletics and their "organized mass noise" were promoted to prevent "students from thinking."[20]

With a plethora of other charges that intercollegiate athletics were commercialized, professionalized, and promoted negative influences at institutions of higher learning, both the American Association of University Professors and the Carnegie Foundation for the Advancement of Teaching entered into studies of the question of college athletics. Predictably the AAUP, which felt that faculties should have greater control over athletics, had little impact on institutions which were controlled by presidents who were themselves subservient to the boards of trustees.[21] The Carnegie Foundation for the Advancement of Teaching, however, did make an impact when its three-year study, a report on *American College Athletics*, was released in 1929. The Carnegie Report was prefaced with these stinging remarks:

> The paid coach, the gate receipts, the special training tables, the costly sweaters and extensive journeys in special pullman cars, the recruiting from the high school, the demoralizing publicity showered on the players, the devotion of an undue proportion of time to training, the devices of putting a desirable athlete, but a weak scholar, across the hurdles of the examination—these ought to stop. . . .[22]

The report concluded with a rather naive belief that college presidents could effect change away from policies of commercialized and professionalized athletics which boards of trustees had previously sanctioned. Writer H. L. Mencken was quick to grasp that college presidents "are far too politic a class of men to take any really effective steps against an enterprise that brings in such large sums of money. . . ."[23] Henry S. Pritchett, who wrote the preface to the Carnegie Report on *American College Athletics*, might well have remembered what he had written two decades before. "Party politics," Pritchett wrote in 1911, "have also played their part in the state institutions in the dismissal of men, notably of presidents who have stood for a sound educational policy against the popular cry for greater numbers or winning athletic teams."[24]

The hoopla of the Carnegie Report caused a ripple of reform, but it resulted in little permanent change in college athletics. Its strongest impact may have been to stimulate the growth of intramural sports in the colleges. Most colleges did not diminish their commercialized intercollegiate programs, but they did begin to make greater provision for those who were not varsity material. In the process it likely quieted some critics who claimed that if sports are good for the elite athletes, they are also beneficial to those who are not. Those who found fault in sport were far outnumbered by those who participated actively or passively in sport. Humorist Finley Peter Dunne, the creator of Mr. Dooley, gave the 1920 answer to those who wanted sport reform. Using college football as his focal point, Mr. Dooley replied: "Futball will niver be abolished [for it] is a gran' game. It's th' kind iv sport that makes an active, aggressive American business man. An' it's good advertisin'."[25] As in other periods of American history, sport in the 1920s echoed the social scene. It was indulged in by the masses and criticized by the minority.

THE DEPRESSION EFFECT

The Carnegie Report on college athletics was released on the day the stock market began its 1929 collapse ushering in the Great

Depression of the 1930s. If there was a diminution of college athletics in the Thirties, it was a result of the Depression far more than the exposé of the Carnegie Report. Hard times coming in athletics was only natural as the national income was cut in half from 1929 to 1932. When football receipts at the Big Ten colleges fell 30 to 40 percent in the early Thirties it was reflective of a similar reduction in workers' wages in the same time period. While college football attendance dropped nearly 30 percent by the depths of the Depression in 1933, few colleges dropped football though some smaller schools like Antioch in Ohio and Reed in Oregon did so.[26] The effect was felt more in the so-called minor sports which were abandoned in some colleges when the shrinkage of football receipts dictated such action.

Sport outside the college was also affected by the economic scene. Golf, on which more money was expended for equipment in 1929 than on the combined total of baseball, football, basketball, boxing, and tennis, was possibly the hardest hit. Golf clubs lost over one million members during the first five years of the Depression, and many of the private clubs were either sold or converted to daily fee courses.[27] Other sports felt the financial pinch but not as severely. If the value of athletic goods sold is a valid indication of the difficulties of sport during the Depression, then sport was probably in a less depressed state than was the economy as a whole. Though there was a sharp decline in the first several years of the Depression, census statistics indicate that 10 percent more was being spent on athletic goods at the end of the Depression in 1939 than in the last year of the Roaring Twenties. One can ponder the question why expenditures on hunting and fishing, two of the oldest sports in America, declined less than most during the 1930s. In fact, fishermen were spending more in 1936 than they had at the height of prosperity in the 1920s.[28]

Professional sport saw the need for innovation and change in order to increase attendance figures. Baseball, the sport least prone to change, found its gate receipts falling from $17 million in 1929 to less than $11 million in 1933. One innovative method of attracting patrons was night baseball which had been experimented with as early as 1883 in Fort Wayne, Indiana, but which was first successful in 1929 when a Des Moines, Iowa minor league team introduced it. Major league teams were reluctant to introduce night baseball as players and team owners complained of the glare of the lights, the possibility of injuries on cold nights, and the lateness resulting in the lack of publicity in morning newspapers. Cincinnati brought night baseball to the majors in 1935, and though criticism continued, economic considerations prevailed. By World War II, all but five of the major league teams had installed lights.[29]

The state of the economy played a role in both professional baseball and football. Blue Laws had prevented professional sports on Sunday in most States until the late 1800s and early 1900s. The prohibition still existed in Pennsylvania when the Depression hit. Both football and baseball teams in Philadelphia and Pittsburgh were anxious to play on Sunday since all other major league teams were playing. Connie Mack, long time manager of the Philadelphia Athletics, stated that his club could not meet the payroll "playing on seventy-seven weekdays at home." The economic argument and the increased amusement taxes from Sunday sports overode the pietistic concerns, and the Pennsylvania legislature allowed cities self-determination on the issue. Both cities approved Sunday sports. That decision not only helped professional sport to survive the Depression in Pennsylvania but led directly to the formation of Pittsburgh's professional football team by Art Rooney.[30]

Economic exigencies also led America's oldest commercialized sport, horse racing, to look for additional sources of income. State governments which were looking for an increased tax base decided that legalized betting outweighed the moral issues about gambling and horse racing. Pari-mutuel (actually Paris-mutuel) betting became the means. Devised by a Frenchman in 1872, the pari-mutuel system pooled all bets, gave a percentage to the state and management, and split the remainder among the first, second, and third place finishers. Only 5 states allowed betting on horse races prior to 1933, but the Depression prompted 10 states to legalize pari-mutuel betting in that year with other states following during the hard times. The Depres-

Pari-mutuel betting was prompted by the need for revenue by states during the Depression. (Courtesy of Library of Congress.)

sion, wrote Damon Runyon, was "responsible for a sudden growth in racing in the United States. . . . The State needed money, and they found that racing could be made to pay huge sums of taxes."[31]

Government, primarily from the impetus of the Federal government, came to play a dynamic role in promoting American sport for the first time. It is true that government had used sport during World War I to train an army and give diversion to the troops, but during the Depression the New Deal government of President Franklin Roosevelt gave millions, nay billions of dollars to promote sport and recreation in America. Massive, direct involvement in the economic sphere was a major departure from any previous governmental role, and sport received its share. When Roosevelt assumed power in 1933, two of the first concerns were to relieve unemployment and to stimulate economic recovery. During the first administration a number of relief and recovery programs were initiated, and most, including the Civilian Conservation Corps (CCC), the National Youth Administration (NYA), the Public Works Administration (PWA), and the Works Progress Administration (WPA), benefited sport. The CCC was composed of young men who, while living in a camp situation, built parks, created trails and lakes, and constructed cabins and ski runs. The NYA employed both young men and women, most of whom were in school. Among its projects were those improving parks and recreational facilities. The PWA was created to prime the economy with large projects such as the building of dams, bridges, sewage systems, and hospitals. About 1 dollar of every 100 of the $4 billion was spent on constructing athletic facilities.

Of the New Deal agencies, the Works Progress Administration did most to promote sport through the construction of athletic fields, playgrounds, parks, swimming pools, tennis and handball courts, golf courses, ice skating rinks, fair and rodeo grounds, and recreation buildings. In all, nearly one billion dollars were expended on sport and recreation facilities by the WPA from 1935 to the beginning of World War II. With over 40,000 sport and recreation projects sponsored by that federal agency, nearly every community in America received some help, though most did not compare to the million dollar Timberline Lodge ski area developed by the WPA near Portland, Oregon.[32]

The Depression and the New Deal relief and recovery legislation had the effect of nourishing less expensive, mass sport. Probably the two sports which grew the fastest during the 1930s were relatively inexpensive—bowling and softball. Bowling was almost certainly the most popular participant sport in the 1930s and possibly a decade earlier. It was estimated that 10 million Americans bowled regularly.[33] A generation before, bowling alleys had been considered as disrepu-

Timberline Lodge Ski Area was a WPA Depression project on Mt. Hood. (Courtesy of Works Progress Administration, Photo no. 69-N-10312C, in the National Archives.)

table places as were pool halls which only the "hoi polloi" often frequented. The American Bowling Congress, organized in 1895, attempted to change the rowdy-saloon image and give bowling standard rules and equipment. By the Thirties, the ABC had been remarkably successful in getting bowling out of the "alleys" and into the "lanes."

"Softball," someone stated during the Depression, "is the Shirley Temple of the sports world." Like the child actress, softball was new to most people and became an "overnight" success. Softball had been called several names from its origin in the late 1800s—kitten ball, playground ball, and recreation ball. It had been played both indoors and outdoors, and when the Depression came it became the number one outdoor game. It could be played, unlike baseball, on many playgrounds, was less costly than the National Game, required less talent to be enjoyable, and could be played at any age by both sexes. St. Petersburg, Florida gained notoriety for its Three-quarter Century Club in which its two teams averaged over eighty years of age per man. Chicago, in 1936, had 900 organized teams, while there were an estimated one million participants nationally.[34]

It is not surprising that bowling and softball were the two most popular sports in a rapidly developing adjunct to American industry called industrial recreation. Whereas most nineteenth century industrialists were little concerned about the social life of their workers, a few owners of industry could see that the promotion of sport and recreational activities for workers might create pleasure, loyalty, and serve to increase production. One of the earliest recreation programs in industry was the Pullman Athletic Association created in 1880 to serve George Pullman's company town on the outskirts of Chicago. This paternalistic program provided for swimming, boating, ice skating, baseball, bicycling, and other sport pursuits.[35] Other industrial concerns joined in the movement to provide recreational outlets for their workers, but the fastest development of industrial recreation awaited World War I when, because of the labor shortage, industries were concerned about securing good laborers and retaining them. Walter Camp, shortly after the war, warned industry of excessive paternalism in its athletic programs. "Let the workers organize their own athletics with management support," cautioned Camp, "but do not organize the sport by management for workers."[36] However, in the 1920s athletics sponsored and run by management were common, and there was a tendency to move toward professional teams of experts for advertising purposes rather than to provide recreation for the masses of workers. One could note that both the Green Bay Packers and the Decatur Staleys (later Chicago Bears) were the results of industrial sport to advertise industries.[37]

When economic hard times arrived, possibly one of every four industrial sports programs was dropped as industries did what they could to cut expenses.[38] At the same time the laborers in the programs which existed tended to share the role of governance more equally with management. The result was to increase less costly sports, while greater numbers of workers became involved in programs still operating. A survey of 600 companies in 1940 indicated that nearly 40 percent of the industries had athletic programs. The chart on page 325 indicates that the most popular programs were bowling and softball for both men and women, though the percentage of programs for women was much less than for men.[39]

Before the attack upon Pearl Harbor abruptly brought the United States into World War II, there was evidence that the American people had shed the austerity of the Depression and were moving toward a period of greater involvement in both active and vicarious participation in sport. On the fateful day of December 7, 1941, a

Sports Sponsored in Industrial Athletics

Sport	% Programs for Men	% Programs for Women
Bowling	87	35
Softball	74	11
Basketball	54	6
Golf	40	5
Baseball	34	1
Tennis	21	10
Ping Pong	24	4
Horse Shoes	24	1
Rifle	14	1
Volleyball	12	1
Swimming	9	1
Roller Skating	7	4
Billiards	10	1
Badminton	7	2

(Adapted from Diehl, L. J., and Eastwood, F. R.: Industrial Recreation. Lafayette, Ind.: Purdue University, 1940.)

crowd of 55,000 saw the New York Giants, Eastern champions of the National Football League, play their final regular season game, while nearly 16,000 saw the New York Rangers defeat the Boston Bruins in professional hockey. The day before, two college football teams, the University of Southern California and University of California at Los Angeles, played before 65,000 fans in sunny California. While Japanese planes left the American Pacific fleet in near ruin, people were reading their Sunday papers announcing that Babe Ruth, out of baseball for a half-dozen years, had signed a contract with Sam Goldwyn to appear in a movie on the life of Lou Gehrig, the honored New York Yankee who had died early that year of a rare muscular disease. Most sport fans were probably not too concerned that Bobby Riggs was ranked the number one amateur tennis player in America, but they likely noted a report about Ted Williams. Williams had finished the baseball season batting .406 for the Boston Red Sox, and on "the day of infamy" it was announced that he was classified 1-A by his draft board. Ted Williams and other professional and amateur athletes soon joined the war effort.

Almost immediately there was concern by the sports world that the war might force organized sport to be drastically reduced for the duration of the fighting as it had been during World War I. Most professional and amateur sports leaders appeared unselfish and patriotic as they called for the government to recognize the need for continuing sport throughout the emergency. "Let us keep our games to stay tough" stated one scribe. For Americans "to Lose is intolerable! We must Win!" wrote sportswriter John Kieran. "It's the spirit that our sports field furnishes in large quantities and it's exactly the spirit the country needs most to win the war." A spokesman for the Orange Bowl wanted to prolong the emphasis on sport for at least another month. Responding to the United States involvement in World War II, he said: "I think the public will raise hell this New Year's Day and then get down to Business."[40]

The war effort was the major business, but most of organized sport continued during World War II. As wars have tended to do, it apparently stimulated a desire for sport in Americans. When the war was concluded, it was soon evident that professional sports, including baseball, basketball, football, hockey, bowling, golf, horse and auto racing, and tennis, would have their greatest growth period. Problems would arise and solutions would be sought. Improved air service would expand both amateur and professional sport with the prospect of new and expanded leagues and competitions. Television, which had in 1939 successfully transmitted a college baseball game between Princeton and Columbia and a professional boxing match between Max Baer and Tommy Nova, was about ready to become the most important factor in promoting organized sport in the twentieth century. Organized labor, which had been given rights under New Deal legislation, would push for the labor sports movement to replace management dominated industrial sports and would attempt to unionize organized sports. Blacks had fought alongside whites for freedom against Germany and Japan and were ready to fight for justice in America. Part of that struggle was for the right to participate in sport, and it involved foremost the movement toward the integrating of professional team sports. World War II had set the stage for a second Golden Age of Sport.

REFERENCES

1. Football As Our Greatest Popular Spectacle, *Literary Digest*, LXXV (December 2, 1922), p. 52.

2. Thomas Foster, Why Our Soldiers Learn to Box, *Outing*, LXXII (May 1918), pp. 114-116; and How Uncle Sam Has Created an Army of Athletes, *Scientific American*, CXX (February 8, 1919), pp. 114-115.

3. *The Inter-Allied Games* (Paris: The Games Committee, 1919), pp. 17-20, 23.

4. Ibid., pp. 85, 114, 154, 174-188, and 324-327.

5. J. R. Hildebrand, Geography of Games, *National Geographic Magazine*, XXXVI (August 1919), p. 103.

6. Randy Roberts, Jack Dempsey: American Hero, *Journal of Popular Culture*, VIII (Fall 1974), pp. 411-426.

7. *New York Times*, September 23, 1927, p. 1.

8. *Chicago Tribune*, September 23, 1927, p. 1; and *New York Times*, September 23, 1927, pp. 1, 18.

9. Gene Tunney, My Fights with Jack Dempsey, in Herbert W. Wind (ed.), *The Realm of Sport* (New York: Simon and Schuster, 1966), p. 218.

10. Hugh Fullerton, Baseball on Trial, *New Republic*, XXIV (October 20, 1920), pp. 183-184; Eliot Asinof, *Eight Men Out: The Black Sox and the 1919 World Series* (New York: Holt, Rinehart and Winston, 1963), pp. passim; and David Q. Voigt, *American Baseball* (Norman: University of Oklahoma Press, 1970), II, pp. 124-133.

11. Voigt, *Baseball*, II, pp. 150-151.

12. Marshall Smelzer, The Babe on Balance, *The American Scholar*, CLVI (Spring 1975), p. 299.

13. Notre Dame's Cyclone Beats Army, *New York Herald Tribune*, October 19, 1924, p. 1.

14. Allison Danzig and Peter Brandwein, *The Greatest Sport Stories from the New York Times* (New York: A. S. Barnes, 1951), pp. 218-220.

15. *New York Times*, November 22, 1925, Sec. 10, p. 1.

16. Ibid., November 12, 1925, p. 31; November 18, 1925, p. 19; November 23, 1925, p. 26; and December 8, 1925, p. 1; and "Pro Football Versus Collegiate," *Literary Digest*, CXXII (October 31, 1936), pp. 40-41.

17. *New York Times*, December 8, 1925, p. 1; and Football History As Made by the Illinois Iceman, *Literary Digest*, LXXXVII (December 26, 1925), pp. 29-34.

18. Yelping Alumni: The Matter with College Football, *Outlook*, CXLII (January 6, 1926), p. 22.

19. Joseph K. Hart, The Faculty Loses the Ball, *Survey*, XLIX (December 1922), pp. 305, 335.

20. Upton Sinclair, Shall We Abolish Football? *Forum*, LXXVI (December 1926), pp. 838, 840.

21. Ernest H. Wilkins, Intercollegiate Football: Report by Committee G, American Association of University Professors *Bulletin*, XII (April 1926), pp. 218-223.

22. Howard J. Savage, et al., *American College Athletics* (New York: The Carnegie Foundation for the Advancement of Teaching, 1929), p. xxi.

23. H. L. Mencken, The Striated Muscle Fetish, *American Mercury*, XXIII (June 1931), p. 156.

24. Henry S. Pritchett, Progress of the State Universities, Carnegie Foundation for the Advancement of Teaching *Annual Report*, VI (1911), p. 108.

25. Futball Will Niver Be Abolished, *Literary Digest*, LXXXVIII (March 13, 1926), p. 71.

26. King Football Answers the Depression, *Literary Digest*, CXVI (September 16, 1933), p. 24; and John R. Tunis, The Slump in Football Common, *Atlantic Monthly*, CL (December 1932), pp. 679-682.

27. *1930 Census*, Manufactures—1929, Vol. II, p. 1365; and "Club Comeback," *Business Week* (June 27, 1936), pp. 20-21.

28. *1930 Census*, "Manufactures—1929," Vol. I, p. 239; *1940 Census*, Manufactures—1939, Vol. II, Part 2, p. 591; Sporting Goods Sales Up, *Business Week* (July 17, 1937), pp. 34-35; and "Industrial Report on Sports," *Newsweek*, XII (December 26, 1938), p. 20.

29. United States House of Representatives, Organized Baseball, Report No. 2002, 82nd Congress, 2nd Session (1952), p. 12; Big League Baseball, *Fortune*, XVI (August 1937), p. 116; More Light on Night Baseball, *Literary Digest*, CVI (September 27, 1930), p. 36; and Voigt, *Baseball*, II, pp. 210, 251.

30. William C. White, Bye, Bye, Blue Laws, *Scribner's Magazine*, XCIV (August 1933), pp. 107-109; J. Thomas Jable, Sports, Amusements, and Pennsylvania Blue Laws, 1682-1973, Ph.D. dissertation, Penn State University, 1974, pp. 150-170; John A. Lucas, The Unholy Experiment—Professional Baseball's Struggle Against Pennsylvania Sunday Blue Laws 1926-1934, *Pennsylvania History*, XXXVIII (April 1971), p. 173; and Stephen Riess, "Professional Sunday Baseball: A Study in Social Reform, 1892-1934," *The Maryland Historian*, IV (Fall 1973), pp. 95-108.

31. Paris-Mutuels Tonic Puts New Life in Race Season, *Literary Digest*, CXVI (July 29, 1933), p. 27; Race-Bets: $500,000,000 A Year Thrills, *Literary Digest*, CXXII (December 26, 1936), pp. 34-35; and Dixon Wecter, *The Age of the Great Depression, 1929-1941* (Chicago: Quadrangle Books, 1971), p. 243.

32. Report on Progress of the WPA Program Works Progress Administration, June 30, 1942, p. 46; Donald S. Howard, *The WPA and Federal Relief Policy* (New York: Russell Sage Foundation, 1943), pp. 125-130; Frederick W. Cozens and Florence S. Stumpf, *Sports in American Life* (Chicago: University of Chicago Press, 1953), p. 324; and Wecter, *Age of the Great Depression*, pp. 222-224.

33. Paul W. Kearney, Ten Million Keglers Can't Be Wrong, *Reader's Digest*, XXX (March 1937), pp. 79-82.

34. America's Fastest Growing Game, *Popular Mechanics*, LXV (June 1936), pp. 834-837.

35. Almont Lindsey, *The Pullman Strike* (Chicago: University of Chicago Press, 1942), pp. 38-56.

36. Walter Camp, Industrial Athletics: How the Sports for Soldiers and Sailors Are Developing into Civilian Athletics, *Outlook*, CXXII (June 11, 1919), pp. 252-253.

37. Outdoor Recreation for Industrial Workers, *Monthly Labor Review*, XXIV (May 1927), pp. 867-882; and Athletics in Industry, *Literary Digest*, XCI (November 6, 1926), pp. 69-72.

38. Jackson M. Anderson, *Industrial Recreation* (New York: McGraw-Hill, 1955), p. 62.

39. Leonard J. Diehl and Floyd R. Eastwood, *Industrial Recreation* (Lafayette, Ind.: Purdue University, 1940), pp. 1-41.

40. *Washington Post*, December 7, 1941, Sports, p. 3; December 8, 1941, pp. 13, 24; December 9, 1941, p. 26; December 10, 1941, p. 31; *New York Tribune*, December 7, 1941, p. 27; and *New York Times*, December 9, 1941, p. 49.

CHAPTER 19

The Growth of American Professional Sport

The late James M. Barrie, in an address to the graduating class at St. Andrews University, noted that "God gave us memory so that we might have roses in December." History, too, in addition to being instructive, allows us to look back at significant remembrances of things past. The Roman dramatist, Terence, said that "there is nothing human that I do not feel to be my concern." Both Barrie and Terence would probably have enjoyed a glance over their respective shoulders at the history of sport. In late nineteenth and early twentieth century America, professional sport grew with fretful uncertainty. So much depended on the exigencies of commerce, the halting growth of the technological revolution, and the uneven distribution of leisure time among the several social classes. During the 1920s—still looked upon as the first "golden age of sport"—new attendance records, male and female sport stars larger than life, unprecedented sporting heroics, made the next era of the 1930s and 1940s appear less than provocative. The thirty years following World War II vacillated between new horizons of prosperity and traumatic human unrest. No such oscillation has occurred in the growth of professional sport—an eruptive process that has preoccupied millions of Americans and involved several billions of dollars.

Leisure consists in freedom from gainful employment and, as Joffre Dumazedier noted, it "appears to be distinguished by a search for a state of satisfaction." The millions who watch professional sport have little purpose other than those legitimate feelings of pleasure and escape. All sport offers this in abundance—professional athletics in great quantities. Our thoroughly technical society has given most of us a glimpse of a post-industrial society, a shift from manufacturing goods to human services, as Daniel Bell calls it. It is not yet sure that in this imminent society of the 1980s, the growth of professional spectator sport will continue. There are signs in our own times that massive participatory play has already made some inroads into the spiraling world of pro sports. Ruskin once said that great nations write their autobiographies in three manuscripts, the book of their deeds, the book of their words, and the book of their art. Sir Kenneth Clark believed we must read all three books, "but of the three the only trustworthy one is the last."[1] Professional sport is an art form, a barometer of the times and a portent of society's tastes. In a modern American society, professional sport must be studied if that culture's history is to be accurately written. If futurist Herman Kahn is right, the Agricultural and Industrial Revolutions are nearly over, and will be followed by a different kind of service or truly postindustrial economy. "This quarternary society," he says, "can be characterized as emphasizing people 'playing games with and against others, and with and against communities.'"[2] In addition to some work, hundreds of millions of people will be preoccupied with ritualistic and aesthetic activities, cultural, social, recreational, and the whole spectrum of spectator and participatory sport.

BASEBALL, FOOTBALL, AND BASKETBALL—MODELS OF SPORTS GROWTH.

From 1946 through the 1949 baseball season, attendance grew enormously—from 10 million to 20.2 million. During the 1950s the time-honored game changed rapidly as franchises moved to even more promising urban areas in an attempt to break the attendance lethargy. The weakened minor leagues were reluctantly kept alive as necessary training centers. Black baseball players, talented athletes from the Caribbean Islands, and, later, a new kind of professional from the American universities, profoundly changed the game during the 1960s. In 1969, baseball expanded to 24 major league franchises, 12 in each league—resulting in sky-rocketing salaries in the frantic search for talent. The tug of television, pressures from football and basketball, the demise of autocratic, conservative leadership, players' strikes, and constant attacks on baseball's favored legal position by players and their representatives, made it a different, yet decidedly recognizable game during the 1970s. Surprisingly, the game retained its popularity with the fans. That "ultimate innovator," Bill Veeck was right with his cliche that baseball is an escape from the problems of daily life. "We're selling an illusion, that's all," he told a *Sports Illustrated* journalist in a March 15, 1976, article titled, "Back Where I Belong." The modern players are faster and stronger. Baseball is the best of sports, the worst of sports, the most

Professional football (Massillon Tigers) used a plump ball and a minimum of padding in 1905. (Courtesy of Library of Congress.)

exciting, yet the dullest, the crudest and at the same time, the most skillful of games, said Englishman Paul Gardner. Thomas Wolfe found baseball to be "a part of the whole weather of our lives, of the thing that is our own, of the whole fabric, the million memories of America."[3]

Nothing in sport rivals the popular rise of professional football in the 1960s and 1970s. It had come a long way from those earliest days of Jim Thorpe, George Halas, Curly Lambeau, Fritz Pollard, Elmer Oliphant, and Red Grange—when the ball was "as plump as an oversize Christmas pudding . . . meant for kicking rather than passing." Hard times marked the game, and even the pre-war greats Bronko Nagurski, Ernie Nevers, Chris Cagle, Benny Friedman, Ken Strong, Don Hutson, Sammy Baugh, Sid Luckman, and Bill Dudley, failed to make it a national pastime. Paul Brown and then Vince Lombardi differed in their coaching approaches, but helped change many aspects of the game during the 1950s and 1960s. The American Football League was born in 1960, a reminder to the National Football League that only big salaries could keep the "super" players in the older conference. Joe "Willy" Namath started the money avalanche with his 1965 price-tag of $400,000. The game was extraordinarily complex, yet talented men made orderliness and clean execution out of it. And it was done at high speed, insuring appeal to millions. Historian Richard Hofstader noted that, "Nothing in this country is done as well as professional football. Compare it with our diplomacy."[4] In the 1970s, teams increased from 12 to 26; disquietude and higher salary demands became commonplace. Yet the measure of the game's greatness was reflected in sport geniuses like O. J. Simpson—the epitome of "speed, balance and E.S.P." Football will continue to be a part of the American scene as long as men like Simpson play the game.

The smaller dimensions of a basketball court lend themselves ideally to television. Beyond this, guaranteeing its success in the American post mid-century, are the enormous pool of giant, talented athletes playing a supremely physical and sophisticated game. The old Celtics, formed in 1912, played their way into shape with two-a-day games. So do the modern teams with their season beginning in November and ending in June. Maurice Podoloff became the first commissioner of the Basketball Association of America in 1946, later called the National Basketball Association. In 1967, the rival American Basketball Association appeared, its red, white, and blue ball plus the incomparable Julius "Doctor J." Erving, made vain efforts to close the gap between the two leagues. But the older league had been blessed with an avalanche of stars like Cousy, Baylor, West, Lucas,

Joe Namath was supreme when football became America's leading spectator sport in the 1960s. (Courtesy of Joe Namath.)

Robertson, Russell, Chamberlain, Havlicek, DeBusschere, Cowens, Frasier, Kareem Abdul-Jabbar, and many others. Salaries were the highest average among professional athletes, the game was the fastest growing sport in the world. More than 20 teams in both leagues formed a network that covered every major urban area in the United States. The two rival leagues merged in 1976 and reduced the total number of teams, but the interest in professional basketball continued to grow. Converts were made every day, reminding one of the long-ago question of Ralph Waldo Emerson to Margaret Fuller, as both watched the

O. J. Simpson was the star of football in the 1970s. (Courtesy of Buffalo Bills.)

world's greatest ballet dancer. "Margaret," he said, "this is poetry." "No, Waldo," replied Margaret; "it is not poetry, it is religion."[5]

THE PRICE OF EXPANSION—SPIRALING SALARIES AND NEW STADIA

There is no athletic record that the modern professional gladiator cannot break. In the United States the twin prospects of fame and fortune have attracted by far the majority of male athletic talent. "The sweep of legend and the impact of competitiveness," as Roger Kahn describes the twin attractions, have created a sporting omnipresence for almost all Americans. It seems almost everyone connected with pro sports makes a lot of money. Attendance records were set when well over 30 million people attended major league baseball games in 1977. Similar things were happening in other sports. Basketball and hockey players made the most money. In 1973, four basketball players earned $400,000 a season and at least 50 earned $100,000. The two basketball conferences paid 22½ million dollars in salaries, baseball paid 22 million, while the payroll for slightly more than a thousand football players was 28½ million dollars.[6] Altogether, more than 150 American athletes earned salaries exceeding $100,000. The majority of them were basketball players. And yet, economist George Scully of Southern Methodist "sees pro football salaries doubling in two years."[7] The National Hockey League grossed about $50 million during 1973— and paid its players one-quarter of the total take. That single year, the three skaters in the front line of the New York Rangers were paid $600,000.[8] The fascination for sport combines with tax write-offs, ticket sales, local governmental subsidization, and large amounts of monies from television to allow such salaries. The lengthy Brookings Institution Study on Sports concluded that "Professional sports leagues have a remarkably complex set of rules and practices that all but eliminate business competition among their members."[9]

Another manifestation of sport's importance was the number of old and new stadia. Most large cities have built or are planning to build new arenas of sport. The Houston Astrodome started the new trend, although Chicago, Philadelphia, and Los Angeles have had 100,000 seating capacity stadia for two generations. But many think that brand new sport complexes are necessary to compete successfully. The Superdome is New Orleans' pride and joy and problem child. It has 79,000 seats, cost $173,000,000, cannot earn a profit unless it operates profitably 200 days a year, "and has money troubles that may go on forever...."[10] The new Yankee Stadium cost more than $100,000,000, but cannot compare with the Hackensack, New Jersey, Meadowlands sport complex—a $330,000,000 adventure. There was concern among many and outrage with a few at such costs. Virginia

The size of the New Orleans Superdome (nearly 700 meters wide) was outdone only by its cost (nearly $200,000,000).

Senator Robert C. Byrd, voiced his anger on the floor of the U.S. Senate:

> What all this means, simply, is that in many cities across this nation, citizens are placing their lives, their children's lives, and even their grandchildren's lives in hock so that they can sit on cushioned seats watching professional athletes who dress in carpeted rooms.[11]

THE OTHER SPORTS GIANTS AWAKEN

The United States was in the middle of another "Golden Age of Sport." There were almost no more so-called "minor sports." Talented men and women roamed the land, bowling, riding, shooting, gliding, running, paddling, fighting, wrestling, jumping, and driving. Small and large monies were made in horse and dog racing, playing tennis and golf, teaching all versions of the eastern martial arts, and, if one stretched the definition of sport, in demolition and roller derbies. There were dozens more. Obviously, the greater the affluence and leisure of a society, the greater variety of sport it possesses. Muhammed Ali earned several million dollars barnstorming through 1976, Johnny Rutherford earned a small fortune as a result of his abbreviated, rain-soaked Indianapolis 500 on Memorial Day of that same year. Professional softball teams, both men and women, had a precarious living. Millionaire soccer player, Pele, led his Cosmos to a 3-1 victory over the Seattle Sounders in April, 1976. Some found it difficult to believe that 58,124 spectators paid their way into that west coast city's new $67,000,000 Kingdome to see a game of European football. There were obvious dangers in the over-serious, totally commercial and frequently crass aspects of pro sports. Social scientists had only recently begun to see the national impact of sport—especially that most visible professional manifestation of the sports world. The *New York Times* political analyst, James Reston, saw in sport not only diversion and illusion, but hope. "The world of sports," he said, "has everything the world of politics lacks and longs for . . .; sports are now more popular than politics in America."[12]

THE OMNIPOTENCE OF TELEVISION

The great understatement is to say that television has profoundly influenced professional sport since the Second World War. NBC, CBS, and ABC were, in a real sense, the biggest sports initials. Over 70 million people watched the 1975 sixth world series game between Boston and Cincinnati. The 1970 football Super Bowl—"that divinely inspired spectacle"—saw the Hartford Insurance Company pay $200,000 for a single sixty-second commercial. All viewers had a front row . . . and an expert by his or her side. In 1974, the three networks paid over $100,000,000 to sports clubs. "For the clubs, this is the best sort of money there is—guaranteed, before the season even starts."[13] William O. Johnson's perceptive book, *Super Spectator and the Electric Lilliputians*, sometimes read like a review of high finance. Mass America took much of its sports "insulated, isolated, miniaturized, and in the gloom of a darkened room." Commercials tampered with the game itself. Johnson may have been serious when he said:

> God only knows what subtle and ugly things can occur to the morale, the momentum, the chemistry, the metaphysics of a team when it is forced to pause in the struggle while television beams out pictures of two men visiting through a shared bathroom cabinet about using a certain brand of underarm deodorant.[14]

Johnson's concern, as well as those deeply involved in the business of sport, was that entire budgets were built around television income; chaos would result if the money were ever withdrawn. Television had thrust sport into a golden era—but an era of near total dependence on American commerce. Thus "major league sport has now sold itself beyond the capacity to control its own destiny."[15]

VIOLENCE AS SPORT'S PROFOUNDLY DISRUPTIVE ELEMENT

It is natural, inherently acceptable, and historically correct to say that professional sport is an extremely rough, physical way of life. It is incorrect to conclude, then, that violence is an inevitable part of contact sports. Philosophy professor, Michael Levin, points out examples of violence, such as automobile accidents, military battles, and cataclysms. "Their mark is an uncontrolled, spasmodic release of energy that threatens the organic integrity of anything in its vicinity."[16] This hardly describes football, basketball, or hockey as it *should* be played. Violence—physical action beyond roughness, and outside the purview of the game's rules—has become more frequent in American sport. Such action may temporarily attract more fans, but will eventually reduce the sport's appeal. Serge Savard of the Montreal Canadiens made a blunt comment after they swept the violent (and talented) Philadelphia Flyers in the 1976 Stanley Cup finals. "The Flyers were the worst thing to happen to hockey. The way they fight, the way they set the example for the young kids. To sweep them, maybe we put an end to all the crap they stand for." Significantly stiffen the penalty for violence, say some. "Admirable finesse would no longer be obscured by blind violence," concluded a *Sports Illustrated* editor.[17]

Violence in sport reached epidemic proportions in the 1970s. Journalists, fans, coaches, athletes, college professors and, recently, the law courts, had strong and frequently divergent views on its significance. Public acceptance or public outrage will largely determine the future direction of sport and violence. The Toronto lawyer, William McMurtry, believed that professional hockey was sick. It is:

> the only sport where physical intimidation outside the rules is encouraged as a legitimate tactic, leading to the glorification of brawlers in attempts to sell the game to the U.S. audience.[18]

Konrad Lorenz and Robert Ardrey have popularized the view that nature and man are violent. There is much supportive evidence. Revisionist scientists like Herbert Seig and Ashley Montagu argue that human aggression is not an instinct at all but learned behavior, which, presumably, can be unlearned. There can be little doubt that certain existing sports are fostering violence and aggression rather than alleviating it. Legitimately pragmatic goals of sport need balance with the humanistic process. Too frequently the canvas of professional sport is "smeared with pain." Most pros can endure pain. Some are like the untiring blue geese, others "like the Sooty tern, which can fly for three years or more before alighting. That is the way of athletes."[19] Once the idea of order goes, so goes the game. Few weep for the injured professional, especially those involved in brawls. When the rules are bent and broken, sport and sportsmen lose their integrity. The real losers are "the children and adults who watch and then repeat what they see on playgrounds and in the stands—and perhaps in their lives."[20] For any individual, example is terribly important. You don't teach morality. You 'catch' it—like an infection, a good one.[21] Restraint in sport, as in life, is being confused with repression. Many have forgotten that "the value of self-control in relation to true freedom is as much an art as it is a discipline."[22]

PROFESSIONAL SPORTS APPROACH THEIR ZENITH

There are more than 7,000 registered professional athletes in the United States. No other country even comes close to these numbers. There are evidences that at least through the remainder of the 1970s,

'You've got a great future in this world, kid!'

Some questionable ethics in sport, brutality and dishonesty, were likely a reflection of the infection of the larger society. (Courtesy of The Milwaukee Journal.)

this number will grow significantly. And yet there are signs that this growth is not altogether permanent. Dozens of sport businesses, like indoor lacrosse, lead fleeting lives. The giant American Basketball Association experiment staggered through the 1976 season, losing millions of dollars. Four of its teams requested permission to buy into the older NBA at $7 million per team. "Madness," cried John Y. Brown, ABA president, pointing out that such a transaction would necessitate each ABA team to fill their arena to capacity every night at $4.50 a ticket for six years just to break even.[23] Madness or not, the ABA folded, and the NBA accepted some ABA teams. The profit motive in professional sport remains quite correctly its main objective. But when profits become the only objective of sport, avarice and unrelenting selfishness tend to dominate the thinking of both players and owners. At the present time, some owners and athletes are infected with this disease. Overly pessimistic author Leonard Shecter, in his *The Jocks*, hints that the woods of sport are filled with crooks . . . lurking just beneath the surface and at the edge of our minds. "And I tell you, you have not heard the last of them."[24] Glenn Dickey is convinced the professional sports empire is doomed. "Fans and athletes," he says, "are locked in a symbiotic embrace," neither understanding one another, as excess and overemphasis are piled one upon the other.[25]

Professional sport, beset by serious fiscal and ethical problems, serves an important commercial, recreational, and cathartic function for millions of Americans. The high-salaried, consummately skillful professional athlete has been an American tradition since the mid-nineteenth century. Today, the dangers and rewards are greater than ever before. Huge monies, glamor, travel, adulation—all compete with the risks of serious injury, gambling, drugs, and the rising intervention of strike lockouts, legal suits, and player-owner confrontations.[26] The best of sport reminds one of the idealized version in ancient societies. At its worst, it is as Bob Lipsyte calls it, "a grotesque distortion of sports . . . turning our best athletes into clowns."[27] Athletics, like most popular culture, supplies the material for daydreams. Commercial sport in the United States may have reached its zenith in the creation of individualized myth-making and collective adulation. The business psyche so dominates professional sport that the profit motive has nearly completely eradicated whatever remains of the idea that it is something especially apart from the world of commerce. America needs professional sport, and will continue to demand it for many years to come. And yet there is a groundswell, a perceptible, measurable, national yearning for participatory sport, a sport-for-all, recreational, life-time exercise movement that could alter the face (and waistline) of millions of people during the 1980s. The immediate future will see a temporal and financial struggle between these two provocative leisure activities. Somehow, a continuing affluent American will live easily admidst both.

References

1. Kenneth Clark, *Civilization—a personal view* (New York: Harper and Row, Pub., 1969), p. 1.

2. Herman Kahn *et al.*, *The Next 200 Years—a Scenario for America and the World* (New York: William Morrow and Co., Inc., 1976), p 22.

3. Thomas Wolfe, *The Letters of Thomas Wolfe*, ed., by Elizabeth Nowell (New York: Scribner, 1956), p. 722.

4. Richard Hofstader as quoted in Richard Kostelanetz, "Fanfare for TV football," *Intellectual Digest*, (August 3, 1973), p. 53.

5. See D. W. Brogan, *The American Character* (New York: Alfred A. Knopf, 1944), pp. 141-142.

6. Leonard Koppett, "In pay, N.B.A. is biggest league," *The New York Times*, March 11, 1973.

7. George Scully as quoted in "Economist sees pro football salaries doubling in two years," *The New York Times*, January 24, 1974.

8. Richard John Pietschmann, "Salaries in Professional Sports," *Mainliner—United Airlines Magazine*, (December 2, 1973), p. 22.

9. Roger Noll (ed.), *Government and the Sports Business* (Washington, D.C.: The Brookings Institute, 1974), p. 9.

10. J. D. Reed, "Really running in the red," *Sports Illustrated*, 44 (March 15, 1976), p. 27.

11. Robert C. Byrd, "Give education an equal chance," *Congressional Record* (Senate), July 25, 1974.

12. James Reston as quoted in Joseph Durso, *The All-American Dollar—the big business of sports* (Boston: Houghton Mifflin Co., 1971), p. 249.

13. Paul Gardner, *Nice Guys Finish Last—Sport and American Life* (New York: Universe Books, 1975), p. 34.

14. William O. Johnson, *Super Spectator and the Electric Lilliputians* (Boston: Little, Brown and Co., 1971), p. 60.

15. *Ibid.*, p. 236.

16. Michael E. Levin, "Rough, not Violent," Letter to the Sports Editor, *The New York Times*, February 29, 1976, p. 2 Sports Sec.

17. Robert W. Creamer, "Scorecard," *Sports Illustrated*, 44 (May 31, 1976).

18. William McMurtry as quoted in Parton Keese, "Violence in Sports: What it could mean," *The New York Times*, January 26, 1976, Sports section.

19. Mark Kram, "The Face of Pain," *Sports Illustrated*, 44 (March 8, 1976), p. 66.

20. Stefan Kanfer, "Doing violence to sport," *Time*, 107 (May 31, 1976), p. 65.

21. Kenneth Boulding as quoted in Charlotte Saikowski, "Regaining America's unity of purpose," *The Christian Science Monitor*, April 22, 1976, p. 15.

22. Godfrey John, "The Beauty of restraint," *The Christian Science Monitor*, April 22, 1976, p. 25.

23. John Y. Brown as quoted in Bill Hendrick, "ABA's demise expected," *The Philadelphia Inquirer*, June 9, 1976, p. 5E.

24. Leonard Shecter, *The Jocks* (Indianapolis: The Bobbs-Merrill Co., 1969), p. 268.

25. Glenn Dickey, *The Jock Empire—Its Rise and Deserved Fall* (Radnor, Pa.: Chilton Book Co., 1974), p. 209.

26. The entire volume 38 (Winter-Spring, 1973) issue of *Law and Contemporary Problems* is devoted to "Collective bargaining and professional team sports industry."

27. Robert Lipsyte, *Sportsworld—An American Dreamland* (New York: Quadrangle, 1975), p. xiv.

CHAPTER 20

Women's Sport: A Trial of Equality

The entry of American women in sport was for the most part a phenomenon of the latter nineteenth century. The acceptance of women in sport, where it was achieved, was primarily a latter twentieth century occurrence. At the end of the 1800s the question was asked: "Should a lady ride a bicycle?" A generation later following World War I, the question often discussed was: "Shall women compete in highly competitive athletics?" Another forty years later one asked: "Should women have equal opportunity with men to compete in athletics at all levels?" Considering the status of women at the various times, the questions were logical. The answers were complicated. The results were mixed.

Women who participated in sport in the early twentieth century seemed out of place with the norms of society—later in the century they appeared to be more in tune with the times. One great sportswoman, Eleanora Sears, who was considered an eccentric in the early years of the twentieth century, would have been far more acceptable at the end of it. Eleanora Sears, a great, great grandaughter of Thomas Jefferson, was born into the affluence of a Boston "Brahmin" family in the early 1880s. It was from this position of prominence and wealth that she flaunted society by participating in a variety of sports, most of which were not acceptable under the social restrictions of the time. As she broke with Victorian tradition, Sears showed expert horsemanship in riding, jumping, and showing. She played tennis at a championship level winning 4 national doubles titles, and she was the first woman's national champion in the racket sport, squash. Displaying her showmanship in a way similar to James Gordon Bennett a generation earlier, she competed in distance walking contests. Some of her pedestrian feats covered distances over

342

100 miles and once, at the age of forty-four years, she won a $1,000 bet by walking from Providence, Rhode Island to Boston in less than ten hours. Not content with participation in only a few sports, she was a fine rifle and pistol shooter, participated in golf, swimming, canoeing, and yachting, and even played baseball, football, and donned boxing gloves. As she refused to be denied sports enjoyed by men, Sears was one of the first women to race autos and to fly airplanes. When she was refused participation on the American polo squad because she was a woman, Sears organized her own team. Only a wealthy woman who refused to be tied to society's values could have succeeded in such sporting escapades in the early years of the 1900s. Eleanora Sears seemed out of place even as America terminated World War I by granting women the right to vote.[1]

WOMEN'S RIGHTS AND WOMEN'S SPORT AFTER WORLD WAR I

The women's rights movement which began at Seneca Falls, New York in 1848, saw its greatest triumph, many believed, in the passage of the XIX Amendment to the Constitution in 1920 granting women suffrage. Those who took this viewpoint including a large number in the women's rights movement felt that women had now achieved equality in America. The ballot, it seemed, came to symbolize the long struggle for women's equality. If the vote meant equality, one would have expected to see a significant increase in women's interscholastic and intercollegiate athletics as well as in intramural programs, and vast extensions of both private and public involvement by women in a multitude of sports which had previously been dominated by men.

One woman believed that this was true even at the onset of World War I. She said: "Women used to do nothing but ride horses and play croquet. Now they are coming to the front in every sport." Expanding on her theme she indicated, without strong evidence, that "there is practically nothing a woman cannot do that she would be likely to do, and she is likely to wish to do nearly everything."[2] Even an Eleanora Sears, who came closest to doing everything, would have had difficulty accepting that statement. In the long run Elizabeth Cady Stanton, the nineteenth century leader of the women's rights movement, was more accurate in her prediction of the meaning to women of the right to vote. She dismissed it as "not even half a loaf: . . . only a crust, a crumb." In sport and in society, the franchise for women, while it had a short time effect in producing women's involvement, did not appear to have a dynamic, lasting effect. As one historian has shown: "The ballot had supplied a symbol before it was gained. Almost as soon as the franchise was gained, the symbol was lost."[3]

To Carrie Chapman Catt, leader of the suffrage movement, a signal victory, symbolically and literally, had been won. In 1926, six years after the XIX Amendment, nineteen-year-old Gertrude Ederle became the first woman to swim the English Channel. "It is a far cry from swimming the Channel," Catt noted, "to the days which my memory goes back, when it was thought that women could not throw a ball or even walk very far down the street without feeling faint."[4] In some ways it was amazing that attitudes could change so significantly from the late nineteenth century to 1926. In the 1890s, young college women the age of Gertrude Ederle could hardly bear to be seen in a gymnasium in physical education bloomer outfits, even by members of their own sex.[5] Yet, in the mid-1920s, it was not unthinkable that a champion swimmer should gain international exposure in a tight fitting swim suit as she broke the male Channel record by nearly two hours.

The exploit of Gertrude Ederle gave some women a new sense of dignity in their physical abilities. Ederle, who had won a gold and two bronze swimming medals in the 1924 Olympics, trained diligently in her quest to become the first female to swim from France to England. One of the first important women athletes to come from working class parents, she won a 3-mile ocean race at age sixteen. Two years later she became the first woman to complete the 21-mile race from the Battery to Sandy Hook in New York Bay, and she shattered the men's record in accomplishing it. A short time later she tried to swim the English Channel from Cape Gris Nez in France. Failing as had all other swimmers on their first attempt, she trained for another year. On August 6, 1926, Ederle swam from Cape Gris Nez coming to the beach at Kingsdown, England fourteen hours and twenty-three minutes later.[6]

Ederle was only one of a group of prominent women athletes in the Golden Age of American sport. Unlike male athletes who generally gained more prominence in team sports, especially baseball and football, women athletes tended to cluster in individual or dual sports like swimming, golf, and tennis. These sports were considered more feminine and were more socially acceptable, just as they had been from the late 1800s. Except for the momentary fame of Ederle, Glenna Collett in golf and Helen Wills in tennis were the two most prominent American sport heroines of the 1920s.

Glenna Collett (Vare), like most women athletes of the times, came from a prosperous family. She won her first of 6 national amateur championships in 1922 as a nineteen-year-old. She was the first woman to shoot a round of golf in less than 80 strokes in national competition. One might note that in the 1915 national tournament more than half of the qualifiers recorded scores of 100 or more and

Gertrude Ederle swam the English Channel in record time two years after participating in the 1924 Paris Olympics. (Courtesy of Swimming Hall of Fame, Ft. Lauderdale.)

85 strokes won the medal for low score. Much of Collett's success came from her long drives off the tee which were attributed to her superior strength and coordination. She might have been considered the best in the world had not England's Joyce Wethered dominated the scene. Wethered won the British Ladies' Amateur four times in the 1920s and helped foil Collett's attempt to become the first American to win the British Women's golfing crown. Not until Babe Didrikson (Zaharias) won in 1947 did the United States women claim the English championship. Collett's golfing ability combined with her grace and feminine charm contributed to making golf more popular with American women. She did not, like Eleanora Sears before her or Babe Didrikson after her, challenge the existing social code for women athletes. Like most women athletes during the twentieth century, Collett showed that the social acceptance of the clothes worn was nearly as important as the desire to excel. She once wrote that "clothes be, above all else, comfortable, and so correct that they will cause no embarrassment." Her social awareness and her longevity helped to keep golf, next to tennis, the most popular women's sport. Collett won her last national championship in 1935 beating youthful Patty Berg, terminating a career in golf that paralleled the Helen Wills' era in tennis.

The most publicized woman athlete of the 1920s was Helen Wills who stood supreme in American tennis for most of that decade and into the next. Wills, like a multitude of twentieth century athletes, came from California. Her physician father and interested mother gave her the financial and moral support to sustain her in the game she learned as a young girl in Berkeley. Her upwardly mobile, upper middle class parents might also help to explain why Wills was such a goal-oriented and competitive woman in a society which gave little support to these qualities in a woman. Wills later revealed that while in college she pursued the Phi Beta Kappa scholastic honor successfully because "it was desirable to be the possessor of a Phi Beta Kappa key," and not because learning was enjoyable. Her tennis conquests outwardly appeared to be similarly contested. Her unchanging, grim countenance in competition soon earned her the title, "Little Miss Poker Face." With a Puritan-like appearance and a similar work ethic, she knew she would win—that hard work would eventually be rewarded with victory.[8] Like most outstanding athletes, Wills sought "some degree of perfection" though she feared others might believe it to be a "form of conceit."[9]

Helen Wills won a total of 7 U.S. singles titles at Forest Hills, 8 English singles championships at Wimbledon, and a rather meaningless gold medal in singles at the 1924 Olympics in Paris, the last time that tennis was contested in the Olympics. She captured her first title in 1923 at Forest Hills and her last in 1938 at Wimbledon. The competitive nature of Helen Wills and women's tennis in the period after World War I is worth noting as there was considerable social pressure, as will be seen, against high level athletic competition for women in the 1920s. Wills won her first major title at age seventeen when she beat Malla Mallory who had won 7 of the previous 8 American titles at Forest Hills. Mallory had won considerable fame in 1921 when she had beaten the incomparable Frenchwoman, Suzanne Lenglen in the same tournament. Lenglen lost only that one match between 1919 and 1926 when she turned professional, and it was a rather sensational loss. Using pre-game psychology, Mallory asked Lenglen if she was ready "for the licking I am going to give you" after Lenglen had predicted a 6-0, 6-0 triumph. The match started with Mallory winning the first set 6 games to 2 as she "raced around the court, driving furiously, making no mistakes." Lenglen then double faulted in her service of the first game in the second set. Thereupon she clutched her chest, coughed, and walked off the court, defaulting the match rather than apparently facing greater humiliation in the match.[10]

Helen Wills did not have the opportunity to challenge Lenglen until 1926 when Wills journeyed to the Riviera in southern France to play in a winter of tournaments. After the two played a "cat-and-mouse" strategy in entering or not entering various tourneys, the two finally entered the tournament at Cannes. While the early rounds were being played, an American film company was negotiating a $100,000 contract to film the finals between the two best women players in the world. As predicted, both made the finals setting up what was called "the most important woman's athletic contest of modern times." It matched the quickest, shrewdest, and smoothest player, Lenglen, against the calm, hard hitting, and doggedly determined Wills. The match was played before an overflow crowd of 4,000 noisy spectators paying an equivalent of $9.00 a ticket or even higher scalper's prices. Lenglen won the first set with superb control, 6-3, and the second, 8-6 in an intense struggle which saw two key official's calls, one against each woman, affect the outcome. Lenglen stood supreme.[11]

Wills remained an amateur and was a veteran at the age of twenty years. For the next seven years, with Lenglen having turned professional, Wills won every tennis tournament she entered. By the early 1930s her chief rival was Helen Jacobs, another Californian. Their most controversial match occurred in 1933 at Forest Hills where Wills had won each of the seven years she had entered in the previous decade. Jacobs, though was the reigning champion as Wills had not competed the year before. At this time Wills was having back trouble both prior to and during the tournament. Playing in the finals, Jacobs

Helen Wills was great, but France's Suzanne Lenglen was supreme. (Courtesy of Library of Congress.)

won the first set, 8-6 while Wills took the second, 6-3. Jacobs then jumped to a quick 3 game lead in the final set. Suddenly Wills went to the judges stand and said: "My leg is bothering me. I can't go on." The press, spectators, and especially Malla Mallory were surprised and angered at the sudden default. Mallory remembered her match with Lenglen in 1921 when Lenglen quit, sparing her further humiliation. Mallory believed Wills had done the same. Even Wills hinted later that she had been "selfish," having preferred, like many animals and humans, "to suffer in a quiet dark place."[12]

It seemed that Wills could not take the loss psychologically after so many years of winning—victory had dominated her life so long that it was nearly impossible to accept defeat. That some women had as strong a desire to win as male athletes had shown for generations, was an indication that women's sport at the higher levels was becoming more competitive than social as it had been in its early development. The indominable spirit of Wills remained as she returned to tennis action after a two year rest. She won at Wimbledon in 1935 and again in 1938. The competitive spirit of women's athletics which Helen Wills typified had increased with the advance of the movement to gain the right to vote. This athletic "killer instinct" by which Wills was often labeled was tempered, however, by a drive in the 1920s to do away with highly competitive sports for women. The partial success of that movement had much to do with the lag in competitive athletics for an important group of girls and women.

THE WOMEN'S ANTI-COMPETITIVE MOVEMENT

While Helen Wills, Glenna Collett, Gertrude Ederle, and others were making their mark in competitive athletics, an opposing group led by women physical educators was condemning this growth of highly visible women's athletics. The concerted drive in the 1920s and 30s was not directed primarily at tennis, golf, or swimming, but at the general concept of highly competitive athletics. If any sport was picked to be condemned, it appeared to be track and field for it came to symbolize in women's sports what were considered to be the evils of a system of athletics in which a few might gain prominence, though exploited, at the expense of the masses of girls and women. An understanding of this phenomenon will help to explain in part the slow development of women's athletics in the twentieth century.

Women's Track and the Paris Games

The Olympic Games, begun by Baron Pierre de Coubertin in 1896, came to be the focal point for much of amateur athletics in the world shortly before the First World War. But women who wanted to participate were frustrated in their efforts as the International Olympic Committee, headed by de Coubertin, was reluctant to open the doors wide to women's athletics. De Coubertin saw women as a hinderance to his Olympic ideal of "citius, altius, fortius," ever faster, higher, stronger, for women could never reach the physical achievement of men. He wanted the Olympics to be a chivalric athletic elite of "brothers in arms," striving for individual athletic records. This excluded women whose place in society he believed should be governed by "heredity, tradition, and everyday habits." He thought that women's participation in the Olympics, even after they were first accepted, was "impractical, uninteresting, inaesthetic, and we are not afraid to add: wrong." Furthermore, de Coubertin said that the public spectacle of women's athletics was undignified.[13]

The door to Olympic participation had been breached in 1900 when women first entered golf and tennis competition. Later archery and ice skating were allowed before swimming was accepted in the 1912 Games. Though a Chicagoan, Margaret Abbott won the 1900 golfing medal and Lydia Scott Howell captured three events in archery in the 1904 Games in St. Louis, American women took little interest in the early Olympic Games. The all-male American Olympic

Committee took even less interest as it was opposed to any sport for women in which they could not wear long skirts. Following World War I and a change in policy, 15 American swimmers were sent to the 1920 Games in Antwerp, Belgium and were competing at the same time women's suffrage was ratified by the required 36th state. The entry and the winning of 4 out of 5 swimming and diving events marked the permanent entry of American women in the Olympic movement. Progress, nevertheless, was slow in its development.[14]

By the early 1920s there was pressure to include women in track and field, the most important competition in the Olympics. When the International Olympic Committee rejected the entrance of women in track for the 1920 Games, the newly formed Federation Sportive Feminine Internationale decided to sponsor the "Women's Olympics" in Paris in 1922. In the United States, Dr. Harry E. Stewart of the New Haven School of Physiotherapy, formed the National Women's Track Athletics Committee which prepared a women's team for the Paris Games. The Amateur Athletic Union, which desired to control amateur sport in America including women's sport, was concerned that Stewart's group was seizing power that rightfully belonged to the AAU. The AAU, after all, had taken control of women's swimming in 1914, and set up the first national championships in 1916. They wanted to do no less in track and field.

Meanwhile a group of women physical educators primarily in the colleges believed they could not sit idly by and watch the control of women's sport be taken away from what they thought should be the official governing body, the Committee on Women's Athletics of the American Physical Education Association. The Committee on Women's Athletics (CWA) had been organized in 1917 as an expansion of the nearly two decade old Women's Basketball Rules Committee which had been formed to give women's basketball in the schools and colleges a common set of rules. The CWA was late to form a committee on track and field because its members had only been interested in pursuing standards in team rather than individual sports.[15]

As the AAU met to discuss taking over women's track and field, the CWA passed a resolution:

> Since the Women's Committee on Athletics of the American Physical Education Association is convinced the American Physical Education Association is the only logical organization to direct the policies in women's athletics, it goes on record as disapproving of any affiliation with the Amateur Athletic Union with relation to athletics for women.[16]

The Committee on Women's Athletics further strongly opposed the participation of American women in the Paris Games of August,

1922. Despite the protestations, the Games went on with American women competing. The AAU then organized the first indoor and outdoor track and field championships for women which were won by an industrial sport organization, the Athletic Association of the Prudential Insurance Company of Newark, New Jersey.[17] The CWA was bypassed and removed from an important role in women's competitive athletics outside the educational setting, though the fighting had just begun, and a new organization was formed and joined the battle.

Women's Division of the NAAF

At the same time the fight over women's track and field was taking place, a new organization was founded, the National Amateur Athletic Federation. This organization, at first independent of the track and field confrontation, was the outgrowth of World War I statistics which indicated low levels of physical fitness among American youth. This led to the belief that there was a need of a national group to pull together the various organizations involved in the physical activity of American young people. In early 1922, the Secretary of War and the Secretary of Navy, Cabinet officers of the Warren Harding administration, contacted Lou Henry Hoover, wife of Herbert Hoover, then Secretary of Commerce, asking if she would take the leadership of the women's side of a new amateur athletic group. Mrs. Hoover suggested a separate unit for women, and when the National Amateur Athletic Federation (NAAF) was organized in December of 1922, a Women's Division was created which she headed.[18]

The creation of an independent Women's Division of NAAF made it possible for the first time for women to control a national amateur group involved in women's sport. Unlike any other sport group, outside of educational institutions, the Women's Division was controlled almost exclusively by women. For the most part they were physical educators, most of whom were teaching in colleges. The individuals on the original eight member executive committee, except for Lou Hoover, were physical educators including such leaders as Agnes Wayman, Blanche Trilling, and Ethel Perrin.[19] All seven physical educators were active members of the Committee on Women's Athletics of the American Physical Education Association. This was the beginning of a system of interlocking directorates in which the same group of college women physical educators came to control a number of different organizations working for the same goals in women's sport. Said Agnes Wayman early in the history of the Women's Division: "We are setting forth under our own sail with women at the helm and women manning the whole craft."[20] As

Agnes Wayman was one of the women physical educators who helped place strong controls on women's competitive athletics.

history would show, they were also sailing away from the mainstream of American athletics.

Out of the first conference of the Women's Division of the NAAF, held in early April, 1923, came the belief that women's sport should be "play for play's sake," that competition which involved travel and the winning of championships be minimized, and that all international competition be condemned. It strongly denounced the intensive training of the few at the expense of participation for all.[21] The platform developed by the Women's Division was to be the "Magna Carta" for women's sport and was summed up in the motto of the group: "A game for every girl and every girl in a game." Had the organization worked for highly competitive athletics, in addition to the avowed goal of a system of sane athletics, it might have had a more positive role to play in the development of women's sports in the twentieth century. But, the Women's Division chose to emphasize only sport for the masses, rejecting the elite athlete. How did it come about that women physical educators who favored sport for women gave little thought to those who wanted to excel?

The Basis for the Anti-Competitive Philosophy

Women physical educators had a unique role to play in education of women in colleges from their beginning. When women first began attending college in the mid-1800s either by integrating previous all-male institutions or in separate women's colleges, one of the first tasks in almost every school was to hire a physical educator to provide for their physical activity and health needs. This maternalistic provision was logical when one understands that in the nineteenth century it was believed that women would have greater difficulty than men withstanding the physiological and psychological rigors of four years of a classical education. Whether it was organizing a daily walk for the young women, setting up a system of gymnastics, or providing for some form of sport activity such as archery, tennis, or even rowing, it was generally the woman physical educator who dominated the scene. This contrasted with the male physical educator who, when there was one, had almost nothing to do with sport and commanded little respect from students, faculty, or administration.

Whereas men's college athletics from the beginning had been formed and directed almost entirely by students, and men physical educators had almost no influence on athletics until the twentieth century, women's sport was dominated by women physical educators from the first. This one condition gave women in physical education leverage over the philosophy developed and the direction which college women's sport would take. By 1900, the various sports had begun to replace formal gymnastics as the basis of women's physical education programs.[22] Foremost among these was basketball. In 1899, a group of women physical educators met to form a standard set of basketball rules for women—a group that eventually became the Committee on Women's Athletics of the American Physical Education Association. The philosophy of women's sport in the colleges began to be more clearly outlined. Lucille Eaton Hill of Wellesley College, using the utilitarian philosophy of John Stuart Mill, wrote that women's sport should contribute the "greatest good to the greatest number; not the greatest good to the smallest number. . . ."[23]

Team sports, such as basketball or field hockey, fit nicely into the thinking of the Progressive period in turn-of-the-century America in which concern for the welfare of society began to place limitations on unfettered individualism that had dominated much of nineteenth century thought. Women physical educators considered team sports vital for college women, who, like other girls having been brought up in the home with less chance for social interaction than boys, needed the experience of the "give-and-take" which team sports provided. Team sports also satisfied the new progressive educational philosophy expounded by John Dewey who saw as one purpose of education the transformation of society.[24] This change in society toward more social goals could best occur if the educational process produced individuals who knew how to cooperate. What better way to learn cooperation, physical educators could ask, than through team sports? For best results, cooperation would be stressed while competition would be minimized.

By the early 1900s, women physical educators, who had been more practical than theoretical, could base their beliefs regarding coopera-tive team sports on the philosophy of a small group of men physical educators who claimed that sport should be used for the social, moral, and ethical as well as the physical development of young people. The philosophy of Thomas D. Wood, Clark W. Hetherington, and Luther H. Gulick[25] gave support to women physical educators who saw their sport programs as being radically different from men's programs.

Men's highly specialized, competitive, and commercialized intercol-legiate programs had been viewed with concern by women physical educators in the late 1800s. It intensified in the early years of the twentieth century. Senda Berenson, leader in college women's basket-ball, warned her colleagues in 1901 to "profit by the experience of our brothers and therefore save ourselves from allowing those objection-able features to creep into our athletics. . . ." She was not alone. Resolutions opposing intercollegiate athletic contests for women were soon passed.[26]

Why, though, would women physical educators be more altruistic than leaders in men's athletics as they looked at the welfare of the masses of women who might benefit from an experience in sport? One answer is based on a traditional belief of women as moral uplifters of society. This credence came from a strict interpretation of the Bible, of the original sin of Eve—not Adam—at the Garden of Eden, and woman's need to redeem herself through good works.[27] This religious influence was felt well into the twentieth century. Elizabeth Cady Stanton, a nineteenth century feminist, as late as 1895, believed that "from the inauguration of the movement for women's emancipation the Bible has been used to hold her in the 'divinely ordained sphere,' prescribed in the Old and New Testaments."[28] The "divinely ordained sphere," many believed, was exhibited in women upholding morality of society as well as the traditional caring for the home and bearing and raising children. It seems likely that the socialization process, whether Biblically influenced or not and which set higher ethical standards for women than for men, weighed heavily upon women physical educators to uplift their institutional sports, cleansing them from the evil influence which resulted from the male impact upon them.

That women physical educators accepted their role as uplifters of society is not surprising. They were college educated and were products of the women's rights movement which by the early 1900s had gained greater respectability by emphasizing the distinctiveness of women. Females, the women's rights movement increasingly emphasized, were primarily spiritual creatures who believed in the sanctity of the home and of women's special place in it, but whose participation in the political system would also elevate the moral level of American society.[29] It seems logical to believe that women physical educators saw themselves as a unique group dedicated to high ideals and service to the public through an uncompromising sports program dedicated to serving all women, especially those in need of physical activity.

The Women's Olympic Participation Controversy

The rationale for women physical educators' opposition to intense competitive athletics had been in the making for a generation before the Women's Division of the NAAF took its stand against women's participation in international competition such as the Paris Games of the Federation Sportive Feminine Internationale and the Olympics in the 1920s. The Woman's Division was running against the tide of world competition for women. The Federation Sportive Feminine Internationale (FSFI) decided to continue its quadrennial games in 1926. At this point, the International Amateur Athletic Federation, the world body for amateur sports, made an agreement with the FSFI to take control of women's athletics in exchange for recommending to the International Olympic Committee (IOC) that five track and field events for women be placed on the 1928 Olympic program. When the IOC agreed to accept the five track events, the FSFI changed the title of its competitions, as the IOC desired, from the "Women's Olympic Games" to the "International Ladies Games."[30]

The opposition of the Women's Division of the NAAF had little effect upon the entry of women in the 1928 Olympic track competition. The participation, especially in the 800 meter race for women, did have an influence—a negative one. Eleven women entered the 800 meter race. With insufficient training, five dropped out before the race was completed, five collapsed after reaching the finish, and the remaining starter fainted in the dressing room following the race. Sportswriter John R. Tunis called the participants, the fastest of whom ran the distance in two minutes and 16.8 seconds, the "eleven wretched women." The implications for Tunis and numerous other men and women was that women should not copy the athletics of men when they are not capable.[31] Unfortunately for women's athletics and for this event which was subsequently dropped from the Olympics, consensus was that women were considered to be physiologically incapable of prolonged physical activity. This fiasco supported the myth.

The 1928 Olympic track episode provided fuel for the American women physical educators and the Women's Division of the NAAF (supported by a group of men physical educators and several important sportswriters) to campaign heavily to prevent women from participating in the Los Angeles Olympics in 1932. The Women's Division sent petitions to the International Amateur Athletic Federation and the International Olympic Committee in 1930 asking them to remove women's track and field competition from the Olympics.[32] Baron Pierre de Coubertin agreed, but the IOC voted to continue the track events. The IOC, though, deleted the 800 meter race and added 2 other events, the 80 meter hurdles and the javelin throw. These two events were won in Los Angeles by America's greatest woman athlete of the first half of the twentieth century, Mildred "Babe" Didrikson.

Babe Didrikson: The Dominating Athlete

No woman athlete, with the possible exception of Billie Jean King a generation later, did more to promote highly competitive athletics for women than did Babe Didrikson. From 1930 until the mid-1950s, Didrikson, like Eleanora Sears before her, was proficient in a variety of sports. The similarity with Sears ends there for Didrikson's lower socio-economic status stemming from her parent's Norwegian immigrant background was far removed from the Boston Brahmin background of Sears. Didrikson was fifteen years old when the coach of the Golden Cyclone Athletic Club of the Employers Casualty Company of Dallas noticed her in a basketball tournament while playing for the Beaumont, Texas high school. She was quickly put on the payroll of the company with an office job, and was soon playing industrial basketball for the Golden Cyclones. She participated in the AAU sponsored Women's National Basketball Tournament which was started in 1926. For three years Didrikson made all-American while leading the team to a runner-up and a national title. While working for the Dallas firm, she participated in track and field. Just prior to the Olympic Games of 1932, she entered the Women's National AAU track and field meet as the Cyclones' sole representative. In this meet, which was also the trials for the Olympics, Didrikson won five events: the 80 meter hurdles, javelin and baseball throws, shot put, and long jump; was second in the high jump and fourth in the discus throw; and set three world records. That was enough to win the team championship for the Cyclones and to qualify Didrikson for three Olympic events, the limit set for women.[33]

Babe Didrikson's exploits at the 1932 Olympics gave her national fame. In all three events she set the Olympic standard. She attained world records in the 80 meter hurdles and the high jump even though in the latter event she placed second. In the high jump her winning jump was disallowed because it was claimed she used an incorrect form while "diving" over the bar. Of her record javelin throw, she characteristically boasted: "I coulda throwed it farther, but I slipped."[34] Renown did not come without cost as there were those who questioned her femininity. The male chauvinism of sports writer Paul Gallico showed through as he described the "hirsute," hairy performance of 5 feet 6½ inches, 130 pound, eighteen-year-old Didrikson. Others questioned

Babe Didrikson could have thrown the javelin farther but she "slipped."

her estrogen levels, believing that her hormone levels were approaching those of men. These allegations followed her through her career even after she married George Zaharias, the professional wrestler, and began donning more "feminine" clothes, even adding lace, curling her hair, and putting on high heels. It was difficult in an America, which revered the male athlete, to accept a female athlete who had the speed, power, and competitive spirit to dominate nearly every woman's sport she entered, and to be able to compete with the best of male athletes.[35]

Following her Olympic success, Didrikson was disqualified for further amateur track and field by the AAU for appearing in an auto advertisement. She quickly moved into other areas. Possibly as a publicity stunt, she said she planned to swim the English Channel, a task she likely could have done knowing her determination and skill as a swimmer. At one time she was timed in the 100 meter free style and was only one second off the world's record. She turned instead to forming the Babe Didrikson All-American Basketball team in which she was the only female competitor. Later she played with the bearded House of David baseball team. Her baseball throw which approached 300 feet drew spectators as did her pitching ability. She pitched in an exhibition baseball game for the St. Louis Cardinals and once pitched several effective innings against a professional Negro team. Said Bill Holland, one of the better black pitchers: "She was a good athlete. . . . She could pitch pretty good, but not like a man." If not, she could throw a football 50 yards with accuracy and could play billiards well enough to tour the country giving exhibitions. Her product endorsements and barnstorming tours and exhibitions in various sports earned Didrikson an estimated $50,000 to $100,000 a year during the depth of the Depression. This income enabled her to hire the best professional golfing teachers as she decided to become the top woman golfer in America. She soon proved to the golfing world what she felt about herself—that she was "best at everything."[36]

Didrikson played her first round of golf following the 1932 Olympics in something less than 100 strokes, and she took up the game seriously in 1934 at the age of twenty. In the spring of 1935, she won the Texas Woman's State Championship. Two weeks later she was declared a professional by the United States Golfing Association (USGA). She soon went on an exhibition tour with the leading golf professional, Gene Sarazen, for $600 to $1,000 per week. Professional golf for women, though, was almost non-existent, and in order for Didrikson to dominate golf she had to return to amateur status. Strangely the USGA would reinstate an individual if the professional would repent and stay out of competition for three years. This Didrikson did. In 1940, after again being accepted by the USGA as an amateur, she won the woman's Western and Texas Opens. In another decade she had won every major golf championship. Between 1944 and 1947 she won 22 tournaments, 14 of them in a row (though it was not the 17 she claimed she won). From that point until the end of her career cut short by cancer, she won a remarkable 34 of 88 tournaments she entered.[37]

Didrikson had shown in her twenty-six years of competition a brilliance in athletics which an American woman had not shown before. Despite the fact that she tended to perpetuate the myth that women athletes were something less than true women—that they were partly masculine—Didrikson showed society that women could participate in competitive athletics and reach excellence. She, more than any other women, changed women's golf into an attacking game with scores under 70 strokes not being uncommon.[38] It was Didrikson's presence which gave the Ladies' Professional Golfers Association, formed in 1949, visibility. It is not likely that any one person will again dominate so many sports as did Didrikson for she participated before masses of women were involved in competitive athletics. Most women, when Didrikson dominated the scene, participated in social play days if they took part at all.

A Generation of Play Days

Babe Didrikson never participated in an educational institution play day. She might have, for play days in schools and colleges began to take the place of interscholastic and intercollegiate athletics during the 1920s and 1930s. Women physical educators, who favored the philosophy of the Women's Division of the NAAF, were opposed to the type of interscholastic basketball in which Didrikson took part because of the tendency to exploit the girl's talent for the chance to win championships, to advertise the school, or to promote the town. It seems obvious that most any athletic exhibition which produces excellence will be exploited because, for most, excellence makes performance interesting, and people are willing to pay for the opportunity to observe that which is best. The philosophy of many women physical educators opposed high caliber athletic performance since it would attract attention and bring about the commercialization of the sport. This, they deemed, was like a malignant growth which would eat at the soul of sports. Sports were valuable, they claimed, for the socialization, not the professionalization, of the individual. Thus, when Babe Didrikson was showing America what a woman athlete could achieve, another movement was taking place in the schools to limit women's competition. One critic of the non-competitive play day wrote in 1926:

> The movement now on foot to restrict and abolish, or denature sport for girls, is part of the enslavement from which women have suffered through the ages. It can not finally succeed, altho it may gain sufficient present vogue . . . to cheat a generation of girls of the contact with the world which is their right.[39]

Women physical educators would have disagreed vociferously, arguing that by not stressing competition, women were allowed to be free to enjoy athletics.

The idea of the play day was to bring together girls from a number of schools for a day of sport activities ranging from basketball, volleyball, field hockey, and swimming to hopscotch, dodge ball, relays, and folk dancing. Individual schools would not compete against one another, rather teams composed of players from a number of schools would play. Victory would obviously mean less in a basketball game in which none of the participants had previously played together than if a team from one school had practiced as a unit for a period of weeks. Competition was deemphasized in the play day; socialization was maximized. Frequent breaks with "cookies and juice" prevented over-exertion while increasing social interaction. California, which led the states in bringing the play day into widespread use, adopted a slogan: "A team for everyone and everyone on a team." In the city of Oakland, home of the fierce competitor Helen Wills, the Department of Recreation coined the saying: "Play for every girl and woman—but no championships."[40]

The play day idea made rapid progress in the colleges in the 1920s and began to have an impact in the public schools as well. A 1923 study showed that the anti-intercollegiate athletic movement for women was strong. Of 50 colleges surveyed only 22 percent allowed intercollegiate competition, while 93 percent of the physical educators were opposed to varsity competition. The fear of commercialized sport was intensified by the untrue belief that highly competitive sport was detrimental to women's reproductive systems.[41] Surveyor Mabel Lee, the first woman president of the American Physical Education Association, followed up her study eights years later with statistics to "prove how absolutely determined are the women of the physical education profession and . . . the women college students of today, not to permit women's athletics to follow in the steps of men's athletics." At this time only 12 percent of the 100 colleges surveyed permitted intercollegiate athletics, but 80 percent had play days.[42] The women's belief in the recreative, not competitive, value of sport was continually being reinforced by men physical education leaders such as Frederick R. Rogers who said in 1930: "Games like basketball and baseball are combative sports. They develop ugly muscles—muscles ugly in girls—as well as scowling faces and the competitive spirit.[43]

Mabel Lee provided statistics and moral force to limit highly competitive athletics for women.

There was an intense social pressure of leaders of women's physical education upon those within the profession to limit competition to play day situations, or later sports days.[44] One case in point was seen when Gladys Palmer and other women at the Ohio State University women's physical education staff organized the first Women's National Collegiate Golf Tournament in 1941.[45] Several years before the tourney, Palmer had put up a trial balloon before other college physical educators in which she called for "excellence of play," an admiration of excellence for its own sake," and a provision for competition to "maximize expertness."[46] When Palmer and her staff proposed conducting the golf tournament to the Executive Committee of the National Section on Women's Athletics of the American Association for Health, Physical Education and Recreation, not only did the leaders reject the proposal outright, but they stopped speaking to the Ohio State women. "It was awful," recalled one of the tournament backers. "Not only were we 'outlaws,' but we were ostracized in the national association and for years none of us was elected to any offices."[47]

Martyring themselves for women's athletic competition, the Ohio State women launched their tournament in the face of their colleagues' scorn. Gladys Palmer even suggested that a Women's Na-

Ohio State hosted the first national college golf tournament in 1941, creating an outburst of criticism among women physical educators. (Courtesy of the Ohio State University Photo Archives.)

tional Collegiate Athletic Association be formed, a theoretical forerunner of the Association of Intercollegiate Athletics for Women created a generation later. The Women's NCAA was not created, but the tournament went on. Thirty eight collegians took part in the first meet which was carefully orchestrated to attain the best of sportsmanship while preventing unfavorable publicity. The tournament directors ensured that all contestants wore acceptable golf dresses, not shorts and halters. The successful continuation of the tournament was cut short by the outbreak of World War II. Since 1946, though, it has continued uninterrupted—a tribute to the much maligned promoters of excellence in college athletics.[48]

Despite inroads of competition such as the Women's National Collegiate Golf Tournament, the play day remained for a generation the pinnacle of athletic participation for most college women. Surveys in the 1950s showed that play days were still the most popular form of competition. There were, however, some signs that the play day idea was a slowly dying concept. In eastern colleges by the end of World War II, about one-third of the institutions were taking part in intercollegiate athletics, considerably more than fifteen years earlier.[49] Eleanor Metheny, an outspoken physical educator brought up during the period of play days, reflected upon the non-competitive era:

> In the days when there was a stigma attached to the concept of playing to win, the women who were responsible for our welfare devised the idea of a play day that would permit us to enjoy sports participation with girls from other schools. . . . We had fun at these play days, and we enjoyed the tea and the sociability—but the better players among us felt frustrated by the lack of meaningful team play. . . . These play days did little to satisfy our desire for all-out competition with worthy and honored opponents.[50]

THE REVOLUTION IN WOMEN'S SPORTS

Radical changes have taken place in women's sport since the latter nineteenth century when women's participation in physical activity was questioned. The first half of the twentieth century saw the increased involvement with an emphasis on participation, not competition. The revolt in women's athletics, with a thrust toward highly competitive contests, awaited the period following World War II, and made the most rapid progress on the heels of the women's movement of the 1960s.

World War II, Civil Rights and the Women's Movement

Women's competitive athletics had not made rapid strides for the generation following the 1920s. In some areas, such as college athletics, women's involvement had retrogressed. What gains had occurred following women's suffrage had been largely negated by the 1930s. The Depression had thrown millions out of work. There was great social pressure to keep women out of the job market so that the traditional head of the family, the male, might find work. Women, in the meantime, became more dependent, less assertive, and more inclined to remain in the traditional role of homemaker. As always, social expectations reinforcing women's place as being in the home were more important than psychological or physiological characteristics inherent in females which might dictate their sport involvement.

As late as World War II there still was a widespread and ungrounded belief that vigorous competitive athletics would have a damaging effect upon a woman's childbearing function. Appearing in *Scientific American* a few years before the war was the statement that "feminine muscular development interferes with motherhood."[51] More common was the misguided assumption that there should be a cessation of all physical activity during menstruation. Even the AAU which sanctioned highly competitive athletics believed this. Shortly after the Second World War the AAU conducted a study of the effect of athletic competition on girls and women. It concluded without evidence, by simply quoting a woman medical doctor, that competition during a woman's period might have a harmful effect upon a woman's capacity for "being a normal mother."[52] The Freudian assertion that "anatomy is destiny" continued to hinder the growth of women's athletics.

World War II was an important precipitator in the women's movement, as it was in the crusade to give blacks greater equality in sport as in society. With the dire need of workers to replace men drawn into military service, women in unprecendented numbers entered the job market. Significantly, it increasingly was older, married women—a group which had previously been home bound and lacking gainful employment—who filled the gap. The experience of millions of women being out of the home and fulfilling a useful function in the traditional male world was, as one historian has stated, "a milestone for women in America."[53] It also took the events of World War II to bring about the first professional team sport for women, baseball.

The All-American Girls' Baseball League began in 1943 when Philip K. Wrigley, the chewing gum king and owner of the Chicago Cubs National League baseball team, became concerned that the government might disband Major League baseball for the duration of the war. It was thought that the All-American Girls' Baseball League could help fill this war time need for spectator sport if organized baseball should be forced to suspend activity. With the initial financial backing of a quarter-million dollars by Wrigley and moral support of

Major League owner Branch Rickey, the Girls' League began operation in four middle-sized cities in three midwestern states, Rockford, Illinois; South Bend, Indiana; and Kenosha and Racine, Wisconsin. In its dozen years of operation the league never expanded beyond Minnesota and Michigan. The conservative midwest dictated that femininity was as important, if not more so, than the quality of performance.[54]

For the most part the young women chosen to represent the teams had previously played organized softball. Those picked in the try-outs were chosen, of course, on the basis of their skill level, but some were rejected because of their too-masculine mannerisms. During pre-season training the women players were instructed during the day in the particular type of softball-baseball established by the league. At night they were given charm lessons. The nocturnal etiquette included lessons in posture, wearing clothes, applying cosmetics, as well as "how to take a called third strike." During the regular season the players wore specially designed feminine dresses which could be cut no more than 6 inches above the knee. Each team hired a chaperone for the players as the league strove to give the public the image of femininity.[55]

The league failed financially by the early 1950s after reaching a

The All-American Girls' Baseball League was as concerned with femininity as with winning. (Courtesy of Merrie Fidler.)

peak attendance of nearly a million spectators in 1948. It began to decline, along with minor league baseball, at the time television started becoming popular. The league attempted to increase its popularity by reducing the size and increasing the liveliness of the ball, making legal the overhand pitch, and extending the distance of the pitching mound and the bases—all while keeping the basic feminine image. When the league died in 1954, the ball used was the regulation baseball.[56]

Too few appreciated the skill level achieved by a small group of women who learned the rudiments of the game in a society which did not readily sanction ball playing for girls or women. The schools from which players might have gained skills had been philosophically opposed to highly skilled women athletes, and this acted as a negative factor on the talent pool of available athletes. It was apparent that both men and women in American society were not ready to accept women's professional sports on a large scale, especially team sports. It is likely that the novelty of women's baseball carried it through the first years of existence. Who in America had ever witnessed women professionals playing the "national pastime," previously a male's domain? After the novelty wore off, neither the skill level nor the attitude toward women's sport was great enough to sustain the league. Women's sport was to await the women's movement of the 1960s before it would advance more rapidly.

The decade from the early 1960s to the early 1970s will likely be remembered for the battle for equal rights for minorities as well as for the devisive ten year involvement in the Vietnam War. The time seemed ripe for blacks to assert their rights to equality through intense civil rights actions and for women to begin to throw off the social bonds which had traditionally tied them to the home. A freedom to achieve an identity other than through her children or her husband was sought by a growing number of women, primarily of the better educated class. Leaders such as Betty Friedan, who criticized the "feminine mystique" built around motherhood and the home, were not presenting anything new. But, the message struck a responsive chord in the class of college educated women who had benefitted by the slowly changing role of women from their traditional roles.[57] What the women leaders were able to do was to raise the public consciousness about the inferior place of women in the American society. Eventually women's role in sport was given close scrutiny by those who wanted a more just society.

BILLIE JEAN KING, TITLE IX, AND THE COMPETITIVE SCENE

Greatest progress in women's sport was made in the socially acceptable sports, such as tennis and golf, and in the educational institutions during the women's movement of the 1960s and 1970s. Symbolic of the strides toward equality in women's athletics were the leadership of Billie Jean King in professional sport and the passage of a 1972 amendment, Title IX, to a civil rights act of the previous decade. Both the dynamic leadership of women in sport and involvement of the government were important to the women's competitive sports movement.

On September 30, 1973, before a prime time television audience, Billie Jean King rode out to the tennis court in the Houston Astrodome on an Egyptian litter to meet challenger Bobby Riggs. Riggs, a well worn, pre-World War II Wimbledon and Forest Hills champion, was almost twice the age of twenty-nine-year-old Billie Jean King, probably the best woman player in the world. Riggs represented the reactionary male chauvinists, while King symbolized the feminist movement. It is ironic that an athletic event should have been chosen by the American people to signify the merits of the two sexes, since for physiological reasons women are not equal to men in those athletic performances where strength and speed are important. The event proved that a woman athlete in her prime could beat a male champion past his peak. King easily beat Riggs, 6-4, 6-3, 6-3. Much more importantly, the match focused attention on the high level of performance that women could achieve in athletics. King became the most celebrated woman athlete, and her interest in woman's equality gained greater attention.

It was not clear from Billie Jean King's early background that she would lead women athletes toward greater equality. As did a number of women tennis champions, she had an early interest in softball but was either persuaded or desired to be in a sport "where she could be considered a lady."[58] She attained distinction early by winning the Wimbledon doubles championship at age seventeen, though she did not capture the singles title until five years later. In 1967, King along with two other women tennis players attempted to boycott the U.S. Nationals at Forest Hills in an effort of women players to gain increased influence over the conduct of the tournament. What King wanted was an organization of women players to control major aspects of the game. Through her tenacity, the Women's Tennis Association was formed in opposition to the control of the United States Lawn Tennis Association. The result was the substantial increase in prize money for women professionals. King also campaigned for equality of pay with the male professionals in meets where both sexes participated. Equity was achieved at Wimbledon and at Forest Hills in the mid-1970s. This was far different from tournaments only a few years before in which women received as little as 12 percent of the men's prizes. To further the cause of women's tennis,

King and a small group of players began a women-only tour in 1972 which became a success when advertisers, such as tobacco companies, came to support it. King's efforts had helped make women's tennis a glamour sport and the most financially lucrative venture in women's athletic history. In the process King became the first woman athlete to win over $100,000 in prize money in a year, enough to help her establish the magazine dedicated to promoting and liberating women's athletics, *womenSports*.[59]

In some ways Billie Jean King was to women's professional athletics what Title IX of the Education Amendment Act of 1972 was to women's sport in educational institutions. Both were liberating forces in competitive athletics. Title IX was quite likely the most important action to further women's sport in the twentieth century. The act read simply:

> No person in the United States shall, on the basis of sex, be excluded from participation in, be denied the benefits of, or be subjected to discrimination under any education program or activity receiving federal financial assistance.

The act, administered by the Department of Health, Education and Welfare, applied to nearly every school and college in America. When it was passed, it became obvious that sport in educational institutions was one of the most blatant areas of sexist discrimination in America. Where competitive sport existed for women in the early 1970s, it was often financed with a budget less than 1 percent of the men's athletic programs.[60]

Title IX required equality of opportunity, facilities, practice time, coaching, and travel. It began to break down even more rapidly the generations-old "protective" actions traditionally taken by women physical educators which were designed to prevent exploitation in women's sports but which also retarded the movement toward equality of women in sport. Equality under the act meant that if there were 10 men's sports there should be 10 women's sports providing sufficient interest existed. It also meant that athletic scholarships at the collegiate level should be equally available to women as to men. Women leaders in college athletics had been so opposed to this custom in men's athletics that it took federal court action to convince the women's ruling body, the Division for Girls and Women's Sports of the American Association for Health, Physical Education and Recreation, to change its controlling legislation to allow grants-in-aid for athletes.

While there was some opposition to aspects of Title IX by women leaders, it was insignificant to the fear and antipathy toward it exhibited by those in control of men's athletics. Male resistance came chiefly from those who believed that the financing of women's programs would further jeopardize the tenuous stability of men's athletic programs. The most important ruling body in college men's athletics, the National Collegiate Athletic Association (NCAA), claimed that implementation of Title IX would be "disruptive, often destructive, and surely counterproductive."[61] While the NCAA criticized Title IX, it moved to take over the management of competitive college women's athletics from the fledgling body formed in 1972 solely by women, the Association for Intercollegiate Athletics for Women (AIAW).

The AIAW was the outgrowth of a Commission on Intercollegiate Sports for Women formed in the mid-1960s. The purpose of the Commission was to encourage intercollegiate competition, a reflection of the direction in women's movement in sports had taken during the same decade. As the number of national championships for women expanded, there was a need for a stronger national body. The AIAW was thus created. The deadly fear of women leaders that men might attempt to take control was realized in 1975 when the NCAA at its annual convention came close to taking a vote to assume governance of women's intercollegiate athletics.[62] Threatened by the possible loss of autonomy of its sports programs, the AIAW fought to maintain what it considered a sane approach to intercollegiate athletics. As women's sport became more prominent, there was increasing pressure for the men's and women's programs to have a combined governance.

The revolution in women's athletics continued. It was clear that progress toward highly competitive athletics and greater participation at all levels was occurring at the same time that setbacks, like the NCAA unilateral attempt at takeover, existed. Since World War II and the woman's movement of the 1960s, women had made appreciable gains in most areas of amateur and professional sport. Despite beliefs by some male jockeys that "racing is not a woman's game," women were riding horses at the best thoroughbred race tracks. Though some people objected to women participating in male dominated sports, women were capable of running over 26 miles in marathon races in considerably less than three hours. Girls were found competent to participate in Little League baseball, previously forbidden by the League until court orders brought about girls' rights to compete. Young women were beginning to gain recognition in school athletics where previously they could only do so as the cheerleading sex symbols of male sports. College women athletes were becoming highly skilled for the first time so that arenas were filled by interested spectators for women's basketball games and gymnastic meets, while commercial television sought to broadcast the best in women's athletics. People even began to define feminine as that which a woman does. Sport was becoming a larger part of being feminine. The revolution in women's sports was continuing. The jury for the trial of equality in woman's sport was still deliberating. The decision had not yet been reached.

REFERENCES

1. *New York Times*, Mar. 27, 1968, p. 37; A Horseless Lady Paul Revere, *Literary Digest*, LXXXVIII (Jan. 16, 1926), 58-62; Lady From Boston, *Time*, XXVII (Mar. 16, 1936), 38-39; Joanna Davenport, Eleanora Randolph Sears, Pioneer in Women's Sports, North American Society for Sport History, *Proceedings*, (1976), p. 17; and Maury Z. Levy and Barbara J. Walder, Eleanora Sears, *WomenSports*, I (June 1974), pp. 31-32.

2. Isabel Harvey Hoskins, Golf Problems for Women, *Outing* LXIV (Aug. 1914), p. 561.

3. William H. Chafe, *The American Woman: Her Changing Social, Economic and Political Roles, 1920-1970* (New York: Oxford University Press, 1972), pp. 25, 30.

4. How a Girl Beat Leander at the Hero Game, *Literary Digest*, XC (Aug. 21, 1926), p. 67.

5. Mark Sullivan, *Our Times, The United States 1900-1925* (New York: Charles Scribner's Sons, 1930), II, pp. 191-192.

6. *New York Times*, Aug. 7, 1926, pp. 1, 3.

7. Donald Steel and Peter Ryde, *The Encyclopedia of Golf* (New York: Viking Press, 1975), pp. 84-85; William D. Richardson, The Woman on the Links, *Country Life*, XLVIII (July 1925), pp. 41-42; Will Grimsley, *Golf, Its History, People & Events* (Englewood Cliffs, N.J.: Prentice-Hall, 1966), pp. 150-151, 206, 228-229; and Feminine Laurel Bearers, *Review of Reviews*, LXXIV (Sept. 1926), p. 315.

8. Helen Wills, *Fifteen-Thirty* (New York: C. Scribner's Sons, 1937), pp. 4-5, 13, 29; and Helen Wills Moody, Education of a Tennis Player, *Scribner's Monthly*, XCIX (May 1936), p. 270.

9. Helen Wills, letter to Will Durant, philosopher and historian, June 10, 1931, in Wills, *Fifteen-Thirty*, p. 191.

10. Helen H. Jacobs, *Gallery of Champions* (London: Alvin Redman, 1951), pp. 95-96; Willis, *Fifteen-Thirty*, p. 17; and Temperament at the Tennis Net, *Literary Digest*, LXXXVII (Feb. 27, 1926), p. 64.

11. *New York Times*, Feb. 17, 1926, pp. 1, 15; Wills, *Fifteen-Thirty*, pp. 82-95; Phyllis H. Satterthwaite, Suzanne Lenglen and Helen Wills, *Living Age*, CCCXXVIII (Mar. 27, 1926), 666-667; and Temperament at the Tennis Net, pp. 62-67.

12. Jacobs, Gallery of Champions, pp. 30-33; Wills, *Fifteen-Thirty*, pp. 260-262; and United States Lawn Tennis Association, *Official Encyclopedia of Tennis* (New York: Harper & Row, 1971), pp. 35-39.

13. Pierre de Coubertin, The Philosophic Foundation of Modern Olympics, (Aug. 4, 1935). *The Olympic Idea* (Schorndorf, Germany: Druckerei und Verlag Karl Hofmann, 1966), pp. 133-134; de Coubertin, Chronique du Mois, *La Revue Olympique* (July 1910), pp. 109-110, and Coubertin, Les Femmes Aux Jeaux Olympiques, *La Review Olympique* (July 1912), 111, as quoted in Mary Leigh, The Evolution of Women's Participation in the Summer Olympic Games, 1900-1948, Ph.D. dissertation, Ohio State University, 1974, pp. 64-65, 78; and Mary Leigh, Pierre de Coubertin: A Man of His Time, *Quest*, XXII (June 1974), pp. 19-24.

14. Betty Spears, Women in the Olympics: An Unresolved Problem, in Peter J. Graham and Horst Ueberhorst (eds.), *The Modern Olympics* (Cornwall, N.Y.: Leisure Press, 1976), p. 66; Leigh, The Evolution of Women's Participation in the Summer Olympic Games, passim; Paula Welch, American Women: Early Pursuit of Olympic Laurels, North American Society for Sport History, *Proceedings* (1975), pp. 34-35; and Ellen W. Gerber, et al., *The American Woman in Sport* (Reading, Mass.: Addison-Wesley, 1974), pp. 138-139.

15. Cynthia M. Wesson, Purposes of the Committee on Women's Athletics of the APEA and Its Progress Up To the Present, *National Educational Association Addresses and Proceedings*, LX (1922), p. 1097.

16. *Ibid.*

17. George H. Vreeland, Track and Field Women Champions, *The National Athlete*, V (June 1924), pp. 7-8.

18. Alice A. Sefton, *The Women's Division of the National Amateur Federation* (Palo Alto: Stanford University Press, 1941), pp. 1-5; and Katherine L. Ley, Women's Intercollegiate Athletics, *The Encyclopedia of Education* (New York: Macmillan, 1971), I, p. 375.

19. Sefton, *The Women's Division*, pp. 1-5.

20. Agnes R. Wayman, Women's Athletics—All Uses—No Abuses, *American Physical Education Review*, XXIX (Nov. 1924), p. 517.

21. Athletics for the Girls and Women, *Playground*, XVII (May 1923), 116-118, 122-125; and Agnes Wayman, Women Division of the NAAF, *Journal of Physical Education*, III (Mar. 1932), pp. 3-7, 53-54.

22. Betty Spears, The Emergence of Sport in Physical Education, Paper presented at the American Association for Health, Physical Education and Recreation Convention, Minneapolis, Apr. 16, 1973, p. 20.

23. Lucille Eaton Hill, Introduction, in her *Athletic and Outdoor Sports for Women* (New York: Macmillan, 1903), p. 5.

24. Ellen Gerber expands upon this and other factors in her The Controlled Development of Collegiate Sport for Women, 1923-1936, *Journal of Sport History*, II (Spring 1975), pp. 1-28.

25. See, for example, Thomas D. Wood, Physical Education, *The Ninth Yearbook of the National Society for the Study of Education* (Par I), 1910, pp. 75-104; Clark W. Hetherington, Fundamental Education, *American Physical Education Review*, XV (1910), 629-635; and Luther Gulick, Interest in Relation to Muscular Exercise, *American Physical Education Review*, VII (1902), pp. 57-62.

26. Senda Berenson, *Basket Ball for Women* (New York: American Sports Publishing Co., 1901), p. 20; and Wisconsin Physical Education Society—Report, *American Physical Education Review*, IX (1904), p. 57.

27. For the negative influence of religion on women's sport see Ronald A. Smith, American Women's Sport in the Victorian Era, *Proceedings* of the Third Canadian Symposium on the History of Sport and Physical Education, Dalhousie University, Halifax, Nova Scotia (August 18-21, 1974), p. 7.

28. Elizabeth Cady Stanton, *The Woman's Bible* (New York: Arno Press, 1972, originally 1895), p. 7.

29. William H. Chafe, *The American Woman, Her Changing Social, Economic and Political Roles, 1920-1970* (New York: Oxford University Press, 1972), pp. 12-15.

30. Spears, Women in the Olympics, pp. 68-70; and Gerber, *The American Woman in Sport*, pp. 140-141.

31. John R. Tunis, "Women and the Sports Business," *Harper's Monthly*, CLIX (July 1929), p. 213.

32. Sefton, *The Women's Division of the National Amateur Athletic Federation* (Palo Alto; Stanford University Press, 1941), pp. 55-56, 82-84.

33. Babe Didrikson Zaharias, *This Life I've Led* (New York: A. S. Barnes, 1955), pp. 34-38; Babe Zaharias, *Current Biography* (1947), 701-703; *New York Times*, Sept. 28, 1956, pp. I, 30; and Betty Hicks, Babe Didrikson Zaharias, *womenSports*, II (Nov. 1975), pp. 24-25.

34. Golf: 'Best at Everything,' Babe Garners Another Trophy, *Newsweek*, V (May 4, 1935), p. 18.

35. Betty Hicks, Babe Didrikson Zaharias, *womenSports* II (Nov. 1975), p. 27.

36. Twas a Comedy of Errors, But Babe Didrikson Has Gone Pro, *Literary Digest*, CXV (Jan 7, 1933), p. 33; Babe Zaharias, *Current Biography* (1947), 701-703; *New York Times*, Sept. 28, 1956, p. 30; John Holway, Bill Holland, Star Pitcher of the Thirties, *Black Sports*, V (May 1976), p. 61; and Golf: 'Best at Everything,' p. 19.

37. Betty Hicks, Babe Didrikson Zaharias, *womenSports*, II (Dec. 1975), pp. 18-20.

38. Betty Hicks, Babe Didrikson Zaharias, *womenSports*, II (Nov. 1975), p. 28.

39. How Much Competition is Good for Girls? *Literary Digest*, LXXXIX (April 17, 1926), p. 74.

40. Ethel Perrin and Grace Turner, *Play Day The Spirit of Sport* (New York: American Child Health Association, 1929), p. 11; and Ruth M. Findlay, Team Play and the American Girl, *Playground*, XVIII (Oct. 1924), p. 428.

41. Mabel Lee, The Case For and Against Intercollegiate Athletics for Women and the Situation as It Stands Today, *Mind and Body*, XXX (Nov. 1923), pp. 246-255.

42. Mabel Lee, The Case For and Against Intercollegiate Athletics and the Situation Since 1923, *Research Quarterly*, II (May 1931), pp. 127, 116.

43. *New York Herald Tribune*, Jan. 11, 1930, p. 2.

44. The sports day was an interschool activity in which the participating teams were composed of players from the same school, but it was not considered as competitive as interscholastic competition as many teams were involved and scores were relatively unimportant.

45. See Ralph J. Sabock, A History of Physical Education at The Ohio State University—Men's and Women's Division 1895-1969, Ph.D. dissertation, Ohio State University, 1969, pp. 200-215.

46. Gladys Palmer, Policies in Women's Athletics, *Journal of Health, Physical Education and Recreation*, IX (Nov. 1938), pp. 586-587.

47. Sabock, A History of Physical Education at the Ohio State University, pp. 207-208.

48. *Ibid.*, pp. 209-214.

49. M. Gladys Scott, Competition for Women in American Colleges, *Research Quarterly*, XVI (Mar. 1945), pp. 57, 67.

50. Eleanor Metheny, Where Will You Go From Here? in her *Connotations of Movement in Sports and Dance* (Dubuque, Ia.: Brown, 1965), p. 158.

51. Donald A. Laird, Why Aren't More Women Athletes? *Scientific American*, CLIV (Mar. 1936), p. 143.

52. *A. A. U. Study of Effect of Athletic Competition on Girls and Women* (New York: Amateur Athletic Union, 1953), p. 8.

53. William H. Chafe, *The American Woman, Her Changing Social, Economical and Political Roles, 1920-1970* (New York: Oxford University Press, 1972), p. 195.

54. For an extensive study of the league see Merrie A. Fidler, The Development and Decline of the All-American Girls Baseball League, 1943-1954, M.S. thesis, University of Massachusetts, 1976.

55. Fidler, The Development and Decline of the All-American Girls Baseball League, pp. 42, 75, 84-89, 263; Baseball: Babette Ruths, *Newsweek*, XXVIII (July 29, 1946), 68; Girls' Baseball, *Life*, XVIII (June 4, 1945), 63-66; and W. G. Nicholson, Women's Pro Baseball Packed the Stands, *womenSports*, III (Apr. 1976), pp. 23-24.

56. Fidler, The Development and Decline of the All-American Girls Baseball League, p. 110.

57. Chafe, *The American Woman*, pp. 226-244.

58. Billie Jean King, *Current Biography*, (1967), p. 225. Others who moved away from the masculine image of softball or baseball to tennis were Mary K. Browne, U.S. singles champion, 1912-1914; Helen Wills; and Alice Marble, U.S. singles champion, 1936 and 1938-1940.

59. Billie Jean King, Publisher's Letter, *womenSports*, II (Mar. 1975), 4; Women's Liberator, *Forbes*, CX (Sept. 15, 1972), 29; and Curry Kirkpatrick, There She Is, Ms. America, *Sports Illustrated*, XXXIX (Oct. 1, 1973), p. 32.

60. Ellen Weber, Title IX Controversy, *womenSports*, I (June 1974), p. 74; Ellen Weber, Revolution in Women's Sport, *womenSports*, I (Sept. 1974), p. 37; and Bil Gilbert and Nancy Williamson, Are Women Being Two Faced, *Sports Illustrated*, XXXVIII (June 4, 1973), pp. 44-54.

61. Weber, Title IX Controversy, p. 74.

62. Candace L. Hogan, NCAA & AIAW: Will the Men Score on Women's Athletics, *womenSports*, IV (Jan. 1977), pp. 46-49.

CHAPTER 21

Blacks in Sport: From Jim Crow Toward Integration

The period in America after World War I has often been called the "Golden Age of Sport." For one group, Afro-Americans, it would more properly be called the "Despairing Age of Sport." By the First World War much of America was legally segregated with Jim Crow laws existing in all states below the Mason-Dixon line, and social segregation common north of it. In the north as in the south most organized sport was for whites only. Jackie Robinson, the eventual twentieth century desegregator of professional baseball, was six months old in 1919 when Jack Dempsey won the heavyweight boxing championship from Jess Willard and immediately announced that he would pay "no attention to Negro challengers."[1] Major League baseball for the previous thirty-five years saw no black participants as it had early felt the crunch of Jim Crow. Only white America would sing the nearly century old song:

O Jim Crow's come to town as you all
   must know,
An' he weel about, he turn about, he do
   jis so,
An' every time he weel about he jump
   Jim Crow.

Few whites would have agreed with Justice Harlan who, as the lone dissenter in the historic "separate but equal" Plessy v. Ferguson Supreme Court ruling in 1896, believed that if evils result from the comingling of the two races, they will be infinitely less than the evils resulting from the infringement of civil rights.[2]

In the nineteenth century, black liberator Frederick Douglass pointed out that "the relations between the white and black people of this country is the central question of the age." Early in the twentieth century historian W. E. B. DuBois proclaimed that "the problem of the twentieth century is the problem of the Color Line." Not until the post-World War II period were black Americans to make significant progress toward their civil rights and equality. As that occurred blacks moved more freely into white dominated sport. Possibly the most significant factor in the development of twentieth century sport was the movement toward integration of blacks into the mainstream of American sport.

THE STATUS OF BLACKS IN SPORT BETWEEN THE WARS

Blacks were not totally absent from white dominated sport in the period following World War I, but it is also clear that the black athlete was not readily accepted in any sport. Some sports like professional baseball and golf were completely segregated—baseball by a "gentleman's" agreement and golf through its Professional Golfer's Association Caucasian only clause. Amateur track and field and professional boxing were more open though prejudice was still apparent when, for instance, Jack Dempsey refused to fight blacks.

Baseball—The Symbolic Sport

Professional baseball had shut its doors to blacks in the mid-1880s, mirroring the Jim Crow exclusion from full participation in American life of that era. Forced out of organized baseball by whites, blacks formed their own teams and from time-to-time attempted to organize leagues. Not until 1920 were leagues successful. Rube Foster, a premier pitcher and manager of the Chicago American Giants, proposed a black baseball league patterned after the major leagues. The National Negro Baseball League was the result, composed of teams from Indianapolis, Kansas City, Detroit, St. Louis, and two from Chicago. Three years later the Eastern Negro League was formed. The leagues never reached the financial stability or discipline which white organized baseball achieved as clubs lacked ownership of the baseball parks and interleague "wars" over rights to ball players resulted. Rube Foster's league lasted until the Depression when it folded in 1931. The Eastern Negro League collapsed in 1928. Negro barnstorming teams continued.[3]

Black baseball regrouped in 1933, and a second Negro National League was created. Four years later the Negro American League began competition. These two leagues were quite stable through the Depression years and probably reached a peak during the Second World War. The famous Homestead Grays of Western Pennsylvania in the Negro National League and the Kansas City Monarchs of the Negro American League dominated play in the 1930s and 1940s.

The annual Negro all-star games, more than the championship games at the season's end, were the capstone events in the black leagues. Beginning in 1933 and ending with the collapse of black baseball leagues around 1950, the all-star games focused attention on a number of all-time greats in baseball. Several players should be noted. Josh Gibson, a home run hitting catcher for the Homestead Grays and the Pittsburgh Crawfords from 1930-1946, combined with Buck Leonard, a first baseman with the Grays, as Ruth and Gehrig did a few years before with the New York Yankees. Cool Papa Bell, an outfielder, and Judy Johnson, a third baseman, played together with the Pittsburgh Crawfords. Satchel Paige pitched with numerous teams but was probably best known when he played with the Kansas City Monarchs. Paige began his professional career in 1926 when he was about twenty years old. Through his twenty-two years of black baseball, he was the biggest gate attraction because of his showmanship and ability. Had he been allowed to play in the major leagues during the 1920s and 1930s, he could have pitched against players like Cobb and Ruth and been compared with pitchers of the stature of Walter Johnson and Dizzy Dean. After baseball was desegregated he became a major league rookie at the age of forty-two in 1948 winning 6 games and losing 1 for the World Champion Cleveland Indians and drawing over 200,000 fans to watch him in his first three pitching assignments.[4]

These five players, who have been honored by being chosen to the Baseball Hall of Fame in Cooperstown, may not be as good as three men who preceded them in the early 1900s, Oscar Charleston, John Henry Lloyd, and Smokey Joe Williams. Oscar Charleston began his professional career in 1915 with the Indianapolis ABCs, combining speed and power. John McGraw, the manager of the New York Giants, believed Charleston was the best player in all of baseball. John Henry Lloyd joined the professional ranks in 1905 and played until 1931 when he retired from big-time Negro baseball. His fielding at shortstop was superb; his batting average was often over .400. When Honus Wagner, the celebrated major leaguer, was asked who was the best player in the major leagues he said it was Babe Ruth, but in all of baseball he believed it was John Henry Lloyd. For greatness in pitching there are those who believe that Smokey Joe Williams was the best of any race. His fast ball was legendary and was often compared to that of Walter Johnson and Satchel Paige. He pitched for twelve years in Texas before he began his tenure with the best black teams beginning in 1910. He won 41 games and lost only 3 for Rube Foster's Chicago American Giants in 1914. Williams continued in black baseball until 1932 when he retired at the age of fifty-six years.[5]

Baseball was symbolic of the plight of blacks in American society.

The situation in Kansas City showed the hypocrisy which existed. That city had a white team in the American Association minor league as well as the Kansas City Monarchs of the Negro National League. Both teams used the same park. When the American Association team used the facility, blacks were segregated from whites, but when the Monarchs played, whites could sit together with the black spectators. Blacks were thus taught to accept the segregation barriers when it suited whites, and they often swallowed their pride in the period between the wars and accepted, with bitterness and resentment, Jim Crow accommodations.[6]

Jim Crow Arrives Late in Pro Football

While blacks were forced to go their own way in baseball well before the twentieth century, they have been part of professional football for much of its history. Pro football began in Western Pennsylvania in the mid-1890s and had a tenuous existence chiefly in three states, Ohio, Pennsylvania, and New York, into the 1920s. Most of the better professional players had college experience, for football was primarily a college game. The first two black players in professional football, however, did not attend college. Charles Follis was the first in 1904, when he signed a contract with the Shelby Athletic Club in Ohio. Follis had starred as a running back for the first football team at Wooster High School which he helped to organize a few years before. With the Shelby A. C. during his first year as a professional, his team lost only one game—that being to Ohio's Massillon Tigers who were considered the professional champs. Follis played for three years, and he also played on a professional black baseball team from Wooster before dying prematurely of pneumonia in 1910. The next year Henry McDonald, a high school graduate from Rochester, New York, became the second known black to play professional football when he signed with the Rochester Jeffersons. McDonald was a speedy back like Follis and played for thirteen years with Rochester and the Buffalo All Stars.[7]

Follis' and McDonald's entries into professional football preceded two all-Americans from Brown and Rutgers, Fritz Pollard and Paul Robeson. Pollard, who in 1916 had helped Brown defeat both Yale and Harvard on successive Saturdays, joined the Akron Pros in 1919 as a star half back. Robeson, a 215 pound end turned professional in 1920 ending the season with Pollard on Akron's undefeated team. Pollard knew Robeson personally and had played against Robeson in college. As the first black professional football coach, Pollard had asked Robeson to play for the Akron team. Robeson played only two more seasons, while Pollard starred on various teams through most of the 1920s. He, of course, had the opportunity to play against the great Indian, Jim Thorpe and his Canton Bulldogs on several occasions during his eight years. Though blacks found racial prejudice in their dealings with whites, Indians may have shown greater antipathy. There is the story of two football hall of fame Indians, Jim Thorpe and Joe Guyon of the Canton Bulldogs, in a game against Fritz Pollard's Akron team. The two Indians wanted to put Pollard out of the game so they told their kicker to punt high and short to Pollard. This done, Pollard waited for the ball as Thorpe and Guyon attempted flying tackles from both sides. The 150 pound Pollard caught the ball and immediately dropped face down on the ground. The two Indians' heads collided and as they lay unconscious, Pollard, as the rules allowed, leaped to his feet and returned the ball for a long gain.[8] Later Pollard and Thorpe became good friends.

Other blacks played in the fledgling National Football League in the 1920s and early 1930s until the "color line" was drawn in 1933. Included were two on the Chicago Cardinals, Duke Slater, an all-American tackle from Iowa, and Joe Lillard, a back from the University of Oregon. Slater played for a decade beginning in 1922, while Lillard competed for only two years. Lillard, however, is significant for he was the last black to be allowed to play in the

Duke Slater, without helmet, blocks the Notre Dame line for Iowa before playing pro ball for the Chicago Cardinals. (Courtesy of University of Iowa Archives.)

National Football League until after World War II, when, like professional baseball, the sport was again desegregated. The most likely explanation of the Jim Crow principle was that owners decided that blacks were not wanted or needed for professional football to continue during the depression. Chicagoan Fritz Pollard, who likely would have known, believed strongly that it was the result of the prejudice of George Halas, owner of the Chicago Bears, who during the 1920s generally refused to compete against teams which had black players. It might be noted that Halas' Bears were one of the last teams in the National Football League to have a black player after World War II. Thus, while blacks continued to compete on a few college teams in the north, and, of course, in Negro colleges, the pros excluded the best of them for thirteen years.[9]

The Special Cases of Jesse Owens and Joe Louis

That professional football closed its doors to blacks the same year Hitler's Nazi Party of the "pure" Aryan race came to power is probably a coincidence, although both events were surrounded by an aura of racial superiority. It is ironic, then, that two blacks in the 1930s, Jesse Owens in track and Joe Louis in boxing, became celebrated Americans for denying that the Nazis were physically or athletically superior. Owens would star in the 1936 "Nazi" Olympics held in Berlin, while Louis would defeat Germany's best boxer two years later.

Jesse Owens and Joe Louis were born only months apart of Alabama sharecropper parents in the year preceding World War I. They were both products of the Negro migration north to industrial America; Owens to Ohio's largest city, Cleveland, and Louis to Michigan's metropolis, Detroit. Born at the nadir of blacks in sport at a time when Jack Johnson was the despised black heavyweight boxing champion of the world, both Owens and Louis picked individual sports in which to compete rather than team sports in which blacks gained little recognition. Both white-controlled track and boxing allowed blacks to participate when they were ready for competition, which was not true of professional baseball or football.

Jesse Owens was not the first American black to win an Olympic track and field medal. That distinction belonged to George Poage who won two medals in hurdle races in the third Olympics held in St. Louis in 1904. Several others showed distinction during the next three decades including Eddie Tolan and Ralph Metcalfe who finished in a memorable near dead heat in the record setting 100 meter dash at the Los Angeles Olympics of 1932. The track and field aggregation sent to the 1936 Berlin Olympics included nine medal winning blacks, one of whom was, of course, Jesse Owens, the star performer.[10]

The previous year Owens had participated in probably the greatest individual performance in a track and field meet in American history. Owens was a sophomore at Ohio State University when he competed at Ann Arbor, Michigan before 10,000 spectators at the 1935 Big Ten championships. A questionable performer because he was recovering from a back injury incurred during a college scuffle only several days before, he decided to try the 100 yard dash. Without the help of starting blocks, he tied the world record in 9.4 seconds. He quickly moved to the long jump area for his only jump of the day, a world record of 26 feet 8¼ inches. As he leaped with jubilation at his record, the announcer called for all participants in the 220 yard dash. By now Owens was "floating," as he later said, and broke the world record by three-tenths of a second in 20.3 seconds. One more event remained for Owens. He rested for the first time that May afternoon while the two mile race was run. As soon as it was over Owens dug his starting holes into the track and looked at the hurdles set for the 220 yard low hurdle race. The gun sounded and 22.6 seconds later, four-tenths of a second better than anyone else had ever run the event, Owens had completed his fourth world record performance—all within about one hour.

Jesse Owens was the clear American choice to dominate the 1936 Olympics, and he did not disappoint the spectators nor his admirers. He troubled only the racists. Arriving in Germany, Owens was the best known of the American blacks of whom there were 18 on the entire team. The German press, reflecting Hitler's idea of the "pure Aryan" master race, denigrated America and these American performers by calling them the "Black Auxiliaries." However close to the truth these allegations might have been, Owens chose not to get into the controversy, desiring only to show his physical superiority on the track. This he did. On the second day of the track and field competition, Owens won the most popular Olympic event, the 100 meter dash, tying the world record of 10.3 seconds, one yard ahead of Ralph Metcalfe who had also finished second four years before. The next day Owens long jumped 26 feet 5⁵/₁₆ inches setting an Olympic mark after he had nearly failed to qualify. The 200 meter dash was contested the following day, and he set a world record in 20.7 seconds, while Matt Robinson, older brother of baseball's desegregator Jackie Robinson, came in second tying the previous world record time. Owens' fourth gold medal came in a world record performance in the 400 meter relay run in 39.8 seconds. Even before the close of the Olympics, Jesse Owens was clearly its major hero.

Outstanding performances like that of Owens are of myth-making

Jesse Owens won four gold medals at the 1936 Berlin Olympics and was termed a "Black Auxiliary" by Hitler. (Courtesy of Library of Congress.)

proportions. If myths are the poetic appearance of historical events, then Owens became the chief mythological character in the most important modern Olympic Games ever contested. When his name and that of probably the most momentous twentieth century figure, Adolph Hitler, are combined in one event, then it is easy to see how the myth about Jesse Owens being snubbed by Hitler could develop. During the Games, a leading New York newspaper reported that "Hitler has not yet shaken hands with a Negro Olympic champion. . . ." As Jesse Owens was the most publicized black on the American team, the press and others soon circulated the story that Jesse Owens had been snubbed by Hitler. The distinction, if one must be given, should be awarded to another black, Cornelius Johnson, who won the high jump on the first day of the track competition. Before the high jump was completed on that August day, Hitler had personally congratulated the other track and field winners, all of whom were Germans or Finns. When the German high jumpers were eliminated near the day's end, Hitler left the stadium leaving behind three Americans who were eventual medal winners including Cornelius Johnson who won the event. One can conjecture that Johnson was snubbed by Hitler. Before any more winners were decided the president of the International Olympic Committee informed Hitler that he was only a guest and that he should congratulate all or none. He chose the latter, though in private he continued to greet German champions.[12]

Owens and the four other black Olympic gold medal winners did not explode the Aryan supremacy myth, though they did help keep Americans from being completely embarrassed by Germany's domination of the Berlin Olympics. Hitler could look at his country's 89 Olympic medal winners with added confidence that Germany's ideology and its physical performance was far superior to that of any other country including the United States which could garner only 56 medals. Yet, ironically enough, there were those in the United States who exalted Jesse Owens for his role in gaining some American prestige in the face of greater Nazi strength, while back at home he and other blacks had to submit to Jim Crow legislation and other equally baneful racial prejudice. Owens chose not to become involved in the political debate and merely accepted with appreciation and modesty the adulation which came his way. A hero to the blacks, Owens impressed much of the white public because, unlike Jack Johnson before him, he did not speak out for civil rights. Accepting the racial situation as it was, Owens was considered by many a credit to his race. Said Owens about his public image: "I came along at the time when images were being formed. The Negro people needed an image and Joe Louis and I came along. It gives you a real sense of responsibility to your fellow man."[13]

Joe Louis became an even stronger figure in black athletics than did Owens, for his career had longevity, while Owens had only a momentary period of glory. However, Owens, because he had superior verbal skills, was in demand for most of his life as a public speaker. Joe Louis had little formal education, and his popularity was destined to come only through his boxing record, retaining the heavyweight championship longer than any other boxer. Louis took his first lesson in boxing when he was fifteen years of age. At the depths of the Depression, as Franklin Roosevelt prepared to take office, Louis fought his first amateur fight. He was knocked out in the second round, but he earned a $7 merchandise check. Soon he was eyed by a black boxing aficionado, John Roxborough, who saw a future for Louis in the fight game.[14]

Louis quickly joined the professional ranks and accepted a code of conduct which helped make him the most highly acceptable black athlete that American society had yet seen. Among the rules his black advisors asked him to follow were that Louis live and fight clean; never gloat over a fallen opponent; never go into a night club alone; and above all never have his picture taken with a white woman. These were obviously devised to make Louis acceptable to the larger American public and to reject any comparison to the other black heavyweight champion, Jack Johnson, who had followed none of the rules. Later, Jackie Robinson had a similar set of rules designed to

Joe Louis became heavyweight champion in the 1930s with an image acceptable to white America. (Courtesy of Library of Congress.)

make him acceptable as the first black major league baseball player of the twentieth century. It was likely true that for a black man to reach the top and be acceptable to the dominant white society, he was required to be modest, humble, and a "clean" liver. One sportswriter described Louis in this manner: "The colored boy is clean, fine and superb, modest and unassuming as a chauffeur or as the man who cuts and rakes the lawn once a week."[15]

Joe Louis was also a superb boxer, strong with fast hands. Within a year as a professional, Louis fought and won 22 fights and gained the opportunity to fight the ex-champ Primo Carnera. Carnera, an Italian, came along just at the right time for Louis. Italy, under Fascist Mussolini, had just made war on a weak African nation, Ethiopia, ruled by Hailie Selassie, and had turned American public opinion against Italy. Louis, it seemed, could retaliate by knocking out Carnera. This he did before 60,000 spectators in New York's Yankee Stadium. Black Americans took special pride in Louis' accomplishment, but white Americans also felt pride in the symbolic defeat of Fascism. Louis soon disposed of another previous title holder, Max Baer, which led to a match with ex-champion and pride of Nazi Germany, Max Schmeling.[16]

Max Schmeling had briefly held the crown following Gene Tunney's retirement in 1928. He was thirty-one years old and over his fighting peak when he met Louis in their first fight in June of 1936, only three months after Hitler had violated the Treaty of Versailles by marching his troops into the Rhineland. Overconfident, Louis was surprisingly knocked out by the underdog Schmeling in 12 rounds. For the Nazis this was one more proof of Aryan supremacy. German Minister of Propaganda, Joseph Goebbels, wired Schmeling: "Congratulations, I know you won for Germany. Heil Hitler."[17] Schmeling then returned to Germany, having defeated Louis as the number one threat to take the heavyweight crown held by James Braddock. He was immediately given a place of honor at the Berlin Olympic Games. While Jesse Owens was basking in the glory of his four gold medals, Joe Louis was rebuilding his tarnished image by beating another ex-champ, Jack Sharkey and six other boxers on his way to a championship fight with Braddock. One year after his defeat by Schmeling, Louis defeated Braddock and won the heavyweight championship. Louis, who fought more times than any other champion, placed his title on the line three times before he met Schmeling again exactly one year after becoming champion.

The second Schmeling match in June of 1938 was probably the highlight of Louis' career. Politically it was by far the most important. Germany had annexed Austria only months before the fight. Hitler was soon to take part of Czechoslovakia and endanger the rest of

Europe. It was meaningful to the American public that the physical idol of Hitler be defeated, and Louis saw the fight as a chance for revenge. A crowd of 70,000 packed Yankee Stadium for the second of three million-dollar fights of Louis' career. It was estimated that nearly two-thirds of all American radios were tuned into the fight. About double the number of people listened to the fight as they did to the most popular radio show of the 1930s, Charlie McCarthy. In two minutes and four seconds of the first round—after 41 punches and three knockdowns by Louis—Schmeling lay prone on the canvas, victim of one of the most impressive beatings in ring history. Americans were proud that a native son had beaten a Nazi supporter.[18]

Joe Louis continued as champion another decade including four years during World War II when he only fought exhibitions as a corporal in the Army. Throughout this time his public life remained untainted, and his popularity with blacks and whites continued to grow. The rise of Louis to a position of prominence gave blacks during the Depression years someone to relate to who was successful in white society. It is likely that Joe Louis, as well as Jesse Owens, were positive forces which led to a thaw in racial segregation during and after World War II.

WORLD WAR II—THE THAW IN SEGREGATION

Segregation in American sport was never complete for there were always examples like Joe Louis and Jesse Owens to deny complete Jim Crowism. This was true even in the south where total separation came closest. Prior to World War II, there were examples of blacks on northern college teams playing against all-white southern colleges, though generally southern schools required that contracts with northern colleges contain clauses forbidding Yankee colleges from competing with blacks. In 1938, a New York University black played in a football game against North Carolina. Following the game the player expressed surprise that North Carolina did not attempt to injure him and thus remove him from the game. "They didn't go for me at all," he said. The same year Duke University allowed Syracuse's quarterback, Wilmeth Sidat-Singh, an adopted black son of an Indian doctor, to compete.[19] These were exceptions to the rule in north-south relations. Jim McDaniel, probably the top black tennis player when World War II began, once played against Bobby Riggs in high school and had an exhibition game with reigning professional Don Budge in 1941, but he was never allowed to participate in important tournaments.[20] At that time both participants and uniforms were required to be white. The social pressures to prevent blacks from participation were nearly as great in the north as were legal sanctions of the Jim Crow laws passed in southern states. As an example, the coach of a teacher's college in Wisconsin felt compelled to ask his president if he had any objections to a Negro athlete entering the school—this at a time when Wisconsin had only several years before passed a civil rights law to protect the rights of blacks.[21]

The greatest change in rights for blacks since emancipation occurred during the generation begun when the world was engaged in the second great war of the twentieth century. In the early 1940s, blacks were still going to court to obtain the equal portion of the 1896 Plessy v. Ferguson "separate but equal" decision.[22] Blacks were just coming out of the Depression which had been much more severe for them than for whites. It took a proposed March-on-Washington of 100,000 led by A. Philip Randolph, the black president of the Brotherhood of Sleeping Car Porters, to persuade President Roosevelt to issue an Executive Order in 1941, which created the Committee on Fair Employment Practices preventing discrimination in the hiring of workers in national defense industries. When Pearl Harbor was attacked, the United States Army, as well as its blood bank, was still segregated as it had been during the First World War, while the Marines allowed no blacks in its branch of service.[23]

Much was said about fighting for freedom and democracy, and blacks considered again what it might mean to them. Wrote a twenty-two-year-old black soldier:

> I won't fight or die in vain. If I fight, suffer or die it will be for the freedom of every black, and any black man to live equally with other races. . . . A new Negro will return from the war—a bitter Negro if he is disappointed again. He will be taught to kill, to suffer, to die for something he believes in, and he will live by these rules to gain his personal rights.[24]

Two major questions were raised when a black went to court to challenge being drafted into a segregated army: Was segregation in itself discrimination, and was a Jim Crow army compatible with a war fought for democratic aims?[25] Heavyweight champion, Joe Louis, did not publicly question the war effort. Despite being draft exempt, Louis joined the segregated army as a private and claimed he was glad he was an American citizen fighting for liberty and justice. Yet, Louis spoke out against the discrimination he found in the military. Once the war was concluded he continued in a low key fashion to oppose the injustice of Jim Crow laws and racial discrimination. When a black military veteran was attacked by a southern policeman, Louis said what many blacks felt—that blacks "didn't fight to preserve fascism at home."[26] The war gave reason for both blacks and whites to reconsider the position of blacks in American society and in its sport structure. Two weeks after the Japanese agreed to surrender ending World War II, Jackie Robinson took the first step toward the desegregation of America's "National Pastime" when he agreed to play baseball in the Brooklyn Dodger system.

PAUL ROBESON AND JACKIE ROBINSON: A CONTRAST

Ask an American who Jackie Robinson was, and the answer will likely be that he was the first black major league baseball player. While that is not quite correct for blacks were in the majors in the 1880s, people still recognize Robinson correctly for desegregating (some say integrating) baseball. Ask the same person who Paul Robeson was, and there will likely be silence, unless the person is black. Robeson, an all-American football player at Rutgers, was once called the greatest defensive end of all time by Walter Camp. He was also winner of 12 varsity letters in football, basketball, baseball, and track and field in the late 1910s; leader of his class in scholarship and a Phi Beta Kappa scholar; a professional football player on the first championship of what today is the National Football League, a lawyer, a Shakespearean actor, and a world renowned singer. Yet he is, for most, a forgotten man. The contrast between two great athletes is both striking and instructive of the place of blacks in American society and in sport during the first half of the twentieth century.

The April day in 1947 that Jackie Robinson got his first major league hit for the Brooklyn Dodgers, the city Council of Peoria, Illinois voted unanimously to oppose Paul Robeson's appearance in their city. Robinson had been requested by Branch Rickey, owner of the Brooklyn team, not to speak out, not to complain to umpires, nor retaliate to insults\from opposing ballplayers or spectators. Robeson, to the contrary was speaking his mind, deploring the Jim Crowism in America, and praising the racial harmony he found in the Soviet Union. It was his sympathy for communism which caused Paul Robeson to become a "persona non grata" to many Americans and to the United States government after World War II.

Legal and social segregation was an embarrassment to the American government during the Cold War following the Second World War as it had been during the war when Americans were supposedly fighting to uphold democratic institutions. Communists agitators, foreign and domestic, could point to the racial policies in America and make propaganda gains. Early in World War II, Satchel Paige and the Kansas City Monarchs beat Dizzy Dean and a group of major league players then in the service. A week later, Paige was pitching to the great black catcher, Josh Gibson, and his Homestead Grays, and they again badly defeated Dizzy Dean and his white service team. This culminated a campaign by the organ of the American Communist Party, the *Daily Worker*, to pressure Commissioner Landis and or-

Paul Robeson of Rutgers was called the greatest defensive end of all time by Walter Camp. (Courtesy of Rutgers University Archives.)

ganized baseball to allow blacks to enter. The paper challenged Landis:

> The stars could get only two hits off Satchel Paige in seven innings of trying. Why does your silence keep him and other Negro stars from taking his [sic] rightful place in our national pastime at a time when we are at war and Negroes and whites are fighting and dying together to end Hitlerism?[27]

At the same time Jimmy Dykes, manager of the Chicago White Sox told a young black shortshop, Jackie Robinson: "I'd love to have you on my team and so would all the other big league managers. But it's not up to us. Get after Landis."[28] Other managers felt the same way, but no progress for ending Jim Crowism was then made in major league baseball.[29] Communist agitation was not the effective way to end segregation in America, though this was the method Robeson used.

While Robeson entered the post-World War II era as an outspoken critic of American racial policies and praising those of the socialistic Soviet Union, Jackie Robinson endured the torture of desegregating major league baseball in 1947. During his first year with the Brooklyn Dodgers he received death threats to himself and his family, while he

Jackie Robinson endured the torture of desegregating baseball after six decades of segregation. (Courtesy of National Baseball Hall of Fame and Museum.)

stoically took verbal abuse, the worst from manager Ben Chapman's Philadelphia Phillies. A challenge by the St. Louis Cardinals to boycott the Brooklyn Dodgers had to be cut short by league president Ford Frick who warned the Cardinals that those who take part "will be suspended and I don't care if it wrecks the National League for five years." Later, the Cardinals released their anger upon Robinson as both Enos Slaughter and Joe Garagiola spiked him, as Robinson believed, maliciously. Despite this he became Rookie of the Year and helped Brooklyn reach the World Series.[30]

After two years of generally ignoring insult and injury, Robinson and Branch Rickey discussed the situation and agreed that beginning in 1949, Robinson would be his own man to express his inner feelings. This he did, and instead of being a "martyred" hero, some of the press began to treat him as an ungrateful Negro or an "uppity nigger" as it was often called—something which Jesse Owens and Joe Louis had been careful to avoid. Meanwhile Paul Robeson, during those two years, spoke out for freedom from Jim Crowism so prevalent in America. Because he referred to the superior social conditions in the Soviet Union, he was castigated by the controversial House of Representatives Un-American Activities Committee as being a communist sympathizer. Across the nation Robeson was challenged to his right to speak by those who felt he was a threat to America. Robeson, after being banned from giving a concert by the Albany, New York School Board, said: "Whether I am a communist or a communist sympathizer is irrelevant. The question is whether American citizens, regardless of their political beliefs or sympathies, may enjoy their constitutional rights."[31] The situation reached a crisis stage in 1949, when Robeson spoke in Paris before the World Congress of the Partisans of Peace and told those assembled it was unthinkable that American Negroes "would go to war on behalf of those who have oppressed us for generations" against the Soviet Union "which in one generation has raised our people to the full dignity of mankind."[32] There was an outcry by the American press and fear by the American government that blacks would be unwilling to fight the Soviets if the need arose. The chairman of the House Un-American Activities Committee telegrammed Jackie Robinson asking him to testify before his committee "to give the lie to statements by Paul Robeson."

Jackie Robinson, probably the best known black in America, was asked to give testimony against another black—both of whom were fighting racial prejudice in their own ways. The decision to testify or not was difficult, and it created a dilemma for Robinson. If he testified he might merely be the black pawn in a white man's game which pitted one black against another, and he might be considered a "traitor" to his own people. If he did not testify he feared that

Robeson's statement might discredit all blacks in the eyes of whites. At the time, Robinson had faith in the ultimate justice whites would render to blacks. Robinson did testify. He said that he believed Robeson's statement that blacks would not fight in a war with the Soviet Union was "silly," that it was "a siren song sung in bass." He also spoke out against communism. These assertions pleased the white press and especially governmental officials. Robinson, however, said much more. He did not, like some Americans, believe Robeson's freedom of speech was "silly." Robinson confirmed Robeson's conviction that blacks would continue to fight racial discrimination in the military, on buses, and in employment in America "until we get it licked," and he challenged America "to go the rest of the way in wiping Jim Crow out of American sports."[33]

At mid-century, blacks, sport, and Cold War politics came to a head as the "red scare" of the Joe McCarthy era revealed itself. Robeson, in speaking out for the rights of blacks, couched his words in sympathy with the communist line, and he was ostracized and deprived of foreign travel for a decade by the State Department.[34] Robinson took a strong stand eventually, but did not use the fiery words of communism to aid or hinder the cause. Robeson, the athlete and singer, sacrificed himself, wealth, and productive career for his beliefs. Robinson, the breaker of the color line in baseball, survived to carry on his own betterment and that of blacks in America.

THE MOVEMENT TOWARD INTEGRATION IN SPORTS

The breakthrough of Jackie Robinson into organized baseball was the most important event in desegregating sport in America. The course of integrating sport will likely continue well into the future, for the movement toward full acceptance of all people without reference to racial, religious, or ethnic differences is a difficult process. Robinson's entry into baseball was only one step toward achieving full equality of status and condition. One observer has noted that in sport as in society, integration, if it is ever complete, will cease to exist when it has been achieved.[35]

Professional football, not baseball, was the first of the major team sports to be desegregated following World War II. After the 1945 season in which the championship Cleveland Rams of the National Football League lost money, the team moved to Los Angeles. In an attempt to shore up attendance in the California city which had another professional team in the newly formed All-American Football Conference, owner Dan Reeves signed two blacks, Kenny Washington and Woody Strode. They were former teammates of Jackie Robinson in the late 1930s at the University of California, Los Angeles. In a 1939 national survey of 1,600 college football players, Washington had been the only player who was cited for all-American by every player he competed against. By 1946 he had had a knee operation and, although he played well for several seasons in the NFL, he never approached his collegiate status. Strode, thirty-one years of age as a rookie, played two years before moving into the acting business both in professional wrestling and in Hollywood. In addition to Washington and Strode in the NFL, the All-American Football Conference began competition its first year with blacks on one of its teams. The Cleveland Browns under coach Paul Brown signed Bill Willis, a lineman from Ohio State, and Marion Motley of Nevada. Willis was an all-pro guard 7 of his 8 seasons while fullback Motley, often compared with the great Jim Brown, was the second black, following Emlen Tunnell, to make the Pro Football Hall of Fame after eight years of competition.[36]

Following the desegregation in professional baseball and football, other sports soon broke the color line. The National Basketball Association admitted blacks for the first time in 1950. Chuck Cooper of Duquesne played for the Boston Celtics and Nat "Sweetwater" Clifton of the Harlem Globetrotters, an all-black team, signed with the New York Knicks. The year 1950 saw Althea Gibson being allowed to compete at Forest Hills in the United States tennis championships breaking the whites only custom in this traditionally upper class sport. The year before the American Bowling Congress had opened its lanes to blacks. Emmett Ashford, the first black to umpire in major league baseball in 1966, first entered white baseball as an official in 1951 in the Southwest International League. The following year organized hockey saw its first black performer in America, Art Dorrington of the Johnstown Jets in Pennsylvania. Barriers in the first few years after Jackie Robinson entered baseball were slowly being pushed aside, but it was a painful process. To be accepted as a player was obviously less difficult than to be chosen to lead a team as coach or manager. In basektball, the sport eventually dominated by blacks, the first black head coach was John McLendon of the Cleveland Pipers of the American Basketball Association in 1961. The ABA eventually merged with the National Basketball Association which hired its first black coach in 1966, Bill Russell of the world champion Boston Celtics. Baseball hired its first black manager, Frank Robinson of the Cleveland Indians, in 1975, more than a century after the first major league was formed. Professional football, by the nation's bicentennial, had only one black coach since Fritz Pollard coached in the fledgling National Football League in the 1920s. He was Willie Wood, former Green Bay Packer, who headed the Philadelphia entry in the World Football League, a league which folded quickly because it was financially destitute.[37]

Golf could well symbolize the difficulty in desegregating sport in America. The United States Open Golf Tournament was only three years old in 1896 when John Shippen, son of an Indian mother and Negro father, competed at Shinnecock Hills, Long Island. He competed for several years, but blacks were eventually excluded. In 1926, blacks organized their own tournament, and it was out of this competition that the United Golfers Association for blacks was formed two years later. By the 1930s, there were about 50,000 black golfers out of 12 million blacks living in the United States. In the whole nation there were only about 20 private golf courses for blacks. The Professional Golfers Association had written into its constitution a Caucasian-only clause, and this effectively kept blacks out of important golf tournaments. When some tournaments co-sponsored with the PGA were opened to blacks in the 1950s, Charlie Sifford first became known to a wide audience. As many of the tournaments were held in the south, it was more difficult for golfers to succeed in this sport than in others. For instance, the city of Atlanta did not desegregate its golf courses until a Supreme Court decision forced it to do so in the mid-1950s. Charlie Sifford first played in the southern Greensboro Open in 1960, but he was harrassed so intensely by a small group of whites who threw beer cans, shouted, and jumped around that his game broke down. The Masters Tournament in Augusta, Georgia, claimed to be the most prestigious tournament in America, only invited a black, Lee Elder, to participate for the first time in 1974. In golf, one of the most expensive of the popular sports, it has been extremely difficult for blacks to make important contributions.[38]

Sports in American colleges reflected the trying athletic scene which professional sports were experiencing in the period after World War II. Two incidents from the 1950s give a graphic view of the difficulties. In the midwest, Drake University of Des Moines, Iowa, had an outstanding football team led by Johnny Bright, its black quarterback and nation's leading ground gainer for the third year in 1951. When Drake played Oklahoma A & M, there were rumors of betting pools on when the Aggies would injure and remove Bright from the game. On the first play of the game Bright handed the ball off, and while far removed from the action and from the officials' eyes, the A & M defensive tackle hit him on the jaw with a forearm blow with so much force that the attacker's feet were a foot off the ground at impact. Bright's jaw was broken. Despite this he threw a 60 yard touchdown pass on the next play. Soon Drake got possession of the ball again, and the same tackle once more hit him on his blind side and well away from the play. This time Bright was taken from the field. Pictures

Blatant racism is shown against Drake's Johnny Bright as he is slugged by an Oklahoma A & M player in 1951. (Copyright 1951, courtesy of Des Moines Register and Tribune Company.)

clearly show the assault. That Drake broke relations with Oklahoma A & M is of less historical importance than the symbolism of the act.[39]

In the south in the 1950s the Drake scene was nearly impossible because the southern colleges, which had no blacks, would sign

"Caucausian only" contracts if they desired to compete with northern institutions during the regular season. Georgia Tech and the University of Pittsburgh were chosen to play in the 1956 post-season Sugar Bowl football game on New Year's Day in New Orleans. The Governor of Georgia, Marvin Griffin, discovered that Pittsburgh had a second string black fullback, and he wrote the State Board of Regents in Georgia asking that it vote to forbid Georgia Tech from playing the game. It is significant that less than two years before, the United States Supreme Court ruled that segregation in schools was illegal. The 1954, Brown vs. Board of Education decision was a landmark in the push for civil rights in America. The white controlled south, though, was fighting a last ditch effort to keep blacks from achieving racial equality through its segregation policies. Governor Griffin's involvement in the Georgia Tech-Pittsburgh game was a clarion call to the racial bigotry which then existed. Griffin trumpeted:

> The South stands at Armageddon. The battle is joined. There is no more difference in compromising the integrity of race on the playing field than in doing so in the classroom. One break in the dyke and the relentless seas will rush in and destroy us.

The fact that Georgia Tech had played Notre Dame which had blacks in 1953 seemed unimportant at the time. Georgia Tech students picketed the Governor and paraded through Atlanta shouting, "We'll play who we want." The Georgia Tech president stood firm on the game. "I'm 60 years old, and I have never broken a contract," he said. "I'm not going to break one now." Finally the Georgia Board of Regents voted to allow the game, but future games against teams with blacks were to be prohibited. The game went on. Georgia Tech won, 7-0, after it scored following a disputed interference call on Bobby Grier, the black who created the furor.

The repercussion from the backlash of the segregationists was felt throughout the south. In several months Louisiana voted to prohibit Negroes and Caucasians from competing in athletic contests anywhere in the state. Said the field secretary of the National Association for the Advancement of Colored People: "Hitler was criticized for his unsportsmanlike attitude toward colored athletes during the 1936 Olympics, but if the 1956 Olympics were to be held right here, colored athletes could not even compete."[41] Blacks felt this backlash for the remainder of the 1950s and through the next decade.

The 1960s, for black amateur and professional athletes, were crucial years as they were in the civil rights movement. What activist W. E. B. DuBois stated in the early twentieth century appeared true a half century later: "The problem of the twentieth century is the problem of the Color Line." The resolution of problems between blacks and whites was intensified as the nation fought a war in Southeast Asia that was neither declared nor clearly rationalized. The turmoil of war in Vietnam and the civil rights movement during the same decade affected the direction of sport. Blacks began to question more subtle discriminitory practices as the move toward integration took place. They asked: Why were black athletes treated differently than white athletes? Why did predominately white colleges only give athletic grants-in-aids to star blacks so that blacks were seldom occupying second string positions on teams? Why were blacks recruited in colleges if they were not expected to graduate? Why were off-season jobs obtained primarily by whites? Why were athletes accepted rather equally on the playing field but rejected in the clubs and fraternities? Why were most black professional athletes rejected for lucrative product endorsements for television and the press? Why were black players of caliber equal to whites paid less? Possibly most important in sport itself was the question: Why were quota systems and player position discriminations allowed to exist?

Looking at the two dominating professional sports of the twentieth century, football and baseball, it is evident that though desegregation had taken place, integration was far from achieved. After Robinson's entry into baseball, there was an unwritten 50 percent color line rule for several years that no team would have five blacks on the field at any one time. This was broken in 1954 when the Brooklyn Dodgers opened a game with Jackie Robinson, Roy Campanella, Junior Gilliam, Don Newcombe, and Sandy Amoros in the line-up.[42] In football as in baseball there was clear evidence that blacks were not generally chosen to play in central positions on teams. In baseball this meant that peripheral positions such as the outfield and the outside positions of the infield, third and first base, had many more blacks than did the central positions of catcher, pitcher, second base, and shortstop. In football blacks also occupied the peripheral positions, generally being excluded from the central positions of quarterback, center, and guards on offense and linebacker on defense. There may have been several explanations for this, but the most logical one was that white management, through subtle discrimination, decided that whites should be in control of the central, thinking positions; that blacks could play in the peripheral, reaction positions.[43]

Even less obvious than the question of the centrality of player position was the discrimination against the black sub-star player. In baseball this was most easily discerned through the massive amount of statistics recorded in the "national pastime." There is little question in the first generation of blacks in major league baseball that the black player, to be treated equally, had to be better than the white player. For the first quarter century following desegregation in baseball, blacks consistently had batting averages about 20 percentage points higher than had whites and about 40 percentage points higher in slugging averages, which take into account extra-base hits. In addition they consistently hit more home runs, stole more than double the bases, and the pitchers had a higher winning percentage and lower earned run averages than did whites. This subtle discrimination can be explained by noting that fewer black sub-star players were on major league teams so that the star players brought up the averages well above the white players.[44]

Some discrimination was not subtle or hidden; it was obvious and blatant. The best example, perhaps, was that concerning the heavyweight champion of the world, Muhammad Ali (previously known as Cassius Clay). Ali, as Cassius Clay, won the Olympic light-heavyweight championship in 1960. That was the year the United States started committing troops to Vietnam. Four years later, at age twenty-two, Ali fought and won the heavyweight championship of the world by beating Sonny Liston. Only a month before, Ali had failed the Army induction test. Two years and several championship fights later, Ali was reclassified 1-A by his draft board. Ali said: "I ain't got no quarrels with them Viet Congs," and claimed conscientious objector status because of his Black Muslim religious beliefs. The Justice Department hearing officer agreed with Ali, but the Justice Department asked his draft board to turn it down. The draft board rejected Ali's pleas. When he was called to be inducted into the Army, he challenged the ruling and refused to serve. Almost immediately and well before he was brought to trial, the New York State Athletic Commission stripped Ali of his title, essentially convicting him and taking away his livelihood. Later Ali was convicted of draft evasion which was eventually appealed to the the United States Supreme Court. He affirmed, at one point, the beliefs similar to those held by Paul Robeson a generation before. "You want me to do what white man says," testified Ali, "and go fight a war against some people I don't know nothing about, get some freedom for some other people when my own people can't get theirs here? Every day they die in Vietnam for nothing, I might as well die right here for something." For over three years Ali challenged the decision. In the early summer of 1971, the Supreme Court threw out the conviction in a unanimous decision stating that the Justice Department had misled the draft board.[45]

Before the case was finally settled in 1971, Ali was again allowed to box. After winning two comeback bouts, he was given a chance to regain his title from the new champion Joe Frazier. In a classic New York Madison Square Garden fight with ringside seats selling for $150 and scalped for $1,000, Frazier won a 15 round decision. Within a day the South Carolina legislature invited Frazier, the less vocal black fighter, to address its body—a compliment it undoubtedly would not have offered to Ali even if he had been a South Carolina native. Said Ali: "We ain't through yet." And he was not. Three years later at the age of thirty-two years, he knocked out unbeaten George Foreman at dawn in Kinshasa, Zaire—the first championship heavyweight boxing match held in Africa. More than a decade had elapsed since Ali had claimed: "I am the greatest" and coined his slogan, "Float like a butterfly, sting like a bee." In those ten years the Vietnam war had raged and was terminated, and the civil rights battles had been fought. The country was at peace. Muhammad Ali regained the title which had been unjustly taken from him. It appeared that many who had been threatened by the presence of Ali in a prominent position in the 1960s felt in the mid-1970s that his victory was justice for the wrongs which society had done to him the decade before. Fifty years before, Jack Dempsey had been highly criticized for not serving in World War I and was brought to trial for draft evasion. He, too, was cleared of the charge. Ali as champion never declined to fight whites though Dempsey had refused to be challenged by a black.[46]

Ali, unlike most superior athletes, was on the cutting edge of social change. Those who have the prominence to actuate change generally do not—they have too much at stake, socially and economically, to venture forth. Ali did so, and while he created much hatred in the process, he won certain victories in the battle for civil rights and prominence for himself as probably the best known athlete in the world in the 1970s. Others who had blatantly tried to challenge the racial and economic system had not been as successful. For example, Curt Flood fought the reserve clause in baseball. While Ali was challenging his draft status and his right to box, Curt Flood, the star black center fielder for the St. Louis Cardinals, was carrying out a fight to challenge the anachronistic reserve clause which since 1879 prevented baseball players from offering their talent to the highest bidder in a free market economy. There was good reason why complete freedom-of-player movement in sport might create unequal talent pools and thus lead to failure of the competitive system. Yet, there was also logic in allowing athletes, like other working individuals, flexibility in their employment. When Flood was traded to the Philadelphia Phillies without his consent in 1969, he brought suit against major league baseball for violation of federal antitrust legislation (Sherman Antitrust Act of 1890) and for violation of civil rights statutes. Despite a $100,000 salary offer, Flood claimed the major leagues were imposing a form of peonage and involuntary servitude contrary to the Thirteenth Amendment which had freed the slaves after the Civil War. He claimed he was not "a piece of property to be bought and sold irrespective of my wishes." Flood demanded to be a free agent, to be able to bargain with any other major league team.

The Flood case was decided by the United States Supreme Court less than a year after Ali's judgment, but this time the petitioner lost. The Court in previous cases concerning the baseball reserve clause had found that baseball was exempt from antitrust action in a 1922 decision (Federal Baseball Club v. National League) and in a 1953 case (Toolson v. New York Yankees). The 1972 decision to exempt baseball from antitrust action reaffirmed its earlier decision even if, as the Court reasoned, "this ruling is unrealistic, inconsistent, or illogical." The Court knew that it made little sense to exempt baseball from monopoly legislation when other sports were not, but it reasoned that Congress, not the courts, should take the needed action to remedy the situation.[47] With this decision, Flood also lost his baseball career, for he found that after being out of baseball while he was challenging the reserve clause, he could no longer perform at a satisfactory level. His baseball career was ruined—the reserve clause remained, though it was to be challenged again under different circumstances.

Both Curt Flood and Muhammad Ali were spokesmen for black athletes who clearly expressed their rights to full participation in American life. That they spoke up and were listened to by a predominant white audience indicated that the integration process in sport was making some progress. That there was some reaction to them because of their race rather than solely because of their ideas indicated that although the movement from Jim Crow toward integration was in process, it certainly had not been achieved.

REFERENCES

1. *New York Times*, July 6, 1919, p. 17.

2. Justice J. Harlan, Dissenting Opinion, Plessy v. Ferguson, *United States Reports: The Supreme Court*, Vol. 163, No. 210, p. 562.

3. Robert Peterson, *Only the Ball Was White* (Englewood Cliffs, N.J.: Prentice-Hall, 1970), pp. 80-102; The Negro Baseball Leagues, *Black Sports*, II (May-June 1972), pp. 74-75; and A.S. "Doc" Young, *Negro Firsts in Sports* (Chicago: Johnson Publishing Co., 1963), pp. 54-68.

4. Peterson, *Only the Ball Was White*, pp. 116-144.

5. John Holway, Oscar Charleston: Scrappy Outfielder of Black Baseball Era, *Black Sports*, V (Mar. 1976), 18-19, 59; and Peterson, *Only the Ball Was White*, pp. 74-79, 131, 216-218, and 241-243.

6. George S. Schuyler, Keeping the Negro in His Place, *American Mercury*, XVII (Aug. 1929), pp. 469-475.

7. Milton Roberts, Charles Follis: First Black Pro Gridder Labored in Obscurity, *Black Sports*, V (Nov. 1975), pp. 42, 57-58; and "Henry McDonald, First Black Pro Football Player," *Black Sports*, II (Jan. 1973), pp. 38-39.

8. Harry A. March, *Pro Football, Its "Ups" and "Downs"* (Albany, N.Y.: J. B. Lyon Company, 1934), pp. 151-152.

9. Edwin B. Henderson, *The Black Athlete: Emergence and Arrival* (New York: Publishers Co., 1970), pp. 46-47, 197; Ocania Chalk, *Black College Sport* (New York:

Dodd & Mead, 1976), pp. 190-191; Fritz Pollard, Brown's Black All-American Pre-World War I Vintage, *Black Sports*, I (Nov. 1971), pp. 16-17, 20, 31, 53 and (Dec. 1971), pp. 60-63, 77, 80; and Fritz Pollard, Taped Interview with Marilyn Gingrich and Lenny Moore, June 1973, in Pollard's home in New York City, recording in Pattee Library Archives, Penn State University.

10. The Black Olympian, *Black Sports*, II (May-June 1972), pp. 58-62.

11. Stephen E. Ambrose, Jesse Owens Breaks 4 Track Records, *American History Illustrated*, I (June 1966), pp. 51-52.

12. *New York Times*, August 5, 1936, p. 25; and Young. *Negro Firsts in Sports*, pp. 104-105. Richard D. Mandell tells the same story in his *The Nazi Olympics* (New York: Macmillan, 1971), p. 228.

13. Henderson, *The Black Athlete*, p. 33.

14. Anthony O. Edmonds, *Joe Louis* (Grand Rapids, Mich.: William B. Eerdmans Publisher, 1973), p. 28.

15. Ibid., p. 64.

16. John Durant, *The Heavyweight Champions* (New York: Hastings House, 1976), pp. 99-102; and Edmonds, *Joe Louis*, pp. 37-42.

17. Gerald Aston, '*And a Credit to His Race*' (New York: Saturday Review Press, 1974), p. 138.

18. Industrial Report on Sports, *Newsweek*, XII (Dec. 26, 1938), 20; Aston, '*And a Credit to His Race*,' p. 181; *New York Times* (June 23, 1938), pp. 1, 14; and Anthony O. Edmonds, The Second Louis-Schmeling Fight: Sport, Symbol and Culture, *Journal of Popular Culture*, VII (Summer 1973), pp. 42-50.

19. Sports, *Newsweek*, XII (Oct. 31, 1938), p. 32.

20. Jim Crow Tennis, *Time*, XXXIV (Aug. 28, 1939), pp. 41-42; and Ken Bentley, Jim McDaniel, *Black Sports*, III (Sept. 1973), pp. 10-11.

21. Coach L. J. Leitl, Platteville, letter to President A. M. Royce, Platteville, Aug. 21, 1934, *Platteville Presidential Correspondence*, unprocessed material, Box 5, Faculty, 1934-35, State Historical Society of Wisconsin Archives, Madison; and Milton R. Konitz, Legislation Guaranteeing Equality of Access to Places of Public Accommodations, *Annals of American Academy of Political and Social Science*, CCLXXV (May 1951), pp. 48-49.

22. See the Mitchell Case regarding equal accommodations on railroads in Negroes and Pullmans, *Commonweal*, XXXIV (May 9, 1941), pp. 51-52; and No More Jim Crow? *Time*, XXXVII (May 12, 1941), pp. 15-16.

23. President's Order Against Discrimination, *Monthly Labor Review*, LIII (Aug. 1941), 398; Lester B. Granger, Barriers to Negro War Employment, *Annals of the American Academy of Political and Social Science*, CCXXIII (Sept. 1942), pp. 72-80; Charles S. Johnson, The Negro, *American Journal of Sociology*, XLVII (May 1942), pp. 854-864; Negroes Open Campaign Against 'Jim Crow,' *Christian Century*, LIX (June 24, 1942), p. 797; and Walter White, What the Negro Thinks of the Army, *Annals of the American Academy of Political and Social Science*, CCXXIII (Sept. 1942), pp. 67-71.

24. Lucile B. Milner, Jim Crow in the Army, *New Republic*, CVIII (Mar. 13, 1944), p. 339.

25. Dwight MacDonald, Novel Case of Winfred Lynn, *Nation*, CLVI (Feb. 20, 1943), pp. 268-270.

26. Edmonds, *Joe Louis*, pp. 85-86; 99-100.

27. *Daily Worker*, May 26, 1942, p. 8.

28. Ibid.

29. Negroes and Baseball, *Newsweek*, XX (Aug. 10, 1942), pp. 58-59.

30. *New York Times*, May 10, 1947, p. 16; Sermon to St. Louis Baseball Players, *Nation*, CLXIV (May 17, 1947), p. 559; Rookie of the Year, *Time*, L (Sept. 22, 1947), pp. 70-76; Jackie Robinson, *I Never Had It Made* (New York: G. P. Putnam's Sons, 1972), pp. 66-83; and Milton J. Shapiro, *Jackie Robinson of the Brooklyn Dodgers* (New York: Julian Messner, 1966), pp. 94-108.

31. Pastors Support Robeson's Rights, *Christian Century*, LXIV (May 14, 1947), p. 631.

32. *New York Times*, Apr. 21, 1949, p. 6.

33. Ibid., July 9, 1949, p. 8; and Robinson, *I Never Had It Made*, pp. 94-98.

34. Paul Robeson, *Here I Stand* (London: Dennis Dobson, 1958), pp. 71-81; and Harold D. Weaver, Jr., Paul Robeson: Beleagured Leader, *Black Scholar*, V (Dec. 1973-Jan. 1974), pp. 23-32.

35. Ira De A. Reid, Forward to Racial Desegregation and Integration, *Annals of the American Academy of Political and Social Science*, (Mar. 1956), pp. ix-x.

36. Henderson, *The Black Athlete*, pp. 49, 210-211; Young, *Negro Firsts in Sports*, pp. 145-147; David S. Neft, et al., *The Sports Encyclopedia: Pro Football* (New York: Grossett & Dunlap, 1974), pp. 84, 105, 210, 213; and Ronald L. Mendell and Timothy B. Phares, *Who's Who in Football* (New Rochelle, N.Y.: Arlington House, 1974), pp. 238, 364, 375-376.

37. Joann Stevens, The Man: John McClendon, *Black Sports*, V (Mar. 1976), pp. 38-40; Young, *Negro Firsts in Sports*, passim; Henderson *The Black Athlete*, passim; and Larry Fox, *Illustrated History of Basektball* (New York: Grosset & Dunlap, 1974), pp. 161-162.

38. Guil Jones, Past Greats, *Black Sports*, III (July 1973), pp. 64-65; Negro Open, *Time*, XXXII (Sept. 12, 1938), pp. 35-36; Dick Edwards, 19 Years Is a Long Time to Be in the Rough, *Black Sports*, III (July 1973), pp. 32-35; A. S. Young, The Black Athlete in the Golden Age of Sports, *Ebony*, XXIV (June 1969), pp. 114-124; Is Golf Necessary? *Time*, LXVII (Jan. 2, 1956), pp. 14-15; and *New York Times*, Apr. 15, 1974, p. 44.

39. Caught by the Camera, *Life*, XXXI (Nov. 5, 1951), pp. 121-124; *New York Times*, Oct. 22, 1951, p. 28 and Oct. 25, 1951, p. 40.

40. Armegeddon To Go, *Time*, LXVI (Dec. 12, 1955), p. 24; James P. Wesberry, Football Spoils Georgia Rumpus, *Christian Century*, LXXII (Dec. 21, 1955), pp. 1504-1505; Rebels at Georgia Tech, *Newsweek*, XLVI (Dec. 12, 1955), p. 104; When Symbols Clash, *Commonweal*, LXIII (Dec. 16, 1955), p. 274; and *New York Times*, Jan. 3, 1956, p. 33.

41. Segregation Snafu in Louisiana, *Newsweek*, XLVIII (July 30, 1956), pp. 79-80.

42. John Lardner, The Old Emancipator, *Newsweek*, XLVII (Apr. 9, 1956), p. 84. On September 1, 1971, the Pittsburgh Pirates fielded an all-black team.

43. John W. Loy, Jr. and Joseph F. McElvogue, Racial Segregation in American Sport, *International Review of Sport Sociology*, V (1970), pp. 5-23.

44. Aaron Rosenblatt, Negroes in Baseball: The Failure of Success, *Transaction Magazine*, IV (Sept. 1967), pp. 51-53; David S. Neft, et al., The Black, Latin, White Report, *The Sports Encyclopedia: Baseball* (New York: Grossett & Dunlap, 1974), pp. 477-478; and Gerald W. Scully, Discrimination: The Case of Baseball, in Roger G. Noll (ed.), *Government and the Sports Business* (Washington, D.C.: The Brookings Institution, 1974), pp. 221-273.

45. Bert Sugar, An Ali-gorical Tale, *Black Sports*, III (July 1973), pp. 14-15; and *New York Times*, Jan. 12, 1971, p. 40; June 29, 1971, p. 1; and July 1, 1971, p. 68.

46. *New York Times*, Jan. 27, 1971, p. 22; Mar. 9, 1971, p. 29; Mar. 10, 1971, p. 49; and Oct. 30, 1974, p. 1; Through the Years with Ali, *Sports Illustrated*, XLV (Dec. 20-27, 1976), pp. 104-120; and Nat Fleischer, *Jack Dempsey* (New Rochelle, N.Y.: Arlington House, 1972), pp. 85-88.

47. Flood v. Kuhn, 407 U.S. 258, *Supreme Court Reporter*, 405-408 U.S., October Term, 1971, June 19, 1972, pp. 2099-2119; and Curt Flood, My Rebellion, *Sports Illustrated*, XXXIV (Feb. 1, 1971), pp. 24-29.

CHAPTER 22

The Amateur Spirit and the Olympic Games Experiment

The French Baron, Pierre de Coubertin (1863-1937), founder of the modern Olympic games, never promised that watching and participating in the games would guarantee that we would all love one another. He was convinced, however, that these quadrennial sport festivals lifted the level of physical fitness for hundreds of thousands, and breathed out an atmosphere of chivalry, courage, beauty, and a mutual respect for and between young men and women from all over the world. "Games for all nations" was his creed. "I believe in the future of mankind," he said in the same year of his death. The pageantry of the Olympic Games, its symbolisms, even mystical meanings, so often the target of some journalists, were all Coubertin's efforts to build into these games a Greek dignity and intensity, a medieval chivalric idealism, and a modern sense of pride and passion. He succeeded in this to an astonishing degree, despite powerful intrusions from ultra nationalists and the money crises of Olympic sites construction. Coubertin was old-fashioned enough to believe that a sense of personal destiny, individual toughness combined with dignity, might remain with young people who trained for and participated in the Olympic Games. The great experiment began on Easter Sunday, 1896, appropriately, in Athens, Greece—site of the ancient games and spiritual origin of sport as it is understood in the western world. Speaking at the Athenian Parnasse Society, Baron de Coubertin paid tribute to both the ancient Greeks as creators of the ideal formula for sport, and to nineteenth-century Englishmen for having spread the doctrine of honorable and competitive sport throughout the western world.[1]

Pierre de Coubertin, seated on left, with the 1896 International Olympic Committee.

Athens, Greece 1896

The modest first games were accepted with unvarnished enthusiasm by tens of thousands of Greeks. The rest of the world was only vaguely aware of its importance. American athletes did well; a dozen more nations sent representatives. German gymnasts and the Greek marathon runner Spiridon Loues gained a measure of sport immortality. A modern sporting impulse had begun and Coubertin prayed that a kind of redemptive cosmopolitanism might characterize his Olympic games. American hurdler Thomas P. Curtis won a gold medal and was invited to a reception at the home of Madame Heinrich Schliemann, wife of the famed archaeologist. A picnic followed where the two Greek·monarchs, Constantine and George, insisted on learning the mysteries of baseball. Nothing would do except a demonstration and Tom Curtis blasted an orange into the bosom of Constantine's best court uniform. "He was a good sport," recalled Curtis, "and joined in the somewhat subdued laughter, but I think the Americanization of Greece ended right there."[2]

Paris, France 1900

The second games of the modern era were not so successful. Baron de Coubertin fretted about his countrymen's lack of enthusiasm for athletics despite a widespread athletic renaissance and a new millennial European air of cosmopolitanism. He even wrote Harvard University president, Charles Eliot, asking for the school to send its best athletes to Paris. "The only thing we shall look for," entreated the Baron, "will be good sport and first class athletes—also, of course, pure amateurs."[3] The Paris World's Fair took away most of the glitter from the tangential and poorly organized sporting event. Coubertin was hurt, but still strongly convinced that international sport, only in its infancy, would grow to startling proportions. All quality was not lost, however. The 200 meter freestyle was won by Frederick C. V. Lane, in 2:25.2—exactly thirteen seconds faster than the world's record. The sober Olympic historian, Erich Kamper, notes that "the swimming events . . . were held in the River Seine and swum with the current, which explains the amazingly good times."[4]

St. Louis, U.S.A. 1904

Another world's fair resulted in a repetitious overshadowing of the Olympic Games' future. North Americans won far too many medals, proving that these third games were not representative of the world's best athletes. The Baron and his ten-year-old International Olympic Committee were alarmed and feared that the passage of four more years would see a further erosion of Olympic interest. An "emergency" Olympics back in friendly Athens was needed. The ever-enthusiastic Greeks supported a 1906 games; North American and European athletes came to the aid of the movement, and the concept of sport internationalism was saved. Coubertin, the Anglophile, had praised both the Greek origins of sport as well as the modern English "Muscular Christian" renaissance; "sport and physical education," he said, "have proven beyond doubt their great importance as a powerful national force."[5] Even in these tremulous, early days of the modern Olympics, the I.O.C. demanded that it and not any person, city or nation was responsible for the games. President of the United States, Theodore Roosevelt, for one, was furious.[6]

London, England 1908

A thousand-year-old love affair with outdoor sports made the English people nearly perfect hosts for the fourth official Olympic games. American aggressiveness did chafe the English athletes and officials, but an energetic, well-conceived games prompted Coubertin to hypothesize that his version of international sport, the kind where money was not the prime motive, was capable of cutting through the strong but still artificial barriers of race, creed, and ultra-nationalism. An irreverently perceptive criticism of Coubertin's committee came from the American sportsman, Caspar Whitney, who said that the I.O.C. was ill-equipped to handle the big operation of an Olympic games. They were rich dilettantes—amateurs trying to do a job requiring professional sports administrators. They were inexperienced men, he said, "chosen quite after the fashion that obtains in nominating patronesses to smart garden parties. . . ."[7]

Stockholm, Sweden 1912

Small and large arguments proved the fragility and humanness of the Olympic games. They failed to dim the obvious fact that the fifth games signaled the true beginning of "bigtime" international athletics. Technological and scientific advancement, still only in their infancy, heralded a new era in athletic competitions. The struggle in the traditional pentathlon, in the newly-created military pentathlon (a Coubertin creation), and the the decathlon was noteworthy. Three Americans emerged into the finals—Avery Brundage, George S. Patton . . . and Jim Thorpe! Coubertin looked about and commented that "the human body and human spirit are inseparable; I have worked hard for a universal vehicle to make this obvious to all the world."

Antwerp, Belgium 1920

Pierre de Coubertin was profoundly disturbed by World War I, and attempted to join the French army in 1914. At age fifty-one, he was rejected. The scheduled Berlin games of 1916 were cancelled, although the chronologic classification of 1916-1920 was unassailable and labeled, "The Sixth Olympiad." Brave and foolhardy efforts culminated in the games of the Seventh Olympiad in war-ravaged Antwerp. Things worked out, although imperfectly. Coubertin was getting repetitious as he addressed the King of Belgium and guests at an August 17th banquet—pleading with them to view the Olympic games and its sport philosophy of "Olympism" with objectivity, with a sense and hope for universal peace, progress, and human service. The Olympic experiment, imperfect as always, made a brave effort to shake off the years of war. Forty thousand spectators saw the angry Czech soccer team, trailing Belgium 2-0, walk off the field after forty minutes, giving victory to the home team. Young and talented athletes made their mark in the post-war world. The French engineer-inventor, Edouard Berlin, successfully transmitted a photographic image by telephone from Antwerp to Paris. The historic first picture was that of the Swedish women's Olympic team.[8]

Paris, France 1924

Nothing stands still in sport. Paavo Nurmi of Finland startled Parisians and the world with his relentless distance running. Paris was broiling in daily temperatures over 100° F. Tempers flared, and the London *Times* cried, "No more Olympic Games." The aging Coubertin, quite correctly replied that it is precisely at times of international tension, that world physical education and well-organized sport can play an essential role in the healing process. French intellectuals, rarely interested in sport, mused on their nation's futile but brave efforts in this direction. "Something has changed," one of them said. "We take pride in the manliness of our broad-shouldered lads. Even more so, forty-year-olds are running even with autobuses!"[9]

Amsterdam, Holland 1928

The ancient Greek custom of combining art, music, and cultural events in harmony with athletic competition was continued in 1928. Larger numbers of women entered and competed in the games, much to the disgust of the retired Olympic president, Pierre de Coubertin. He was, after all, a Victorian-Edwardian child of his times. As was his custom, Coubertin returned to his theme that the Olympic movement, bathed in redolent idealism, its origins in Periclean Greece,

Paavo Nurmi of Finland, in the middle, continued to dominate the distance running at the 1928 Amsterdam games.

chivalric Christianity, and robustly honorable English sport, could move the world.[10] Responsible critics of the Olympic games mounted their guns, but Douglas MacArthur, American Olympic Committee president, could not be counted among them. His 1928 report to the American people called the nation's athletic heritage "talismanic." If called upon to indicate his country's most characteristic element, he said, "my finger would unerringly point to our athletic escutcheon."[11]

Los Angeles, U.S.A. 1932

Journalist Bill Henry was director of the Games of the Tenth Olympiad. The world was deep in a depression. Henry drastically reduced prices and daily filled the Colosseum of 100,000 seats. The sun warmed the city for twenty days, and Olympic records tumbled in wholesale lots. Coubertin didn't make the trip from his Olympic headquarters in Lausanne, Switzerland, but he reminded the world's youth, once again, that "the main issue in life is not the victory but the fight; the essential thing is not to have won but to have fought well." President of the United States, Herbert Hoover, unable to be in Los Angeles, ate bread flown in from the Olympic training table. Vice-president Curtis proclaimed the opening of the games, and the brilliant college president, Robert Gordon Sproul, reminded the huge audience that:

> Those [ancient] games were not only physical contests. They were a solemn reunion in Greek energy, the totality of human activity, physical, mental and spiritual. . . . May these games upon which we are about to embark, like their ancient pattern, help the life of men to higher physical, spiritual, and moral values. . . . May they promote the love of play, the reciprocity of good will, the solvent of sportsmanship in which shall be washed away the immemorial feuds of mankind that now obscure the realizable ideal of "Peace on earth, good will toward men."[12]

Berlin, Germany 1936

The International Olympic Committee fought a bitter, partially successful, and hidden struggle with Adolf Hitler for ideological control of the 1936 games. German physical culture had reached a high point. These games, sometimes called "The Nazi Olympics," sometimes called "The Jesse Owens Olympics," were the last to be staged for many years. The games of the 12th and 13th Olympiads were never held, as all mankind was plunged into war. Baron de Coubertin was spared that horror, for he died in September of 1937. His sporting philosophy of "Olympism," incorporated a kind of religious reverence for honest athletics, a kind of aristocracy of effort available to all mankind. It was all very romantic, somehow unreal—and the old man knew it. He clung to his principle of nonprofessional sport to the end. Administrative control of the Olympic movement from 1925 to 1942 was directed by Belgium's Count Baillet-Latour, the mantle picked up by Sweden's J. S. Edstrom from 1946-1952. During the crisis years, 1938-1948, the single greatest ideological influence for Olympic sport was the towering figure of the German physical educator, Carl Diem (1882-1962). His jingoist-tinged *The Olympic Idea in the New Europe* was decidedly not typical of Dr. Diem. Rather, his three volume *Olympische Flamme*, also published during the war, is a monumental tribute to mankind's universal preoccupation with the joy of sport. During the deepest violence of World War II, Diem tried to remind the world that it was also the fiftieth anniversary of the International Olympic Committee. Its spiritual leader will always be Coubertin, he said—a man ahead of his time in his comprehension that nonprofessional sport contains a physical, aesthetic, and even metaphysical dimension.[13]

London, England 1948

An austere, dignified, rain-drenched Olympics—"a pleasurable rather than grandiose affair"—marked the first post-war games. New heroes and heroines emerged and would begin anew the old tradition, so well expressed by Edstrom, who believed that "the Olympic Games cannot enforce peace in the world . . . but they give the opportunity . . . to find out that all men on earth are brothers." Arthur Daley of *The New York Times* was for the elimination of yachting, canoeing, shooting, equestrian events, field hockey, and the entire winter games. Veteran Olympic watcher, Ronald Stead, strongly supported the entire Olympic concept, but rejected run-away growth of the games, and suggested they be "shorn of spectacular irrelevancies, rescued from under cover exploitation, restored to simplicity and integrity."[14] Both men were flying in the face of the Olympic direction from that day to the present.

Helsinki, Finland 1952

Avery Brundage, new leader of the movement called the Helsinki games "the perfect Olympics"—just the right size, perfectly organized, and almost completely free of disharmony. The "Czechoslovakian Train," Emil Zatopek, won gold medals in the 5,000 and 10,000 meter runs plus triumphing in the marathon. A new era in scientific and ruthlessly tough training programs—in all sports—had begun. Bob Mathias won his second consecutive decathlon gold medal, Sammy Lee proved his platform diving domination, and pound-for-pound, Tommy Kono was the world's greatest weightlifter. Marjorie Jackson of Australia, Pat McCormick of the U.S.A., and a host of brilliant female athletes complemented the men with

Avery Brundage, president of the IOC, was an Olympic idealist.

their own brand of skill and tenacity. Brundage loved the Olympic games, and as he left the Olympic stadium, he reminded those who would listen, "This dream is far more important than winning a race. Whatever happens in the world, the dream does not wholly die."[15]

Melbourne, Australia 1956

The Australian friendliness and love of sport were unbounded. Organizational difficulties were overcome, good weather and astonishing performances were the order of the day. Avery Brundage preached his litany that a world of ideological difference lay between the professional sports entertainer and the Olympic amateur athlete. And yet enormous pressure was mounting to modify the Olympic rules, if only minutely. On the eve of the November games, the International Olympic Committee agreed to eliminate from the athlete's pledge that he or she would "remain an amateur"—even after the games. Another note of realism was struck by Gaston Meyer, editor of *L'Equipe*, who warned of the future consequences of runaway Olympic growth.

Rome, Italy 1960

Olympic athlete, former world-record holder, and journalist, Chris Chataway, brought a refreshing balance to the value of the Olympic games. There is, undoubtedly, he said, "a sort of freemasonry among the competitors,"—a common bond of mutual understanding similar to that existing between international scientists. The athletes gain more from the experience than anyone else. Are the Olympics a force for good or ill? He answered his own question with the irreverent comment that "they are not much of a force at all. They are worth while for what they are—the best sports meetings in the world."[16] A hot spell reminiscent of the 1924 Paris Olympics drove most affluent Italians to the shore, leaving Olympic stadia to foreign visitors. The spectre of Olympic "gigantism" emerged and was to grow alarmingly. Cities, provinces, whole national governments were now necessary to mobilize and coordinate these new games—a clear violation of the original Olympic spirit. The very success of the Olympic games magnified problems that had always existed. "The Olympic games are not to be a career," said Mr. Brundage; "they are incidental to a symmetrical and harmonious physical, mental and spiritual development."

Tokyo, Japan 1964

A half-billion dollars was spent by the meticulous and zealous Japanese. The pageantry and symbolism of the three-week Olympic ceremony was never more impressive as the mystical-minded Japanese seemed to catch the Olympic spirit. No one could catch Bob Hayes, however, as he stamped himself the fastest runner of the twentieth century. Peter Snell, Abebe Bikila, Gaston Roelants, Valerie Brumel, Wyomia Tyus, Vera Caslavska, and Dawn Fraser all won gold . . . and a measure of immortality. Athletes around the world were training hard for thirty hours a week; few were glamorously high salaried professional athletes in the American tradition; most were subsidized by the state or private business. The line between amateur and professional was still there, but became increasingly indistinct. Some like Doug Gardner declared the games should either be "open" to all, or very much restricted to that small group of unvarnished worshipers of amateurism. In a perceptive article titled, "Can it ever be a temple again?," he concluded that:

> If the I.O.C. wants a Temple, then they must take the first steps themselves by reducing the size and status of the Games so that none but the worshippers will wish to attend.[17]

Mexico City, Mexico 1968

In his own way, the old man, Avery Brundage continued his fight against gigantism, commercialism, and the intrusion of radical international politics. Although unprepared in a number of critical areas, the unvarnished friendliness of the Mexican people was more than compensation. Extraordinary advances in technology and technique plus mile-high thin atmosphere produced breath-taking results that prompted many to ask, "How long can mankind continue to break world's sport records?" Eighty-one-year-old Brundage reminded us that "the man who climbs a Matterhorn or who runs a four-minute mile does not expect to find a pot of gold when he arrives. He has not conquered nature; he has conquered himself." Indeed, it was as difficult as ever to emphasize that skill and valor are personal virtues and not tools of sovereign states. The trace of childishness about the philosophy of Olympism was, for some, the surest warrant for its continuance. The medical doctor, physical education-humanist, Ernst Jokl, urged an international audience to work for an Olympic peace—a dream, of course, "but like Heine, who once said: 'The thought precedes the deed, so as lightning precedes thunder.' "[18]

Munich, West Germany 1972

The city of Munich and the Bavarian state spent $640,000,000 on the greatest sport spectacle in the history of the world. It was too big, too expensive, and marked by violence. In many significant ways it was a great Olympic games; German thoroughness and love of sport was much admired and shone through it all. Lord Killanin succeeded Brundage that year. Both men recognized in their Olympic movement a revolt against modern materialism, an effort toward universal physical fitness, and a mystical kind of universal cosmopolitanism. Brundage looked to the past for the fruition of these gifts. The younger man, Killanin, looked forward, his hands bearing gifts—the one offering the purest kind of athletic altruism, the other promising massive financial subsidization for future aspiring Olympic athletes of the world.

Montreal, Canada 1976

Ironic as the statement may be, the Montreal Olympic Games of 1976 would have been an unqualified success had it not been for serious political intrusions. Olympic and world records for both men and women tumbled in greater profusion than ever before. Paid admissions to twenty-one sporting events were tabulated at 3,137,287. The Canadian organizing committee (COJO) did a magnificent job in copying many of the 1972 Munich innovations plus adding a distinct

French-Canadian flavor. Super-stars were legion. A significant portion of the world's population saw, during the brief period, July 17 through August 1, gold medalists, Nadia Comaneci, Bruce Jenner, Alberto Junatorena, Laasi Viren, Tatyana Kazankina, John Nabor, Kornelia Ender, Edwin Moses, Vasily Alexeyev, Klaus Dibiasi, Teofilo Stevenson, and a host of others. Protecting ABC-TV's 31 million dollar commitment was anchor-man, Jim McKay, who established an Olympic record of sorts, with 116 hours of broadcasting (not including nearly endless advertisement breaks for which ABC collected $72,000 per minute). The dignified and always impressive opening ceremonies were matched by perhaps the most colorful and spectacular Canadian-tinged closing ceremonies. In between, athletic drama of the highest order and political machinations of a different order proved again that the athletes and organizers are not gods, but men and women—all vulnerable as well as capable of great deeds.

In a complex web involving the I.O.C., COJO, the People's Republic of China, the Republic of China on Taiwan, and the Canadian government, it was finally decided not to allow Taiwan's participation in the Montreal games.[19] Slowly, but then in rapid succession, almost all African nations walked away from Montreal, heading home, refusing to participate if New Zealand was allowed to do so. Alleged racial policies by a New Zealand rugby football team were given as reasons. Thirty African nations and several hundred grim-faced athletes were recalled.[20] The double blow underscored the Olympic movement's vulnerability to political pressures, and a host of articles appeared predicting the rapid demise of the games.[21] These Olympic games, so unique and fragile as an international social experiment, are worth keeping. But only some fairly rapid and radical reforms will save them. The IOC has been deluged with suggestions, including those of the authors.

The Urgency of Olympic Reform

The future of the Olympics is uncertain; they may not last out the twentieth century. Some significant changes in the structure and management of the Olympic games are necessary if they are to become more pacific, more fiscally responsible, and with even greater sensitivity to the needs of youth. Greater stability in world governments will, of course, have a far greater positive effect on the Olympic movement than any combination of internal reforms. Theories and suggestions abound regarding Olympic change. Only two fairly well defined views will be mentioned here. Bill Bradley, Rhodes scholar, Olympic winner, and professional basketball player, believes the Olympics should be open to everyone. He is opposed to Olympic team sports, believes in a permanent Greek site with a two-month span rather than a two-week time period for the Olympic experience. Lastly:

> Everyone in the Olympics should get a participant's medal. Silver and bronze medals should be eliminated and the gold medal should go only to someone who breaks an Olympic record. Then an athlete would compete against a standard, not against another athlete or another country.[22]

The authors advocate a permanent Olympic city to be built in Switzerland or Greece. During its construction, previous Olympic sites should be used. More sports should be included over a thirty-day period. During the Olympic year, each participating nation would voluntarily contribute 1/100,000th of its gross national product (GNP). The playing of the national anthems at the games need not take place; all remaining ceremonies should be retained. The I.O.C. should accelerate its commitment to self-appraisal and select for membership, qualified men and women from wider social and economic backgrounds. A team of Olympic ambassadors should be assigned the on-going task of disseminating the philosophy of "Olympism." The recent by-laws to the I.O.C.'s Rule 26 need much wider implementation. Limited financial subsidization for the productive athletic life of qualified nonprofessionals is now legal. Sport federations, national olympic committees, state governments, and, especially in capitalist countries, private businesses may now help young men and women prepare for national and international athletic competitions. The olympic committee of the Soviet Union and the city of Moscow ready themselves for the 1980 Eurasian version of the modern Olympic games.

REFERENCES

1. Pierre de Coubertin, L'athletisme dans le monde moderne et les jeux olympiques, *Bulletin du comite international des jeux olympiques*, 2 (January, 1895), p. 4.

2. Thomas P. Curtis, High Hurdles and White Gloves, *The Atlantic Monthly*, 198 (December, 1956), p. 62.

3. Letter, Pierre de Coubertin to Charles Eliot, March 9, 1898, Harvard University Archives, Box 133, Folder 905, *Eliot Papers*.

4. Erich Kamper, *Encyclopedia of the Olympic Games* (New York: McGraw-Hill Book Co., 1972), footnote No. 158, p. 332.

5. Pierre de Coubertin, La force nationale du sport, *Revue des deux mondes*, 7 (February, 1902), p. 924.

6. See Roosevelt's speech in The Olympian Contests, *The New York Daily Tribune*, August 22, 1902, p. 14.

7. Caspar Whitney, The View-Point, *Outing*, 52 (September, 1908), p. 763.

8. A photograph sent by telephone, *The Independent*, 103 (September 18, 1920), p. 336.

9. Marcel Berger, Les sports. Coup d'oeil sur les jeux olympiques, *La Revue de France*, 4 (Juillet, 1924), p. 224.

10. See Coubertin's twelve page manuscript *Olympie* (Geneve: Imprimerie Burge, 1929).

11. Douglas MacArthur as quoted in *American Olympic Committee Report 1928* (New York: AOC, 1928), p. 6.

12. Robert Gordon Sproul, Dedicatory speech, Riverside, California *Press-Enterprise*, August 1, 1932. The full text of his speech is reproduced in *Olympic Review*, 66-67 (May-June, 1973), pp. 184-186.

13. Carl Diem, Pierre de Coubertin, *Olympic Review* (April, 1944), pp. 1-17.

14. Ronald Stead, A Spartan Touch . . . , *The Christian Science Monitor*, July 10, 1948, p. 9.

15. Avery Brundage as quoted in Footnote to the Olympics, *The New York Times*, August 16, 1952, p. 14.

16. Chris Chataway, An Olympian appraises the Olympics, *The New York Times Magazine Section*, October 4, 1959, p. 58.

17. Doug Gardner, Can it ever be a temple again?, *World Sports* (January, 1965), p. 5.

18. Ernst Jokl, Pax Olympica, *Proceedings*, First International Seminar on the history of physical education and sport, Wingate Institute, Israel, April 9-11, 1968, p. 19.

19. The IOC's position may be gleaned from Killanin's remarks in *The New York Times*, August 3, 1976, pp. 23, 25; Taiwan's adamant stand is discussed in an article China can be called anything, *The Pennsylvania Mirror*, July 9, 1976, p. 10; the Canadian government's official response to the furor is Olympics and Taiwan. Canadian Embassy Public Affairs Division, No. 4, July 22, 1976; the enigmatic mainland Chinese, not even members of the Olympic community of nations, exerted strong influence, but issued no official bulletins.

20. Aspects of this mysterious African pull-out may be found in Steve Cady, Black nations continue withdrawals, *The New York Times*, July 18, 1976, p. 1, Sports Section and Frank Deford, Dark genius of dissent, *Sports Illustrated*, 45 (July 26, 1976), p. 16.

21. For example, see Red Smith, Greeks had words for it, *The New York Times*, July 25, 1976, p. 3; Roscoe Drummond, The last Olympics? *The Christian Science Monitor*, July 28, 1976, p. 2; The Flickering Flame, and The Dying Flame, on editorial pages of *The New York Times*, July 17 and August 2, 1976.

22. Bill Bradley, Five ways to reform the Olympics, *The New York Times*, July 21, 1976, p. 31.

CHAPTER 23
Sport for All

No nation in the world can even remotely compare with the United States in its obsession for watching sporting events. Enormous national wealth, an ever-increasing amount of individual time free from work, and a long tradition of highly organized amateur and professional athletics account for this passive state. And yet there is substantial data to indicate that participatory sporting and recreational activities are presently competing for both purse and time. The majority of American people have already entered an era where millions of choices are being made between spending money and time on passive, spectator sport and the even larger commitment toward life-time, sport-for-all. In significant numbers, Americans are turning to fun activities, exotic sporting, recreational, and life-time physical activities. The tug between watching sports and participating in them will go on for a long time. Statistical evidences from Europe and the United States indicate that the participatory sport-for-all movement is growing more rapidly than the sedentary pastime of watching sport. It is entirely possible that within a generation the one will catch up with the other.

SPORT FOR ALL AS BIG BUSINESS

A careful survey by the A. C. Nielsen Company, a prominent market research firm, established the extraordinary popularity of the American sport-for-all movement. According to this survey (p. 415), swimming, bicycling, fishing and camping were favorite pastimes. Tennis has since moved into the top ten with well over 30 million "players"—each of whom spends an average of $250.00 per year.[1] Golf is rapidly moving up the list into fourteenth place. Back in 1969, *U. S. News and World Report*, reporting on the role of recreation, play,

Favorite American Pastimes

Total Popularity (Projected Estimate in Millions)

Swimming	107,191,000
Bicycling	65,613,000
Fishing	61,263,000
Camping	54,435,000
Bowling	38,218,000
Table Tennis	33,501,000
Pool and billiards	32,920,000
Boating (other than sailing)	32,629,000
Softball	26,362,000
Ice Skating	24,875,000

(Adapted from data in *The New York Times*, March 23, 1974)

and leisure, noted that affluent and leisured Americans have boomed it into an 83-billion-dollar enterprise—"the fastest-growing business in America."[2] In 1970, over 8 million bicycles sold for $300 million, 7 million people owned pleasure boats, $3 billion was spent on hunting and fishing equipment. Leisure authority, Max Kaplan, points out that the total expenditure for recreation by Americans is over one-fifth of our total consuming expenditures—a total of "well over $110 billion."[3] The leisure business reaches out and touches almost every single citizen. More Americans have more time on their hands and money to spend than ever before. Millions of dollars will be spent watching sports; billions will be spent in playing at sport, in the coming national involvement in life-time, sport for all.

THE FITNESS DIMENSION OF SPORT FOR ALL

Although the President's Council on Physical Fitness and Sport started during Dwight Eisenhower's administration and grew during the brief tenure of the physically vigorous John Kennedy, the massive concern with fitness during the decade of the sixties is a European phenomena. Switzerland has a well-organized fun and fitness course available to every citizen. Financed by the government and national insurance companies, Switzerland has 150 "parcourses"— each providing jogging, flexibility and strength exercises. The vest-pocket nation, highly-organized and in love with the out-of-doors, has found parcourse programs enormously appealing. A massive West German sport for all program called "Trimm trab-Trimm-trab" has evolved into a national campaign and affected the lives of millions.

Massive governmental programs of winter lifetime sports involvement have already become a tradition in Norway, Finland, Sweden, and the Netherlands. Even England, usually slow to move, has launched a nation-wide program that The Sports Council calls "Sport For All." Other nations, including the two Chinas, and the entire communist-socialist block of nations, have organized and well-publicized programs of lifetime sports, sport for all. The United States, so much more amorphous in its national political and ideological control has greater difficulty in convincing millions of Americans that The President's Council on Physical Fitness and Sports is correct in its slogan, "Physical fitness is beautiful, beautiful, beautiful." Author-athlete, Kenny Moore, is close to the mark with his observation that places like Finland and Sweden:

> are a very active culture beyond the top level of athletics, that there is a commitment to sports as something good for the people, as a means toward education. Here [USA] I get the feeling that sport is very vicarious, that it is a means of entertainment.[4]

Persistent good humor and an abundance of factual data from the medical profession, sport scientists, the physical education professionals, the media, and the business community, will probably alter America's uncertain attitudes toward physical fitness. In the vaguest sort of way, millions of Americans are becoming better informed, understanding what a classic scholar said over fifty years ago. "All our people," he said, "should emulate the physical fitness of Ulysses. We are no more protected from physical decadency by our Olympic games than were the Greeks by theirs."[5]

Mass participation in sport may become one of the most significant movements in the United States. Hiking, orienteering, climbing, cross-country skiing, the whole range of Eastern martial arts, all the racquet sports, swimming, weight-lifting, rowing and paddling, volleyball, and scores of other relatively vigorous activities are being savored by an ever-increasing number. The Boston Marathon with 2,000 fit runners, and the 6,000 men and women who race the San Francisco Bay-to-Breakers road race typify the largest group of fitness apostles—the runners and joggers. Although Archibald MacLeish was referring to football, he might well have included any vigorous sport in his reminder that a "precise sense of participation" is one of the many rewards for the daily retreats into physical reeducation.[6]

SPORT AND THE EXISTENTIAL-HUMANISTIC PREOCCUPATION

The awful truth that American competitive sport has frequently gone mad is countered by the intrinsic value of sport participation—a

Skiing is one of the mass participant sports.

turning away from the winning preoccupation to a point of view which sees sport as a three-letter word, "F-U-N." According to the new sport humanists, and in a seemingly contradictory, existential way, the reduction of winning's importance actually heightens the value of the individual sporting experience. This old-new attitude gained momentum in the 1960s and 1970s, adding hundreds of thousands of participants to a sporting cult that did not in the least consider the winning edge of great importance. Only a few, however, were willing to go as far as George Leonard's catchy, glittering generality, "Winning isn't everything. It's nothing." Competition, like a little salt, add zest to the game and to life, he noted, tempering his lead statement somewhat. When winning becomes the only thing, "it can lead only to eventual emptiness and anomie."[7] This existential-humanist disgust for the winning obsession created a new and less threatening environment, and large numbers joined the ranks of sport enthusiasts. For a short time, Jack Scott preached an anti-sports establishment, anti-win-at-all-costs litany. He gained instant fame during the late 60s and 70s. Personal confusion and frequent philosophical contradictions led to his rapid demise. Nonetheless, as Scott predicted, this new renaissance in athletic thought will strongly affect sport and school physical education for the remainder of the century.[8] Competition out-of-bounds is an obvious sickness; the play element must be fused with the serious competitive spirit to give the life-time, sport-for-all thrust a healthy and therefore more permanent cycle. Human development, both physical and spiritual, must be the goal of all sport competitors and participants. Joy and high emotion must co-mingle, and, as Central Michigan University's Charles Ping noted in quoting Nietzsche, man must experience "the ideal of truly exuberant, alive and world affirming man." "The nurturing of the expressive sense is one of the key justifications of an athletic program."[9]

METAPHYSICAL DIMENSIONS OF SPORT

More and more, there is fuller realization of sport's physical, recreational, intellectual, and even spiritual dimensions. Obviously, sport continues to touch the lives of millions, and newer battalions of Americans now see opportunities for lifelong involvement in sporting, recreational activities. Any new passion brings with it new disciples and a multiplication of creeds. The new politics, the new psychologies and philosophies of the decades of the 1960s and 1970s, also gave birth to an animated metaphysical dimension to sport. Whatever the truths and excesses of this contemplative and philosophically irrational preoccupation with sport, it definitely has opened up the possibilities of mass public involvement. The tendency to individual exaggeration is countered by the truism that thinking tends to make it so. In his book *Positive Addiction* psychiatrist William Glasser is convinced that running is the hardest but surest way to healthful positive addiction. The multiplication of particular kinds of addictions "strengthen us and make our lives more satisfying," is his medical and metaphysical prognosis.[10] There appears a growing realization that sport is much more than cheap entertainment—that it is capable of giving us a vision of beauty and an extraordinary experience, both physical and metaphysical. Nineteen hundred seventy-six Boston Marathon victor, Jack Fultz, thought it odd that late in the race "your mind moves away from the body. It wanders. You start to transcend the physical pain." The literature is replete with such remarks from golfers, weight-lifters, swimmers, and other men and women involved in individual sports. The modern precursor to this mystical, irrational component might be Eugen Herrigel in his 1953 *Zen in the Art of Archery.* He continually speaks of the self-detached, egoless, spiritually-minded athlete as the truly effective sportsman and human. The "unspiritual archer" can never compete successfully against the one immersed in "unbroken equanimity."[11]

Golf champion, Tony Jacklin, attributed some of his success to a mystical perception of sport—a state where everything is pure and clear, "a cocoon of concentration. And . . . I'm invincible," he said.[12]

Had the first three place winners of the 1953 Boston Marathon reached the transcendance of physical pain?

The current vogue of Eastern philosophies, yoga and transcendental meditation, raised levels of consciousness techniques, all have had real but ill-defined impacts on professional athletes, serious and recreational sporting men and women. Michael Murphy in his *Golf in the Kingdom* talks in terms of a return of the human to the divine—through sport. George Leonard does the same thing in his 1975 *The Ultimate Athlete*. There are many more writers equally reverential about the metaphysical side of sport. Such talk is exciting, somewhat new, and contains much truth. But it is unbridled, lacking balance or a Grecian sense of sophrosyne. Several writers have helped in this latter regard. Scott Kretchmar and William Harper conclude that there is no rational answer to the question, "Why does man play?" Excessive preoccupation with explanations are to be avoided. Larry Locke rejects sport as educative. Sport is just what it is, he says. Articulate educators, skeptical and seriously concerned about the recent wave of literature giving moral, aesthetic, and even religious adornments to sport, are emerging at the same time that such metaphysical sport literature is still on the increase. "It used to be the things worth dying for were abstract ideas," noted *New York Times* cultural reporter,

Richard Shepard. The excessive passion for sport ideology is ruining sport and "hampering the spread of ideology the world over."[13] Olympic marathon champion, Frank Shorter, possibly summed up this impatience with the over-passionate sportsman with his remark that he has nothing but respect for the average guy who runs. "What I can't stand," he says, are those "who make a cult out of it. It ruins the whole thing to take it so seriously."[14] What each of us must learn to do is to immerse ourselves in sport, enjoy the game as something vitally important for that moment, and yet as soon as it is over, realize its relatively inconsequential nature.

THE FUTURE SPORT FOR ALL SCENARIO—A CASE FOR OPTIMISM

It has been said that sporting events are almost the only thing in life that has a conclusion. Pessimists (or as Herman Kahn calls them, "catastrophists") declare that today's sports are actually the funeral games of modern western civilization. And yet there is an almost infinite variety of choices between the Super Bowl and a casual hour of frizbee play—between gladiatorial competition and the ephemeral suspicion of sport. The over-rapid ascendancy of intellect is presently being met by a healthy, countervailing sporting impulse. Our machine culture often fails us; men and women who pursue lifetime sports may be looking for and often find what Max Lerner calls "new accessions of experience."

The expanding sport-for-all movement in the United States is important for its physical fitness implications. During the 1960s and 1970s, medical and physiological evidence mounted steadily that sound health habits combined with regular, vigorous exercise are of vital importance in daily work and in making our leisure time meaningful. During this era, huge numbers accepted the self-evident declaration of prominent physician, Per-Olaf Astrand, that "the human body is built for action, not for rest." Regular exercise or "active recreation" has been dramatically forwarded as a prerequisite for good body function and to the quality of life. The American Medical Association, in a rare moment of sermonizing, recommended a lifelong commitment to the broadest concept of fitness in order that one may "live best and serve most."[16] The long argument between diet or exercise as more important in the prevention of heart disease seems resolved in favor of exercise. More and more, physicians, physiologists, physical educators, and nutritionists have thrust regular, pleasant exercise into the fore of cardiovascular medicine. *Time* magazine, on February 23, 1968, both admonished us and urged us with its essay, "Don't just sit there; walk, jog, run." Psychological and social benefits are frequently forwarded as possible benefits. "What all of the experts are wholeheartedly against is nonexercise." The scientific and popular literature on human fitness is replete with titles like, "Therapeutic physical exercise," "the road to fitness," "Can exercise improve your brain power," "The new aerobics—key to fitness at any age," and "Exercise: the new miracle drug." No doubt that all of this and more led to the extravagant national advertisement which proclaimed "Not one of the top U.S. corporations has a fat president."

Playing games is increasingly important to millions of people. Games permit a respite from customary pattern, said Marshall McLuhan. They can provide many varieties of satisfaction—from the mundane to the sublime. When Swedish film director Ingmar Bergman was in his late 50s and contemplating his advancing years, he commented, "It's like climbing a mountain. The higher you get, the more tired and breathless you become, but your view becomes much more extensive." The new sport and recreational surge in the United States has embraced millions, motivated by thoughts as private as Bergman's view. Should sport be spontaneous, uninhibited, unstructured, noncompetitive, nonaggressive, nonviolent play for its own sake? Or does it mean daring, risking, bearing uncertainty, and enduring tension for a prize.[17] The options available are both extremes and all the subtleties in between. The post industrial scenario should open significant recreational and sporting opportunities to all social and economic classes (except the shrinking number of poor). The quaternary society—a truly postindustrial economy—might very well contain a significant population participating in nonwork activities, marking "the third great watershed of human history."[18] There is much room for optimism in a realistic anticipation of a continued strong American economy where significant leisure will be available to more and more individuals. Just as significant, possibly, is the growing awareness that participation in lifetime sports can measurably enhance the quality of life.

SPORT ALTERS AMERICAN LIVING PATTERNS

It is an acceptable cliche that sport is a mirror of society. For some time now, the reverse has also been true. The extraordinary pervasiveness of sport in American society—especially the new lifetime sport involvement—has actually altered the lives of countless individuals. Recently, historians have generally accepted sport as a genuine area of exploration. The same is true of many psychologists, sociologists, physiologists, physicians, and philosophers. Learned societies of scholars from each of these disciplines look keenly at the effects of individual and collective sporting experiences. Like quicksilver, however, definitive statements about sport and play are hard to come by.

Like any form of human behavior that has antecedents both in the predispositions of the species and in the specific cultures within which individuals grow and develop, the meaning to be derived from participation in physical play is almost impossible to dissect given our correct level of analysis.[19]

The new sport humanists, Stuart Miller, George Leonard, Bil Gilbert, Neil Amdur, and many others may be unfamiliar with the older philosophies of R. Tait McKenzie, Clark Hetherington, Jay B. Nash, and Arthur H. Steinhaus. A close analysis of the modernists reveals a sport-for-all attitude precisely the same as those of the traditional educators. There is no essential philosophical difference in Esalen Institute's Stuart Miller and that of the late physical education scientist, Arthur Steinhaus. Miller's "new" directions sees sport as "a powerful psychological searchlight, teaching the player about himself . . . consciously used in the development of the whole personality. . . ." Steinhaus' classic essay, "Fitness beyond muscle," concluded that "for the highest human accomplishments man must be strong in totality." The laudable message of the new sport humanists is old, very old. The new advocates of self-actualization through sport have no more hard evidence of sport's efficacy in this direction than did the old-timers who talked so convincingly about character-building through athletic competition. The strong evidences from both directions, except in the physiological dimension, still tend to remain semi-scientific. Exactly what sport does to the individual human mind and spirit is still uncertain. No doubt remains, however, that it is capable of profoundly affecting men and women, young and old.

In the year 1976, 15 million Americans drove, chipped, and putted over 300 million rounds of golf. Multiply this a hundred fold in a hundred different sporting directions and one begins to see the enormity of this still new, sport-for-all, lifetime sports direction. "The vibrant dynamic feeling that comes from being more than just well" is an intellectual realization and a body feeling that is gaining acceptance at a remarkable rate in contemporary America. The response you get from moderate, regular, and joyous exercise "is so great," say Laurence Morehouse in his almost too casual text, *Total Fitness in 30 Minutes a Week.* "Functional wellness," "minimum maintenance," are terms he uses to emphasize that sport is necessary to us and can be fun. "Inactivity will kill you," he warns. The American free citizen, who both worships material abundance and who feels entitled to his share of it, may slowly spiral out of the narrow definition of wealth and emerge more expansive, realizing what Sebastian de Grazia knew. Work may make a man stoop-shouldered or rich or both; it may even ennoble him. Worthy use of leisure may perfect him, and in this lies its future. Through leisure man "may realize his ties to the natural world and so free his mind to rise to divine reaches."[20]

REFERENCES

1. Neil Amdur, Swimming still rated top participant sport, *The New York Times*, March 24, 1974, p. 1, Sports section.
2. 82 Billion dollars for leisure, *U.S. News and World Report*, 67 (September 15, 1969), p. 58.
3. Max Kaplan, *Leisure: Theory and Practice* (New York: John Wiley and Sons, Inc., 1975), p. 123.
4. Ken Moore as quoted in Skip Myslenski, U.S. decathlon star knows sacrifice, *The Philadelphia Inquirer*, June 13, 1976, p. 7E.
5. Allan H. Gilbert, Olympic Decadence, *The Classical Journal*, 21 (May, 1926), p. 698.
6. See MacLeish's sport philosophy in Neil Amdur, *The Fifth Down* (New York: Coward, McCann, and Geoghegan, Inc., 1971), pp. 11-14.
7. George B. Leonard, Winning isn't everything. It's nothing. *Intellectual Digest*, 4 (October, 1973), p. 47.
8. John Lucas, as quoted in Neil Amdur, The New Awakening in Athletics, *The Washington Star*, April 2, 1972, p. c6.
9. Charles J. Ping, Education and Athletics are worthy college experiences, *N.C.A.A. News*, 11 (March 15, 1974), p. 7.
10. William Glasser, Positive Addiction (New York: Harper & Row, Pub., 1976), 2, passim.
11. Eugen Herrigel, *Zen in the Art of Archery* (New York: Random House Vintage Books, 1971), pp. 78, 80, passim.
12. Tony Jacklin as quoted in Dudley Doust, Mystical perception in sport, *Intellectual Digest*, 4 (April, 1974), p. 32.
13. Richard F. Shepard, Time to end sports, opiate of the masses, *The New York Times*, November 17, 1974, p. 2 Sports section.
14. Frank Shorter, as quoted in Lawrence Shainberg, The obsessiveness of the long-distance runner, *The New York Times Magazine*, February 25, 1973, p. 28.
15. See Per-Olof Astrand, *Health and Fitness* (Stockholm, Sweden: Universaltryck, 1973).
16. Fitness of American Youth, *The Journal of the American Medical Association*, 163 (February 23, 1957), p. 648.
17. For one person's view, see John P. Sixk, Hot Sporting Blood, *Intellectual Digest*, 4 (November, 1973), pp. 46-47.
18. Herman Kahn *et al.*, *The Next 200 Years. A Scenario for America and the World* (New York: William Morrow and Co., Inc., 1976), p. 23.
19. Daryl Siedentop, *Physical Education–Introductory Analysis* (Dubuque, Iowa: William C. Brown Co., 1976), p. 27.
20. Sebastian de Grazia, *Of Time, Work, and Leisure* (Garden City, New York: Anchor Books—Doubleday and Co., Inc., 1964), p. 414.

Index

Page numbers in *italics* refer to illustrations.

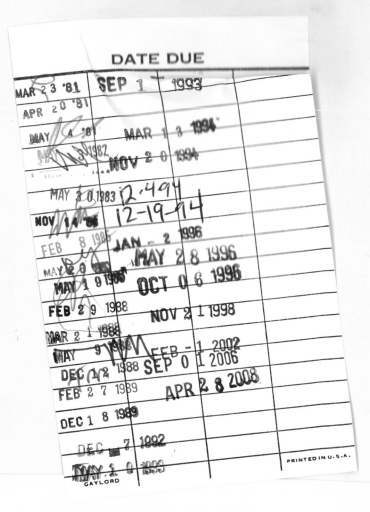
GV
706.5
L82

Lucas, John Apostal, 1927-
   Saga of American sport / John A.
Lucas, Ronald A. Smith. --
Philadelphia : Lea & Febiger, 1978.
   x, 439 p. : ill. ; 24 cm.
   Includes bibliographical references
and index.
   ISBN 0-8121-0485-4

   1. Sports--Social aspects--United
States. 2. Sports--United States--
History. I. Smith, Ronald Austin,
1936- joint author. II. Title.